**A National Bureau
of Economic Research
Conference Report**

Health and Labor Force Participation over the Life Cycle
Evidence from the Past

Edited by **Dora L. Costa**

The University of Chicago Press

Chicago and London

DORA L. COSTA is associate professor of economics at the
Massachusetts Institute of Technology and a research associate of the
National Bureau of Economic Research.

The University of Chicago Press, Chicago 60637
The University of Chicago Press, Ltd., London
© 2003 by the National Bureau of Economic Research
All rights reserved. Published 2003
Printed in the United States of America
12 11 10 09 08 07 06 05 04 03   1 2 3 4 5
ISBN: 0-226-11618-2 (cloth)

Library of Congress Cataloging-in-Publication Data

Health and labor force participation over the life cycle : evidence from
    the past / edited by Dora L. Costa.
        p. cm.—(A National Bureau of Economic Research conference
    report)
    Includes bibliographical references and index.
    ISBN 0-226-11618-2 (cloth : alk. paper)
    1. Medical economics—United States. 2. Industrial hygiene—
United States. 3. Aged—Health and hygiene—United States.
4. Aged —Employment—United States. I. Costa, Dora L. II. Series.

RA410.53 .H4115 2003
331.3'98'0973—dc21

                                                            2002042977

⊗ The paper used in this publication meets the minimum requirements of
the American National Standard for Information Sciences—Permanence
of Paper for Printed Library Materials, ANSI Z39.48-1992.

Contents

Preface

The twentieth century witnessed remarkable improvements in the health and longevity of older Americans. At the beginning of the twentieth century a fifty-five-year-old American man could expect to live seventeen more years. By century's end he could expect to live twenty-three more years. This increase in life expectancy was extremely slow at first, rising by only about half a year during the first three decades of the twentieth century. More recently it has been more rapid, rising by four years in the last four decades of the century. Whether the increase in life expectancy has been accompanied by increases in health has been the subject of much debate among scholars (Crimmins 1990; Cutler and Richardson 1997; Manton, Corder, and Stallard 1997; Verbrugge 1984; Waidmann, Bound, and Schoenbaum 1995), but the preponderance of the evidence suggests that the overall trend is one of improving health. Particularly striking is the high burden of chronic disease and of functional impairments at older ages at the beginning of the twentieth century, a burden that lightened only slowly during the first half of the twentieth century but more rapidly later on (Costa 2000, 2002, 2003; Fogel and Costa 1997).

The increase in life expectancy in the United States has raised issues about the fiscal solvency of our health care and pension systems. The net effect of increases in life expectancy and improvements in health on the aggregate cost of health care remains uncertain. More than 80 percent of men older than sixty-four are retired, and continued increases in the share of the population over age sixty-four seem likely, given current fertility and mi-

Dora L. Costa is associate professor of economics at the Massachusetts Institute of Technology and a research associate of the National Bureau of Economic Research.

gration projections, because of the continuing long-term decrease in the probability of dying.

Attempts to forecast the paths of health care and pension costs over several decades have led researchers to pay increasing attention to the historical record. The past is still with us both because older generations are still with us and because physiological and economic processes have a long reach. Each cohort carries with it a set of expectations, values, human capital, and health capital, often formed at very young ages, and transmits these to future generations. The oldest generation alive today was born when life expectancy at birth was only fifty. A growing body of evidence indicates that chronic disease at older ages and premature older-age mortality are, to a considerable extent, the result of exposure to infectious disease, occupational hazards, malnutrition, and other types of biomedical and socioeconomic stress throughout the life cycle and particularly early in life and that health capital is transmitted to future generations through the mother's womb (Barker 1992, 1994; Costa 2000; Doblehammer and Vaupel 2001; Elo and Preston 1992; Emmanuel et al. 1999; Manton, Corder, and Stallard 1997).

The need to understand changes in health and in retirement rates has led to the creation of several longitudinal surveys, including the Framingham Heart Study, the Panel Study of Income Dynamics; the Retirement History Longitudinal Survey; the National Long Term Care Survey; and the Health and Retirement Study. These surveys, however, generally interview individuals starting only in middle age and cover only the latter half of the twentieth century, when most of the increases in retirement rates and improvements in elderly health and longevity were already well under way. These data sets may not provide a long enough period of observation to differentiate adequately between short-term fluctuations and underlying long-term trends over the twentieth century.

Economic historians have recently begun to create data sets that will help us understand health trends in the past. These have established that past populations were shorter-lived, smaller, and lighter, and that they faced a heavy disease burden in old age. Among Union Army veterans aged sixty to seventy-four in 1910, more than one-third had difficulty walking, almost one-third had valvular heart disease, more than half had arthritis, and more than one-third had decreased breath and adventitious sounds (Costa 2000, 2002). The high prevalence of chronic conditions among these men was directly related to such infectious diseases as rheumatic fever, respiratory infections, typhoid, and malaria and to such occupational hazards as exposure to dust and fumes and the adverse effects of manual labor in an unmechanized society (Costa 2000). High disease prevalence combined with the inefficacy of medical care led to such functional limitations as difficulty in walking (Costa 2002).

Anthropometric measures suggest that even at younger ages, men in the past did not fare well. Union Army soldiers in their thirties and Union Army veterans in their late fifties and early sixties had an average body mass index (BMI) of only 23, compared to one of 26 for men in the same age groups in 1961 (Costa and Steckel 1997), implying that net nutritional status was poorer in the past. The abundant information that we have on adult heights, a measure of net nutritional status during the growing years, suggests that health cycled in the past. Troops who fought in the French and Indian Wars and in the American Revolution nearly attained the heights of those born in the 1930s (roughly 175 cm), but then average height fell by 4 cm in the ensuing half-century, reaching a trough among those born in the 1880s before rising 6 cm for those cohorts born in the middle of the twentieth century. Life expectancy at age ten underwent similar cycles. Explanations include the increase in infectious disease with the rise of immigration and internal migration, growing crowding with urbanization and the spread of factories, and declines in nutritional intake (Haines, Craig, and Weiss 2000; Costa and Steckel 1997; Fogel 1986).

Economic historians have also created data sets to help us understand trends in migration and in labor force participation in the past. Steckel (1989) established the east-west pattern, along a very similar latitude, of migration in the mid–nineteenth century. As the century progressed, rural-to-urban migration became increasingly important even though city dwellers faced higher mortality rates from infectious disease. Despite their poor health, men in the past spent a much greater percentage of their lives in the labor force than do men today. Labor force participation rates of men older than sixty-four were 84 percent in 1870 but by 1920 had fallen to 60 percent, and by 1940 to 42 percent (Costa 1998). Since the mid-1980s labor force participation rates have fluctuated between 15 and 18 percent (Bureau of Labor Statistics Series LFU606501, available at http://www.bls.gov/). Costa argued that increases in income explain much of the rise in retirement rates, but that over time men have become less responsive to changes in income. That is, the income elasticity of retirement has fallen, perhaps because of rising incomes, changes in social norms, or the growth of a retirement lifestyle.

The papers in this volume all use new data that help us obtain a better understanding of health, migration, and work in the past. Joseph P. Ferrie's chapter 2 uses merged mortality and population schedules from the United States federal censuses of 1850 and 1860. These data on 175,000 individuals enable him to examine the link between wealth and mortality.

The other papers in this volume are based largely upon a unique longitudinal database that covers the life histories of men born between 1820 and 1850, and who reached age fifty-five between 1875 and 1905. These data allow researchers to extend their studies of aging patterns to earlier cohorts who retired under very different institutions and who grew old when infectious disease was still common, when most men labored in manual jobs, and when medicine could provide diagnoses but few cures. The sample is based upon 35,570 men out of a randomly drawn sample of 39,616 white males who were mustered into the Union Army during 1861–65. Socioeconomic and biomedical histories of the recruits from childhood to death were created by linking information from different sources, including military records, pension records, reports from examining surgeons, and the 1850, 1860, 1900, and 1910 censuses. Work is currently in progress on linking these men to the 1880 census. Auxiliary data sets that provide epidemiological information on cities and counties have been collected as well (the data are available for download from http://www.cpe.uchicago.edu).

How a data set with 15,000 variables on 35,570 individuals was created from manuscript records, many of them free-form, barely legible doctors' examinations, is the subject of chapter 2 in this volume, by Larry T. Wimmer. Much of the credit goes to Robert Fogel's unwillingness to take no for answer, even when it was clear that the task of collecting the data was much more complex and time consuming than anyone had previously imagined. At least as much of the credit goes to Wimmer, who led the data collection, patiently explaining to Fogel what could and could not be done. Without his efforts, the data would not exist. All of us who have used the data in our research owe him a very large debt.

While the Union Army data is an unusually rich data source, one of its disadvantages is that we cannot examine the mortality experiences of women, children, and Southerners. By using manuscript schedules from the 1850 and 1860 mortality censuses for rural populations, Ferrie's paper sheds light on the experience of these groups. By linking individuals found in the population censuses to the mortality censuses, Ferrie is also able to bring new evidence to bear on the old question of the role of socioeconomic factors on mortality. To date, work on historical populations suggests that the relationship between mortality and income was weak, but became stronger in the twentieth century. Low or negative time-series correlations between income or real wages and mortality rates have been reported for historical data in countries such as England and Italy (Livi-Bacci 1991; Kunitz and Engerman 1992). Among groups that in the United States have been studied at the individual level, the relationship between wealth and survival rates suggests an egalitarian pattern of death. Wealth conveyed no systematic advantage for survival of women and children in households matched in the 1850 and 1860 censuses (Steckel 1988; Davin 1993). Preston and Haines (1991) report that race and place of residence were the most important correlates of child survival in the late nineteenth century. Unlike previous researchers, Ferrie is able to examine mortality by cause for all age groups over a one-year period. His findings show that even when the United States was largely rural and agricultural, when money could not buy access to sophisticated medical care, health differentials by wealth were substantial.

Chulhee Lee's chapter 3 provides insights into mortality patterns in an environment in which infectious and parasitic diseases are common. Union Army camps provide a unique opportunity to examine the mortality effects of being thrust into a high-disease environment. Lee finds that prior exposure to unfavorable epidemiological environments reduced the chances of contracting and dying from disease while in service. Recruits at particularly high risk were farmers and rural residents, the native-born, and those from counties with high child death rates. Wealth reduced the chances of contracting a disease but had no favorable effects on mortality. Lee's results suggest that one reason researchers report such egalitarian patterns of death in the nineteenth century is that it may be hard to identify the effect of wealth under a very severe disease environment in which acute infectious diseases are common. The effects of other factors, such as differences in immunity status or rates of exposure, may dominate the effect of wealth.

Daniel Scott Smith's chapter 4 also examines the roles of prior exposure to disease and individual characteristics on mortality while in the army. Examining companies from New York State, he uses both the Union Army data and published records that provide crude death rate measures, rejection rates, and information on the region in which soldiers served. By examining published sources he can compare the mortality of officers and enlisted men. His findings suggest that simple self-protection measures such as better food and latrines led to a much lower mortality rate for officers than for enlisted men. He also finds that prior exposure to disease was important. The healthier and wealthier were not unambiguously more likely to live than the less healthy and the poorer.

In chapter 5, Sven E. Wilson and Clayne L. Pope examine the effects of family and community variables on the height of recruits. Data on heights provides the most abundant evidence on long-term health trends because height was recorded by military organizations to help identify deserters, to assess fighting strength, and to ensure that soldiers received their proper pay. Adult height depends upon nutritional intake and upon the demands made on that nutritional intake by disease, climate, and work effort during the growing years. In the United States, occupational differences in stature were relatively small by European standards, but widened in the first half of the nineteenth century at the same time that average heights fell. Wilson and Pope find that among Union Army soldiers linked to the 1860 census, urbanization and region were particularly important predictors of height probably because urban areas were centers of infectious disease. Farmers had a height advantage even in remote areas, suggesting that access to food was also important. They also find a positive relation between wealth and height at low levels of wealth. Finally, they also find that movers who are the children of the native-born are shorter than nonmovers, perhaps because migration to the frontier states contributed to environmental stress among children.

Sven E. Wilson's paper on respiratory disease (ch. 6) turns to examining the health of Union Army veterans at older ages. He finds that the prevalence of respiratory disease increased between 1895 and 1910. Several factors could explain this increase: Urbanization (and therefore exposure to respiratory illnesses) increased, the continued growth of manufacturing decreased both indoor and outdoor air quality, cigarette smoking became increasingly popular, and later cohorts suffered worse early childhood health and nutrition (as evidenced by the decline in height and the increase in mortality). During early infancy, when the alveoli are still growing and expanding, a respiratory infection will retard infant growth and lead to worsened lung capacity at late adult ages, a condition associated with respiratory disorders. Although Wilson cannot examine the impact of respiratory infections in early childhood, he finds that having had a respiratory infection during the war, when the veteran was a young adult, is the strongest predictor of respiratory disease later on. His findings suggest that life-cycle factors should be further investigated in explaining cycles in health.

In chapter 7, Werner Troesken and Patricia E. Beeson turn to health hazards at adult ages in large cities. Most researchers are aware of the hazards from inadequate sanitation and from crowding, but another danger that city dwellers faced was cities' use of lead water mains. Troesken and Beeson find that veterans in cities with lead water mains experienced greater dizziness and ear problems. Although they did not disproportionately suffer from even more serious sequelae, such as kidney failure, this may be because they had the good fortune to obtain their water from lead water mains only at later ages, not in early childhood.

Chapter 8, by Mario A. Sánchez, uses the rich residential histories available in the Union Army data to study the migration decision, the return migration decision, and the effect of migration on life expectancy. Sánchez is able to provide new numbers on the extent of migration in the United States and to estimate migration probabilities as a function of individual characteristics. He finds that migrants are especially at risk of dying from infectious disease, regardless of whether they migrated to urban or rural areas (although those who migrated to urban areas were at greater risk), suggesting that moving in and of itself was stressful. His findings suggest that the high level of internal migration experienced by the United States in the nineteenth century contributed to the observed worsening of health and that we may be underestimating the costs of migration to urban areas.

Tayatat Kanjanapipatkul (ch. 9) examines the effect of pensions on the labor force participation of Union Army veterans. Although this issue was addressed in Costa (1998), the results need to be replicated on the much larger sample that is now available and extended to investigate differential responsiveness to pension income among different groups and robustness to different specifications of pension income. Kanjanapipatkul finds that, in the larger sample, the elasticity of retirement with respect to pension income was larger in 1910 than in 1900 and that while his estimate for 1910 was in line with Costa's results, his estimate for 1900 was much smaller. His findings suggest declines in the income elasticity of retirement date more to the second than to the first half of the twentieth century. Kanjanapipatkul also finds that the elasticity varied by occupation. Professionals were most sensitive to pension income, whereas today they are the group least sensitive to pension income.

Chapter 10, by Chen Song and Louis L. Nguyen, focuses on the health and retirement decision. In virtually all studies of either recent or past populations, poor health leads to retirement. Song and Nguyen focus their research on the labor-supply effects of one specific health condition: hernias. Although easily cured today, at the beginning of the twentieth century hernias were chronic, painful, and debilitating. Song and Nguyen find that even when hernias were considered severely disabling by the doctors who examined them, they had relatively little effect on retirement rates, implying that many men continued to work in pain. However, they also find that if men were in less manually demanding occupations, then they were less likely to retire. Their results are consistent with higher costs of switching to a less manually demanding occupation for men with relatively little human capital.

The papers in this volume owe a large debt to the financial support of National Institute of Health grant AG10120 and of the National Bureau of Economic Research. They benefited from the comments of Peter Blanck, John Brown, William Collins, Claudia Goldin, Michael Haines, Charles Holmes, Robert Margo, Anne McCants, Rebecca Menes, Irwin Rosenberg, Nevin Scrimshaw, and Richard Steckel. This book owes a particularly large debt to Robert Fogel, because without him the data that made most of these papers possible would not exist. Larry Wimmer, Joseph Ferrie, Sven Wilson, Clayne Pope, Mario Sánchez, Tayatat Kanjanapipatkul, and Chen Song were all his students and have been involved in the Union Army project. Nguyen became involved in the project while a student at the University of Chicago. Troesken and Smith are relative latecomers to the data, but quickly mastered it. This volume is therefore dedicated to Robert Fogel.

References

Barker, D. J. P. 1992. *Fetal and infant origins of adult disease.* London: British Medical Journal Publishing Group.

———. 1994. *Mothers, babies, and disease in later life.* London: British Medical Journal Publishing Group.

Costa, D. L. 1998. *The evolution of retirement: An American economic history, 1880–1990.* Chicago: University of Chicago Press.

———. 2000. Understanding the twentieth century decline in chronic conditions among older men. *Demography* 37:53–72.

———. 2002. Changing chronic disease rates and long-term declines in functional limitation among older men. *Demography* 39 (1): 119–38.

———. 2003. Understanding mid-life and older age mortality declines: Evidence from Union Army veterans. *Journal of Econometrics* 112 (1): 175–92.

Costa, D. L., and R. H. Steckel. 1997. Long-term trends in health, welfare, and economics growth in the United States. In *Health and welfare during industrialization,* ed. R. Floud and R. H. Steckel, 47–89. Chicago: University of Chicago Press.

Crimmins, E. 1990. Are Americans healthier as well as longer-lived? *Journal of Insurance Medicine* 22:89–92.

Cutler, D. M., and E. Richardson. 1997. Measuring the health of the United States population. *Brookings Papers on Economic Activity, Microeconomics:* 217–71.

Davin, E. L. 1993. The era of the common child: Egalitarian death in antebellum America. *Mid-America: An Historical Review* 75 (2): 135–63.

Doblehammer, G., and J. W. Vaupel. 2001. Life span depends on month of birth. *Proceedings of the National Academy of Sciences, USA* 98:2934–39.

Elo, I. T., and S. H. Preston. 1992. Effects of early-life conditions on adult mortality: A review. *Population Index* 58 (2): 186–212.

Emmanuel, I., et al. 1999. The Washington State Intergenerational Study of Birth Outcomes: Methodology and some comparisons of maternal birthweight and infant birthweight and gestation in four ethnic groups. *Paediatric and Perinatal Epidemiology* 13 (3): 352–69.

Fogel, R. W. 1986. Nutrition and the decline in mortality since 1700: Some preliminary findings. In *Long-term factors in American economic growth,* ed. S. L. Engerman and R. E. Gallman, 439–555. Chicago: University of Chicago Press.

Fogel, R. W., and D. L. Costa. 1997. A theory of technophysio evolution, with some implications for forecasting population, health care costs, and pension costs. *Demography* 34 (1): 49–66.

Haines, M. R., L. A. Craig, and T. Weiss. 2000. Development, health, nutrition, and mortality: The case of the "antebellum puzzle" in the United States. NBER Working Paper no. H0130. Cambridge, Mass.: National Bureau of Economic Research.

Kunitz, S. J., and S. L. Engerman. 1992. The ranks of death: Secular trends in income and mortality. *Health Transition Review* 2 (Supplement): 29–46.

Livi-Bacci, M. 1991. *Population and nutrition: An essay on European demographic history.* Cambridge: Cambridge University Press.

Manton, K. G., L. Corder, and E. Stallard. 1997. Chronic disability trends in elderly United States populations: 1982–1994. *Proceedings of the National Academy of Sciences* 94 (6): 2593–98.

Preston, S. H., and M. R. Haines. 1991. *Fatal years: Child mortality in late nineteenth century America.* Princeton, N.J.: Princeton University Press.

Steckel, Richard H. 1988. The health and mortality of women and children, 1850–1860. *Journal of Economic History* 48:333–45.

———. 1989. Household migration and rural settlement in the United States, 1850–1860. *Explorations in Economic History* 26:190–218.

Verbrugge, L. M. 1984. Longer life but worsening health? Trends in health and mortality of middle-aged and older persons. *Milbank Quarterly* 62 (3): 475–519.

Waidmann, T., J. Bound, and M. Schoenbaum. 1995. The illusion of failure: Trends in the self-reported health of the U.S. elderly. *Milbank Quarterly* 73 (2): 253–87.

Reflections on the Early Indicators Project
A Partial History

Larry T. Wimmer

While many events have clearly defined starting points, the origin of a research project is often more difficult to identify. It is more likely a function of whom you ask and the point of reference used. So it is with the beginning date of the project "Early Indicators of Later Work Levels, Disease, and Death" (EI). It might seem logical to date the project from the year our proposal (Fogel 1991) first received funding from the National Institutes of Health (NIH) and the National Science Foundation (NSF). That award, however, came five years after our initial application (1986), when we were politely told, "An interesting idea, but we are not convinced that you can actually collect these records. When you can demonstrate feasibility come back." I suspect that some on the panel did not expect to see us again. In the interim, at the urging of Bob Fogel, we completed the collection software that was of concern to the panel and collected a sample of twenty companies in order to demonstrate the feasibility of our collection procedures. That twenty-company sample quickly became the basis of several significant research papers. Approval of the project and its funding initiated seven years of intense collection. Even before that first application (1986), support from the National Bureau of Economic Research (NBER) deserves much of the credit for the "start" of the EI project. As early as 1981, NBER found the idea sufficiently promising to contribute advanced funding as part of their ongoing support of the Development of the American Economy (DAE), which had begun in 1979.

In my mind, however, I believe it is reasonable to date the origin of the EI project back to 1972! In that year Bob Fogel and Stan Engerman were proposing the collection of probate data in order to study American slav-

Larry T. Wimmer is professor of economics at Brigham Young University.

ery. While visiting Emory University, Bob went to the archives in Atlanta to examine the records that were expected to provide a critical source of data on slave prices. He was told that the original probate records were often spread throughout county archives across the South, making collection expensive and oversight very difficult. As if that were not sufficiently discouraging, he was also informed that many of the records were too fragile to allow public use. "However, you might consider using the microfilmed probate records collected and available in one location at the Family History Library of the Church of Jesus Christ of Latter-day Saints in Salt Lake City." My recollection is that within minutes Bob was on the phone to Clayne Pope and me asking, "What do you know about the Family History Library?" Both of us, former students of Bob's, were at Brigham Young University just south of Salt Lake City. As I recall, our answers were approximately the same. "The library is where my mother has done family genealogy work, but other than that I have no idea. But, we will find out!" Earlier, Alice Hanson Jones, while completing her dissertation at Chicago on colonial wealth, made extensive use of the library; knowing that I was from Utah, she told me what "helpful people" they were at the library. Unfortunately, her comments had not made much of an impression upon my mind. In retrospect, our answers to Bob's question seem unbelievably naive as we look back upon almost thirty years of our own work and that of many other social scientists using the immense microfilm collection of personal, church, city, county, state, and federal records found in the Family History Library.

The year 1972 dates the start of collaborative work and common interests that culminated in our joint EI project. Initially, Bob and Stan used the probate records of the Family History Library for age-specific slave prices, an important contribution to their "new" data in *Time on the Cross* (Fogel and Engerman 1974). From the outset, Bob seemed interested in almost every aspect of the history and collection of the library. Eventually, the Family History Library recognized him during its centennial year in 1994 for his contributions and ongoing association. Meanwhile, Clayne, Jim Kearl, and I were using the archival data to study wealth determinants and distributions in early Utah (Kearl, Pope, and Wimmer 1980). Bob and Stan's work on the height of slaves and its correlation with their mortality experience suggested the value of height data as another means of estimating overall health and standard of living. Subsequently Bob, Stan, and Roderick Floud (of the London Guildhall University) began investigating other archives for height data as a proxy for net nutritional intake. Pope used the library's published family histories to begin a reconstruction of the mortality experience of nineteenth-century U.S. populations. The work of these several authors merged in 1978 with a study on "The Economics of Mortality in North America, 1650–1910" (Fogel et al. 1978).

Much of this early work suggested a deterioration in height, health, and life expectancy during the mid-nineteenth century while wages continued to rise. This perplexing puzzle led to the search for further data that might shed light on socioeconomic and health conditions during this critical period. It was in the search for such data that the extensive collection of military records in the National Archives involving Civil War recruits and veterans came to our attention. These military records, combined with the census manuscripts and published family histories, suggested the possibility of a surprisingly complete prospective study of aging among Northern white males during the specific time period in question. These data, linked across individuals and across multiple records, yield information starting with the national origin, wealth, and occupation of the parents of our young recruits in 1861; identify each battle, disease, and hospitalization of a recruit during his wartime service; provide a documented record throughout the remainder of the veteran's life as he entered the massive pension system stemming from the Civil War; and finally conclude with later-life family structure, living circumstances, and employment found in the 1900 and 1910 federal census records.

The early phase of the project involved five years of development and testing of alternative software and collection methods, followed by seven years of actual data collection. It was clear from the outset that such a study required collaboration across different academic fields. Thus, concurrent with the collection, a number of demographers, economists, and medical researchers began examining the data for a wide range of issues. These issues include the influence of height and other socioeconomic and biomedical factors on the development of specific infectious and chronic diseases; labor force participation at middle and late ages; and elapsed time to death. The initial team included Bob Fogel (economist, University of Chicago), James Trussell (demographer, Princeton), Nevin Scrimshaw (medicine, Massachusetts Institute of Technology [MIT] and Harvard), Irwin Rosenberg (medicine, Tufts), Michael Haines (economist, Colgate), and Clayne Pope and me (economists, Brigham Young University [BYU]). To this list eventually were added a number of other senior investigators, including Robert Mittendorf (medicine, University of Chicago) and a growing number of graduate students of Bob's from Chicago. Many of the latter have gone on to play major roles in the direction of the project, even becoming senior investigators themselves in future proposals—this list includes Dora Costa, Sven Wilson, Chulhee Lee, and John Kim.

The EI project proposed the collection of a life-cycle sample of 39,616 men mustered into 331 randomly selected companies of the Union Army. The sample is drawn from eight different federal record sources and is supported by additional information regarding local health, water conditions, and incidence of disease. Four of the eight records are the federal censuses of 1850, 1860, 1900, and 1910. The military records constitute the core of the sample, and include the Military Service Records, the Carded Medical

Records, the Pension Records, and the Surgeons' Certificates. The Military Service Records (MSR) contain information on each recruit before enlistment (location, occupation, and physical characteristics such as height, etc.), plus a daily muster record including health, battles, wounds, hospitalization, desertion, POW status, cause of death, or muster-out information. The Carded Medical Records (CMR) contain information from field and regimental hospitals, including length of stay, reason for admission, and condition or disposition upon release. The most valuable records and those making this study unique are the Pension Records (PEN) and the Surgeons' Certificates (SCRT) from the federal pension system. These records begin with the introduction of a veteran into the pension system whenever an initial claim is made and, after a lifetime of claims, affidavits, documents, letters, counterclaims, etc., conclude in most cases with evidence relating to the veteran's death—a death certificate or accompanying letters confirming the time and cause of death. It is not uncommon for the pension to continue beyond the death of the veteran through claims stemming from the veteran's widow or family. The PEN records frequently contain several hundred documents that, unlike the census manuscripts, exist for the explicit purpose of authenticating every aspect of a veteran's claim relative to his true identity, age, military service, past and present residence, previous and current employment, general and specific health-related conditions, and fitness for manual labor—plus general economic circumstances and later-life health, retirement, and family structure.

It was immediately clear that the records of the federal pension system constituted a very promising data source that might be used to answer a wide range of questions regarding health, migration, and labor force participation for a large segment of our population from the mid-nineteenth century through the first quarter of the twentieth century. These records provide us with an important benchmark on infectious and chronic diseases before our modern understanding of germ theory, before widespread public health programs, and before the introduction of modern intervention into disease treatment—a benchmark against which to judge the enormous improvements in medicine and life expectancy taken for granted in the twentieth century. These data reveal much about labor force participation among an aging population a generation before the introduction of Social Security and other pension programs. First, however, we were confronted with a number of roadblocks that had to be overcome for the project to succeed.

One of our first challenges was that of devising a system for linking each recruit across all eight records covering a period of as much as eighty years. Little was known then of linking except within communities where migration meant leaving the sample. Complicating our task was the sheer size of the sample, plus a large number of common names, considerable interstate migration, and frequent name changes or use of aliases. What today is commonplace was then a serious set of questions: What form should a unique identification number take? (We even experimented with unique letters and combinations of numbers and letters.) Would it be sufficient, and if so, how should such a number be devised? The task of linking seemed possible only because of the location and other identifying information found in the military pension records. It was not self-evident that we could practically or reasonably produce a historical data set large enough to make inferences specific to age, location, occupation, and disease.

One of the most serious challenges involved our need to produce an interactive software system capable of linking the different purposes among skilled programmers, professional researchers, and the people who would input the data. We were faced with problems that today are part of any commercially available software but then were major hurdles for us. No interactive, commercial packages were available that could give us real-time feedback or could handle the size of our data set. Our earliest collections were written down by hand at the archives, sent to BYU to be keypunched, and subsequently entered into the university's mainframe for further analysis both here and at the University of Chicago. Such procedures were extremely time consuming and expensive, and multiplied the probability of introducing errors into the data set. The introduction of "new," thirteen-pound portable computers was promising for collection at source—earlier laptops had been judged to be too expensive and the screens too difficult to read! In this way, the EI project bridges the interval from keypunched cards to laptop computers that were more powerful than our university's early mainframe! Mark Showalter's association with the project illustrates another example of the time and cost of developing our own software. As an undergraduate at BYU he helped with our first efforts at software development. Subsequently, Mark has completed his Ph.D. at MIT and been a colleague in our department for ten years. Randy Campbell, Shawn Jordan, and Steve Shreeve took over software development from Mark and were ultimately responsible for the software used throughout the collection phase of the project.

That we might be able to use laptop computers and develop our own interactive software to link across multiple years and records answered only one of many difficult questions. The much larger question involved the complicated nature of the records themselves. While we had collected census data for the Utah wealth project, searching for almost 40,000 recruits spreading quickly across the United States presented a formidable challenge. In addition, information found in each federal census year differs from that of previous years. Nevertheless, as daunting as these records seemed initially, census collection became the least of our problems. Janet Bassett, a genealogist working with our programmers at BYU, was responsible for the development of a series of fixed-field collection screens for each census year using our interactive software. Subsequently, she supervised the training of our student teams who actually performed the tasks of searching, verifying, linking, and collecting the census records. With adequate money and student time we were confident that we could collect the census records, although questions remained regarding retrieval and linkage rates that could be answered only with time and experience.

The MSR and CMR presented us with a different set of problems. All collection involving these records had to be done on site at the National Archives, where we were fortunate to find generous administrators and exceptionally skilled and experienced staff. Once on site we found that, unlike with the census records, locating the military records was a minor problem. These data often appeared in a fixed format; however, the format itself changes frequently and contains several open-ended responses.

After several months of working with these records, we were able to decide upon fixed-field collection screens that enabled data-entry persons to identify and collect the relevant information from each record and iteration of forms. Julene Bassett and Noelle Yetter, two former BYU students working for us at the archives, helped achieve this second success. There are a total of eleven collection screens involving the MSR and CMR, including information regarding the recruit's age, residence, and occupation before enlistment, plus military and medical data from the date of enlistment to his departure resulting from his death, going AWOL, or being mustered out.

The PEN and SCRT records with their hundreds of free-form letters, affidavits, and documents presented by far the greatest software and collection challenges. Initially, Clayne and I feared that the task associated with the PEN records might be insurmountable, that student data-entry persons would simply have no idea what to include and what to leave out of such a mass of information. Even if we could construct a manageable set of collection screens there was the real possibility that it might require such extensive supervision, take so long, and cost so much that it would make collection impractical. In addition, we worried about consistency and error rates associated with collection. Bob assured "us" that "we" could solve these problems! After a year of living with the PEN records and a number of false starts, we had a set of eight fixed-field collection screens, with accompanying backups and expansion screens containing more than 3,200 variables covering the life cycles of these recruits from before enlistment to their death. These screens enabled carefully trained and supervised students to turn page by page through the pension records, identifying the desired information and retrieving the relevant data from each document. At the National Archives, Noelle Yetter provided the commitment, continuity, and consistency that made this collection possible. She trained, supervised, performed de novo testing of error rates, scolded, and encouraged almost 100 students from BYU, working in teams of eight to twelve at a time, over the ensuing seven-year period.

Bob had been right about the feasibility of collecting the PEN records—although Clayne and I reminded him that his "optimism" led us to substantially underestimate the time and effort in bringing about that outcome. Celebration necessarily waited upon solving what Clayne and I were convinced was the greatest obstacle of all, the Surgeons' Certificates (SCRT)! How could we expect undergraduates with no medical background or training to collect data from century-old records, using archaic nineteenth- and early twentieth-century medical terminology? The typical veteran experienced an average of almost five examinations during his time within the pension system, with some having over thirty. Each exam is the result of an appearance by the veteran before three pension-board-certified physicians, and stems from his initial claim or subsequent petition for changes in his classification. These examinations cover a wide range of health-related conditions, from accidents and wounds either during or after the war to infectious and chronic diseases.

Clayne and I warned Bob that unlike the census, MSR, CMR, or PEN, about which we had previously expressed our doubts, in the case of the SCRT we might truly be facing a hopeless task. Not surprisingly, Bob insisted that it was possible and even offered to have Chicago take on this task. The first set of SCRT collection screens we received consisted of individual, fixed-field screens for each disease. In a fixed-field format each disease set must anticipate all possible responses that might be encountered for that specific disease. As a result, some collection sets contained as many as fifty to sixty separate screens per disease. We tested these screens using several of our best data-entry persons, and found that they typically became lost early in the detail of a single disease. After a very large investment of time, and through the joint efforts of our medical personnel, programmers, and experienced collection supervisors, we produced what may be the major accomplishment of the collection phase of the project. The impossible ultimately became an impressive set of thirty-nine screens combining fixed-field, variable-width, and open-ended comments that has enabled the collection of these incredibly complicated and yet extraordinarily valuable SCRT. Each screen includes the flexibility of multiple backup screens for additional information, and can be amended as new information and conditions are encountered. If each variable is found only once there are a total of over 2,300 variables—counting is more probabilistic in the case of SCRT since they include open-ended questions. Our success with the SCRT depended very heavily upon the efforts of Nevin Scrimshaw and Irwin Rosenberg, two of our senior medical investigators. Their input was absolutely essential, but as is so often the case, the tedious hours of writing, testing, and re-rewriting screens over this period fell upon students: Julene Bassett and Sharon Nielsen (two former BYU students) and Louis Nguyen (then a medical student at Chicago). Subsequently, Julene and Sharon, and finally Brant Williams, supervised almost every stage of the collection project. Louis, now a physician at the Barnes Jewish Hospital, St. Louis, remains an active participant in the project and in the analysis of the data.

During the seven years of collection, over 200 students collected 303 companies of census records, MSR, CMR, PEN, and SCRT involving 35,571 recruits of the Union Army. A subsequent proposal has been approved which will complete the full 331 companies; add samples from the 1870 and 1880 censuses, a sample of 6,000 Black recruits, and a sample of 10,000 males rejected for military service—as well as add information from private family histories to the Civil War sample (Fogel 2001). The decision was made to conclude this initial collection by recollecting the original twenty-company sample as a quality check against our data collection procedures. Other quality controls consist of over 100 automated checks upon upper and lower bounds of numeric values, acceptable dates, place names, and occupations. Two-field checks are used to compare date intervals involving ages at marriage, death, etc. These built-in, automated checks are in addition to training, supervision, weekly supervisors' meetings, and de novo testing of 5 to 10 percent of the data to track error rates. These quality control instruments and error rates are reported in the data user's manuals prepared by the Center for Population Economics (CPE) at the University of Chicago and the Department of Economics at BYU. Finally, all the data were visually inspected by our BYU project supervisor for any apparent outliers before our phase of the collection was considered complete and the raw data sent to the CPE.

Of the 35,571 initial recruits in the current EI sample, 98 percent (34,775) were linked to the MSR and 85 percent (30,286) to the CMR (Fogel et al. 2001, 70). The size of the sample is suggested by the 1,230 and 1,495 variables found in the relatively small MSR and CMR (CPE 2000, 1). Of those veterans who survived the war and therefore were at risk of being found in the pension system, 79 percent (24,185) have a PEN (Fogel et al., 170). Of those with a PEN, 69 percent have at least one SCRT, with an average of 4.63 examinations per veteran. The SCRT contain 81,877 observations on 2,312 variables for the 16,713 veterans with SCRT (CPE 1999, 1–3). After the liberalizing Pension Law of 1890, an increasing number of veterans enter the system; and of these, 83 percent appear with at least one SCRT (Fogel et al., 115). The average age at which a veteran entered the system was 47.3 years and the average longevity after the first examination is 24.8 years (Fogel et al., 116–17).

Sixty-two percent of the recruits are linked to at least one census record. The lowest linkage rates were those associated with the early census years, 36 percent for 1850 and 41 percent for 1860. Such low rates result primarily from two factors: First, many of the recruits were immigrants who had not yet arrived in 1850; and second, census indexes for those early years exist only for heads of households. During those early years, most of our recruits were, of course, children living within the households of their parents. For those at risk of being found in the 1900 and 1910 census records, defined as those known not to have died prior to the census year, we achieve very high linkage rates of 82 and 70 percent (Fogel et al., 2001, 170). Detailed descriptions plus photocopy examples of each of the eight data sources, examples of the collection screens associated with each record, and a listing and identification of all variables can be found in the data user's manuals available from the CPE.

As each company of digitized records is received by the CPE at Chicago, another equally challenging and important set of procedures take place before the "Early Indicators of Later Work Levels, Disease, and Death" becomes a public-use record. I slight that part of the history not because it is less important, but because it is a different history, much of it waiting to be written as that final phase of the project is completed. It is the work at CPE that will make the efforts at BYU increasingly meaningful and accessible to scholars as yet another large number of students and their supervisors are responsible for the final cleaning and processing of the data. Further software development has been required for cleaning, testing, and coding the original data before the final step, the preparation of a public-use tape. In the past much of this work has been done by Min-Woon Song, John Kim, and Dietrich Kappe under the supervision of Dora Costa, Chris Acito, Julene Bassett, Sven Wilson, and Peter Viechnicki. The current managing director of research at the CPE is Joseph Burton. One can find further information on the project and the public-use tape at http://www.cpe.uchicago.edu.

"Collaboration," as it pertains to the EI project, involves far more than providing helpful suggestions or contributing to a joint report. Collaboration has required major commitments of time and effort by fifteen senior investigators from eight universities at almost every stage of the project, and has included not only research, but also the shared tedium of constructing, reading, and revising screens again and again. Collaboration has occupied the time of numerous graduate students who have gone on to become scholars and senior investigators in their own right, and, last but surely not least, benefitted from more than 200 students and full-time employees without whom this project literally could not have happened.

References

Center for Population Economics (CPE), Graduate School of Business, University of Chicago, and Department of Economics, Brigham Young University. 1999. *Public use tape on the aging of veterans of the Union Army: Data user's manual. Surgeons' Certificates 1860–1940.* Version S-1. Chicago: CPE.

————. 2000. *Public use tape of the aging of veterans of the Union Army: Data user's manual.* Military, Pension, and Medical Records 1820–1940, Version M-5. Chicago: CPE.

Fogel, Robert W., with Dora Costa, Charles Holmes, Matthew Kahn, Diane Lauderdale, Chulhee Lee, Louis Nguyen, Clayne Pope, Paul Rathouz, Irwin Rosenberg, Nevin Scrimshaw, Chen Song, Werner Troesken, and Sven Wilson. 2001.Early indicators of later work levels, disease, and death. Grant submitted to the National Institutes of Health. Center for Population Economics, Graduate School of Business, University of Chicago. Typescript.

Fogel, Robert W., and Stanley L. Engerman. 1974. *Time on the cross: The economics of American negro slavery.* Boston: Little, Brown.

Fogel, Robert W., Stanley L. Engerman, James Trussell, Roderick Floud, Clayne L. Pope, and Larry T. Wimmer. 1978. The economics of mortality in North America, 1650–1910: A description of a research project. *Historical Methods* 11 (2): 75–109.

Fogel, Robert W., with Michael Haines, Clayne Pope, Irwin Rosenberg, Nevin Scrimshaw, James Trussell, and Larry Wimmer. 1991. Aging of Union Army men: A longitudinal study, 1830–1940. Grant submitted to the National Institute of Health. Center for Population Economics, Graduate School of Business, University of Chicago. Typescript.

Kearl, J. R., Clayne L. Pope, and Larry T. Wimmer. 1980. Household wealth in a settlement economy: Utah, 1850–1870. *Journal of Economic History* 40 (3): 477–96.

The Rich and the Dead
Socioeconomic Status and Mortality in the United States, 1850–1860

Joseph P. Ferrie

2.1 Introduction

Research on the link between socioeconomic status and mortality in the late-twentieth-century United States has demonstrated that those lower in status die at earlier ages and suffer from more sickness and disease throughout their lives (Williams 1998; Lantz et al. 1998). Although a great deal of attention has now been devoted to explaining why those lower in status have worse outcomes, and the possibility that the causal link between health and status runs in both directions (with poor health leading to low status), such investigations lack a long-run perspective (Smith 1999). For example, although wide disparities in mortality rates by status were observed as early as the 1960s (Kitagawa and Hauser 1973), we do not know whether the disparities observed over the last four decades are large or small by historical standards.

Perhaps these disparities are merely the continuation of poor outcomes for poor people that generations have failed to erase—the result of poor nutrition, inadequate housing, or harsh working conditions. Or perhaps disparate health outcomes by status are a product of developments in medicine and technology in the late twentieth century that have given a new advantage to those with the incomes to purchase them. Knowing how health out-

Joseph P. Ferrie is associate professor of economics and faculty fellow at the Institute for Policy Research, both at Northwestern University, and a research associate of the National Bureau of Economic Research.

The author thanks participants at Northwestern University's Economic History Workshop and Institute for Policy Research faculty seminar, the 2001 American Economic Association meetings, the NBER conference participants, (particularly discussants Richard Steckel and Irwin Rosenberg), and Deirdre McCloskey and Stan Engerman for extremely helpful comments. Financial support was provided by the National Science Foundation.

comes differed by economic status in an earlier era (e.g., at a time when medical knowledge was rudimentary at best) can help distinguish between these explanations.

This study introduces new evidence on the individual-level correlates of mortality, particularly socioeconomic status measured by occupation and family wealth, created by merging the mortality and population schedules of the 1850 and 1860 federal population censuses. The experiences of several populations that have been overlooked in previous analyses of mortality in the middle of the nineteenth century are explored. For example, although the mortality of young children has been studied, it has been impossible to examine the mortality of older children and most young adults at the individual level. Although studies of the mortality of Union Army veterans have provided insights into the mortality of older adults, this work has of necessity ignored the experiences of Southerners, women, and children.

2.2   What We Know about Nineteenth-Century Socioeconomic Status and Mortality

There is a consensus today that low status is associated with increased risk for a variety of diseases, as well as a substantially increased risk of premature mortality. Attention has now largely turned to discovering the mechanisms that produce these disparate outcomes. An understanding of the long-run progress made in narrowing disparities in health outcomes by status, however, has been more difficult to attain. There are few sources of data on mortality with information on status available before the Second World War. In fact, no nationally uniform system of reporting deaths was in place until the completion of the Death Registration Area in 1933. Before that time, those interested in the link between status and mortality were forced to rely on data less representative of the national experience. Three published studies and one ongoing research project have attempted to assess the link between status and mortality for the second half of the nineteenth century.

The first of these estimated crude death rates of taxpayers and nontaxpayers for 1865 in Providence, Rhode Island (Chapin 1924). The annual crude death rate for taxpayers was 11 per thousand, while the corresponding rate for nontaxpayers was 25 per thousand. Although this suggests a substantial gap in crude death rates by status, it is less than satisfying in a number of respects. The first is the year examined: 1865 was the last year of the U.S. Civil War. Given the disruptions to commerce, industry, and agriculture, as well as the large number of Rhode Island's inhabitants who enlisted, this is unlikely to have been a year representative of the mid-nineteenth-century mortality experience. The second difficulty is the narrow geographic coverage of the study: It examines a significant urban center, but in 1860 only 21 percent of the U.S. population lived in places of 2,500 or more inhabitants. An additional shortcoming is that the study is unable to distinguish among different causes of death, although we know today that not all causes are equally susceptible to the influence of status. Finally, the experience of a single city for a single year tells us little about trends in the link between status and mortality over the late nineteenth century; data from several years are necessary to establish a pattern of increase or decline in the relationship between status and mortality.

The second study to examine the relationship between status and mortality for the late nineteenth century used data from the 1900 U.S. Census of Population, which for only the second time contained a question on "children ever born" (Preston and Haines 1991). The authors used this information, together with the composition of the household actually observed in the 1900 population schedules, to infer infant and child mortality for each household. There was no significant relationship between higher status and lower infant and child mortality, when status was measured by the occupation of the husband's occupation or imputed income (Preston and Haines, 154–56). Although there was higher mortality among those in households headed by unskilled laborers than among those in households headed by other workers, there were no substantial differences in mortality by occupation among households headed by individuals who were not unskilled laborers. They did find, however, that property ownership was associated with lower infant and child mortality than renting (Preston and Haines, 157–58).

Although this study is useful for its broad geographic coverage and the representativeness of the population it examines, it also has some important limitations. The first is the inability to assess the mortality experience of adults: Mortality was inferred from the question on "children ever born" and the observed household composition in 1900, so it was not possible to say whether individuals at older ages who were absent from the households where their mothers were enumerated had died or simply moved out. This study is also somewhat limited in the components of socioeconomic status that it can examine: Although the household head's occupation was recorded, there was no information collected in the 1900 census on the value of the household's wealth.[1] Such information was included in the 1850–70 population censuses, and can thus be used in the sample that will be constructed in the present project. Another difficulty with the Preston and Haines (1991) study is that, like the 1865 Providence, Rhode Island, study,

---

1. Although the census asked whether the family's residence was owned or rented, it did not inquire as to the value of the property, or the value of any other assets held by the family. If there are differences in the impact of different types of wealth on mortality, even the data on home ownership would then present an incomplete picture of the link between the family's socioeconomic status and its mortality experience.

it provides information at only one date (1900). Although deaths that occurred prior to 1900 can be inferred, it is impossible to say much about deaths that occurred much prior to 1885, nor to say with much precision when the deaths that can be inferred actually occurred. This may substantially attenuate any underlying link between observed household socioeconomic status (measured in 1900) and the household's infant and child mortality experience over the preceding years. It is also impossible with these data to examine causes of death and uncover links between status and specific mortality risks.

Finally, one study has examined the link between status and mortality with a sample that covers the entire United States and includes the information on wealth provided in the 1850 and 1860 federal population censuses (Steckel 1988). The project used 1,600 households linked from the 1850 census population schedules to the 1860 population schedules. Mortality within the household was inferred by comparing the household's composition in 1850 and in 1860. Like Preston and Haines (1991), Steckel found no relationship between status (measured by real estate wealth, literacy, and father's occupation) and infant and child mortality. Like the other studies described above, however, this project was unable to disaggregate by cause of death and provides information on status and mortality at but a single point in time.

The University of Chicago's Center for Population Economics (CPE) is using information from Union Army pension records to assess the link between socioeconomic status (among other factors) and later disability and premature mortality. Although this work is able to provide tremendously detailed information on diseases and causes of death as documented by health science professionals, it covers a relatively narrow population: veterans of the Union Army who survived late enough into the nineteenth century to obtain a federal pension. It says nothing about mortality among infants, children, women, or younger men. Furthermore, it is limited to the Northern population. The present study complements this work: Although the data on causes of death are less precise, they cover the populations and regions missed in the Union Army veterans project.

A recent unpublished study (Haines, Craig, and Weiss 2000) examined county-level crude death rates for 1850 (calculated from the mortality schedules used here) and found that wealthier counties actually had higher crude death rates. The authors conclude that this surprising finding "is consistent with the view that wealthier areas were those with more urbanization and greater levels of commercialization and better transport connections" (Haines, Weiss, and Craig, 8). Although their methodology makes it possible to say how aggregate wealth in a county affected aggregate mortality levels, their findings cannot tell us how status at the individual level affected individual-level mortality—and it is at the individual level that the link between status and mortality is probably strongest, if it exists.

Table 2.1   **Sample Records from Mortality Schedules (1850) for Perry County, Illinois**

Name	Age	Occupation	Sex	Month of Death	Cause of Death	Birthplace
Cunningham, Margaret J.	25	None	F	December	Fever	South Carolina
Curlee, James	22	Student	M	February	Fever	Tennessee
Dermon, Jane	60	None	F	May	Bowel inflammation	Ireland
Dunn, James	33	Farmer	M	August	Fever	South Carolina

2.3 The Data

As part of the regular decennial federal censuses of 1850 through 1880, census marshals asked each household how many members had died in the twelve preceding months. Although published totals from these inquiries were included in the 1850 through 1880 census volumes (and these figures form the basis for many mid-nineteenth-century U.S. life tables; e.g., Haines 1998), the data have never been examined at the individual level.[2] Several difficulties have prevented their full exploitation.[3]

The greatest difficulty is the inaccessibility of the original manuscript schedules. After the census office's tabulations were completed, the schedules were returned to archives in the states where the data had been gathered. Records from a few states have not survived, some have not been microfilmed, and none were available in machine-readable form until recently. Entries for over 400,000 decedents from the 1850 through 1880 mortality schedules have now been either transcribed and published (Volkel 1972, 1979; Hahn 1983, 1987) or computerized (Jackson 1999). Table 2.1 shows several records from the 1850 mortality schedules from Perry County, Illinois, to illustrate the range of information available from this source.

There are four likely sources of bias in these data. The first is that, based on model life tables and the published totals, it appears that mortality at very young and very old ages is underreported, and that overall mortality is underestimated by as much as 40 percent. The second bias is that surviving households are probably more likely to report deaths that occurred closer in time to the date of the census enumeration. The third bias is the underenumeration of deaths in households where all members died and thus left no survivors to report their deaths to the census enumerator. The final bias results from the reporting of the cause of death by household members rather than by health care professionals. This no doubt leads to common mistakes (like reporting "typhus" when the cause of death was "typhoid"),

---

2. Among those who have made use of the published totals, in addition to Haines (1998) are Fogel and Engerman (1974, 101) to calculate slave death rates, and Jacobson (1957).

3. These difficulties are summarized in Condran and Crimmins (1979).

but can be remedied to some extent by grouping diseases into broad categories, reflecting either easily identified physical symptoms or the likely susceptibility to the influence of socioeconomic status. For the present study, which will examine mortality rates by comparing the mortality schedules to the population schedules for a set of identical counties, these biases are substantial problems only if underreporting or misreporting varies by status differently in the mortality and population schedules. If an undercount of deaths in low-status families results from such families' being missed entirely by the census, then both the survivors and decedents will be absent from the combined data, leaving the mortality rate unaffected.[4]

Although it is not possible to test whether reporting of the *number* of deaths varied by status, it is possible to assess whether the reported *timing* of the deaths that were reported varied by status. If low-status families were as likely as high-status families to report deaths more distant in time from the census date, we can have somewhat greater confidence in the reliability of the reporting of deaths by status.[5] After decedents from the 1860 mortality schedules were matched to their surviving families in the 1860 population schedules (as described below), the distribution of the months in which deaths occurred was calculated for high- (total wealth > 0) and low- (total wealth $= 0$) status families. Figure 2.1 shows that the distributions are

4. An example can help assess the possible magnitude of the bias from underenumeration (failure of an entire family to appear in the population schedules, and the lack of information reported by these families in the mortality schedules) or underreporting (failure of families reported in the population schedules to inform the census marshal that a death had occurred that should have been included in the mortality schedules) in the estimated effect of wealth on mortality. Imagine a population containing 100,000 individuals, half in families with zero wealth and half in families with positive wealth. The mortality rate among those in families with zero wealth is 30 per thousand; it is 10 per thousand among those in families with positive wealth. The possession of positive wealth reduces mortality by 0.020. Suppose now that 40 percent of those in families with zero wealth (both survivors and decedents) were missed by the census marshals (and none of those with positive wealth were missed). The difference in the mortality rate by wealth ownership for the remaining 80,000 observations is still 0.020. Suppose now that underenumeration was zero for both groups, but that 20 percent of the deaths in zero-wealth families were not reported. Wealth now appears to reduce mortality by 0.014. If the 20 percent underreporting rate was instead applied to the positive-wealth families, wealth appears to reduce mortality by 0.022. This suggests that (a) the failure of entire low-wealth families to appear in the census (in both the population and mortality schedules) leads to no bias in the effect of wealth on mortality; (b) the failure of low-wealth families to report deaths when the rest of the family was enumerated can bias the effect of wealth downward from its true value (by 30 percent in this case); and (c) the failure of high-wealth families to report deaths can bias the effect of wealth upward from its true value (by 10 percent in this case).

5. This abstracts from the possibility that the timing of deaths in the year prior to the census was systematically related to status (e.g., if poor nutrition or poor housing made deaths in the winter more likely for families of low status). If such was the case, we might observe months when low-status families reported a larger fraction of their deaths than high-status families. There would be no reason to expect, however, that the gap between the fractions reported by high- and low-status families would widen continuously as time from the census date increased if both high- and low-status families are able to remember accurately the months in which deaths occurred.

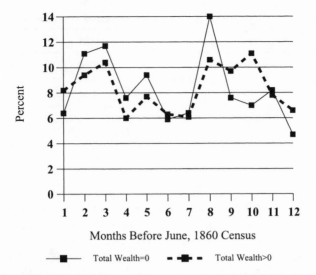

Fig. 2.1   Distribution of months of death by family total wealth in three Illinois counties and two Alabama counties, 1860

Notes: For "Total Wealth = 0," $N = 171$; for "Total Wealth > 0," $N = 587$. The chi-square statistic for the homogeneity of the two distributions is 7.5622 ($p = 0.8180$).

similar except at ten months prior to the census (August 1859). The overall distributions are statistically indistinguishable.

The advantages of using individual observations from the mortality schedules more than outweigh the shortcomings. For example, when combined with the information on each family's socioeconomic status in the population schedules, the mortality schedules provide the best and most broadly representative view we are likely to get of the socioeconomic correlates of mortality by cause of death. The range of places that can be examined makes it possible to assess the impact of a variety of environmental forces (such as climate and the presence of sanitation and public health systems) on the relationship between status and mortality.

By themselves, the data in the mortality schedules are an extremely valuable and heretofore unexploited source of information on the health of the nineteenth-century U.S. population. As table 2.1 shows, the mortality schedules themselves contain some information on status—each decedent's occupation at the time of death was reported. But a great deal more can be done after linking the mortality schedules to the population schedules collected at the same time. Table 2.2 shows the information relating to status than can be obtained from the 1850 and 1860 population schedules. Each piece of information is reported for each surviving member of the family.

Two data sets will be employed. In the first, individuals from a particular

Table 2.2   Variables in Population Schedules Related to Socioeconomic Status

	1850	1860
	Occupation	Occupation
	Real estate wealth	Real estate wealth
		Personal wealth
	Literacy	Literacy
	School attendance	School attendance
	Pauper	Pauper
	Criminality	Criminality
	Disability	Disability

county in the mortality schedules will be merged with individuals from the corresponding county in the population schedules. This will make possible an examination of the correlates of mortality at the individual level that controls for characteristics common to the two schedules (age, birthplace, occupation, and characteristics of the county). Since occupation will be the only measure of socioeconomic status available in this merged data set, attention will be confined to males over the age of twenty.[6] Fifty counties, shown in figure 2.2, were selected for which the 1850 population schedules have been entirely transcribed and for which decedents were included in the computerized mortality database.[7] The counties are concentrated in the Midwest, the upper South, and Alabama.[8] The linkage produced a sample of 927 adult male decedents and 82,246 adult male survivors in the fifty-county area.

6. An alternative strategy would be to combine decedents from all places in the computerized mortality schedules with individuals from the population schedules for the same places who appeared in the public-use sample of the 1850 census. The strategy employed here (focusing on places that have been completely transcribed) will allow for more detailed controls for location-specific effects at the level of minor civil divisions when, at a later date in the project, the manuscripts of the mortality schedules for these fifty counties are searched to determine the town or township of residence for the decedents. In recording deaths, census marshals often remarked upon the quality of the soil, the local climate, the prevalence of endemic diseases, and general economic conditions observed in the town or township. For example, James Searcy, the assistant census marshal who enumerated the southern division of Henry County, Alabama, in 1850, noted: "Bilious fevers or diseases are the most prevalent malady in my district caused by excessive drought and heat. Well watered and qualely light gray soil—generally oak, pine, hickory, cedar timber, lime and marl . . ." (Volkel 1972, 94).

7. The computerized mortality schedule transcriptions were obtained from Jackson (1999). The computerized population schedule transcriptions were obtained from the on-line archives of the USGenWeb project at http://www.usgenweb.org.

8. Alabama: Baldwin, Blount, Conecuh, Henry, Jackson, Jefferson, Lowndes, Madison, Marengo, Monroe, Shelby, Washington, and Wilcox; Illinois: Clark, Crawford, Gallatin, Grundy, Hamilton, McDonough, Perry, Saline, Sangamon, Schuyler, Scott, Stark, Washington, and Wayne; Indiana: Boone, Fayette, Kosciusko, and White; Iowa: Appanoose and Cedar; Kentucky: Simpson and Spencer; Michigan: Ionia and Lapeer; North Carolina: Northampton and Wake; Ohio: Henry, Pike, Sandusky, and Williams; Pennsylvania: Carbon, Sullivan, and Tioga; Texas: Galveston; Virginia: Charlotte, Fauquier, and Madison.

Fig. 2.2   Fifty counties used in 1850 analysis of mortality by occupation

For a smaller set of counties, it was possible to do better than this. A second data set was created for these places by merging decedents with the families in which they were living before their deaths. This was done by choosing locations for which the population and mortality schedules have been completely transcribed, and for which it was possible to sort both schedules in the order in which they were visited by the census marshal. Since the mortality schedule was filled out at the same time as the population schedule, it was possible to set the schedules side by side and locate the families in the population schedules who reported the deaths in the mortality schedules.[9]

9. It would have also been feasible here to use individuals from the mortality schedules and a sample of individuals from the public-use sample for 1850 or 1860. But because the entire population schedule had to be examined to locate the surviving households of decedents, the set of decedents had to be limited to those places with both mortality and population schedules sorted in their original order—simply examining a 1 percent sample from the population schedule would identify the households of very few decedents with certainty. This suggested using the completely transcribed population schedules for the set of survivors. This will also make possible the analysis of "neighborhood effects" later in the project. As was the case for

Table 2.3 shows an example of this linkage for part of Shelby County, Illinois in 1860. The mortality schedule listed the following individuals in order: Louisa Compton (age 38), Emma A. Compton (age 1), John W. Lanning (age 6), and Jane B. Graybill (infant). Using the names, ages, and birthplaces, these individuals were then inserted back into the population schedules in the families who reported their deaths.

For 1850, it was possible to merge decedents with their surviving families for five counties in Illinois (Morgan, Jackson, Union, Saline, and Washington) and one in Alabama (Shelby). For 1860, it was possible for three counties in Illinois (Perry, Shelby, and Vermilion) and two in Alabama (St. Clair and Tuscaloosa). These counties are shown in figures 2.3 and 2.4.[10] For each family member, the linked data contain the individual's age, sex, race, birthplace, family wealth (the sum of the wealth reported for each family member), the occupation of the family head, family size, whether the family member died in the twelve months before the census, and the cause of death for decedents. A family is defined here and throughout the analysis as a group of individuals with a common surname residing in the same household. A household is a group of individuals living in the same residence, regardless of their surnames.[11]

Table 2.4 shows the marginal effects from a probit regression in which the dependent variable is 1 if the individual was linked to the population schedules and zero otherwise. The overall linkage rate was 85 percent, but age reduced the probability of successful linkage, males were 3 to 4 percentage points more likely to be matched, and those born in the same state of their residence at death were 5 percentage points less likely to be linked. The effect of age reflects the increasing probability than an individual will be living away from the family as he or she becomes older: Unless the mother died in childbirth, an infant was survived by at least one person with the same surname; children at higher ages have a higher probability of having been orphaned and having taken up residence with another family; young adults may have left their families to work on nearby farms or in local businesses; and older adults are more likely to have seen their children move out and to have been a family's last surviving member. The negative effect of having been born locally probably reflects the difficulty in linking single persons

the linkage of adult males described above, this linkage could in theory be done for any locations with extant manuscripts of the population schedules and extant manuscripts of the mortality schedules. The counties chosen for analysis here were those with transcribed population schedules and transcribed mortality schedules, to limit the time spent in data transcription.

10. The transcribed mortality schedules were taken from Volkel (1972 and 1979) for Illinois and from Hahn (1983 and 1987) for Alabama. The computerized population schedule transcriptions were obtained from the on-line archives of the USGenWeb project at http://www.usgenweb.org.

11. For example, in table 2.3, Jane Gallagher and George Thompson in household number 590 are members of the same household as the three Kinsels, but Gallagher and Thompson are each counted as separate families in the analysis.

Table 2.3   Example of Linked Population and Mortality Schedules, Shelby County, Illinois, Southern District (1860)

Household Number	Name	Age	Sex	Occupation	Birthplace	Real Estate	Personal Estate	Cause of Death
589	Compton, Charles	45	M	Farmer	Virginia	$4,200	$1,880	
589[a]	Compton, Louisa	38	F		Ohio			Consumption
589	Compton, Jonathan	18	M	Laborer	Ohio			
589	Compton, Thomas	16	M	Laborer	Ohio			
589	Compton, Marion	14	M		Ohio			
589	Compton, Mary Jane	12	F		Ohio			
589	Compton, Charlie	10	M		Ohio			
589	Compton, Sarah E.	8	F		Illinois			
589	Compton, Louisa	5	F		Illinois			
589[a]	Compton, Emma A.	1	F		Illinois			Unknown
590	Kinsel, John	27	M	Farmer	Ohio		$1,195	
590	Kinsel, Cemantha	21	F		Ohio			
590	Kinsel, Simon J.	1	M		Illinois			
590	Gallagher, Jane	11	F		Illinois			
590	Thompson, George	24	M	Laborer	Ohio			
591	Lanning, William	39	M	Farmer	Pennsylvania	$1,200	$795	
591	Lanning, Mariah	39	F		Ohio			
591	Lanning, Delila J.	17	F		Ohio			
591	Lanning, Thomas M.	15	M	Laborer	Ohio			
591	Lanning, Derick D.	12	M		Ohio			
591[a]	Lanning, John W.	6	M		Ohio			Scarlet fever
591	Lanning, Daniel G.	1	M		Illinois			
591	Sinn, Rhoda	66	F		New Jersey			
592	Graybill, Samuel R.	37	M	Farmer	Ohio	$2,500	$1,300	

(continued)

Table 2.3 (continued)

Household Number	Name	Age	Sex	Occupation	Birthplace	Real Estate	Personal Estate	Cause of Death
592	Graybill, Sarah H.	36	F		Ohio			
592	Graybill, Thomas J.	13	M		Ohio			
592	Graybill, Isaac G.	12	M		Ohio			
592	Graybill, Henry C.	10	M		Ohio			
592	Graybill, Carlisle	9	M		Ohio			
592	Graybill, George	8	M		Ohio			
592	Graybill, Sarah Olive	3	F		Ohio			
592	Graybill, James B.	0	M		Illinois			
592	Graybill, Jane B.	0	F		Illinois			Brain congestion

[a]Entry inserted from mortality schedules.

Fig. 2.3   Illinois counties in 1850 and 1860 analysis by wealth: (1) Morgan, (2) Vermilion, (3) Shelby, (4) Washington, (5) Perry, (6) Jackson, (7) Union, and (8) Saline

Fig. 2.4   Alabama counties in 1850 and 1860 analysis by wealth: (1) Tuscaloosa, (2) St. Clair, (3) Shelby

who resided with nonfamily members and whose deaths, although reported to the census marshal, would have left no persons in the population schedule with the same surname.

Three adjustments were made to the linked sample before it was analyzed. To reduce the influence of extreme outliers, 2,958 individuals in families with more than $10,000 in real estate wealth were deleted. Because individuals residing in households where their surnames were unique were not at risk to be successfully linked from the mortality schedules to the population schedules, although the deaths of such individuals would have been reported in the mortality schedules, the sample was further limited by discarding 1,382 additional individuals whose surnames appeared only once in the households where they were enumerated after the decedents were inserted into their surviving households.[12] Finally, because it was unclear how

12. If an individual was the only person with a surname in a household and that person died, his or her death would have been reported in the mortality schedule. But because there was no one else with the same surname in the household that reported the death, it would not be possible to identify which household reported the death when trying to link individuals from the mortality schedules back to the population schedules, so such deaths would remain unlinked. If a person with a surname unique within a household did not die, that person would appear in the population schedule. The linkage procedure would thus be biased toward survivors among those with surnames unique in their households of residence. To eliminate this bias, it is necessary to remove those with surnames unique in their households of residence from the

Table 2.4   **Marginal Effects from Probit Regressions on Successful Linkage from Mortality to Population Schedules**

Variable	(1)	(2)	(3)	(4)
Ages 1–4	–0.0827	–0.0824	–0.0827	–0.0820
	(2.21)**	(2.18)**	(2.22)**	(2.18)**
Ages 5–19	–0.1203	–0.1235	–0.1244	–0.1249
	(2.73)***	(2.75)***	(2.83)***	(2.79)***
Ages 20–44	–0.1531	–0.1633	–0.1511	–0.1595
	(3.43)***	(3.51)***	(3.41)***	(3.45)***
Ages 45+	–0.2253	–0.2339	–0.2248	–0.2309
	(3.78)***	(3.83)***	(3.80)***	(3.80)***
Male	0.0347	0.0366	0.0371	0.0388
	(1.63)	(1.71)*	(1.76)*	(1.83)*
Born in state of enumeration	–0.0464	–0.0449	–0.0493	–0.0480
	(1.54)	(1.48)	(1.66)*	(1.62)
Foreign-born	–0.0634	–0.0619	–0.0592	–0.0587
	(1.11)	(1.08)	(1.05)	(1.04)
Controls				
Year	Yes	Yes	No	No
County	Yes	Yes	Yes	Yes
Cause of death	No	Yes	No	Yes
Month of death	No	No	Yes	Yes
Predicted probability	0.8526	0.8529	0.8575	0.8580
Pseudo-R^2	0.0384	0.0399	0.0540	0.0566
Observations	1,193	1,193	1,193	1,193

Notes: Absolute value of z-statistics in parentheses. Omitted categories are "Infant," "Female," "Born outside state of enumeration," and "Native-born."
***Significant at the 1 percent level.
**Significant at the 5 percent level.
*Significant at the 10 percent level.

well household wealth would approximate the resources available to household members in group housing or in families with several boarders, 19,562 individuals in households of ten or more members were discarded. The sample that resulted from the linkage and from these adjustments contains 304 decedents and 38,996 survivors in 1850, and 511 decedents and 52,268 survivors in 1860.

In both the 1850 sample of adult male decedents merged with surviving adult males and the 1850 and 1860 samples of individual decedents merged with their surviving families, the counties for which the analysis can be per-

population schedules. In table 2.3, the individuals discarded were Jane Gallagher, George Thompson, and Rhoda Sinn. Although the fact that these individuals were living with families other than their own is potentially useful information on their economic status, it was thought prudent for now to keep analysis of their mortality experience separate from that of individuals living in multiple-person family units. For 1870 and 1880, such merging of decedents who had surnames unique in the household of residence back into the household of residence is feasible, as the mortality schedule reports the number of the households that reported each death.

formed were determined largely by whether genealogists had transcribed mortality and population schedules. These counties are uniformly rural. In 1850, only four places with populations over 3,000 are included: Mauch Chunk, Pennsylvania (pop. 5,203), Springfield, Illinois (pop. 4,533), Raleigh, North Carolina (pop. 4,518), and Galveston, Texas (pop. 4,177). In 1860, only two places with 2,000 or more inhabitants are included: Tuscaloosa, Alabama (pop. 3,989), and Elwood, Illinois (pop. 2,000). It was not possible to locate any counties in the Middle Atlantic or New England states for which linkage was possible.[13] Descriptive statistics for both samples as well as the most common causes of death are shown in tables 2A.1 through 2A.3 in the appendix to this chapter.

2.4   Analysis of Socioeconomic Status and Mortality among Adult Males in 1850

The first hypothesis to be tested is that in 1850 individuals in higher-income occupations had lower mortality rates than individuals in lower-income occupations. The exact mechanism through which this relationship operates will not be tested, but it seems reasonable to imagine that higher-status individuals may be able to purchase better nutrition (both more calories and a greater variety of calorie sources) and better housing (larger, better ventilated, farther from sanitary hazards, more thoroughly protected against rain and cold). The relationship between status and mortality will not be the same for all causes of death. It will be strongest for those causes of death most susceptible to living circumstances. Death from tuberculosis (best transmitted among individuals weakened by poor nutrition or exposure to other diseases and living in cramped, poorly ventilated places) will be more strongly associated with low status than death from drowning.

Occupations are grouped into four broad categories: white-collar (professional, managerial, clerical and sales, and government), craft, farmer, and laborer (including operatives and unskilled workers). Those with no reported occupation are listed as unknown. Farmers and white-collar workers had higher incomes than craft workers, who in turn had higher incomes than laborers, so if income differences are an important source of differences in mortality, laborers should have higher mortality than otherwise identical craftsmen, who should have higher mortality than otherwise identical white-collar workers.[14]

---

13. The 1860 mortality and population schedules for Albany, New York, have been linked by David Davenport, and the author has linked 1860 mortality and population schedules for several wards in Chicago. Results for these places will appear at a later point in the project.

14. Although we have no reliable estimates of farmers' income in 1850 or 1860, Margo (2000, 45) reports that in 1850, assuming twenty-six workdays per month, common laborers in the Midwest earned $20.80 per month, craftsmen earned $35.10 per month, and white-collar workers earned $47.12 per month. In the South Central region, common laborers earned $22.10 per month, craftsmen earned $47.06 per month, and white-collar workers earned $60.84 per month.

There are several likely influences on mortality that must be controlled for to isolate the role of status. The most important is obviously age. It is also possible to identify individuals born outside the state in which they resided at the time of the census. Migrants may have had lower mortality if they are more physically fit than nonmigrants, but their introduction to a new disease environment may have a countervailing effect on their mortality. There may also be differences in the physical or economic environment across counties or regions that influence mortality. Haines, Weiss, and Craig (2000) include a measure of the availability of transportation. The multivariate analysis includes this county-level variable as well as regional dummies for the West (Indiana, Michigan, Illinois, Iowa, and Texas) and South (North Carolina, Virginia, Alabama, and Kentucky).

Columns (1) and (3) of table 2.5 present baseline probit regressions with death (from any cause) as the dependent variable, and age and occupational categories as the only independent variables. Columns (2) and (4) introduce additional controls for individual and county characteristics. Separate regressions are shown for younger (aged twenty to forty-four) and older (aged forty-five and older) males to allow the effects of age and occupation to change as age increases.

As expected, there is a clear age pattern: The risk of death increases with age. But the pattern of increase is nonlinear, as age has a larger impact for those aged 45 and above. Death rates were higher among the foreign-born and lower in the South. The results for occupation provide little support for the hypothesis that those in lower-income occupations suffered from higher mortality rates: Among those with reported occupations, only white-collar workers in column (1) had a mortality rate different from laborers that was statistically significant and large in magnitude (with white-collar workers' mortality rate 3 per thousand lower than that of laborers, the omitted category). Even this difference is eliminated when the additional controls for individual and county characteristics are added in column (2).[15] The predicted probabilities in columns (2) and (4) in fact suggest that the mortality rate of unskilled laborers was roughly the same as that of white-collar workers, and perhaps somewhat below that of craftsmen, despite the low incomes earned by laborers.[16]

Table 2.6 presents a similar regression, with death from consumption (tuberculosis) as the dependent variable. The results in column (2) for males aged twenty to forty-four do indeed reveal substantial and statistically sig-

---

15. The much higher mortality of those with no reported occupation may be the result of the withdrawal from regular work of those debilitated by chronic health conditions in the time before their deaths. One in five males aged twenty and over in the mortality schedules used here had no reported occupation; for the corresponding population schedules, only one in ten had no reported occupation.

16. The predicted probabilities are calculated for a baseline individual (a native-born male born outside his state of enumeration, in a Northern county with no transportation access) at age thirty in columns (1) and (2) and at age fifty in columns (3) and (4).

Table 2.5   **Marginal Effects from Probit Regressions on Mortality From All Causes among Males Aged 20+, 1850**

	Ages 20–44 (1)	Ages 20–44 (2)	Ages 45+ (3)	Ages 45+ (4)
Age	0.0002	0.0001	0.0008	0.0008
	(3.51)***	(2.73)***	(5.06)***	(5.17)***
White-collar	–0.0030	–0.0007	–0.0033	0.0001
	(1.84)*	(0.40)	(0.64)	(0.02)
Farmer	–0.0014	0.0008	–0.0052	–0.0024
	(1.36)	(0.73)	(1.48)	(0.69)
Craftsman	0.0004	0.0016	–0.0007	0.0014
	(0.30)	(1.26)	(0.17)	(0.36)
Unknown	0.0247	0.0298	0.0302	0.0343
	(10.64)***	(11.63)***	(4.67)***	(5.07)***
Born in state of enumeration		0.0001		0.0024
		(0.13)		(0.85)
Foreign-born		0.0103		0.0139
		(7.86)***		(4.35)***
Transportation access		–0.0000		–0.0023
		(0.04)		(1.18)
West		0.0014		0.0025
		(1.54)		(1.00)
South		–0.0023		–0.0049
		(2.40)**		(1.93)*
Predicted probability				
White-collar	0.0054	0.0052	0.0137	0.0148
Farmer	0.0070	0.0064	0.0125	0.0127
Craftsman	0.0087	0.0071	0.0163	0.0161
Laborer	0.0084	0.0058	0.0171	0.0147
Unknown	0.0352	0.0322	0.0217	0.0208
Pseudo-R^2	0.0298	0.0452	0.0266	0.0374
Observations	64,241	64,241	18,932	18,932

Notes: Absolute value of z-statistics in parentheses. The figures shown are partial derivatives. Omitted categories for the categorical variables are "Laborer," "Born outside state of enumeration," "Native-born," "North," and "No access to rail or water transportation." Transportation access was taken from Craig, Palmquist, and Weiss (1998); the authors graciously provided their data in machine-readable format.
***Significant at the 1 percent level.
**Significant at the 5 percent level.
*Significant at the 10 percent level.

nificant differences in mortality from consumption by occupation, controlling for other characteristics. The differences, however, are decidedly *not* those we would expect if income was all that occupational category indicated. Laborers have consumption mortality rates that are only half those of both white-collar workers and craftsmen.

This may reflect the importance of the workplace environment. Farmers and common laborers, most of whom in these rural counties would have

Table 2.6   Marginal Effects from Probit Regressions on Mortality From Consumption among Males Aged 20, 1850

	Ages 20–44 (1)	Ages 20–44 (2)	Ages 45+ (3)	Ages 45+ (4)
Age	–0.0000	–0.0000	0.0001	0.0001
	(0.37)	(0.20)	(1.66)*	(1.75)*
White-collar	0.0009	0.0018	–0.0013	–0.0008
	(1.11)	(1.98)**	(1.13)	(0.66)
Farmer	0.0002	0.0005	–0.0023	–0.0011
	(0.38)	(1.33)	(2.09)**	(1.22)
Craftsman	0.0011	0.0014	–0.0014	–0.0010
	(1.82)*	(2.35)**	(1.69)*	(1.19)
Unknown	0.0017	0.0027	0.0009	0.0020
	(2.06)**	(2.85)***	(0.66)	(1.29)
Born in state of enumeration		0.0005		–0.0007
		(1.52)		(0.93)
Foreign-born		0.0008		0.0006
		(1.76)*		(0.79)
Transportation access		0.0001		0.0004
		(0.25)		(0.69)
West		–0.0006		–0.0012
		(2.16)**		(1.96)**
South		–0.0012		–0.0014
		(3.86)***		(2.19)**
Predicted probability				
White-collar	0.0015	0.0026	0.0011	0.0021
Farmer	0.0010	0.0015	0.0014	0.0023
Craftsman	0.0018	0.0023	0.0011	0.0018
Laborer	0.0009	0.0009	0.0037	0.0042
Unknown	0.0023	0.0035	0.0023	0.0038
Pseudo-R^2	0.0073	0.0270	0.0252	0.0460
Observations	63,729	63,729	18,631	18,631

Notes: Absolute value of z-statistics in parentheses. The figures shown are partial derivatives. Omitted categories for the categorical variables are "Laborer," "Born outside state of enumeration," "Native-born," "North," and "No access to rail or water transportation." Transportation access was taken from Craig, Palmquist, and Weiss (1998); the authors graciously provided their data in machine-readable format.
***Significant at the 1 percent level.
**Significant at the 5 percent level.
*Significant at the 10 percent level.

been farm laborers, generally worked outdoors and had fewer workplace opportunities to come into direct contact with other people than white-collar or craft workers. It may also reflect some self-selection into occupations consistent with health: Those debilitated by consumption may have taken up less physically demanding employment in workshops and offices rather than the strenuous manual work of farmers and common laborers. The results for consumption demonstrate the inadequacy of a simple measure of socioeconomic status (occupation) as a determinant of mortality, and leave open the possibility that socioeconomic status is at least in part determined by health status.

2.5 Analysis of Socioeconomic Status and among Families in 1850 and 1860

The sample of decedents merged with their surviving families in 1850 and 1860 presents two advantages over the data used in the preceding analysis of the link between occupation and mortality for adult males. The first is that it contains total family wealth (real estate wealth in 1850 and 1860, as well as personal wealth in 1860), which is likely to be a more meaningful measure of the economic resources at a family's disposal than the family head's occupational title (which may signify environmental conditions as well). The second is that it provides an opportunity to examine the mortality experienced by all family members, not just adult males. This is useful in itself, as the mortality of older children (aged five to nineteen) has been overlooked in previous studies of the socioeconomic correlates of mortality in the late nineteenth and early twentieth centuries. But the ability to look at several age categories is also useful in that it can eliminate the possibility that socioeconomic status itself is caused by health status, by focusing on the mortality of infants and children who were too young to provide income to the family.[17]

Table 2.7 presents marginal effects from probit regressions by age categories in which mortality is the dependent variable, with controls only for whether the family owned real estate and age in panel A and a full set of individual, family, and location controls in panel B.[18] In no case is the impact of possession of real estate by the family associated with a statistical or substantive reduction in mortality.[19] In six of the ten regressions, the sign of the coefficient on the possession of real estate is actually positive. Of the other controls, the most interesting results are for the occupation of the family head: For adults (aged twenty and over) in columns (4) and (5), residence in a family headed by either a farmer or an unskilled laborer was associated with lower mortality than residence in a family headed by a white-collar

17. This approach to overcoming the problem of reverse causation is suggested by Case, Lubotsky, and Paxson (2001).

18. Additional specifications for the wealth variable are employed in appendix tables 2A.4 through 2A.13—the natural log of wealth and dummies for various levels of wealth. None of the qualitative findings described here are altered by the use of these alternative specifications. The set of controls used in the following regressions differs slightly from that used in the regressions for males aged twenty and over in the previous section: family wealth and the family head's occupation replace the individual's own occupation as the measure of socioeconomic status (as children seldom had reported occupations), and dummies for state and year replace the controls for location (dummies for region and transportation access), which was preferable given the small number of locations and their relative homogeneity within states. Other family-level variables (e.g., parents' literacy and birthplaces) were introduced into the analysis, but did not have much influence on mortality and so were excluded.

19. Steckel (1988, 338–39) finds no relationship between family real estate holdings in 1850 and the survival of infants, children aged one to four, and female spouses between 1850 and 1860.

Table 2.7   **Marginal Effects from Probit Regressions on Mortality from All Causes, 1850 and 1860**

Variable	Infants (1)	Ages 1–4 (2)	Ages 5–19 (3)	Ages 20–44 (4)	Ages 45+ (5)
A.					
Real estate > 0	0.0091	0.0024	−0.0002	−0.0003	0.0042
	(1.29)	(1.26)	(0.29)	(0.38)	(1.60)
Age		−0.0076	−0.0000	0.0002	0.0004
		(8.06)***	(0.60)	(2.63)***	(3.67)***
Predicted probability	0.0473	0.0135	0.0035	0.0058	0.0131
Pseudo-R^2	0.0012	0.0331	0.0003	0.0031	0.0123
Observations	3,662	13,610	34,629	31,369	8,809
B.					
Real estate > 0	0.0085	0.0028	−0.0004	−0.0009	0.0033
	(1.15)	(1.43)	(0.53)	(1.06)	(1.41)
Age		−0.0074	−0.0000	0.0001	0.0005
		(8.09)***	(0.28)	(2.17)**	(4.34)***
Male	0.0128	0.0049	0.0013	0.0002	0.0082
	(1.82)*	(2.66)***	(2.00)**	(0.28)	(3.74)***
Family size	0.0018	0.0004	0.0002	0.0010	0.0019
	(0.96)	(0.68)	(0.93)	(4.72)***	(3.79)***
Born in state of enumeration	−0.0009	−0.0033	0.0006	0.0038	0.0125
	(0.05)	(1.05)	(0.88)	(3.57)***	(1.55)
Foreign-born		0.0090	−0.0013	0.0017	−0.0019
		(0.79)	(0.66)	(1.13)	(0.53)
Head was farmer	−0.0105	−0.0038	−0.0001	−0.0034	−0.0127
	(1.24)	(1.64)	(0.11)	(3.61)***	(4.61)***
Head was laborer	−0.0047	−0.0002	0.0004	−0.0027	−0.0074
	(0.35)	(0.05)	(0.28)	(1.90)*	(1.71)*
Illinois	0.0005	0.0022	−0.0001	0.0001	−0.0031
	(0.05)	(1.00)	(0.13)	(0.12)	(1.29)
1860	0.0045	0.0061	−0.0000	−0.0001	0.0047
	(0.60)	(3.12)***	(0.04)	(0.12)	(2.10)**
Predicted probability	0.4692	0.0128	0.0034	0.0052	0.0107
Pseudo-R^2	0.0057	0.0446	0.0046	0.0229	0.0568
Observations	3,647	13,610	34,629	31,369	8,809

Notes: Absolute value of z-statistics in parentheses. The figures shown are partial derivatives. The sample consists of all individuals in the population schedules and all individuals in the mortality schedules who were merged with families in the population schedules. Wealth is measured at the family level. Omitted categories for the categorical variables are "Real estate = 0," "Female," "Born outside state of enumeration," "Native-born," "Head was white-collar or craftsman," "Alabama," and "1850."

***Significant at the 1 percent level.

**Significant at the 5 percent level.

*Significant at the 10 percent level.

worker or craftsman. This is consistent with the finding for adult males in the previous section, although it applies to both males and females here.

Table 2.8 uses personal wealth rather than real estate wealth. The census did not begin to collect personal wealth data until 1860, so table 2.8 omits observations from 1850. The results are generally more favorable for the hypothesis that wealth was negatively associated with mortality. Either with or without the additional individual, family, and location controls, possession of personal wealth reduced mortality for infants, older children, and younger adults. For these groups, death was half as likely in the twelve months prior to the census in families that possessed personal wealth as it was in families that did not.

The finding that personal wealth has more impact on mortality than real estate wealth may reflect the greater liquidity of personal wealth, and the importance of the household's assets in smoothing consumption: When a negative shock to household income occurs, personal wealth can be liquidated more easily than real estate wealth to compensate for the shock. It would be easier for the household to sell some of its furniture or implements than it would be to sell some of its land—by their nature, moveable assets (personal estate) can be relocated to where there is a demand for them, while immoveable assets (real estate) must find a buyer at their fixed location. These effects are exacerbated if shocks to household income are correlated across the community (say, because of bad weather), since even fewer local buyers for the land a household wishes to liquidate will be available, while the option of transporting some personal property to a market center for liquidation remains.

There are noteworthy differences in the impact of wealth on mortality at different ages. The effect is greatest for infants but small in magnitude and statistically insignificant for children aged one to four. The effect of wealth is greater for infants than for older children aged five to nineteen.[20] In modern data, the effect of the family's economic circumstances on the health of its children increases as the age of the child increases (Case, Lubotsky, and Paxson 2001). This appears to be the case because children in low–socioeconomic status households receive a larger number of adverse shocks to their health as they age, rather than because they are less able to recover from a given shock (Currie and Stabile 2002). The absence of such a pattern for the period examined here may be the result of high infant death rates: Infants in low–socioeconomic status households, who would be at risk to die later in response to an adverse shock under modern conditions where infant deaths are rare, are in effect "weeded out" by high infant mortality.

For 1860, it is also possible to examine the simultaneous influence of real and personal wealth on mortality. Table 2.9 includes both. The finding of a

20. Condran and Crimmins (1979, 14) believe that the five-to-twenty age group was the most accurately reported in the mortality schedules. If they are correct, then the impact of wealth for this group's mortality shown in table 2.8 is perhaps the strongest evidence that wealth's effect is more than an artifact of inaccuracies in the mortality schedules.

Table 2.8   **Marginal Effects From Probit Regressions on Mortality from All Causes, 1860**

Variable	Infants (1)	Ages 1–4 (2)	Ages 5–19 (3)	Ages 20–44 (4)	Ages 45+ (5)
A.					
Personal estate > 0	−0.0438	−0.0011	−0.0027	−0.0048	0.0086
	(2.71)***	(0.25)	(1.90)*	(2.51)**	(1.50)
Age		−0.0107	−0.0001	0.0001	0.0006
		(8.00)***	(0.66)	(1.72)*	(3.61)***
Predicted probability	0.0486	0.0148	0.0034	0.0056	0.0152
Pseudo-R^2	0.0081	0.0513	0.0042	0.0066	0.0173
Observations	2,154	7,730	19,480	18,279	5,136
B.					
Personal estate > 0	−0.0386	−0.0005	−0.0025	−0.0050	0.0090
	(2.32)**	(0.12)	(1.66)*	(2.64)***	(1.76)*
Age		−0.0106	−0.0000	0.0001	0.0007
		(8.03)***	(0.23)	(1.38)	(4.09)***
Male	0.0175	0.0071	0.0004	−0.0014	0.0061
	(1.88)*	(2.77)***	(0.46)	(1.38)	(1.91)*
Family size	0.0000	0.0006	0.0002	0.0010	0.0022
	(0.01)	(0.85)	(0.96)	(3.94)***	(2.81)***
Born in state of enumeration	0.0076	−0.0009	0.0017	0.0031	0.0220
	(0.37)	(0.22)	(1.89)*	(2.45)**	(1.92)*
Foreign-born		0.0413		−0.0000	−0.0002
		(1.58)		(0.02)	(0.03)
Head was farmer	−0.0098	−0.0037	−0.0007	−0.0017	−0.0075
	(0.89)	(1.19)	(0.65)	(1.46)	(1.87)*
Head was laborer	−0.0047	0.0008	0.0009	−0.0021	−0.0061
	(0.31)	(0.17)	(0.50)	(1.21)	(0.89)
Illinois	0.0057	0.0031	−0.0000	−0.0000	−0.0076
	(0.58)	(1.11)	(0.06)	(0.03)	(2.22)**
Predicted probability	0.0479	0.0142	0.0033	0.0050	0.0136
Pseudo-R^2	0.0141	0.0615	0.0109	0.0274	0.0448
Observations	2,149	7,730	19,009	18,279	5,136

Notes: Absolute value of z-statistics in parentheses. The figures shown are partial derivatives. The sample consists of all individuals in the population schedules and all individuals in the mortality schedules who were merged with families in the population schedules. Wealth is measured at the family level. Omitted categories for the categorical variables are "Personal estate = 0," "Female," "Born outside state of enumeration," "Native-born," "Head was white-collar or craftsman," and "Alabama."

***Significant at the 1 percent level.
**Significant at the 5 percent level.
*Significant at the 10 percent level.

Table 2.9   **Marginal Effects from Probit Regressions on Mortality from All Causes, 1860**

Variable	Infants (1)	Ages 1–4 (2)	Ages 5–19 (3)	Ages 20–44 (4)	Ages 45+ (5)
A.					
Real estate > 0	0.0119	0.0037	0.0001	0.0023	0.0049
	(1.19)	(1.32)	(0.09)	(1.87)	(1.20)
Personal estate > 0	−0.0535	−0.0034	0.0028	−0.0070	0.0067
	(2.94)***	(0.68)	(1.74)*	(3.04)**	(1.05)
Age		−0.0107	−0.0001	0.0001	0.0006
		(8.00)***	(0.66)	(1.53)	(3.57)***
Predicted probability	0.0484	0.0147	0.0034	0.0055	0.0151
Pseudo-R^2	0.0098	0.0525	0.0042	0.0094	0.0190
Observations	2,154	7,730	19,480	18,279	5,136
B.					
Real estate > 0	0.0134	0.0048	−0.0002	0.0013	0.0039
	(1.28)	(1.70)*	(0.18)	(1.14)	(1.02)
Personal estate > 0	−0.0479	−0.0031	−0.0023	−0.0063	0.0077
	(2.60)***	(0.64)	(1.44)	(2.86)***	(1.38)
Age		−0.0105	−0.0000	0.0001	0.0007
		(8.03)***	(0.22)	(1.31)	(4.06)***
Male	0.0174	0.0070	0.0004	−0.0014	0.0062
	(1.88)*	(2.76)***	(0.46)	(1.38)	(1.93)*
Family size	−0.0005	0.0004	0.0002	0.0010	0.0021
	(0.21)	(0.58)	(0.97)	(3.80)***	(2.78)***
Born in state of enumeration	0.0057	−0.0016	0.0018	0.0030	0.0223
	(0.27)	(0.40)	(1.89)*	(2.37)**	(1.94)*
Foreign-born		0.0401		−0.0001	−0.0003
		(1.56)		(0.05)	(0.05)
Head was farmer	−0.0100	−0.0041	−0.0006	−0.0019	−0.0078
	(0.90)	(1.30)	(0.63)	(1.55)	(1.95)*
Head was laborer	−0.0004	0.0024	0.0008	−0.0018	−0.0052
	(0.02)	(0.49)	(0.47)	(1.00)	(0.73)
Illinois	0.0059	0.0032	−0.0000	0.0000	−0.0072
	(0.60)	(1.15)	(0.06)	(0.03)	(2.12)**
Predicted probability	0.0476	0.0140	0.0033	0.0049	0.0135
Pseudo-R^2	0.0160	0.0635	0.0109	0.0284	0.0460
Observations	2,149	7,730	19,009	18,279	5,136

Notes: Absolute value of z-statistics in parentheses. The figures shown are partial derivatives. The sample consists of all individuals in the population schedules and all individuals in the mortality schedules who were merged with families in the population schedules. Wealth is measured at the family level. Omitted categories for the categorical variables are "Real estate = 0," "Personal estate = 0," "Female," "Born outside state of enumeration," "Native-born," "Head was white-collar or craftsman," and "Alabama."

***Significant at the 1 percent level.
**Significant at the 5 percent level.
*Significant at the 10 percent level.

strong negative relationship between personal wealth and mortality for several age groups (particularly infants and adults aged twenty to forty-four) remains. The results for real wealth in panel A now present a puzzle, however. For adults aged twenty to forty-four, possession of real estate increased mortality risk, controlling for personal wealth. This effect is both large in magnitude and statistically significant. For adults aged forty-five and over, mortality is also higher among those in families with real estate than among those in families without it, although not at conventional levels of statistical significance. Although it seems plausible that personal wealth would provide more protection against mortality than real wealth, it is unclear why real wealth would actually lead to increased mortality. Part of the answer lies in the absence of the full set of controls: When other personal, family, and location controls are added in panel B, the negative effect of real estate wealth is reduced.

In order to explore this anomaly further, however, a final specification was adopted that allows the effects of wealth and age to differ across locations. Table 2.10 examines mortality with controls for age and for the possession of real wealth and personal wealth, as well as interactions between these and residence in Illinois. The effect of wealth is not uniform across locations. The perverse positive relationship between possession of real estate wealth and mortality is observed only in Alabama; in Illinois, it is exactly offset by the interaction for ages twenty to forty-four and more than offset for ages forty-five and over. In the latter case, the possession of real estate wealth is now associated with unambiguously lower mortality in Illinois. The interactions between Illinois and both age and personal wealth are statistically and substantively insignificant, so these effects are similar in Illinois and Alabama. Two possible explanations for why real estate ownership is associated with higher mortality in Alabama but not in Illinois come to mind. The first follows from differences in physical geography. In the South, some of the most valuable land was alluvial property near rivers and streams, at low elevations. These places had soil and climate conditions particularly conducive to the cultivation of cotton and commanded high prices per acre. But such places may have been particularly unhealthy locations in which to live, compared to land at higher elevations. Families with high levels of real estate wealth may have been more likely to own land in these relatively less healthy locations.

The second obvious difference between the two states is the presence of slaves in Alabama. Although neither St. Clair County nor Tuscaloosa County had unusually high numbers of slaves per farm compared to other counties in Alabama or in the rest of the South, they nonetheless had more slaves than Perry, Shelby, and Vermilion Counties in Illinois.[21] Families in

21. St. Clair County had an average of only two slaves per farm, and Tuscaloosa had seven (which was the median for Alabama counties in 1860). Wilcox County had the state's highest ratio of slaves per farm with sixty-two. The mean for the entire state was nine.

Table 2.10   Marginal Effects from Probit Regressions on Mortality from All Causes, 1860

Variable	Infants (1)	Ages 1–4 (2)	Ages 5–19 (3)	Ages 20–44 (4)	Ages 45+ (5)
Real estate > 0	0.0173	0.0072	−0.0012	0.0067	0.0172
	(0.97)	(1.25)	(0.72)	(2.82)***	(2.57)**
(Illinois) · real estate > 0	−0.073	−0.0044	0.0019	−0.0066	−0.0268
	(0.34)	(0.66)	(0.92)	(2.35)**	(2.71)***
Personal estate > 0	−0.0528	−0.0095	−0.0022	−0.0079	0.0020
	(1.83)*	(1.01)	(1.01)	(1.98)**	(0.22)
(Illinois) · personal estate > 0	−0.0027	0.0057	−0.0003	0.0005	0.0132
	(0.09)	(0.62)	(0.11)	(0.14)	(0.86)
Age		−0.0101	−0.0000	0.0000	0.0006
		(3.94)***	(0.02)	(0.21)	(2.74)***
(Illinois) · age		−0.0006	−0.0001	0.0001	−0.0001
		(0.19)	(0.47)	(0.84)	(0.36)
Illinois	0.0129	0.0028	−0.0004	−0.0006	0.0087
	(0.55)	(0.29)	(0.14)	(0.10)	(0.37)
Predicted probability	0.0483	0.0146	0.0033	0.0053	0.0140
Pseudo-R^2	0.0105	0.0543	0.0060	0.0157	0.0341
Observations	2,154	7,730	19,480	18,279	5,136

Notes: Absolute value of z-statistics in parentheses. The figures shown are partial derivatives. The sample consists of all individuals in the population schedules and all individuals in the mortality schedules who were merged with families in the population schedules. Wealth is measured at the family level. Omitted categories for the categorical variables are "Real estate = 0," "Personal estate = 0," and "Alabama."

***Significant at the 1 percent level.
**Significant at the 5 percent level.
*Significant at the 10 percent level.

Alabama, where greater real estate wealth was likely associated with the ownership of slaves, may have had more daily exposure to individuals lower in socioeconomic status, and therefore had a greater likelihood of contracting infectious diseases than families on isolated farms in Illinois whose only contact with non–family members may have been occasional trips to town or visits to neighbors whose socioeconomic status would not have differed markedly from their own.[22]

22. To assess these two hypotheses, future work on the link between wealth and mortality in the South will explore (a) the impact of the characteristics of the minor civil divisions in which families were located (by including information on such local attributes as elevation and soil type, available from the U.S. Geological Survey and from the mortality schedules themselves) and (b) the impact of the presence of slaves on individual farms (by merging families from the population schedules with their data from the slave schedules, which reported the age and number of slaves owned on each farm in the South). Both of the merged samples used here will also be linked to data on wages at the county level in the Census of Social Statistics described in Margo (2000).

2.6 Conclusions and Extensions

Socioeconomic status was an important force shaping the mortality rates experienced by Americans in the middle of the nineteenth century, at least in the sample of rural counties examined here. Although occupation was a poor proxy for status among adult males in 1850, the effect of personal wealth on mortality was quite large in magnitude. For example, using the coefficients in panel B of column (1) in table 2.8, the mortality rate for male infants born and residing in Illinois in five-person families headed by farmers was 97 per thousand in families that did not own any personal wealth; the mortality rate for otherwise identical infants was roughly half as great (53 per thousand) in families that possessed any personal wealth.[23] Using the coefficients in column (4), the mortality rate for thirty-year-old males born and residing in Illinois in five-person families headed by farmers was 11 per thousand in families that did not own any personal wealth; the mortality rate for otherwise identical thirty-year-old males was less than half as great (5 per thousand) in families that possessed any personal wealth.[24]

The analysis presented here suffers from two principal shortcomings. The first is the inability to say anything about the experience of urban dwellers. Data for Chicago and Albany will be added as the project progresses, but more information from the cities of the Northeast—inundated with immigrants and beset with crowding, poor sanitation, and substandard housing—will be essential to understand the full scope of mid-nineteenth-century America's mortality record. The second shortcoming is the only brief attention given to causes of death and their likely different relationships to socioeconomic status. Nonetheless, these findings suggest that when Americans moved into cities and towns and factories as the first half of the nineteenth century closed, they had already experienced substantial disparities in health outcomes in the rural, agricultural settings they left behind. Even on farms and in small towns, the more affluent experienced longer lives than their poorer neighbors.

This is not to say that the disparities in health outcomes by socioeconomic status observed today simply continued through the end of the nineteenth and into the twentieth century. It is possible that, as urbanization occurred and individuals were exposed to an increasing number of health hazards related to crowding and sanitation from which wealth might pro-

23. Slightly less dramatic (although still substantial) differences can be seen if the coefficients in table 2A.9 are employed: Using the same values for the other control variables, infants in families with no personal wealth faced a mortality rate of eighty-eight per thousand. In families with $250 in personal wealth (the 3rd decile of the family personal wealth distribution), they faced a rate of forty-two per thousand, while in families with $2,500 in personal wealth (the top decile), they faced a rate of thirty-three per thousand.

24. If the coefficients in table 2A.9 are employed, using the same values for the other control variables, thirty-year-old males in families with no personal wealth faced a mortality rate of eleven per thousand. In families with $250 in personal wealth, they faced a rate of five per thousand, while in families with $2,500 in personal wealth, they faced a rate of four per thousand.

vide little escape, the socioeconomic status–mortality gradient became less steep. With the eradication of many urban health hazards in the twentieth century, a significant role for high status in preventing disease and death may have reappeared.

The significance of the gap in mortality between high- and low-wealth households in the middle of the nineteenth century is instead its appearance at a time and place lacking many of the advantages thought to contribute to better health and lower mortality among the wealthy today: education and knowledge of sound health practices, and access to health care professionals, sophisticated diagnostic technologies, and efficacious treatments. Large differences in mortality between those with and those without wealth in rural communities in the mid-nineteenth-century United States demonstrate the important role played by general living standards and the material conditions of day-to-day life in shaping mortality patterns.

Appendix

Table 2A.1   **Descriptive Statistics for Male Decedents and Survivors Aged 20 and Over in 50 Counties, 1850**

Variable	Mean	Standard Deviation	Minimum	Maximum
Died in twelve months prior to census				
All causes	0.0111	0.1050	0	1
Consumption	0.0014	0.0371	0	1
Age				
20–44 years	0.7724	0.4193	0	1
45+ years	0.2276	0.4193	0	1
Birthplace				
State of enumeration	0.2972	0.4571	0	1
Foreign-born	0.1118	0.3151	0	1
Transportation access	0.5925	0.4914	0	1
Region				
North	0.2195	0.4139	0	1
West	0.4323	0.4954	0	1
South	0.3482	0.4764	0	1
Occupation				
White-collar	0.0564	0.2306	0	1
Farmer	0.5899	0.4919	0	1
Craftsman	0.1508	0.3579	0	1
Laborer	0.1430	0.3500	0	1
Unknown	0.0599	0.2374	0	1
Observations	83,173			

Note: Decedents were drawn from the mortality schedules of the 1850 U.S. Census of Population; survivors were drawn from the population schedules of the 1850 U.S. Census of Population.

Table 2A.2   Descriptive Statistics for Decedents and Survivors in 11 Alabama and Illinois Counties, 1850 and 1860

Variable	Mean	Standard Deviation	Minimum	Maximum
Died in twelve months prior to census				
All ages	0.0089	0.0937	0	1
Infant	0.0475	0.2128	0	1
Ages 1–4	0.0158	0.1247	0	1
Ages 5–19	0.0035	0.0588	0	1
Ages 20–44	0.0059	0.0764	0	1
Ages 45+	0.0139	0.1169	0	1
Age				
Infant	0.0398	0.1954	0	1
Ages 1–4	0.1478	0.3549	0	1
Ages 5–19	0.3761	0.4844	0	1
Ages 20–44	0.3407	0.4739	0	1
Ages 45+	0.0957	0.2941	0	1
Male	0.5152	0.4998	0	1
Family size	5.9572	1.9853	2	9
Birthplace				
State of enumeration	0.5311	0.4990	0	1
Foreign-born	0.0550	0.2281	0	1
County				
Alabama	0.2443	0.4297	0	1
Shelby (1850)	0.0593	0.2362	0	1
St. Clair (1860)	0.0796	0.2706	0	1
Tuscaloosa (1860)	0.1054	0.3071	0	1
Illinois	0.7557	0.4297	0	1
Jackson (1850)	0.0536	0.2253	0	1
Morgan (1850)	0.1359	0.3427	0	1
Saline (1850)	0.0488	0.2154	0	1
Union (1850)	0.0635	0.2439	0	1
Washington (1850)	0.0657	0.2477	0	1
Perry (1860)	0.0869	0.2817	0	1
Shelby (1860)	0.1281	0.3342	0	1
Vermilion (1860)	0.1732	0.3784	0	1
Family real estate = 0	0.3940	0.4886	0	1
Family real estate > 0	0.6060	0.4886	0	1
Under $500	0.1741	0.3792	0	1
$500–999	0.1182	0.3229	0	1
$1,000–2,499	0.1924	0.3942	0	1
$2,500–4,999	0.0841	0.2776	0	1
$5,000+	0.0371	0.1891	0	1
Log(family real estate + $1.00)	4.1209	3.4464	0	9.2103
Family personal estate = 0	0.1014	0.3019	0	1
Family personal estate > 0	0.8986	0.3019	0	1
Under $500	0.4333	0.4955	0	1
$500–999	0.2121	0.4088	0	1

Table 2A.2   (continued)

Variable	Mean	Standard Deviation	Minimum	Maximum
$1,000–2,499	0.1697	0.3754	0	1
$2,500–4,999	0.0381	0.1915	0	1
$5,000+	0.0453	0.2079	0	1
Log (family personal estate + $1.00)	5.6029	2.2371	0	13.1902
Occupation of Household Head				
Laborer	0.0626	0.2423	0	1
Farmer	0.6926	0.4614	0	1
Observations	92,079			

Note: Single-person families, families of ten or more, and households with real estate wealth over $10,000 are excluded.

Table 2A.3   **Causes of Death (percent)**

	1850 Sample: Males Males in 50 Counties, Ages 20+	1850 and 1860 Samples: 11 Counties in Illinois and Alabama				
Cause		Infant	Ages 1–4	Ages 5–19	Ages 20–44	Ages 45+
Consumption	12.2	0.6	0.5	3.3	19.8	10.7
Fevers[a]	17.6	9.2	16.3	35.8	29.1	22.1
Typhoid/typhus	2.7	—	0.5	0.8	1.1	0.8
Pneumonia	4.2	2.3	3.4	4.2	5.5	7.4
Diarrhea	3.0	2.2	2.3	0.8	—	0.8
Cholera[b]	8.1	4.0	1.9	0.8	5.0	0.8
Dropsy	3.8	—	—	0.8	3.9	9.0
Accident[c]	4.2	0.6	3.1	6.7	3.9	2.5
Apoplexy	1.7	—	—	—	—	1.6
Croup	—	14.9	15.8	6.7	1.1	—
Flux	1.3	1.2	—	1.7	—	—
Whooping cough	—	4.6	2.3	0.8	—	—
Dysentery	0.7	2.3	3.3	1.7	0.6	—
Brain inflammation	1.7	3.2	4.2	2.5	1.2	0.8
Old age	0.5	—	—	—	—	4.9
Unknown	6.4	16.1	8.8	6.7	3.3	4.9
Observations	927	154	215	120	182	122

[a]Includes yellow fever, lung fever, and brain fever.
[b]Includes cholera infantum.
[c]Includes murder, suicide, drowning, burning, scalding, and gunshot.

Table 2A.4   **Probit Regressions on Mortality, 1850 and 1860 (partial derivatives)**

Variable	Infants (1)	Ages 1–4 (2)	Ages 5–19 (3)	Ages 20–44 (4)	Ages 45+ (5)
A.					
Log(real estate + $1.00)	0.0012	0.0005	–0.0001	–0.0000	0.0006
	(1.17)	(1.83)*	(0.77)	(0.24)	(1.66)*
Age		–0.0075	–0.0000	0.0002	0.0004
		(8.06)***	(0.57)	(2.63)***	(3.69)***
Predicted probability	0.0474	0.0134	0.0035	0.0058	0.0131
Pseudo-R^2	0.0010	0.0396	0.0037	0.0030	0.0125
Observations	3,662	13,610	34,629	31,369	8,809
B.					
Real estate					
$100–499	0.0129	0.0031	0.0001	–0.0014	0.0020
	(1.29)	(1.16)	(0.15)	(1.19)	(0.49)
$500–999	–0.0032	–0.0034	0.0010	0.0002	0.0027
	(0.28)	(1.10)	(0.97)	(0.17)	(0.62)
$1,000–2,499	0.0179	0.0013	–0.0003	0.0009	0.0078
	(1.63)	(0.48)	(0.33)	(0.76)	(2.11)**
$2,500–4,999	0.0087	0.0063	–0.0013	–0.0008	0.0032
	(0.55)	(1.49)	(1.20)	(0.51)	(0.71)
$5,000+	–0.0050	0.0269	–0.0021	–0.0024	0.0076
	(0.20)	(3.55)***	(1.33)	(1.04)	(1.23)
Age		–0.0074	–0.0000	0.0002	0.0004
		(8.04)***	(0.46)	(2.56)**	(3.72)***
Predicted probability	0.0471	0.0131	0.0034	0.0057	0.0130
Pseudo-R^2	0.0031	0.0396	0.0037	0.0049	0.0142
Observations	3,662	13,610	34,629	31,369	8,809

Note: Absolute value of *z*-statistics in parentheses.
***Significant at the 1 percent level.
**Significant at the 5 percent level.
*Significant at the 10 percent level.

Table 2A.5   Probit Regressions on Mortality, 1850 and 1860 (partial derivatives)

Variable	Infants (1)	Ages 1–4 (2)	Ages 5–19 (3)	Ages 20–44 (4)	Ages 45+ (5)
Log(real estate + $1.00)	0.0011	0.0005	−0.0001	−0.0001	0.0004
	(0.97)	(1.74)*	(1.08)	(1.01)	(1.29)
Age		−0.0074	−0.0000	0.0001	0.0005
		(8.09)***	(0.21)	(2.16)**	(4.35)***
Male	0.0129	0.0049	0.0013	0.0002	0.0082
	(1.83)*	(2.66)***	(2.02)**	(0.29)	(3.73)***
Family size	0.0018	0.0003	0.0002	0.0010	0.0019
	(0.93)	(0.56)	(1.01)	(4.72)***	(3.76)***
Born in state of enumeration	−0.0007	−0.0035	0.0007	0.0038	0.0125
	(0.04)	(1.10)	(0.97)	(3.57)***	(1.55)
Foreign-born		0.0087	−0.0013	0.0017	−0.0019
		(0.77)	(0.65)	(1.13)	(0.51)
Head was farmer	−0.0104	−0.0038	−0.0000	−0.0035	−0.0126
	(1.23)	(1.67)*	(0.05)	(3.62)***	(4.59)***
Head was laborer	−0.0050	0.0001	0.0003	−0.0027	−0.0074
	(0.37)	(0.03)	(0.20)	(1.90)*	(1.71)*
Illinois	0.0000	0.0020	−0.0000	0.0002	−0.0033
	(0.00)	(0.91)	(0.06)	(0.17)	(1.39)
1860	0.0041	0.0057	0.0001	−0.0000	0.0045
	(0.53)	(2.92)***	(0.10)	(0.06)	(2.01)**
Predicted probability	0.0469	0.0128	0.0034	0.0052	0.0107
Pseudo-R^2	0.0054	0.0451	0.0051	0.0228	0.0566
Observations	3,647	13,610	34,629	31,369	8,809

Note: Absolute value of z-statistics in parentheses.
***Significant at the 1 percent level.
**Significant at the 5 percent level.
*Significant at the 10 percent level.

Table 2A.6 **Probit Regressions on Mortality, 1850 and 1860 (partial derivatives)**

Variable	Infants (1)	Ages 1–4 (2)	Ages 5–19 (3)	Ages 20–44 (4)	Ages 45+ (5)
Real estate					
$100–499	0.0135	0.0051	0.0001	–0.0016	0.0030
	(1.32)	(1.84)*	(0.07)	(1.45)	(0.83)
$500–999	–0.0043	–0.0025	0.0008	–0.0001	0.0018
	(0.37)	(0.79)	(0.79)	(0.12)	(0.48)
$1,000–2,499	0.0163	0.0012	–0.0005	0.0000	0.0061
	(1.45)	(0.44)	(0.66)	(0.04)	(1.87)*
$2,500–4,999	0.0068	0.0044	–0.0016	–0.0014	0.0020
	(0.42)	(1.07)	(1.50)	(0.95)	(0.51)
$5,000+	–0.0087	0.0234	–0.0023	–0.0028	0.0038
	(0.35)	(3.19)***	(1.55)	(1.47)	(0.76)
Age		–0.0073	–0.0000	0.0001	0.0005
		(8.08)***	(0.06)	(2.12)**	(4.35)***
Male	0.0128	0.0048	0.0012	0.0002	0.0082
	(1.82)*	(2.63)***	(2.03)**	(0.30)	(3.73)***
Family size	0.0020	0.0002	0.0002	0.0010	0.0019
	(1.03)	(0.44)	(1.15)	(4.72)***	(3.75)***
Born in state of enumeration	0.0001	–0.0035	0.0007	0.0037	0.0122
	(0.01)	(1.10)	(1.06)	(3.58)***	(1.52)
Foreign-born		0.0091	–0.0013	0.0016	–0.0020
		(0.80)	(0.67)	(1.06)	(0.55)
Head was farmer	–0.0108	–0.0037	–0.0001	–0.0034	–0.0128
	(1.28)	(1.62)	(0.11)	(3.62)***	(4.65)***
Head was laborer	–0.0053	–0.0002	0.0002	–0.0026	–0.0073
	(0.39)	(0.05)	(0.15)	(1.87)*	(1.69)*
Illinois	0.0006	0.0020	0.0003	0.0001	–0.0031
	(0.07)	(0.89)	(0.37)	(0.15)	(1.26)
1860	0.0049	0.0057	0.0004	–0.0001	0.0046
	(0.63)	(2.82)***	(0.58)	(0.13)	(1.99)**
Predicted probability	0.0466	0.0125	0.0033	0.0051	0.0106
Pseudo-R^2	0.0079	0.0501	0.0086	0.0247	0.0581
Observations	3,647	13,610	34,629	31,369	8,809

Note: Absolute value of z-statistics in parentheses.
***Significant at the 1 percent level.
**Significant at the 5 percent level.
*Significant at the 10 percent level.

Table 2A.7   **Probit Regressions on Mortality, 1860 (partial derivatives)**

Variable	Infants (1)	Ages 1–4 (2)	Ages 5–19 (3)	Ages 20–44 (4)	Ages 45+ (5)
A.					
Log(personal estate + $1.00)	−0.0048	−0.0001	−0.0003	−0.0002	0.0016
	(2.44)**	(0.23)	(1.94)*	(1.05)	(2.00)**
Age		−0.0107	−0.0001	0.0001	0.0006
		(7.99)***	(0.61)	(1.74)*	(3.60)***
Predicted probability	0.0488	0.0148	0.0034	0.0057	0.0151
Pseudo-R^2	0.0068	0.0513	0.0045	0.0031	0.0192
Observations	2,154	7,730	19,480	18,279	5,136
B.					
Personal estate					
$100–499	−0.0431	−0.0004	−0.0018	−0.0045	0.119
	(3.10)***	(0.09)	(1.53)	(2.84)***	(1.43)
$500–999	−0.0139	−0.0050	−0.0015	−0.0035	0.0094
	(1.01)	(1.06)	(1.31)	(2.32)**	(1.03)
$1,000–2,499	−0.0283	−0.0003	−0.0027	−0.0019	0.0097
	(1.96)**	(0.05)	(2.32)**	(1.16)	(1.05)
$2,500–4,999	−0.0346	0.0071	−0.0013	−0.0034	0.0297
	(1.61)	(0.79)	(0.70)	(1.40)	(1.90)*
$5,000+	−0.0321	0.0015	−0.0016	0.0005	0.0260
	(1.40)	(0.18)	(0.98)	(0.18)	(1.99)**
Age		−0.0107	−0.0001	0.0001	0.0006
		(8.00)***	(0.63)	(1.67)*	(3.53)***
Predicted probability	0.0476	0.0146	0.0033	0.0055	0.0150
Pseudo-R^2	0.0152	0.0537	0.0068	0.0115	0.0216
Observations	2,154	7,730	19,480	18,279	5,136

Note: Absolute value of *z*-statistics in parentheses.

***Significant at the 1 percent level.

**Significant at the 5 percent level.

*Significant at the 10 percent level.

Table 2A.8   **Probit Regressions on Mortality, 1860 (partial derivatives)**

Variable	Infants (1)	Ages 1–4 (2)	Ages 5–19 (3)	Ages 20–44 (4)	Ages 45+ (5)
Log(personal estate + $1.00)	−0.0043	0.0001	−0.0003	−0.0004	0.0013
	(2.03)**	(0.17)	(1.96)*	(1.73)*	(1.79)*
Age		−0.0106	−0.0000	0.0001	0.0007
		(8.02)***	(0.16)	(1.42)	(4.09)***
Male	0.0174	0.0071	0.0004	−0.0014	0.0062
	(1.86)*	(2.77)***	(0.48)	(1.36)	(1.91)*
Family size	0.0005	0.0006	0.0003	0.0010	0.0021
	(0.19)	(0.79)	(1.08)	(3.91)***	(2.76)***
Born in state of enumeration	0.0078	−0.0010	0.0018	0.0033	0.0216
	(0.38)	(0.24)	(2.01)**	(2.57)**	(1.90)*
Foreign-born		0.0412		0.0000	−0.0001
		(1.58)		(0.00)	(0.02)
Head was farmer	−0.0108	−0.0039	−0.0005	−0.0020	−0.0077
	(0.98)	(1.24)	(0.55)	(1.61)	(1.91)*
Head was laborer	−0.0075	0.0008	0.0007	−0.0023	−0.0055
	(0.51)	(0.17)	(0.38)	(1.34)	(0.79)
Illinois	0.0046	0.0031	−0.0001	−0.0003	−0.0062
	(0.47)	(1.10)	(0.15)	(0.28)	(1.85)*
Predicted probability	0.0480	0.0141	0.0033	0.0050	0.0136
Pseudo-R^2	0.0128	0.0615	0.0121	0.0247	0.0445
Observations	2,149	7,730	19,009	18,279	5,136

Note: Absolute value of z-statistics in parentheses.
***Significant at the 1 percent level.
**Significant at the 5 percent level.
*Significant at the 10 percent level.

Table 2A.9   **Probit Regressions on Mortality, 1860 (partial derivatives)**

Variable	Infants (1)	Ages 1–4 (2)	Ages 5–19 (3)	Ages 20–44 (4)	Ages 45+ (5)
Personal estate					
$100–499	−0.0375	−0.0004	−0.0015	−0.0040	0.0140
	(2.62)***	(0.09)	(1.25)	(2.68)***	(1.73)*
$500–999	−0.0075	−0.0048	−0.0015	−0.0036	0.0122
	(0.49)	(1.00)	(1.16)	(2.48)**	(1.32)
$1,000–2,499	−0.0238	0.0002	−0.0028	−0.0025	0.0109
	(1.54)	(0.05)	(2.26)**	(1.64)	(1.18)
$2,500–4,999	−0.0324	0.0085	−0.0015	−0.0035	0.0263
	(1.45)	(0.92)	(0.83)	(1.76)*	(1.78)*
$5,000+	−0.0281	0.0053	−0.0019	−0.0010	0.0211
	(1.15)	(0.57)	(1.17)	(0.45)	(1.76)*
Age		−0.0105	−0.0000	0.0001	0.0007
		(8.02)***	(0.15)	(1.39)	(4.06)***
Male	0.0166	0.0071	0.0004	−0.0014	0.0062
	(1.81)*	(2.80)***	(0.51)	(1.43)	(1.92)*
Family size	−0.0005	0.0006	0.0003	0.0010	0.0022
	(0.20)	(0.77)	(1.10)	(3.75)***	(2.83)***
Born in state of enumeration	0.0053	−0.0007	0.0018	0.0029	0.0214
	(0.25)	(0.18)	(2.04)**	(2.33)**	(1.89)*
Foreign-born		0.0426		−0.0001	−0.0002
		(1.64)		(0.03)	(0.04)
Head was farmer	−0.0138	−0.0031	−0.0006	−0.0017	−0.0068
	(1.23)	(0.99)	(0.59)	(1.41)	(1.72)*
Head was laborer	−0.0024	0.0008	0.0006	−0.0019	−0.0062
	(0.15)	(0.18)	(0.35)	(1.10)	(0.91)
Illinois	0.0028	0.0041	−0.0000	0.0003	−0.0064
	(0.28)	(1.45)	(0.02)	(0.24)	(1.79)*
Predicted probability	0.0467	0.0139	0.0032	0.0049	0.0135
Pseudo-R^2	0.0217	0.0643	0.0143	0.0298	0.0465
Observations	2,149	7,730	19,009	18,279	5,136

Note: Absolute value of z-statistics in parentheses.

***Significant at the 1 percent level.

**Significant at the 5 percent level.

*Significant at the 10 percent level.

Table 2A.10   Probit Regressions on Mortality, 1860 (partial derivatives)

Variable	Infants (1)	Ages 1–4 (2)	Ages 5–19 (3)	Ages 20–44 (4)	Ages 45+ (5)
A.					
Log (real estate + $1.00)	0.0024	0.0009	0.0000	0.0003	0.0004
	(1.54)	(2.04)**	(0.01)	(1.53)	(0.61)
Log (personal estate + $1.00)	−0.0068	−0.0009	−0.0003	−0.0005	0.0013
	(2.88)***	(1.31)	(1.58)	(1.73)*	(1.43)
Age		−0.0106	−0.0001	0.0001	0.0006
		(7.99)***	(0.61)	(1.57)	(3.59)***
Predicted probability	0.0484	0.0146	0.0034	0.0057	0.0151
Pseudo-R^2	0.0096	0.0542	0.0045	0.0049	0.0197
Observations	2,154	7,730	19,480	18,279	5,136
B.					
Real estate					
$100–499	0.0205	0.0065	0.0011	0.0014	0.0011
	(1.35)	(1.48)	(0.79)	(0.70)	(0.17)
$500–999	−0.0190	−0.0017	0.0001	0.0038	0.0048
	(1.23)	(0.36)	(0.04)	(1.71)*	(0.74)
$1,000–2,499	0.0179	0.0033	0.0005	0.0024	0.0117
	(1.15)	(0.79)	(0.39)	(1.31)	(1.96)*
$2,500–4,999	0.0159	0.0118	−0.0005	0.0005	0.0001
	(0.77)	(1.90)*	(0.31)	(0.24)	(0.02)
$5,000+	−0.0105	0.0338	−0.0012	−0.0013	0.0072
	(0.36)	(3.21)***	(0.60)	(0.46)	(0.87)
Personal estate					
$100–499	0.0454	0.0016	0.0020	0.0052	0.0090
	(3.19)***	(0.35)	(1.63)	(3.15)***	(1.09)
$500–999	−0.0192	−0.0073	−0.0016	−0.0043	0.0036
	(1.29)	(1.53)	(1.25)	(2.66)***	(0.41)
$1,000–2,499	−0.0319	−0.0054	−0.0026	−0.0025	0.0035
	(2.03)**	(1.05)	(1.91)*	(1.37)	(0.39)
$2,500–4,999	−0.0368	−0.0008	−0.0012	−0.0038	0.0186
	(1.75)*	(0.10)	(0.60)	(1.62)	(1.30)
$5,000+	−0.0332	−0.0057	−0.0015	−0.0004	0.0153
	(1.43)	(0.80)	(0.81)	(0.13)	(1.26)
Age		−0.0104	−0.0001	0.0001	0.0006
		(7.98)***	(0.57)	(1.56)	(3.52)***
Predicted probability	0.0462	0.0141	0.0033	0.0054	0.0145
Pseudo-R^2	0.0232	0.0630	0.0086	0.0153	0.0285
Observations	2,154	7,730	19,480	18,279	5,136

Note: Absolute value of *z*-statistics in parentheses.
***Significant at the 1 percent level.
**Significant at the 5 percent level.
*Significant at the 10 percent level.

Table 2A.11   Probit Regressions on Mortality, 1860 (partial derivatives)

Variable	Infants (1)	Ages 1–4 (2)	Ages 5–19 (3)	Ages 20–44 (4)	Ages 45+ (5)
Log (real estate + $1.00)	0.0024	0.0010	−0.0000	0.0002	0.0004
	(1.48)	(2.19)**	(0.26)	(0.99)	(0.74)
Log (personal estate + $1.00)	−0.0060	−0.0006	−0.0003	−0.0005	0.0010
	(2.49)**	(0.88)	(1.51)	(2.00)**	(1.21)
Age		−0.0105	−0.0000	0.0001	0.0007
		(8.03)***	(0.14)	(1.35)	(4.08)***
Male	0.0173	0.0069	0.0004	−0.0014	0.0062
	(1.87)*	(2.75)***	(0.49)	(1.36)	(1.92)*
Family size	−0.0001	0.0003	0.0003	0.0010	0.0021
	(0.05)	(0.48)	(1.09)	(3.81)***	(2.73)***
Born in state of enumeration	0.0062	−0.0018	0.0019	0.0032	0.0217
	(0.29)	(0.44)	(2.03)**	(2.50)**	(1.91)*
Foreign-born		0.0397		−0.0000	−0.0003
		(1.56)		(0.02)	(0.04)
Head was farmer	−0.0105	−0.0042	−0.0005	−0.0020	−0.0078
	(0.96)	(1.32)	(0.54)	(1.66)*	(1.94)*
Head was laborer	−0.0031	0.0026	0.0006	−0.0021	−0.0049
	(0.20)	(0.54)	(0.34)	(1.18)	(0.67)
Illinois	0.0037	0.0026	−0.0001	−0.0004	−0.0065
	(0.37)	(0.93)	(0.12)	(0.34)	(1.91)*
Predicted probability	0.0477	0.0139	0.0033	0.0050	0.0136
Pseudo-R^2	0.0154	0.0648	0.0122	0.0255	0.0451
Observations	2,149	7,730	19,009	18,279	5,136

Note: Absolute value of z-statistics in parentheses.

***Significant at the 1 percent level.

**Significant at the 5 percent level.

*Significant at the 10 percent level.

Table 2A.12   **Probit Regressions on Mortality, 1860 (partial derivatives)**

Variable	Infants (1)	Ages 1–4 (2)	Ages 5–19 (3)	Ages 20–44 (4)	Ages 45+ (5)
Real estate					
$100–499	0.0218	0.0081	0.0010	0.0010	0.0003
	(1.40)	(1.78)*	(0.68)	(0.53)	(0.06)
$500–999	−0.0178	−0.0001	−0.0000	0.0032	0.0036
	(1.15)	(0.02)	(0.01)	(1.56)	(0.60)
$1,000–2,499	0.0198	0.0040	0.0002	0.0016	0.0113
	(1.24)	(0.94)	(0.18)	(0.94)	(1.99)**
$2,500–4,999	0.0201	0.0109	−0.0008	−0.0003	0.0015
	(0.93)	(1.75)*	(0.50)	(0.14)	(0.24)
$5,000	−0.0062	0.0328	−0.0015	−0.0018	0.0092
	(0.20)	(3.10)***	(0.77)	(0.74)	(1.10)
Personal estate					
$100–499	−0.0400	−0.0016	−0.0017	−0.0047	0.0118
	(2.74)***	(0.36)	(1.38)	(2.97)***	(1.45)
$500–999	−0.0136	−0.0067	−0.0015	−0.0041	0.0067
	(0.85)	(1.42)	(1.11)	(2.72)***	(0.75)
$1,000–2,499	−0.0285	−0.0045	−0.0026	−0.0027	0.0046
	(1.77)*	(0.86)	(1.86)*	(1.62)	(0.52)
$2,500–4,999	−0.0353	0.0004	−0.0012	−0.0036	0.0158
	(1.66)*	(0.05)	(0.62)	(1.79)*	(1.19)
$5,000+	−0.0305	−0.0030	−0.0016	−0.0010	0.0111
	(1.26)	(0.39)	(0.85)	(0.42)	(1.02)
Age		−0.0102	−0.0000	0.0001	0.0006
		(8.01)***	(0.07)	(1.31)	(4.04)***
Male	0.0162	0.0068	0.0004	−0.0014	0.0061
	(1.80)*	(2.73)***	(0.51)	(1.40)	(1.93)*
Family size	−0.0006	0.0003	0.0003	0.0010	0.0021
	(0.26)	(0.37)	(1.17)	(3.80)***	(2.76)***
Born in state of enumeration	0.0049	−0.0016	0.0019	0.0028	0.0207
	(0.24)	(0.39)	(2.06)**	(2.29)**	(1.86)*
Foreign-born		0.0408		−0.0003	−0.0008
		(1.61)		(0.14)	(0.12)
Head was farmer	−0.0143	−0.0034	−0.0006	−0.0017	−0.0072
	(1.29)	(1.13)	(0.60)	(1.43)	(1.82)*
Head was laborer	−0.0006	0.0018	0.0006	−0.0017	−0.0050
	(0.04)	(0.39)	(0.33)	(0.94)	(0.72)
Illinois	0.0020	0.0030	0.0003	0.0007	−0.0067
	(0.19)	(1.00)	(0.32)	(0.64)	(1.75)*
Predicted probability	0.0454	0.0134	0.0032	0.0048	0.0131
Pseudo-R^2	0.0300	0.0730	0.0163	0.0334	0.0534
Observations	2,149	7,730	19,009	18,279	5,136

Note: Absolute value of z-statistics in parentheses.

***Significant at the 1 percent level.

**Significant at the 5 percent level.

*Significant at the 10 percent level.

Table 2A.13   **Profit Regressions on Mortality, 1860 (partial derivatives)**

Variable	Infants (1)	Ages 1–4 (2)	Ages 5–19 (3)	Ages 20–44 (4)	Ages 45+ (5)
Log(real estate + $1.00)	0.0054	0.0015	–0.0002	0.0010	0.0040
	(1.65)*	(1.51)	(0.60)	(2.48)**	(3.18)***
(Illinois) · log(real estate + $1.00)	–0.0040	–0.0008	0.0002	–0.0009	–0.0049
	(1.08)	(0.70)	(0.70)	(1.94)*	(3.42)***
Log(personal estate + $1.00)	–0.0099	–0.0009	–0.0003	–0.0004	–0.0004
	(2.63)***	(0.75)	(1.03)	(1.07)	(0.36)
(Illinois) · log(personal estate + $1.00)	0.0049	–0.0001	0.0000	–0.0003	0.0019
	(1.01)	(0.09)	(0.07)	(0.51)	(1.08)
Age		–0.0101	0.0000	0.0000	0.0006
		(3.93)***	(0.02)	(0.25)	(2.88)***
(Illinois) • age		–0.0006	–0.0001	0.0001	–0.0002
		(0.19)	(0.48)	(0.81)	(0.48)
Illinois	–0.0049	0.0080	–0.0007	0.0001	0.0174
	(0.22)	(0.95)	(0.23)	(0.02)	(0.87)
Predicted probability	0.0481	0.0145	0.0033	0.0054	0.0136
Pseudo-R^2	0.0115	0.0558	0.0064	0.0126	0.0401
Observations	2,154	7,730	19,480	18,279	5,136

Note: Absolute value of z-statistics in parentheses.
***Significant at the 1 percent level.
**Significant at the 5 percent level.
*Significant at the 10 percent level.

References

Case, Anne, Darren Lubotsky, and Christina Paxson. 2001. Economic status and health in childhood: The origins of the gradient. NBER Working Paper no. 8344. Cambridge, Mass.: National Bureau of Economic Research, June.

Chapin, Charles V. 1924. Deaths among taxpayers and non-taxpayers, income tax, Providence, 1865. *America Journal of Public Health* 14:647–51.

Condran, Gretchen A., and Eileen Crimmins. 1979. A description and evaluation of mortality data in the Federal Census: 1850–1900. *Historical Methods* 12:1–23.

Craig, Lee, Raymond Palmquist, and Thomas Weiss. 1998. Transportation improvements and land values in the antebellum United States: A hedonic approach. *Journal of Real Estate Finance and Economics* 16 (March): 173–89.

Currie, Janet, and Mark Stabile. 2002. Socioeconomic status and health: Why is the relationship stronger for older children? NBER Working Paper no. 9098. Cambridge, Mass.: National Bureau of Economic Research, August.

Fogel, Robert W., and Stanley L. Engerman. 1974. *Time on the cross: Evidence and methods.* Boston: Little, Brown.

Hahn, Marilyn Davis. 1983. *Alabama mortality schedule, 1850.* Easley, S.C.: Southern Historical Press.

————. 1987. *Alabama mortality schedule, 1860.* Easley, S.C.: Southern Historical Press.

Haines, Michael. 1998. Estimated life tables for the United States, 1850–1910. *Historical Methods* 31 (Fall): 149–69.

Haines, Michael, Lee Craig, and Thomas Weiss. 2000. Development, health, nutrition, and mortality: The case of the "antebellum puzzle" in the United States. NBER Working Paper no. H0130. Cambridge, Mass.: National Bureau of Economic Research, October.

Jackson, Ronald V. 1999. Accelerated indexing systems, compiler. AIS mortality schedules index [database on-line]. Provo, Utah: Ancestry.com. Available at http:// ancestry.com/search/rectype/inddbs/3530a.htm.

Jacobson, Paul N. 1957. An estimate of the expectation of life in the United States in 1850. *Milbank Memorial Fund Quarterly* 35 (April): 197–201.

Kitagawa, Evelyn M., and Philip M. Hauser. 1973. *Differential mortality in the United States: A study in socioeconomic epidemiology.* Cambridge: Harvard University Press.

Lantz, Paula M., James S. House, James M. Lepowski, David R. Williams, Richard P. Mero, and Jieming Chen. 1998. Socioeconomic factors, health behaviors, and mortality: Results from a nationally representative prospective study of U.S. adults. *Journal of the American Medical Association* 279 (3 June): 1703–08.

Margo, Robert A. 2000. *Wages and labor markets in the United States, 1820–1860.* Chicago: University of Chicago Press.

Preston, Samuel H., and Michael R. Haines. 1991. *The fatal years: Child mortality in late nineteenth-century America.* Princeton, N.J.: Princeton University Press.

Smith, James P. 1999. Healthy bodies and thick wallets: The dual relation between health and economic status. *Journal of Economic Perspectives* 13 (Spring): 145–66.

Steckel, Richard H. 1988. The health and mortality of women and children, 1850–1860. *Journal of Economic History* 48 (June): 333–45.

Volkel, Lowell M. 1972. *Illinois mortality schedule, 1850.* N.p.

————. 1979. *Illinois mortality schedule, 1860.* Indianapolis, Ind.: Heritage House.

Williams, Redford B. 1998. Lower socioeconomic status and increased mortality: Early childhood roots and the potential for successful interventions. *Journal of the American Medical Association* 279 (3 June): 1745–46.

3

Prior Exposure to Disease and Later Health and Mortality
Evidence from Civil War Medical Records

Chulhee Lee

3.1 Introduction

Researchers in various disciples have long tried to understand the interrelationship of socioeconomic status, environment, and health. This subject is related to a number of important issues, such as the changing relationship among host, agent, and environmental factors, the socioeconomic differences in health, and the long-term decline in mortality. The medical and epidemiological literature provides many examples of the possible links between early-life conditions and chronic disease at older ages. A series of studies by D. J. P. Barker and his colleagues (Barker 1992, 1994) links many of the degenerative conditions of old age to exposure to infectious disease, malnutrition, and other types of biomedical and socioeconomic stress in utero and in the first year of life. Studies have found that infectious diseases affect the chances of suffering chronic conditions such as heart, respiratory, and musculoskeletal disorders (Elo and Preston 1992; Costa 2000). These findings provide evidence for the "insult accumulation model," which states that each insult from illness or injury leaves the individual more susceptible to disease in the future (Alter and Riley 1989). However, the relationship between the early-life conditions of a cohort and its later health is not entirely

Chulhee Lee is professor of economics at the Seoul National University.

I am grateful to Dora Costa, Robert Fogel, and Nevin Scrimshaw for their help and encouragement throughout the many years since I began this project, to Susan Jones for editorial assistance, and to Joseph Ferrie for kindly providing the mortality data from the 1860 census and useful information regarding the data. I also thank an anonymous referee and conference participants for their helpful comments and suggestions. Financial support was provided by the Center for Population Economics, the National Institutes of Health (P01 AG 10120), and the National Science Foundation (SBR 9114981). Any remaining errors are my own.

straightforward. Individuals who survive infectious disease may acquire partial or complete immunity and therefore may have lower mortality rates (Lee 1997).

It is well documented that there are considerable variations in health across populations of different socioeconomic backgrounds (United Nations [UN] 1973). Inequality in health is an important social problem even in highly wealthy and egalitarian nations today (Kitagawa and Hauser 1973; Notkota et al. 1985; Lehmann, Mamboury, and Minder 1990; Diderichen 1990; Lawson and Black 1993; Deaton and Paxson 1999). Some evidence suggests that the social health gradient has not diminished in spite of rising income during the second half of the twentieth century (Preston, Haines, and Pamuk 1981; Marmot et al. 1991; Marmot 1999). It is widely accepted that such health differentials by socioeconomic status cannot be fully explained by differences in health behaviors or in access to medical care. Numerous hypotheses have been suggested to explain how social and economic environments alter human biological functioning. Some frequently cited mediating factors between wealth and health include work-related stress, family background, and other social support networks. A growing number of studies demonstrate that health at middle and older ages reflects earlier health and may be correlated across and within generations (Barker et al. 1989; Barker 1997; Ravelli et al. 1998; Wadsworth and Kuh 1997). Some studies see the principal impacts of socioeconomic status on health as stemming not from brief episodes but instead from the accumulation of repeated stress over the lifespan (Seeman et al. 1997). Another line of research focuses on the role of income inequality, maintaining that inequality in relative socioeconomic status raises the level of psychosocial stress that negatively affects endocrine and immunological processes (Sapolsky 1993; Wilkinson 1996). In spite of the tremendous amount of previous research, there is still heated debate going on over the magnitude of the socioeconomic differences in health and the causes of the recent rise in the inequality in health (Fogel and Lee 2002).

The patterns of socioeconomic differences in mortality and morbidity provide important clues to the causes of long-term changes in health. Studies have attributed the long-term improvement in health to a number of factors, including the elimination of chronic malnutrition; advances in public health; improvements in housing, sanitation, and food hygiene; and advances in medical technology (Higgs 1973, 1979; Appleby 1975; McKeown 1976, 1983; Condran and Cheney 1982; Livi-Bacci 1982; Kunitz 1983; Fogel 1986, 1991). Recent historical studies have found that health as measured by life expectancy and mean adult height deteriorated through the early nineteenth century in the United States and some European nations in spite of the growth in per capita income (Pope 1992; Floud and Steckel 1997). This finding indicates that economic growth and epidemiological conditions are not independent forces, and (more importantly) that, under certain circumstances, the effects of economic development on the disease environment can be strongly adverse.[1] Despite the extensive research on such issues, the relative importance of the potential factors of health remains unclear. Achieving a proper understanding of these matters is important not only from a historical point of view, but also, perhaps more significantly, for predicting the impact on health of ongoing technological and social changes in developing countries.

The purpose of this article is to deepen our understanding of these issues by exploring the effects of socioeconomic status and local disease environment on the later health and mortality of Union Army recruits. The Union Army sample and supplemental data set containing information on local death rates are ideal for addressing the issues introduced above, since they possess the following major advantages over data analyzed in previous research. First, the semicontrolled conditions of the army camps during the war provide a unique chance to determine the relationship between socioeconomic background and health. The Civil War brought together a large number of men from heterogeneous socioeconomic and ecological backgrounds into an extremely unhealthy environment that caused unusually high rates of disease contraction and consequent mortality.[2] Upon being mustered into the service, rural dwellers were suddenly plunged into close contact with impoverished men from cities where disease and mortality rates were high, but who were nevertheless in good enough health to pass a physical examination. Another unique feature of the army is that recruits were confined to relatively homogeneous living conditions in terms of the quality of diet, housing, and disease environment compared to normal society. Owing to these features of army life, we are able to identify more clearly the effects of socioeconomic and ecological factors—in particular, the extent of previous exposure to disease—on the degree of susceptibility or resistance to disease. Furthermore, detailed descriptions of disease diagnoses, and cause and date of death while in service, which are contained in the Union Army medical records, make it possible to examine the patterns of cause-specific mortality and timing of wartime deaths.

In an earlier paper, I analyzed the wartime disease experiences of Union

1. The possible causes of the downward swings in the trend of health, according to these studies, are rapid urbanization, a decline in the proportion of the population employed in agriculture, increased geographical mobility, more rapid increases in population than in food supply, a rise in the relative food price, an increase in inequality in income distribution, short-term adverse movement in real wages, and the turbulence of the Civil War (Rosenberg 1962; Steckel 1983, 1995; Fogel 1986, 1991; Komlos 1987; Floud, Wachter, and Gregory 1990; Cuff 1992; Costa 1993; Gallman 1995, 1996; Margo 2000, ch. 7).

2. About 12 percent of all recruits who served in the Union Army died while in service (Vinovskis 1990). Death from disease was more than twice as frequent as death from injury (Steiner 1968, 8). Civil War armies actually suffered comparatively less disease mortality than any previous army. The ratio of the number of deaths from disease to the number of soldiers killed in combat was 7 for the American army in the Mexican War, and 8 for British soldiers in the Napoleonic Wars (McPherson 1988, 487).

Army recruits based on a relatively small sample of persons from the state of Ohio (Lee 1997). This study showed that the relationship between personal characteristics and health among army recruits was nearly the opposite of the common patterns of socioeconomic differences in health found in the civilian populations in the nineteenth century. Former farmers, rural residents, and natives, who were healthier on average prior to enlistment, were more likely to contract and die from disease than were nonfarmers, urban dwellers, and non natives, respectively. I suggested that socioeconomic differences in early childhood exposure to disease were responsible for the unusual patterns of mortality differentials while in service.[3]

This article extends and improves my previous study in three major respects. First, I use a much larger sample of Union Army recruits from eighteen different states in the Northeast, Midwest, and upper South. This larger and geographically more balanced sample will provide a more general picture of wartime medical experiences during the Civil War. This also enables me to analyze how the effects of socioeconomic and ecological factors on health varied across different regions. Second, I employ an improved measure of economic status, namely, household wealth per adult male equivalent. This new index will more accurately represent the economic well-being of a person than does household wealth because it considers not only the extent of economic resources but also the need for spending. Finally, and most significantly, I use a more explicit measure of the local disease environment, namely, county-level child death rates, which will enrich our understanding of the link between the extent of exposure to disease and later health.

3.2   Data

This study is based on a sample of the several primary data sources that were collected and linked as part of the project titled "Early Indicators of Later Work Levels, Disease, and Death" jointly sponsored by the National Institutes of Health, the Center for Population Economics at the University of Chicago, and Brigham Young University. The sample used in this paper is composed of 28,546 recruits who enlisted in the states of Connecticut, Delaware, Illinois, Iowa, Kansas, Kentucky, Maine, Maryland, Massachusetts, Michigan, Minnesota, Missouri, New Hampshire, New York, Ohio, Pennsylvania, Vermont, West Virginia, and the District of Columbia.

3. Despite the negative consequences for net nutritional status, survivors of unhealthy environments developed better immunity to some of the infectious diseases that were rampant in army life. Lee (1997) provides suggestive evidence in support of this hypothesis, based on the patterns of disease-specific mortality differentials and of the timing of death. Some diseases are known to have greater potential for the development of immunity. By classifying diseases by this criterion, I found that the "paradoxical" differentials were greater for diseases with greater immunity potential. The difference in the hazard of dying from immunity-sensitive disease was much greater in the earlier stages of military service when enlistees were not seasoned to the unhealthy environment of the army camps.

The service records contain very detailed descriptions of the diseases or wounds that recruits suffered during military service. As soon as a recruit was too ill to report for duty, his condition was noted in morning reports. If his condition required medical attention, it was recorded in the regimental surgeon's report; if he was hospitalized, the diagnosis of the disease was described in the case history together with the ultimate outcome, such as return to service, discharge for disabilities, or death (U.S. Surgeon General's Office 1870, vol. 1). Information on disease and on date and cause of death in service were gathered from these sources. Military service records provide information on demographic and socioeconomic characteristics of recruits, such as age, occupation at enlistment, place of birth, and height, among other variables, as well as on their military careers, including rank, military duty, company, regiment, change in military status, dates of enlistment and discharge, and so on. Additional information on socioeconomic status and on household structure prior to enlistment can be drawn from manuscript schedules of the 1860 census: These contain information on age, occupation, place of birth, household wealth, place of residence, and literacy, not only for recruits but also for their family members.

In order to construct county-level child death rates, an indicator of local epidemiological environment in the areas in which recruits lived prior to enlistment, I utilize a sample of mortality data from the 1860 federal population census.[4] This sample is not a complete compilation of the mortality schedules for 1850 and 1860. The collection contains information on roughly 400,000 decedents in twenty states, with good coverage of Midwestern and Southern states, but has less information for the Northeast (e.g., the collection contains no records for New York, Massachusetts, or Pennsylvania). Each record reports the state and county in which the death occurred, the date and cause of death, the decedent's age at death, and his or her occupation and place of birth.

One obstacle in using these county-level variables on mortality is a potential bias problem. The number of deaths may have been understated in these sources for several reasons. The two most important of these are, first, the retrospective nature of the question (if the interviewee either forgot

---

4. The mortality data used in this study are available at the Web page of the Center for Population Economics, http://www.cpe.uchicago.edu. This sample of mortality data was created by genealogist Ronald V. Jackson during the 1980s. Although Jackson's principal interest was in obtaining nominal information to provide to individuals exploring their family history, he collected the full range of data available in the mortality schedules. These records were generated by census marshals in their house-to-house canvass in the 1850 and 1860 censuses of the United States. The marshals concluded their interviews with each household by inquiring whether anyone from the household had died in the twelve months preceding the day of the interview. If the answer was affirmative, information on decedents was recorded on a separate mortality schedule. Most of these schedules were returned to state archives earlier in this century, and many have since been microfilmed. Some of these were acquired by Jackson and computerized at his facility in Salt Lake City. See the chapter by Ferrie in this volume for detailed features of these data.

about a death or was unaware of one, such death would not be reported on these schedules), and second, should an entire household have died, none of their deaths would be reported. If the magnitude of such potential undercounts differed across counties, there will be a bias problem arising from measurement errors, as described in Condran and Crimmins (1979). I have not made any attempt to correct such potential errors in this study.

Since the data have been constructed from a number of different sources with uneven rates of successful linkage, the use of several different samples depending on the variables used in the analysis is unavoidable. Among the socioeconomic variables needed for this study, household wealth and county of residence as of 1860 are found only in the census data. Of the 28,546 recruits, 11,056 men (about 39 percent) were successfully linked to the 1860 census. Therefore, I limit the sample to these 11,056 recruits whenever household wealth is concerned. In addition to these individuals, we have information on county of enlistment for 8,264 recruits among those who were not linked to the 1860 census. Assuming that these recruits enlisted in the army in the same counties where they lived in 1860, I use the sample of 19,320 men who were linked to the 1860 census or whose counties of enlistment were known, whenever the information on the county of residence prior to enlistment is needed. Finally, of the 11,056 men who were linked to the 1860 census, 3,864 lived in counties for which the county death rates are available. I use this sample where the effects of local epidemiological environment indicated by child death rate are analyzed.

Table 3.1 compares the medical experiences while in service and other personal characteristics of the three major samples that are used in this study. The three samples are generally similar in terms of the number of cases per person and the number of deaths per 1,000 cases for all diseases combined and for each of six major diseases.[5] Among the personal characteristics, only the percentages of farmers and of immigrants are notably different between the full and census-linked samples.[6] Despite the uneven geographical coverage of the Jackson collection of mortality data, the sample linked to the mortality census is comparable to the full sample in terms of regional composition. Although we cannot preclude the possibil-

5. The number of cases is slightly greater for the recruits who were successfully linked to the 1860 census than for the entire sample, which is to be expected due to the nature of the data collections. The rate of linkage to census records is higher for those who are connected to pension records because pension files provide useful information, especially on place of residence, that helps to locate and identify persons in manuscript schedules of censuses. And army veterans with health problems originating from military service were more likely to apply for and receive pensions because early pension laws required such conditions. Therefore, it is not surprising that recruits who were connected to census records present more severe medical experiences while in service.

6. These differences can also be explained by the disparate linkage rates to pension records: Immigrants were less likely to be found in pension records because many of the foreigners who died during the early postwar years had no eligible dependents or were used behind the front and so were less likely to incur war-related disabilities (Fogel 1993).

Table 3.1   **Medical Experiences in Service and Personal Characteristics: A Comparison of Three Samples**

	Full Sample	Population Census– Linked Sample	Mortality Census– Linked Sample
Number of cases per person			
All diseases	2.066	2.338	2.086
Diarrhea	0.431	0.506	0.440
Typhoid	0.061	0.074	0.064
Malaria	0.218	0.228	0.234
Pneumonia	0.034	0.036	0.029
Measles	0.036	0.044	0.042
Smallpox	0.013	0.016	0.013
Number of deaths per 1,000 cases			
All diseases	37.6	40.8	37.8
Diarrhea	60.2	60.5	57.7
Typhoid	308.7	324.4	290.3
Malaria	13.5	15.0	14.4
Pneumonia	170.1	186.9	207.2
Measles	81.5	83.5	73.6
Smallpox	229.0	288.9	326.5
Personal characteristics			
Mean age	25.6	26.1	25.9
Mean height	67.5	67.9	68.0
Percentage of farmers	47.6	57.6	57.5
Percentage of the U.S.-born	69.3	82.1	86.2
Region of enlistment (%)			
New England	9.2	10.3	10.4
Mid-Atlantic	37.3	31.2	37.4
East North Central	35.8	39.1	34.1
West North Central	11.1	12.5	8.0
South	6.6	6.9	10.1
Military position			
Percentage of privates	91.8	89.8	88.9
Percentage of infantrymen	67.5	65.1	67.8
N	28,536	11,073	3,864

ity of sample selection bias based solely on this comparison, the result suggests that such a bias problem is not likely to be serious.

3.3   Socioeconomic Background, Disease, and Mortality

In this section, I basically replicate my previous study (Lee 1997) using a much larger and more representative sample. Let us begin with a description of the overall features of medical experiences of the recruits in the sample. Nearly 12 percent of recruits in the sample died while in service, two-thirds from illness and the rest from wounds. The total casualties and the fraction of deaths caused by disease are well matched with the statistics for the entire Union Army. I identified the six most common diseases in army camps, namely, typhoid, smallpox, measles, diarrhea (including dysentery), pneumonia, and malaria.[7] These diseases are responsible for nearly four-fifths of all deaths caused by illness and two-fifths of all disease cases. Of these diseases, diarrhea is the single most important killer, accounting for 32 percent of all deaths caused by disease, followed by typhoid, which explains 23 percent of disease-caused deaths.

Table 3.2 reports the wartime mortality from disease in general (D), the mean number of cases per person-year (C), and the case fatality rates (F) of all diseases for recruits according to age, occupation, population size of county, household wealth, and nativity.[8] The mean number of cases of disease per person-year reflects how susceptible recruits of a particular socioeconomic background were to disease, while the case fatality rates indicate how robust they were in resisting the diseases they contracted.

Among the variables pertaining to socioeconomic status used in the analysis, household wealth per adult male equivalent may require an explanation regarding the method of construction. Household wealth is one of the most widely used indicators of economic well-being of individuals. In studying the determinants of health in the nineteenth century, household wealth is often interpreted as a measure of nutritional status because the quality of diet was one of the most important links between economic status and health at a time when medical interventions were limited. In order to construct a more accurate measure of a person's economic well-being (or quality of diet), it is necessary to consider the size of the household's needs as well as its material resources. Use of simple per capita household wealth, taking household size into account, only partially satisfies this requirement because the demand for consumption goods differs by age, sex, and labor force status. A common method of measuring the needs of a household is to convert the number of household members into a scale of adult male equivalents based on the demographic structure of the household, such as the number of householders of a particular age and sex. In order to apply this method it is necessary to determine the scale of a particular type of person based on the relative size of his or her consumption. Here, I consider only food consumption as the basis for determining the scale. I utilize the average caloric consumption of a typical male and a female at given ages as a proportion of that consumed by a male aged twenty to thirty-nine, reported in Fogel (1993, 9). For instance, the average caloric consumption of

7. Malaria includes intermittent and remittent fevers; typhoid includes typho-malaria and continuous fevers.

8. The definitions of these figures are as follows: The mean number of cases per person-year of disease k for group j is $(\Sigma_p \text{CASE}_{pjk} / \Sigma_p \text{SERVICE}_{pj})$, and the case fatality rate of disease k for group j is $(\text{DEATH}_{jk} / \Sigma_p \text{CASE}_{pjk})$, where CASE_{pjk} is the number of cases of disease k that a recruit p in group j suffered, SERVICE_{pj} is the length of service in year (measured in days) for a recruit p in group j, and DEATH_{jk} is the number of the recruits who died from disease k.

Table 3.2 Socioeconomic Background and Wartime Mortality from All Types of Disease

Category	All Ages				Ages 19 and Younger				Ages 20–24				Ages 25–29				Ages 30 and Older			
	N	D	C	F	N	D	C	F	N	D	C	F	N	D	C	F	N	D	C	F
Farmer	13,595	103.5	1.27	42.4	4,402	93.6	1.27	37.3	4,209	106.2	1.17	43.1	2,030	111.8	1.24	46.2	2,954	108.7	1.47	47.0
Nonfarmer	14,951	54.3	0.90	31.4	3,514	45.0	0.92	23.5	4,408	45.6	0.81	28.4	2,740	46.7	0.83	29.1	4,289	75.8	1.06	42.2
Rural county	15,521	91.5	1.22	38.1	4,472	85.2	1.21	34.2	4,618	88.8	1.12	37.2	2,485	85.7	1.18	36.6	3,946	105.4	1.40	45.8
Urban county	3,799	45.3	0.72	30.7	847	29.5	0.79	16.7	1,073	36.3	0.59	28.5	682	48.4	0.63	36.8	1,197	62.7	0.84	40.8
Rural farmer	9,153	109.8	1.31	42.5	2,891	102.4	1.31	38.4	2,840	109.2	1.20	41.8	1,362	114.5	1.29	44.3	2,060	118.0	1.53	48.1
Rural nonfarmer	6,368	65.2	1.09	30.9	1,581	53.8	1.05	24.6	1,778	56.2	0.99	27.6	1,123	50.8	1.05	24.8	1,886	91.7	1.26	42.9
U.S.-born	19,709	80.8	1.18	35.9	6,533	72.9	1.17	31.4	6,100	76.4	1.08	34.1	3,096	82.0	1.17	36.5	4,272	98.1	1.39	44.9
Farmer	11,215	100.9	1.32	40.2	3,812	91.3	1.32	35.8	3,533	99.3	1.21	39.2	1,655	110.6	1.32	43.7	2,215	112.9	1.58	47.2
Nonfarmer	8,575	54.6	1.00	28.4	2,510	45.0	0.97	22.9	2,567	44.8	0.89	24.5	1,441	49.3	1.01	25.5	2,057	82.2	1.19	41.9
Foreign-born	8,756	70.7	0.85	42.9	1,594	68.4	0.87	35.4	2,517	72.3	0.76	47.9	1,674	60.3	0.70	43.0	2,971	76.4	1.01	43.7
Farmer	2,380	115.5	1.02	55.2	590	108.5	1.02	48.8	676	142.0	0.93	67.8	375	117.3	0.90	60.8	739	96.1	1.18	46.3
Nonfarmer	6,376	54.0	0.78	36.4	1,004	44.8	0.79	25.5	1,841	46.7	0.68	36.1	1,299	43.9	0.64	35.0	2,232	69.9	0.95	42.5
Wealth, farmer																				
$0–14	903	106.3	1.39	38.9	261	107.3	1.34	38.2	226	119.5	1.25	45.7	158	94.9	1.44	31.7	258	100.7	1.55	38.6
$15–143	1,117	123.5	1.37	47.1	303	108.9	1.37	41.7	276	126.8	1.18	48.5	182	164.8	1.36	60.0	356	112.4	1.58	43.7
$144–325	1,305	123.4	1.37	47.1	428	144.9	1.35	54.2	395	106.3	1.27	38.0	174	97.7	1.44	37.4	308	129.9	1.56	55.5
$326–809	1,514	111.6	1.32	45.0	506	122.5	1.35	45.5	475	105.3	1.19	43.5	187	117.6	1.12	51.4	346	101.2	1.65	43.6
$810–	1,512	108.5	1.32	44.1	489	81.8	1.31	31.8	576	102.4	1.32	39.4	201	129.4	1.21	62.2	246	158.5	1.47	72.2
Wealth, nonfarmer																				
$0–14	1,235	76.1	1.04	36.4	279	60.9	115	25.0	262	61.1	0.90	29.4	198	30.3	0.93	15.8	496	110.9	1.11	56.3
$15–143	1,120	54.5	1.07	27.2	248	40.3	0.92	19.3	223	26.9	1.10	13.2	210	61.9	1.04	28.9	439	72.9	1.25	38.7
$144–325	937	79.0	1.03	40.4	234	68.4	0.94	35.2	242	70.2	1.06	32.9	154	32.5	0.95	18.4	307	117.3	1.14	61.1
$326–809	723	66.4	1.06	33.4	207	72.5	1.10	33.7	213	51.6	0.88	28.3	108	55.6	0.98	30.2	195	82.1	1.30	39.8
$810–	655	64.1	1.02	33.4	195	46.2	1.12	21.1	225	93.3	0.87	55.0	102	58.8	0.95	32.8	133	45.1	1.18	22.6

Notes: N = number of recruits; D = number of deaths per 1,000 men; C = number of cases per person-year; F = number of deaths per 1,000 cases.

a female aged five to nine is 66.67 percent of an adult male's average consumption. Accordingly, a female aged five to nine is regarded as equivalent to 0.6667 of an adult male.

The results presented in table 3.2 confirm the previous finding that the pattern of mortality differentials in the army was nearly the opposite of the relationship between the socioeconomic status and health of civilians. On average, former farmers had about a 35 percent higher case fatality rate, and about 40 percent more cases of disease per year of service than nonfarmers. As a consequence of a higher susceptibility and case fatality rate combined, farmers were twice as likely to be killed by disease while in service as nonfarmers.[9] This result remains unchanged if country of birth and household wealth are controlled for. For instance, farmers had markedly higher case fatality and wartime mortality rates in all five categories of household wealth.

To examine the effect of population size of place of residence, I divided the sample into rural and urban residents. I include in urban areas all counties that are classified as metropolitan areas by the Integrated Public Use Microdata Series (IPUMS) of the 1860 census.[10] The result reported in table 3.2 indicates that rural residents were twice as likely to die from disease while in service as were city dwellers. In particular, recruits from rural areas were much more susceptible to diseases than urban residents, as indicated by the difference in the mean number of cases per person-year.

Since most of the farmers lived in rural areas, the effects of occupation and urban residence can be distinguished by comparing rural farmers, rural nonfarmers, and urban residents. Farmers who lived in rural counties were two and half times as likely to die from disease in service as urban residents. These differences reflect the combined effects of occupation and place of residence. The difference in the number of cases is accounted for almost equally by the effects of urban residence and of occupation, while the difference in the case fatality rate is largely explained by the effect of occupation.

Native recruits were similar to the foreign-born in the risk of dying while in service. Natives suffered more disease per year of service, but had a lower case fatality rate than nonnatives. These two different factors of mortality cancel each other out. This result contrasts with the pattern found in Ohio where native recruits were at considerably higher risk of dying from disease while in service than nonnatives. A regional comparison of the association

9. Nonnatives were overrepresented among nonfarmers, and farmers were wealthier than nonfarmers on average. Hence, it is necessary to control for these factors in order to identify the pure effect of occupation.

10. The following counties were classified as metropolitan areas in 1860: Albany, Erie, Kings, New York, Richmond, Rensseaer (N.Y.); Baltimore (Md.); Middlesex, Norfolk, Suffolk (Mass.); Cook (Ill.); Hamilton, Kenton (Ohio); Jefferson (Ky.); Clark, Floyd (Ind.); Orleans (La.); San Francisco (Calif.); Essex, Hudson, Camden (N.J.); Montgomery, Philadelphia, Allegheny (Pa.); Kent, Providence (R.I.); and St. Louis (Mo.).

between socioeconomic factors and mortality while in service indicates that natives recorded a higher mortality rate than nonnatives only in the East North Central region (see section 3.5). Although the pattern of mortality differentials varies considerably across age categories, the above result is generally true for each age group. As in the case of Ohio, the household wealth of recruits prior to enlistment appears to have had no clear effect on the likelihood of contracting diseases or the risk of dying from those diseases.

I conduct logistic regressions to examine the effect of each of the socioeconomic factors, controlling for all other factors at the same time. Three different models are employed. The first and second regressions estimate the effect of each independent variable on the separate probabilities of contracting a disease and dying from a disease (respectively) while in service, based on the sample of all recruits linked to the 1860 census. For the third regression, the sample is limited to the recruits who had at least one illness while in service. The second regression examines the determinants of the degree of susceptibility to disease while the third is concerned with fatality in case of contraction. The result of the first regression on mortality shows the combined consequence of the differences in susceptibility and lethality.

The recruits in the sample are classified into three groups according to occupation and place of residence: rural farmers (control group), rural nonfarmers, and residents in urban counties. Variables on personal characteristics such as age, age squared, nativity, and log of household wealth per adult equivalent are included. Variables on height are also added as an index of nutritional status of recruits. The year of enlistment represents variations in the severity of military missions, epidemiological conditions, and the length of service. In a previous study I found that military rank and duty had very strong effects on the chances of dying while in service (Lee 1999). This study also shows that military positions were selectively assigned to the newly enlisted according to their socioeconomic backgrounds. To control for this potential indirect effect of socioeconomic characteristics on the probability of dying through the assignments of military positions, I include dummy variables on duty (which equals 1 if infantryman and zero otherwise) and rank (equals 1 if private and zero otherwise).

The results of the regressions are presented in table 3.3. The estimated parameters for occupation and urban county confirm the patterns of mortality differentials described above (see table 3.2). Farmers from rural areas were much more likely to contract diseases and be killed by them than were nonfarmers from rural counties and city dwellers. As suggested by Lee (1997), the most plausible interpretation of these results is that the effect of earlier exposure to disease was particularly important. A number of studies have noted the fragility of isolated populations once they come in contact with different disease pools (McNeill 1976; Curtin 1989; Pritchett and Tunali 1995; Fetter and Kessler 1996; Sköld 1997). Despite the negative con-

Table 3.3   Results of Logistic Regressions: Correlates of Probability of Dying from Disease

Independent Variable	Mean	All Recruits Linked to the 1860 Census					Recruits Who Contracted Disease		
		Dying from Disease (mean = 0.098) (1)		Contracting Disease (mean = 0.700) (2)			Mean	Dying from Disease (mean = 0.139) (3)	
		Parameter	$\partial P/\partial X_i$	Parameter	$\partial P/\partial X_i$			Parameter	$\partial P/\partial X_i$
Intercept		3.104		−5.549			6.410	0.006	
Age	26.039	−0.011	−0.050	−0.100***	−0.451		25.932	0.001	0.028
Age squared × 10⁻¹	74.480	0.004	0.107	0.017***	0.470		74.117		0.026
Height	67.923	−0.179	−0.267	0.246	0.366		67.957	−0.277	−0.411
Height squared × 10⁻¹	461.923	0.014	0.275	−0.018	−0.362		462.543	0.021	0.418
Farmers, rural county	0.573	N.I.	N.I.	N.I.	N.I.		0.609	N.I.	N.I.
Nonfarmers, rural county	0.349	−0.497***	−0.131	−0.432***	−0.113		0.327	−0.380***	−0.098
Urban county	0.078	−0.932***	−0.138	−0.959***	−0.142		0.064	−0.599***	−0.081
Born in United States	0.820	−0.251***	−0.053	0.187***	0.040		0.831	−0.310***	−0.064
Log of adjusted wealth	4.674	0.009	0.012	−0.030***	−0.041		4.675	0.014	0.019
Duty-infantryman	0.649	1.093***	0.288	−0.308***	−0.081		0.621	1.215***	0.325
Rank-private	0.899	0.420***	0.070	0.192**	0.032		0.901	0.385***	0.063
Year of enlistment									
1861	0.247	N.I.	N.I.	N.I.	N.I.		0.273	N.I.	N.I.
1862	0.392	0.053	0.014	−0.125	−0.034		0.422	0.075	0.020
1863	0.045	0.144	0.016	−0.033	−0.004		0.049	0.161	0.019
1864	0.231	−0.968***	−0.225	−1.033***	−0.240		0.184	−0.656***	0.140
1865	0.084	−1.131***	−0.173	−0.874***	−0.134		0.072	−0.890***	−0.127

Notes: The number of observations is 10,124 for regressions (1) and (2), and 7,152 for (3). Dependent variables are dummy variables that equal 1 if a person died from a disease for regressions (1) and (3), if a person contracted a disease for regression (2), and zero otherwise. N.I. = not included.

***Significant at the 1 percent level.

**Significant at the 5 percent level.

*Significant at the 10 percent level.

sequences for net nutritional status, survivors of unhealthy environments developed better immunity to some of the infectious diseases that were rampant in army life.

The results regarding the effects of country of birth reveal two countervailing effects on wartime mortality as observed in table 3.2. First, U.S.-born recruits were more likely to suffer illness (column [2]) but were less likely than immigrants to die when they became sick (column [3]). The advantage of natives over foreigners in terms of fatality outweighs the disadvantage in the odds of contracting diseases. As a consequence, native recruits were about 5 percent less likely to die from disease while in service than were immigrants (column [3]). The lower contraction rate of immigrants may be explained by the circumstance that they were more likely to be confined to unhealthy environments. For instance, many immigrants suffered from the overcrowding, bad ventilation, and spoiled foods of ship cabins on the voyage from Europe to America. Moreover, most of the immigrants came to and first stayed in large cities in the Northeast where communicable diseases were more prevalent than in the countryside. On the other hand, the higher fatality among foreign-born recruits could be attributable to the generally poor health conditions of immigrants compared to natives as indicated by their higher mortality and smaller stature in nineteenth-century America (Haines 1977; Higgs 1979).[11]

Finally, a close relationship between the adjusted household wealth and the odds of contracting disease stands out in the regression result (column [2]). An increase in the log of adjusted household wealth by 1 standard deviation (2.45) around the sample mean is associated with a decline by 7.4 percent in the probability of having at least one case of illness while in service. In contrast, the adjusted household wealth is positively associated with the odds of dying from disease for those who suffered illness, although the relationship is statistically insignificant. The effect of the adjusted household wealth on the probability of dying from illness, a combined outcome of the above two countervailing effects, is relatively small in magnitude and statistically insignificant.[12]

I perform similar regression analyses separately for the six most common

---

11. Height, an indicator of nutritional status, had no significant effect on the probabilities of contracting and dying from disease while in service. A possible explanation for this result is that the link between nutritional status and health was dominated by the strong influence of infectious diseases in the army. The result of the chapter by Joseph Ferrie in this volume is suggestive with regard to this point. In the mid-nineteenth-century United States, household wealth, another proxy of nutritional status, was negatively related with mortality caused by consumption, but not with the chances of dying from cholera, a more fatal infectious disease.

12. I also used the sum of personal property wealth per adult equivalent as a measure of economic status. The results obtained using this alternative index of wealth were similar to those reported in table 3.3. For the odds of contracting disease while in service, the estimated coefficient for personal property wealth was −0.056 and statistically significant. But its effect on the probability of dying from disease was insignificant. The results for other variables were little changed.

diseases, namely, typhoid, smallpox, measles, diarrhea, pneumonia, and malaria. According to epidemiological studies, the significance of immunity influence of prior contraction differs from one disease to another. For some diseases, such as measles, smallpox, and typhoid, an attack would confer immunity and thus reduce the odds of contracting or dying from those diseases in the future (such diseases will be called *immunity diseases* below). For other diseases, such as malaria, diarrhea, dysentery, and pneumonia, a prior contraction has little influence on susceptibility to or resistance against a later contraction (this type will be called *nonimmunity diseases*).[13] If the immunity hypothesis suggested above is true, the difference in mortality between recruits who had come from different environments should be larger for immunity diseases than for nonimmunity diseases.

Table 3.4 presents the results for the probability of contracting each specific disease. The results are largely consistent with the immunity hypothesis suggested above. The advantages of nonfarmers and urban dwellers over farmers and rural dwellers are generally greater for immunity diseases than for nonimmunity diseases. The greater odds of contraction among U.S.-born recruits is statistically significant for two of three immunity diseases (typhoid and smallpox), compared to only one nonimmunity disease (diarrhea). Meanwhile, the effect of adjusted household wealth is statistically significant for one immunity disease (measles) and one nonimmunity disease (diarrhea).

Table 3.5 reports the regression results for the probability of dying from each specific disease conditional on contracting it. The relationship between socioeconomic factors and fatality is less clearly seen for individual diseases than for all diseases. The effect of occupation and urban residence is statistically significant only for typhoid. Natives had a significantly lower fatality than immigrants for an immunity disease (measles) and two nonimmunity diseases (diarrhea and malaria). The wealthier had disadvantages only in the case of pneumonia.

For another test of the immunity hypothesis, I examine the time pattern of wartime mortality. It is documented in the medical histories of the Civil War that the earlier *seasoning period* in the army was most critical for the survival of recruits. During this period enlistees with limited prior development of immunity were exposed to a pool of various infectious diseases in the army (Steiner 1968). If the differences in wartime mortality between farmers and nonfarmers were mainly caused by the difference in immunity status, most of the difference should have occurred in the early stages of military service when the recruits were not seasoned to the severe disease environment of the army camps.

13. For the epidemiological characteristics of these and other diseases see May (1958), Steiner (1968, 12–26), and Kunitz (1983, 351–53). For more recent documentation of the history of specific diseases, see Fetter and Kessler (1996) for measles, Zurbrigg (1997) for malaria, and Sköld (1997) for smallpox.

Table 3.4   Result of Logistic Regressions: Personal Characteristics and Probability of Contracting Particular Disease ($\partial P/\partial X_i$)

	Typhoid (mean = 0.065) (1)	Smallpox (mean = 0.013) (2)	Measles (mean = 0.038) (3)	Diarrhea (mean = 0.277) (4)	Pneumonia (mean = 0.031) (5)	Malaria (mean = 0.151) (6)
Age	0.091	-0.268	-0.549*	-0.040	-0.076	-0.116
Age squared × 10⁻¹	-0.160	0.211	0.030	0.035	0.083	0.048
Height	-0.070	-0.128	1.552	0.516	0.565	-0.224
Height squared × 10⁻¹	0.049	0.117	-1.539	-0.509	-0.448	0.236
Farmers, rural county	N.I.	N.I.	N.I.	N.I.	N.I.	N.I.
Nonfarmers, rural county	-0.068***	-0.254***	-0.216***	-0.061***	-0.159***	-0.053***
Urban county	-0.175***	-2.127	-0.254***	-0.109***	-0.238***	-0.086***
Born in United States	0.043*	0.057	0.066*	0.072***	-0.001	0.022
Log of adjusted wealth	0.022	-0.058	-0.053*	-0.028**	-0.049	-0.003
Duty-infantryman	0.102	-0.049	0.006	-0.041***	0.039	-0.110***
Rank-private	0.031***	0.036	0.023	0.023*	-0.007	0.032**
Year of enlistment						
1861	N.I.	N.I.	N.I.	N.I.	N.I.	N.I.
1862	0.019	-0.002	-0.037	0.036**	0.027	0.017
1863	-0.021	-0.073	0.046*	0.025***	-0.039	0.005
1864	-0.141***	-0.127**	0.002	-0.112***	-0.146***	-0.096
1865	-0.175***	-0.165**	0.029	-0.055***	-0.048	0.019

Notes: The number of observations is 10,124 for all regressions. Dependent variables are dummy variables that equal 1 if a person contracted a particular disease, and zero otherwise. N.I. = not included.

***Significant at the 1 percent level.
**Significant at the 5 percent level.
*Significant at the 10 percent level.

Table 3.5 **Result of Logistic Regressions: Personal Characteristics and Probability of Dying from Particular Diseases in Case of Contraction ($\partial P / \partial X_i$)**

	Typhoid (mean = 0.321, N = 654) (1)	Smallpox (mean = 0.319, N = 135) (2)	Measles (mean = 0.083, N = 387) (3)	Diarrhea (mean = 0.100, N = 2,808) (4)	Pneumonia (mean = 0.171, N = 315) (5)	Malaria (mean = 0.016, N = 1,528) (6)
Age	-0.395	0.057	0.806	0.206	-0.064	-0.580
Age squared $\times 10^{-1}$	0.430	0.392	-0.973	-0.078	0.392	0.703
Height	-1.370	-1.789	3.267	-1.545+	4.119	-0.661
Height squared $\times 10^{-1}$	1.361	1.864	-3.049	1.544+	-4.071	0.929
Farmers, rural county	N.I.	N.I.	N.I.	N.I.	N.I.	N.I.
Nonfarmers, rural county	-0.144***	-0.038	-0.231	-0.045	0.014	0.137
Urban county	-0.157**	N.I.	0.009	-0.005	-0.074	0.144+
Born in United States	-0.051	0.077	-0.349***	-0.072**	-0.058	-0.213**
Log of adjusted wealth	0.037	0.014	-0.127	0.037	0.194*	0.089
Duty-infantryman	0.400***	0.134	0.319**	0.243***	0.499***	0.352**
Rank-private	0.062	0.204	0.043	0.024	0.138	0.008
Year of enlistment						
1861	N.I.	N.I.	N.I.	N.I.	N.I.	N.I.
1862	-0.059	-0.112	0.335**	0.022	-0.188	0.063
1863	0.009	0.012	-1.686	0.057*	0.067	-1.461
1864	-0.153***	-0.244*	0.173	-0.114**	-0.055	-0.080
1865	-0.080	-0.125	0.173	-0.178***	-0.009	-0.113

Notes: Dependent variables are dummy variables that equal 1 if a person died from a particular disease, and zero otherwise. N.I. = not included.

***Significant at the 1 percent level.

**Significant at the 5 percent level.

*Significant at the 10 percent level.

Table 3.6   **Hazard Rates of Dying from Disease: Number of Deaths per 1,000 Men within Four-Month Intervals**

	Any Illness (1)		Immunity (2)		Non-immunity (3)	
Months in Military Service	Farm	Nonfarm	Farm	Nonfarm	Farm	Nonfarm
0–4	23.8	12.8	13.2	4.5	5.7	3.2
4–8	48.5	22.2	20.6	13.4	18.0	8.0
8–12	29.2	21.3	9.3	5.0	12.9	10.5
12–16	24.9	18.6	6.6	3.3	13.5	9.7
16–20	20.3	13.1	6.3	3.2	9.6	6.5
20–24	21.4	10.7	4.4	2.0	12.5	7.2
24–28	18.5	18.1	2.5	1.0	10.8	12.2
28–32	11.0	11.6	2.4	1.5	7.3	8.4
32–36	10.1	7.4	1.3	0.8	6.5	4.7

Notes: The number of recruits who died from a particular type of disease within each four-month interval was divided by the number of recruits who remained alive in service at the beginning of the time interval and then was multiplied by 1,000. If a recruit died from any cause while in service or was discharged alive, he was removed from the pool of population at risk. For the classification of disease see text.

To see whether this was the case, I calculate the hazard rate of dying from a particular type of disease for each of the four-month intervals from enlistment. The hazard rate for the fifth to eighth month, for example, shows what proportion of the recruits remaining alive in service at the beginning of the fifth month died from any illness or some specific type of disease within the following four months. If a recruit died from any cause or was discharged alive between the fifth and eighth months, he is removed from the population at risk when the hazard rate of the next time interval (the ninth to twelfth month) is calculated.

The time patterns of wartime mortality reported in table 3.6 are consistent with the immunity hypothesis. In general, hazard rates of dying from any disease or immunity disease were higher during the first year in service, particularly from the fifth to the eighth months, than in subsequent periods, confirming the remarks on the seasoning period given in medical histories of the Civil War (see fig. 3.1). Moreover, a disproportionately large fraction of the difference between farmers and nonfarmers in mortality caused by immunity diseases was made in the first eight months. For nonimmunity diseases, in contrast, the incidence of wartime deaths is relatively evenly distributed over time in military service (see fig. 3.2). There is no clear time pattern of the difference between farmers and nonfarmers in the hazard rate of dying from nonimmunity-type diseases except that the difference was especially large between the fifth and eighth months in service.

The results presented in this section largely confirm the previous findings based on the sample of Ohio regiments (Lee 1997), building a strong circumstantial case for the importance of earlier disease exposure. However,

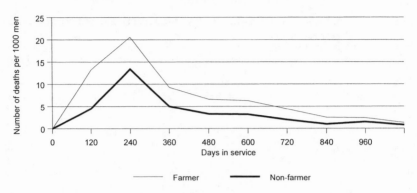

Fig. 3.1   Hazard functions of dying from immunity disease

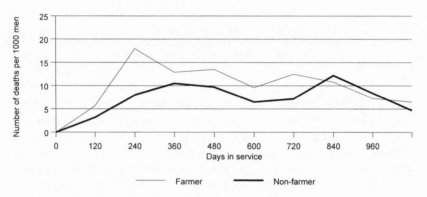

Fig. 3.2   Hazard functions of dying from nonimmunity disease

occupation or urban residence are only indirect indicators of local disease environments. Therefore, the interpretations of the results suggested above are subject to reservations. We now turn to a more direct test using an explicit measure of disease environments that will help to establish the above argument more strongly.

3.4   Local Disease Environment, and Later Health and Mortality

In this section, I analyze the influences of prior exposure to disease using a more explicit measure of local epidemiological environment, namely, the child death rate of each county where recruits resided prior to enlistment. Child or infant mortality is a widely used indicator of the prevalence of infectious diseases. Previous studies have found that infectious diseases increased the chances of suffering chronic conditions such as heart, respiratory, and musculoskeletal disorders at middle and older ages (Barker 1992, 1994; Elo and Preston 1992; Costa 2000). The link between earlier contraction of infectious diseases and later health conditions could be explained in part by the nutritional losses caused by the infections. For example, Haines (1998) found that the crude death rate of the localities where Union Army recruits were reared had a strong negative effect on their heights at the time of enlistment. The analysis of this article is distinct from the existing literature in that it is concerned with the relatively short-term influences of infectious diseases when individuals were exposed to highly severe disease conditions in the army.

As explained above, I calculated the number of deaths in each county for children under age ten and for the population at large from the sample of the 1860 mortality census. By dividing the number of deaths by the county population, I computed the child and crude death rates for each county. Finally, this county-level data set on death rates was linked to the sample of recruits based on the names of the state and county where the recruits lived in 1860. It turned out that 3,864 recruits lived in the counties for which death rates are estimated. For 3,550 of them there is nonmissing information for each variable used in the analysis. The balance of this section is based on the sample of these 3,550 recruits. The sample means of the crude death rate (number of deaths per thousand) and child death rate (number of child deaths per thousand children) are 2.6 and 4.8, respectively. These death rates fall short of the estimate of the crude death rate for the United States circa 1860, 21 deaths per thousand (Poulson 1981, table 10.2). Even if we consider the fact that the Northern death rate was lower than the national average, the estimated county death rates are still much too low, indicating that the number of deaths should be severely undercounted in our mortality data. I use these underestimated county death rates without making any corrections. It should be noted that by doing so I implicitly assume that the extent of undercounting is similar across counties.

Table 3.7 presents the results of logistic regressions that show the effect of local disease environment indicated by county child-death rate on the probabilities of dying from disease (column [1]), of contracting disease (column [2]), and of dying from disease in case of contraction (column [3]). As predicted by the immunity hypothesis, the child death rate is negatively associated with the odds of contracting any disease. The magnitude of the effect is considerably large. An increase in the child death rate by 1 standard deviation (3.6) around the sample mean is associated with a 45 percent decrease in the chances of contracting a disease while in service.[14] However, the child death rate has no significant effect on the fatality rate of those who had one or more disease cases. Largely due to the influence on the odds of contraction, the child death rate has a strong effect on the chances of dying

---

14. The child death rate variable is subject to a measurement error problem because the undercount of deaths may not be constant across counties. If this is the case, the effect of child death rate in the regression would be biased toward zero.

Table 3.7   Result of Logistic Regressions: County Child Death Rate and Probabilities of Contracting and Dying from Diseases

	All Recruits Linked to the 1860 Census						Recruits Who Contracted Diseases		
		Dying from Disease (mean = 0.098) (1)		Contracting Disease (mean = 0.663) (2)				Dying from Disease (mean = 0.120) (3)	
Independent Variables	Mean	Parameter	$\partial P/\partial X_i$	Parameter	$\partial P/\partial X_i$	Mean	Parameter	$\partial P/\partial X_i$
Intercept		-31.445		-12.586			-24.320	
Child death rate	4.771	-0.041**	-0.083	-0.062***	-0.125	4.574	-0.019	-0.035
Age	25.842	-0.0035	-0.148	-0.107***	-0.461	25.636	-0.005	-0.022
Age squared × 10⁻¹	72.881	0.006	0.166	0.017***	0.433	71.910	-0.002	0.050
Height	68.022	0.824	1.154	0.454	0.635	68.109	0.610	0.853
Height squared × 10⁻¹	463.34	-0.057	-1.093	-0.032	-0.607	464.520	-0.042	-0.800
Farmers, rural county	0.572	N.I.	N.I.	N.I.	N.I.	0.611	N.I.	N.I.
Nonfarmers, rural county	0.358	-0.496***	-1.131	-0.353***	-0.093	0.328	-0.392***	-0.101
Urban county	0.070	-1.464***	-0.206	-0.850***	-0.120	0.061	-1.227***	-0.162
Born in United States	0.863	-0.184	-0.035	-0.056	-0.011	0.860	-0.193	-0.037
Log of adjusted wealth	4.871	-0.046	-0.054	-0.056***	-0.066	4.831	-0.032	-0.038
Rank-private	0.888	0.137	0.024	0.076	0.013	0.886	0.115	0.020
Duty-infantryman	0.678	1.066***	0.275	-0.271***	-0.070	0.648	1.179***	0.310
Year of enlistment								
1861	0.250	N.I.	N.I.	N.I.	N.I.	0.283	N.I.	N.I.
1862	0.374	-0.177	-0.047	-0.067	-0.018	0.407	-0.196	-0.053
1863	0.043	-0.070	-0.008	0.036	0.004	0.051	-0.109	-0.013
1864	0.241	-0.939***	-0.221	-1.119***	-0.264	0.180	-0.506**	-0.107
1865	0.091	-1.070***	-0.170	-0.826***	-0.131	0.079	-0.866***	-0.128

Notes: The number of observations is 3,550 for regressions (1) and (2), and 2,355 for (3). Dependent variables are dummy variables that equal 1 if a person died from a disease for regressions (1) and (3) and if a person contracted a disease for regression (2), and zero otherwise. N.I. = not included.

***Significant at the 1 percent level.
**Significant at the 5 percent level.
*Significant at the 10 percent level.

from disease. I tried several different specifications, by including instead of the child death rate the crude death rate, the infant death rate (death rate of children under age one), the log of the child death rate, and dummy variables for five categories of counties according to the size of the child death rate. The results for these specifications, not reported here, provide practically the same implications.[15]

The results for other independent variables are generally similar to the results from the previous regressions in which the child death rate is not included (table 3.3). The only major difference is that the effect of country of birth loses statistical significance. Using the 3,550-man sample, I also conducted similar regressions after excluding the child death rate. A comparison of the results of these regressions, not presented here, with the original regressions presented in table 3.6 shows that the disappearance of the effect of nativity is due mainly to the restriction of the sample, not the inclusion of the child death rate in the regressions. The results also indicate that despite the additional control of the child death rate in the regressions, the magnitudes of the coefficients for occupation and urban county remain little changed. This implies that the two different measures of exposure to disease—population size of place of residence and child death rate—independently affected the chances of dying while in service.

Tables 3.8 and 3.9 offer the results of similar regressions conducted separately for six specific diseases. The effect of the child death rate significantly affects the chances of infection only for two nonimmunity diseases, diarrhea and malaria (table 3.8). On the other hand, measles is the only disease whose fatality was significantly influenced by the child death rate (table 3.9).[16] These results suggest that immunity may not be the only link between local disease environment and health. This point is also relevant for the question of why farmers were disadvantaged even for nonimmunity-type diseases for which their superior nutritional status should have provided an advantage. A possible explanation is that people who lived in unhealthy environments were more aware of how to avoid contracting disease than those with little experience of disease. According to a qualitative record, for example, Germans ate fewer sweets, cooked their food more carefully, and more actively pursued cleanliness (Hess 1981, 66–67). A number of contemporary accounts suggest that rural residents and farmers were particularly unhygienic and ignorant of child health (Preston and Haines 1991, 38–39). Alternatively, it could be explained by a population selection caused by

15. The estimated coefficient for infant death rate for the odds of contracting disease is much smaller in magnitude, −0.011, compared to −0.062 obtained using child death rate. However, since the standard deviation of infant death rate (16.9) is nearly five times larger than that of child death rate (3.6), an increase in either measure of mortality would produce a similar decline in the probability of contracting disease while in service.

16. Using alternative measures of local mortality rate such as crude death rate and infant death rate does not change the result.

Table 3.8   Result of Logistic Regressions: County Child Death Rates and Probability of Contracting Particular Disease ($\partial P/\partial X_i$)

	Typhoid (mean = 0.054) (1)	Smallpox (mean = 0.011) (2)	Measles (mean = 0.036) (3)	Diarrhea (mean = 0.245) (4)	Pneumonia (mean = 0.025) (5)	Malaria (mean = 0.146) (6)
Child death rate	0.002	-0.046	0.018	-0.116***	0.068	-0.113***
Age	0.159	-0.511	0.169	-0.120	-0.079	-0.281
Age squared × 10⁻¹	-0.205	0.460	-0.590	0.115	0.069	0.240
Height	2.041	-0.371	7.276***	0.425	1.311	0.515
Height squared × 10⁻¹	-1.999	0.298	-7.310***	-0.396	-1.181	-0.514
Farmers, rural county	N.I.	N.I.	N.I.	N.I.	N.I.	N.I.
Nonfarmers, rural county	0.010	-0.379***	-0.206***	-0.083***	0.193***	0.064**
Urban county	-0.063	-1.892	-0.345**	-0.084***	-2.020	-0.124***
Born in United States	0.082*	0.108	0.040	0.018	-0.011	-0.032
Log of adjusted wealth	0.003	-0.110	-0.082	-0.067***	-0.054	-0.050*
Rank-private	0.055	-0.016	0.074	0.032	-0.039	0.009
Duty-infantryman	0.078*	-0.138	-0.018	-0.036	0.046	-0.103***
Year of enlistment						
1861	N.I.	N.I.	N.I.	N.I.	N.I.	N.I.
1862	0.004	-0.064	0.001	0.081***	0.089	0.060*
1863	-0.029	0.010	0.040	0.015	0.041	0.007
1864	-0.224***	-0.195	-0.070	-0.106***	-0.147	-0.134***
1865	-0.133**	-0.257	0.001	-0.011	-0.014	-0.030

Notes: The number of observations is 3,550 for all regressions. Dependent variables are dummy variables that equal 1 if a person contracted a particular disease, and zero otherwise. N.I. = not included.

***Significant at the 1 percent level.

**Significant at the 5 percent level.

*Significant at the 10 percent level.

Table 3.9   Result of Logistic Regressions: County Death Rates and Probability of Dying from Particular Disease in Case of Contraction ($\partial P/\partial X_i$)

	All Diseases (mean = 0.120, N = 2,355) (1)	Typhoid (mean = 0.333, N = 201) (2)	Smallpox (mean = 0.040, N = 40) (3)	Measles (mean = 0.084, N = 131) (4)	Diarrhea (mean = 0.101, N = 878) (5)	Pneumonia (mean = 0.237, N = 93) (6)	Malaria (mean = 0.023, N = 522) (7)
Child death rate	-0.035	-0.092	-0.488	-0.693*	-0.080	-0.242	0.160
Age	-0.022	-0.461	5.763	8.939*	0.185	0.582	-1.660
Age squared × 10⁻¹	0.050	0.552	-5.213	-9.414*	-0.101	-0.430	1.853*
Height	0.853	-2.137	36.202	90.255**	-1.349	8.398	-9.882*
Height squared × 10⁻¹	-0.800	2.259	-35.468	-90.959**	1.371	-8.451	10.047*
Farmers, rural county	N.I.	N.I.	N.I.	N.I.	N.I.	N.I.	N.I.
Nonfarmers, rural county	-0.101***	-0.055	2.044*	-0.117	-0.066	-0.195	-0.206
Urban county	-0.162***	-1.592	N.I.	0.467	-0.068	N.I.	-1.337
Born in United States	-0.037	-0.042	0.956	-0.274	0.017	0.120	-0.359***
Log of adjusted wealth	-0.038	0.127	-1.818*	-0.276	0.006	-0.076	0.069
Rank-private	0.020	-0.142	0.565	2.289	-0.027	0.272	0.157
Duty-infantryman	0.310***	0.554***	1.757	0.878**	0.223***	0.162	-0.008
Year of enlistment							
1861	N.I.	N.I.	N.I.	N.I.	N.I.	N.I.	N.I.
1862	-0.053	-0.102	1.321	0.239	-0.108	0.008	-0.053
1863	-0.013	0.034	1.056*	-1.195	0.010	0.216	-1.380
1864	-0.107***	-0.045	0.321	0.267	-0.030	0.143	-0.114
1865	-0.128***	-0.040	-1.204	-0.068	-0.148*	-0.072	0.052

Notes: Dependent variables are dummy variables that equal 1 if a person died from a particular disease, and zero otherwise. N.I. = not included.

***Significant at the 1 percent level.

**Significant at the 5 percent level.

*Significant at the 10 percent level.

differential mortality; that is, individuals who survived an unhealthy environment were on average more robust. Further studies are called for to determine how prior exposure to unfavorable epidemiological environments, if survived, strengthen human resistance to disease.

3.5   Regional Differences

This section documents how the relationship between socioeconomic factors and wartime mortality differed across regions. Let us begin with a regional comparison of the general features of wartime mortality. Table 3.10 reports the cause-specific death rates for five regions. The result indi-

Table 3.10   Number of Cases and Deaths from Specific Causes, by Region

	All	New England	Mid-Atlantic	East North Central	West North Central	South
Number	28,546	2,623	10,643	10,227	3,167	1,886
Cases per person-year						
Wounds	0.29	0.35	0.38	0.25	0.20	0.20
Illnesses	1.07	0.86	0.91	1.28	1.30	0.91
Deaths per 1,000 men						
Wounds	38.5	72.4	39.3	30.3	37.3	33.9
Illnesses	77.7	100.6	50.0	85.0	127.6	79.5
	(100.0)	(100.0)	(100.0)	(100.0)	(100.0)	(100.0)
Immunity diseases	24.5	34.3	15.5	27.3	36.6	25.4
	(30.5)	(34.1)	(31.0)	(32.1)	(28.4)	
Typhoid	18.7	29.7	14.1	18.9	23.7	20.1
	(23.2)	(28.9)	(26.7)	(21.3)	(18.2)	(25.0)
Smallpox	2.9	1.1	0.9	4.1	6.9	2.7
	(3.6)	(1.1)	(1.8)	(4.6)	(5.3)	(3.3)
Measles	2.9	3.4	0.5	4.4	6.0	2.7
	(3.6)	(3.3)	(0.9)	(5.0)	(4.6)	(3.3)
Nonimmunity diseases	37.1	44.6	23.5	41.2	64.7	35.5
	(47.7)	(44.3)	(47.0)	(48.5)	(50.7)	
Diarrhea	26.0	31.3	18.0	28.3	44.8	19.1
	(32.2)	(30.4)	(34.2)	(31.9)	(34.4)	(23.7)
Pneumonia	5.8	4.2	2.1	7.8	11.1	9.0
	(7.2)	(4.1)	(3.9)	(8.8)	(8.5)	(11.2)
Malaria	2.9	5.3	2.3	2.2	4.7	4.2
	(3.7)	(5.2)	(4.3)	(2.5)	(3.6)	(5.3)
Tuberculosis	2.5	3.8	1.1	2.8	4.1	3.2
	(3.0)	(3.7)	(2.1)	(3.2)	(3.1)	(3.9)
Scurvy	1.5	0.4	1.5	2.0	0.9	1.6
	(1.9)	(0.4)	(2.9)	(2.2)	(0.7)	(2.0)
All other diseases	17.5	23.6	12.2	18.0	28.1	18.0
	(21.7)	(23.0)	(23.2)	(20.3)	(21.5)	(22.4)

cates that recruits who were enlisted into the New England regiments were particularly more vulnerable to wounds, compared to other regions. They were nearly twice as likely to die from wounds as were recruits who enlisted in other regions, largely due to a higher case fatality rate. This indicates that New England regiments were presumably sent on more dangerous missions. On the other hand, mortality from disease was the highest for the West North Central (12.8 percent), followed by New England (10.1 percent) and the East North Central (8.5 percent). The Mid-Atlantic regiments had the lowest mortality from disease (5 percent). It is notable that, if New England is excluded, there is a clear negative association between disease-influenced mortality and the extent of urbanization. New England regiments may deviate from such a regularity because they went through more severe military missions, as indicated by the greater casualties caused by wounds. The distribution of the specific causes of death from illness, reported in parentheses in table 3.10, does not differ much between regions.

Table 3.11 presents the mortality from all types of diseases, immunity diseases, and nonimmunity diseases for a number of different socioeconomic categories. Though different from one another in the absolute mortality, the Mid-Atlantic, East North Central, and West North Central are generally similar in terms of the mortality differentials according to socioeconomic backgrounds. Meanwhile, New England and the South demonstrate remarkably different patterns. I first describe the patterns of mortality differentials for the Mid-Atlantic, East North Central, and West North Central. In these three regions, farmers were about 1.7 times as likely to be killed by disease as were nonfarmers. The mortality differential between farmers and nonfarmers is much greater (2.5 times greater for farmers than for nonfarmers) for immunity diseases. A comparison between farmers and nonfarmers who lived in rural counties shows similar patterns. Recruits from rural counties were at much greater risk of dying from disease, especially from immunity diseases, compared to recruits from urban areas. These mortality differentials according to occupation and urban residence remain true if country of birth and household wealth are controlled for. The association between country of birth and mortality from disease differs between farmers and nonfarmers. For nonfarmers, there is no significant difference in mortality between natives and nonnatives. For farmers, on the other hand, the foreign-born were considerably less likely to die than natives.[17] As in the case of the full sample, household wealth had no systematic effect on the likelihood of dying from disease. But mortality from nonimmunity disease is clearly lower for the top wealth category in all regions but the South.

The advantages that farmers and rural residents had over nonfarmers

---

17. This result indicates that the advantages of nonnatives over natives found in the Ohio regiments (Lee 1997), although not observed for the entire sample, are true not only for the state of Ohio but also for the entire Midwest and Mid-Atlantic regions.

Table 3.11 Socioeconomic Background and Wartime Mortality, by Region (number of deaths per 1,000)

Category	New England				Mid-Atlantic				East North Central				West North Central				South			
	N	ILL	IMM	NIM	N	ILL	IMM	NIM	N	ILL	IMM	NIM	N	ILL	IMM	NIM	N	ILL	IMM	NIM
Farmer	897	121.5	55.7	43.5	3,094	70.5	26.5	31.4	6,212	100.8	36.4	46.2	2,375	143.1	42.9	74.5	1,017	112.1	40.3	47.2
Nonfarmer	1,726	89.8	23.2	45.2	7,549	41.6	11.0	20.3	4,015	60.5	13.4	33.4	792	80.8	17.7	35.4	869	41.4	8.1	21.9
Rural county	1,306	117.2	39.8	49.0	4,893	62.9	23.1	28.0	6,526	91.9	31.1	44.0	1,833	138.6	42.0	69.8	963	109.0	40.5	44.7
Urban county	228	100.9	30.7	61.4	2,732	41.4	5.5	24.5	646	44.9	7.7	27.9	1	0.0	0.0	0.0	192	36.4	0.0	36.5
Rural farmer	569	123.0	52.7	43.9	2,137	81.0	30.9	34.6	4,307	105.4	38.1	48.1	1,441	152.6	47.2	80.5	699	125.9	50.1	47.2
Rural nonfarmer	737	112.6	29.9	52.9	2,756	49.0	17.1	22.9	2,219	65.8	17.6	36.1	392	86.7	23.0	30.6	264	64.4	15.2	37.9
U.S.-born	1,394	89.0	30.1	38.0	6,618	56.1	20.1	25.4	8,172	90.8	30.8	43.3	2,269	116.8	41.4	54.2	1,337	73.3	26.2	35.9
Farmer	541	83.2	33.3	31.4	2,548	76.5	30.2	34.1	5,477	106.1	39.1	48.6	1,814	128.4	46.3	60.6	835	93.4	37.1	41.9
Nonfarmer	853	92.6	28.1	42.2	4,070	43.2	13.8	19.9	2,695	59.7	14.1	32.7	455	70.3	22.0	28.6	502	39.8	8.0	25.9
Foreign-born	1,229	113.9	39.1	52.1	4,025	40.0	8.0	20.4	2,055	61.8	13.6	32.6	898	154.8	24.5	91.3	549	94.7	23.7	34.6
Farmer	356	179.8	89.9	61.8	546	42.1	9.2	18.3	735	61.2	16.3	28.6	561	190.7	32.1	119.4	182	197.8	54.9	71.4
Nonfarmer	878	87.1	18.3	48.1	3,479	39.7	7.8	20.7	1,320	62.1	12.1	34.8	337	95.0	11.9	44.5	367	43.6	8.2	16.3
Wealth, farmer																				
$0–100	82	134.1	85.4	0.0	273	102.6	44.0	40.3	555	99.1	41.4	45.0	131	122.1	38.2	68.7	138	159.4	50.7	72.5
$101–500	53	56.6	18.9	75.5	200	105.0	50.0	45.0	439	97.9	25.1	47.8	182	148.4	65.9	65.9	98	132.7	30.6	61.2
$501–1,500	128	156.3	39.1	78.1	281	81.9	32.0	28.5	517	127.7	46.4	63.8	320	162.5	43.8	96.9	136	117.6	51.5	44.1
$1,501–5,000	180	127.8	61.1	33.3	411	85.2	29.2	36.5	808	99.0	43.3	43.3	376	175.5	63.8	87.8	129	108.5	62.0	31.0
$5,001	62	129.0	64.5	48.4	222	90.1	40.5	40.5	506	98.8	33.6	25.7	102	147.1	49.0	98.0	41	24.4	0.0	24.4
Wealth, nonfarmer																				
$0–100	194	128.9	30.9	56.7	827	68.9	14.5	33.9	480	66.7	18.8	29.2	54	148.1	74.1	37.0	91	33.0	0.0	33.0
$101–500	123	97.6	8.1	56.9	447	42.5	6.7	26.8	256	54.7	11.7	39.1	61	82.0	16.4	32.8	42	47.6	23.8	23.8
$501–1,500	137	116.8	43.8	51.1	338	44.4	11.8	32.5	314	54.1	19.1	22.3	68	73.5	29.4	29.4	44	90.9	22.7	68.2
$1,501–5,000	127	110.2	15.7	86.6	299	63.5	16.7	23.4	273	69.6	22.0	44.0	60	116.7	0.0	50.0	26	153.8	38.5	115.4
$5,001–	56	107.1	71.4	17.8	152	32.9	6.8	19.7	168	29.8	11.9	6.0	26	76.9	38.5	0.0	23	173.9	0.0	87.0

Notes: N = number of recruits; ILL = all types of disease; IMM = immunity disease; NIM = nonimmunity disease.

and city dwellers, respectively, are much less visible for New England. For immunity diseases, the difference in mortality between farmers and non-farmers is comparable to the difference found for the above three regions. But farmers and nonfarmers in New England were no different in their likelihood of dying from nonimmunity diseases. The mortality gap between rural and urban residents is even smaller, only 16 percent, because the former had a higher, not lower, mortality from nonimmunity diseases than did the latter. In contrast, the mortality differentials by occupation and county of residence were much more pronounced for recruits from the South. Such greater mortality differentials are largely due to the differences in mortality from immunity disease. For example, Southern farmers were five times more likely to die from immunity disease than were nonfarmers. Among 192 recruits who lived in urban areas in the South prior to enlistment, not a single person was killed by immunity disease, while 4.1 percent of rural residents died from this type of disease.

The farm-nonfarm gap in mortality differs considerably between natives and the foreign-born for these two regions: The advantages of nonfarmers over farmers are much greater for the foreign-born than for natives. In New England, foreign-born farmers were twice as likely to die from illness as were foreign-born nonfarmers, largely due to their lower mortality from immunity disease. In the South, on the other hand, mortality from illness is more than three times greater for foreign-born farmers than for nonfarm immigrants. If household wealth is controlled for, farmers in New England were slightly more likely to die from disease than were nonfarmers, as observed above, for all but one category of wealth. In the South, on the other hand, the farm-nonfarm difference in mortality depends upon the magnitude of household wealth. That is, among the wealthy, farmers were less likely to die from disease than were nonfarmers, mainly due to their lower mortality from nonimmunity disease. Among the poor, in contrast, mortality from disease is greater for farmers than for nonfarmers.

I conduct logit regressions to see how the effects of socioeconomic factors on the probability of dying from disease differed across regions. Table 3.12 presents the results. The regression results for the Mid-Atlantic, East North Central, and West North Central are generally similar to the results for the entire sample. The major difference is that natives are not significantly different from nonnatives in terms of the likelihood of dying from disease while in service. The advantages that recruits from urban areas or nonfarmers had over rural farmers are greater in the Midwest than in the Northeast. This result could be explained by the fact that, in a more urbanized region such as the Northeast, the difference in the extent of exposure to disease between rural and urban population was presumably small relative to that in a more rural region.

The regression results for New England and the South do not support the hypothesis that recruits from healthier environments were more robust in

Table 3.12 Result of Logistic Regressions: Correlates of Probability of Dying from Any Disease, by Region

Independent Variable	New England[a] Mean	New England[a] Parameter	Mid-Atlantic[b] Mean	Mid-Atlantic[b] Parameter	East North Central[c] Mean	East North Central[c] Parameter	West North Central[d] Mean	West North Central[d] Parameter	South[e] Mean	South[e] Parameter
Intercept		-0.059		26.228		-15.141		3.797		8.803
Age										
under 20	0.254	N.I.	0.224	N.I.	0.284	N.I.	0.269	N.I.	0.276	N.I.
20–24	0.309	-0.227	0.301	-0.182	0.291	-0.254	0.273	-0.146	0.287	-0.082
25–29	0.160	-0.015	0.160	-0.462*	0.160	-0.045	0.139	-0.089	0.161	0.140
30 and older	0.277	0.309	0.315	0.359**	0.266	0.109	0.318	-0.278	0.276	0.158
Height	67.7	-0.089	67.3	-0.863	68.1	0.341	68.5	-0.199	68.3	-0.366
Height squared × 10^{-1}	459.7	0.007	454.2	0.062	465.1	-0.024	470.2	0.016	467.1	0.030
Born in United States	0.616	-0.657***	0.806	0.165	0.884	0.278	0.813	-0.317	0.850	-0.472
Farmers, rural county	0.438	N.I.	0.397	N.I.	0.651	N.I.	0.805	N.I.	0.710	N.I.
Nonfarmers, rural county	0.474	-0.028	0.440	-0.375**	0.309	-0.493***	0.195	-0.453*	0.252	-0.253
Urban county	0.088	-0.197	0.163	-0.630***	0.040	-1.044**	0.000	N.I.	0.038	-0.183
Wealth										
$0–100	0.242	-0.204	0.315	0.364*	0.234	-0.217	0.127	-0.204	0.297	-0.205
$101–500	0.158	-0.759	0.187	0.106	0.163	-0.201	0.175	-0.017	0.192	-0.220
$501–1,500	0.225	N.I.	0.183	N.I.	0.192	N.I.	0.279	N.I.	0.240	N.I.
$1,501–5,000	0.271	-0.081	0.209	0.132	0.254	-0.169	0.325	0.024	0.188	-0.021
$5,000–	0.104	-0.018	0.107	0.028	0.157	-0.284	0.095	-0.187	0.082	-0.407

Year of enlistment										
1861	0.281	N.I.	0.231	N.I.	0.221	N.I.	0.248	N.I.	0.403	N.I.
1862	0.544	−0.303	0.359	0.329*	0.385	0.130	0.470	0.212	0.209	−0.649*
1863	0.077	0.487	0.050	0.366	0.024	0.390	0.052	−1.361**	0.076	−0.282
1864	0.091	−0.674*	0.303	−0.690***	0.224	−1.302***	0.204	−0.804***	0.216	−0.796**
1865	0.006	−14.30	0.057	−2.874***	0.144	−0.702***	0.026	−1.515***	0.095	−13.895
Duty-infantryman	0.659	1.371***	0.673	0.912***	0.667	1.262***	0.534	1.154***	0.631	1.363***
Rank-private	0.883	0.513	0.925	0.727**	0.885	0.266	0.892	0.511*	0.898	0.181

Notes: Dependent variable is dummy variable that equals 1 if a person died from a disease, and zero otherwise. N.I. = not included.

[a] Dependent variable mean = 0.125; N = 1,091.

[b] Dependent variable mean = 0.073; N = 3,139.

[c] Dependent variable mean = 0.090; N = 3,927.

[d] Dependent variable mean = 0.155; N = 1,269.

[e] Dependent variable mean = 0.155; N = 707.

***Significant at the 1 percent level.

**Significant at the 5 percent level.

*Significant at the 10 percent level.

resisting disease because of their superior immunity status. If other socioeconomic factors and military positions are controlled for, occupation and county of residence do not have any significant effects on the probability of dying from disease while in service. In New England, natives were much less likely to be killed by disease than were foreign-born recruits. In the South, the mortality differentials according to occupation and place of residence, clearly seen in table 3.11, are no longer present once other variables are controlled for.

These peculiar patterns of New England and the South remain a puzzle to be examined in further studies. A possible explanation for the case of New England is that the effects of socioeconomic backgrounds were relatively weak because New England regiments went through more difficult and dangerous military missions, as indicated by greater casualties caused by wounds. Under circumstances where people are exposed to strong common risk factors that are not associated with their socioeconomic backgrounds, it would be more difficult to identify the effects on mortality of socioeconomic factors. In the South, the weak relationship between socioeconomic background and wartime mortality may be explained as follows: First, since urban development was relatively retarded in the South, urban and rural disease environments were probably not much different in this region compared to those in the North.[18] Second, even the rural population may have been exposed to relatively unhealthy environments in the South due to a climate that is more favorable to the development of various infectious diseases.

3.6 Summary and Implications

The most important result of this study is that prior exposure to unfavorable epidemiological environments reduced the chances of contracting and dying from disease while in service. Farmers and rural residents, who were healthier on average prior to enlistment owing to a greater extent of isolation from other people, were more likely to succumb to illness and to be killed by disease than nonfarmers and urban dwellers, respectively. Native recruits were subject to a greater risk of illness than were foreigners, who had more chances of exposure to infectious diseases in the course of immigration. More direct evidence for the relationship between local disease environment prior to enlistment and health while in service comes from the result that recruits from a county with a higher child death rate were less likely to contract disease than those from a low-mortality county.

The different degree of immunity against pathogens is probably the most

18. In 1860, slightly more than 8 percent of the population in the South lived in cities with a population of 2,500 or more, as compared to 36 percent in the Northeast and 14 percent in the North Central (U.S. Bureau of the Census 1975, A178–179).

important link between the extent of prior exposure to disease and later health. That is, despite the negative consequences for net nutritional status, survivors of unhealthy environments developed better immunity to some of the infectious diseases that were rampant in army life. This hypothesis is supported by the result that the mortality differentials by occupation and place of residence are particularly large for diseases such as typhoid, small-pox, and measles that are known to have greater potential for the development of immunity. Consistent with the immunity hypothesis, moreover, a disproportionately large fraction of the difference between farmers and nonfarmers in mortality caused by immunity diseases was made in the early stage of military service when recruits were not seasoned to the new disease environment in the army camp.[19]

However, immunity may not be the only link between local disease environments and health. The effect of the county death rate on the odds of contracting disease is strong for nonimmunity diseases such as diarrhea and malaria. Also, farmers were disadvantaged even for nonimmunity-type diseases for which their superior nutritional status should have provided an advantage. A possible explanation is that people who lived in an unhealthy environment were better aware of how to avoid contracting disease than those with little experience of disease. An alternative account is population selection caused by differential mortality: Individuals who survived an unhealthy environment were on average more robust.

The results of this study provide a counterexample of the "insult accumulation model" stating that each insult from illness or injury leaves the individual more susceptible to disease in the future (Alter and Riley 1989). The medical experiences of recruits suggests that it is possible that a prior insult provides a resistance to disease, especially when a person is suddenly exposed to a severe disease environment such as Civil War army camps. More generally, this study suggests that we need to reconsider the interrelationship between epidemiological environments and the development of human resistance to disease in order to better understand the links between early-life conditions and later health.

This study provides new evidence pertaining to the link between economic status and health in the nineteenth century. A weak association between wealth and mortality has been a puzzling phenomenon in U.S. economic and demographic history. Steckel (1988) has found that wealth conveyed no systematic advantage for the survival of women or children in households matched in the 1850 and 1860 censuses. As late as 1900, economic status appears to have been a much less important correlate of child mortality than

19. These conclusions are confirmed by the chapter in this volume by Daniel Smith, based on published military service records of New York regiments. Regiments whose recruits came from counties that were more rural and that had lower crude death rates experienced higher mortality during the war. Moreover, the background factors associated with prior exposure to disease were much stronger during the first year in service than thereafter.

place of residence (Preston and Haines, 1991, 150–58). This has led to discussions of egalitarian patterns of death and of relatively small differences in health by social class, perhaps because the poor were better fed in the United States than in Europe.[20] I reported in previous research that there existed a positive effect of wealth on health at least for some diseases on which nutritional influence is great (Lee 1997). I also claimed that the association between wealth and mortality from all causes was weak because the influence of infectious diseases was so strong that it dominated the effect of economic status. The present study has found that economic status measured by household wealth per adult equivalent reduced the chances of contracting diseases while in service. However, wealth had no favorable effect on mortality. This result suggests that in spite of a weak wealth-mortality link, economic status may have been an important determinant of health in the nineteenth century, particularly if morbidity rather than mortality is considered.

This article also strengthens my previous hypothesis that changing human resistance to disease is a potentially important factor in the changes in health in nineteenth-century America. Life expectancy and mean adult height, major indicators of health, declined through the early nineteenth century (Fogel 1986; Komlos 1987, 1992, 1996; Floud, Wachter, and Gregory 1990; Pope 1992; Steckel 1995; Gallman 1995, 1996). A highly plausible explanation for the cycle in health is the epidemiological impact of increased geographical mobility. Higher rates of interregional trade and migration increased morbidity and mortality by spreading communicable diseases and by exposing newcomers to different disease environments. The rise of public schools and changes in labor organization exerted a similar effect by increasing the risk of exposure to infectious diseases (Steckel 1995, 1929–30). The results of this study provide additional evidence for this hypothesis, highlighting the adverse effect of contact with new disease environments caused by geographical migrations.

There was a turnaround in the deterioration in health in the late nineteenth century. Mortality rates started to decline again after the Civil War, and adult height began to increase in the late nineteenth century. Even though a consensus has been reached that the elimination of chronic malnutrition; advances in public health; improvements in housing, sanitation, and food hygiene; and advances in medical technology were important factors which contributed to the decline in mortality, the relative importance of those factors is still under debate (Higgs 1973, 1979; Appleby 1975; McKeown 1976, 1983; Condran and Cheney 1982; Livi-Bacci 1982; Kunitz 1983; Fogel 1986, 1991). The evidence provided in this article suggests that an increase in the degree of resistance, either immunological or social, against infectious diseases could be another potential factor.

Considering the roles of human resistance to disease helps to explain sev-

---

20. In contrast to these studies, the chapter in this volume authored by Joseph Ferrie found that wealth, especially personal wealth, had a strong impact on mortality in rural America.

eral puzzles in the patterns of the improvements in health since the late nineteenth century, particularly regarding the exact timing of the change. According to pioneering regional studies, the upturn of the trend in the mean height did not occur until the 1880s or 1890s, twenty to thirty years later than the beginning of mortality improvements (Steckel and Haurin 1994; Wu 1994; Coclanis and Komlos 1995). The nutrition hypothesis does not explain why mortality began to decline long before any signs of nutritional improvements appeared. On the other hand, the hypothesis regarding human resistance to disease is at least consistent with the timing of the mortality decline. The proportion of the population living in urban areas substantially increased and, owing to the developments of canals and railroads, the degree of geographical mobility rose between 1830 and 1860.[21] These changes presumably increased the fraction of the population who were exposed to but survived various infectious diseases. The results of this study suggest that such shifts in the epidemiological experiences of the population would have lowered the mortality from infectious diseases. This explanation is also consistent with the urban-rural difference in the mortality decline. The decline in mortality rates was faster in urban areas than in rural areas between 1870 and 1900. Previous studies have explained this phenomenon largely by the advances in the urban public health system (Haines 1977; Condran and Crimmins 1980; Preston, Haines, and Pamuk 1981). However, the effectiveness of the advances in public health measures such as the provision of central water supplies, sewage systems, and inspection of food and milk was at best limited even until the last decade of the nineteenth century (Condran and Crimmins-Gardner 1978; Condran and Cheney 1982). On the other hand, the proportion of the population with prior experiences with communicable diseases may have increased more rapidly in cities than in the countryside. If this was the case, we would expect a faster mortality decline in urban areas than in rural areas.

References

Alter, G., and J. Riley. 1989. Frailty, sickness, and death: Models of morbidity and mortality in historical populations. *Population Studies* 43:25–45.
Appleby, A. B. 1975. Nutrition and disease: The case of London, 1550–1750. *Journal of Interdisciplinary History* 6:1–22.

21. In 1830, 4.5 percent of the population were living in large cities with 50,000 residents or more; this percentage rose to 11.0 percent by 1860 and reached 18.7 percent by 1890 (U.S. Bureau of the Census 1965, 14). The proportion of the population residing in small cities with 2,500 to 50,000 inhabitants rose from 5.5 percent in 1830 to 9.9 percent in 1860 (U.S. Bureau of the Census, 14). The decline in the proportion of the population employed in agriculture could have also contributed to the decline in the urban mortality rate, since new migrants to large cities would have been more likely to be nonagricultural workers as the agricultural sector shrank.

Barker, D. J. P. 1992. *Fetal and infant origins of adult disease.* London: British Medical Journal of Publishing Group.

———. 1994. *Mothers, babies, and disease in later life.* London: British Medical Journal of Publishing Group.

———. 1997. Maternal nutrition, fetal nutrition, and disease in later life. *Nutrition* 13 (9): 807–13.

Barker, D. J. P., C. Osmond, J. Golding, D. Kuh, and M. E. J. Wadsworth. 1989. Growth in utero, blood pressure in childhood and adult life, and mortality from cardiovascular disease. *British Medical Journal* 298:564–67.

Coclanis, P. A., J. Komlos. 1995. Nutrition and economic development in post-Reconstruction South Carolina. *Social Science History* 19:91–115.

Condran, G. A., and R. A. Cheney. 1982. Mortality trends in Philadelphia: Age- and cause-specific death rates 1870–1930. *Demography* 19:97–123.

Condran, G. A., and E. Crimmins. 1979. Descriptions and evaluation of mortality data in the Federal Census, 1850–1900. *Historical Methods* 12:1–23.

———. 1980. Mortality differentials between rural and urban areas of states in the northeastern United States, 1890–1900. *Journal of Historical Geography* 6:179–202.

Condran, G. A., and E. Crimmins-Gardner. 1978. Public health measures and mortality in U.S. cities in the late nineteenth century. *Human Ecology* 6:27–54.

Costa, D. L. 1993. Height, wealth, and disease among the native-born in the rural, antebellum North. *Social Science History* 17:355–83.

———. 2000. Understanding the twentieth-century decline in chronic conditions among older men. *Demography* 37:53–72.

Cuff, T. 1992. A weighty issue revisited: New evidence on commercial swine weights and pork production in mid–nineteenth century America. *Agricultural History* 66:55–74.

Curtin, P. D. 1989. *Death by migration.* Cambridge: Cambridge University Press.

Deaton, A., and C. Paxson. 1999. Mortality, education, income, and inequality among American cohorts. NBER Working Paper no. W7140. Cambridge, Mass.: National Bureau of Economic Research.

Diderichen, F. 1990. Health and social inequality in Sweden. *Social Science and Medicine* 31:359–67.

Elo, I. T., and S. H. Preston. 1992. Effects of early-life conditions on adult mortality: A review. *Population Index* 58:186–212.

Fetter, B., and S. Kessler. 1996. Scars from a childhood disease: Measles in the concentration camps during the Boer War. *Social Science History* 20:593–611.

Floud, R., and R. Steckel. 1997. *Health and welfare during industrialization.* Chicago: University of Chicago Press.

Floud, R., K. Wachter, and A. Gregory. 1990. *Height, health, and history.* Cambridge: Cambridge University Press.

Fogel, R. W. 1986. Nutrition and the decline in mortality since 1700: Some preliminary findings. In *Long-term factors in American economic growth,* ed. S. L. Engerman and R. E. Gallman, 439–555. Chicago: University of Chicago Press.

———. 1993. The conquest of high mortality and hunger in Europe and America: Timing and mechanisms. In *Favorites of fortune: Technology, growth, and economic development since the Industrial Revolution,* ed. P. Higonnet, D. Landes, and H. Rosovsky, 33–71. Cambridge: Harvard University Press.

Fogel, R. W., and C. Lee. 1993. New sources and new techniques for the study of secular trends in nutritional status, health, mortality, and process of aging. *Historical Methods* 26:5–43.

———. 2002. Who gets health care. *Daedalus* 131 (1): 107–17.

Gallman, R. E. 1995. Pork production and nutrition during the late nineteenth century: A weighty issue visited yet again. *Agricultural History* 69:592–606.

———. 1996. Dietary change in antebellum America. *Journal of Economic History* 56:193–201.

Gould, B. A. 1869. *Investigations in the military and anthropological statistics of American soldiers.* Cambridge: Harvard University Press.

Haines, M. R. 1977. Mortality in nineteenth century America: Estimates from New York and Pennsylvania census data, 1865 and 1900. *Demography* 14:311–31.

———. 1998. Health, height, nutrition, and mortality: Evidence on the antebellum puzzle from the Union Army recruits for New York State and the United States. In *The biological standard of living in comparative perspective,* ed. J. Komlos and J. Baten, 155–80. Stuttgart: Franz-Steiner-Verlag.

Haines, M. R., and B. A. Anderson. 1988. New demographic history of the late nineteenth-century United States. *Explorations in Economic History* 25:341–65.

Hess, E. J. 1981. The 12th Missouri Infantry: A socio-military profile of a Union regiment. *Missouri Historical Review* 76:53–77.

Higgs, R. 1973. Mortality in rural America, 1870–1920: Estimates and conjectures. *Explorations in Economic History* 10:177–95.

———. 1979. Cycles and trends of mortality in 18 large American cities, 1871–1900. *Explorations in Economic History* 16:381–408.

Kitagawa, E. V., and P. M. Hauser. 1973. *Differential mortality in the United States: A study in socioeconomic epidemiology.* Cambridge: Harvard University Press.

Komlos, J. 1987. Height and weight of West Point cadets: Dietary change in antebellum America. *Journal of Economic History* 47:897–927.

———. 1992. Toward an anthropometric history of African-Americans: The case of the free Blacks in antebellum Maryland. In *Strategic factors in nineteenth-century American economic history,* ed. C. Goldin and H. Rockoff, 297–330. Chicago: University of Chicago Press.

———. 1996. Anomalies in economic history: Toward a resolution of the antebellum puzzle. *Journal of Economic History* 56:202–14.

Kunitz, S. J. 1983. Speculations on the European mortality decline. *Economic History Review* 36:349–64.

Lawson, J. S., and D. Black. 1993. Socioeconomic status: The prime indicator of premature death in Australia. *Journal of Biosocial Science* 25:539–52.

Lee, C. 1997. Socioeconomic background, disease, and mortality among Union Army recruits: Implications for economic and demographic history. *Explorations in Economic History* 34:27–55.

———. 1999. Selective assignment of military positions in the Union Army: Implications for the impact of the Civil War. *Social Science History* 23:67–97.

Lehmann, P., C. Mamboury, and C. Minder. 1990. Health and social inequalities in Switzerland. *Social Science and Medicine* 31:369–86.

Livi-Bacci, M. 1982. The nutrition-mortality link in past times: A comment. *Journal of Interdisciplinary History* 14:293–98.

Margo, R. 2000. *Wages and labor markets in the United States, 1820–1860.* Chicago: University of Chicago Press.

Marmot, M. 1999. Multi-level approaches to understanding social determinants. In *Social epidemiology,* ed. L. Berkman and I. Kawachi, 349–367. Oxford: Oxford University Press.

Marmot, M., G. D. Smith, S. Stansfield, C. Patel, F. North, J. Head, I. White, E. Brunner, and A. Feeny. 1991. Health inequalities among British civil servants: The Whitehall II study. *Lancet* 337 (8 June): 1387–93.

May, J. M. 1958. *The ecology of human disease.* New York: MD Publications.

McKeown, T. 1976. *The modern rise of population.* New York: Academic Press.
————. 1983. Food, infection, and population. *Journal of Interdisciplinary History* 14:227–47.
McNeill, W. H. 1976. *Plaugues and peoples.* Garden City, N.Y.: Doubleday.
McPherson, J. M. 1988. *Battle cry of freedom.* New York: Oxford University Press.
Notkota, V., S. Punsar, M. J. Karvonen, and J. Haapakoski. 1985. Socio-economic conditions in childhood and mortality and morbidity caused by coronary heart disease in adulthood in rural Finland. *Social Science and Medicine* 21:517–23.
Pope, C. L. 1992. Adult mortality in America before 1900: A view from family histories. In *Strategic factors in nineteenth century American economic history,* ed. C. Goldin and H. Rockoff, 267–96. Chicago: University of Chicago Press.
Poulson, B. W. 1981. *Economic history of the United States.* New York: Macmillan.
Preston, S. H., and M. R. Haines. 1991. *Fatal years: Child mortality in late nineteenth century America.* Princeton, N.J.: Princeton University Press.
Preston, S. H., M. R. Haines, and E. Pamuk. 1981. Effects of industrialization and urbanization on mortality in developed countries. In *International Population Conference, Manila, 1981: Solicited papers.* Vol. 2, 233–54. Liege: International Union for the Scientific Study of Population.
Pritchett, J. B., and İ. Tunali. 1995. Strangers' disease: Determinants of yellow fever mortality during the New Orleans epidemic of 1853. *Explorations in Economic History* 32:517–39.
Ravelli, A. C. J., J. H. P. Vander Meulen, R. P. J. Michels, C. Osmond, D. J. P. Barker, C. N. Hales, and O. P. Bleker. 1998. Glucose tolerance in adult after prenatal exposure to famine. *Lancet* 351 (17 January): 173–76.
Rosenberg, C. E. 1962. *The cholera years.* Chicago: University of Chicago Press.
Sapolsky, R. 1993. Endocrinology alfresco: Psychoendocrine studies of wild baboons. *Recent Progress in Hormone Research* 48:437–68.
Seeman, T., B. Singer, J. Row, R. Horwitz, and B. McEwen. 1997. Price of adaptation: Allostatic load and its health consequences. *Archives of Internal Medicine* 157:2259–68.
Sköld, P. 1997. Escape from catastrophe. *Social Science History* 21:1–25.
Soltow, L. 1992. Inequalities in the standard of living in the United States, 1798–1875. In *American economic growth and standard of living before the Civil War,* ed. R. Gallman and J. Wallis, 121–72. Chicago: University of Chicago Press.
————. 1983. Height and per capita income. *Historical Method* 16:1–7.
————. 1988. The health and mortality of women and children, 1850–1860. *Journal of Economic History* 48:333–45.
————. 1995. Stature and the standard of living. *Journal of Economic Literature* 33:1903–40.
Steckel, R. H., and D. R. Haurin. 1994. Health and nutrition in the American Midwest: Evidence from the height of Ohio National Guardsmen, 1850–1910. In *The standard of living and economic development: Essays in anthropometric history,* ed. J. Komlos, 93–116. Chicago: University of Chicago Press.
Steiner, P. E. 1968. *Disease in the Civil War: Natural biological warfare in 1861–1865.* Springfield, Ill.: Charles C. Thomas.
United Nations. 1973. *The determinants and consequences of population trends: New summary of findings of interaction of demographic, economic, and social factors.* New York: United Nations.
U.S. Bureau of the Census. 1965. *Statistical history of the United States from Colonial times to the present.* Washington, D.C.: GPO.
————. 1975. *Historical statistics of the United States, Colonial times to 1970.* Washington, D.C.: GPO.

U.S. Surgeon General's Office. 1870. *Medical and surgical history of the War of the Rebellion.* Washington, D.C.: GPO.

Vinovskis, M. A. 1990. Have social historians lost the Civil War? Some preliminary demographic speculations. In *Toward a social history of the American Civil War,* ed. M. A. Vinovskis, 1–30. New York: Cambridge University Press.

Wadsworth, M. E. J., and D. J. L. Kuh. 1997. Childhood influences on adult health. *Pediatric and Perinatal Epidemiology* 11:2–20.

Wilkinson, R. G. 1996. *Unhealthy societies: The afflictions of inequalities.* London: Routledge.

Wu, J. 1994. How severe was the Great Depression? Evidence from the Pittsburgh region. In *The standard of living and economic development: Essays in anthropometric history,* ed. J. Komlos, 93–116. Chicago: University of Chicago Press.

Zurbrigg, S. 1997. Did starvation protect from malaria? *Social Science History* 21:27–58.

4

Seasoning, Disease Environment, and Conditions of Exposure
New York Union Army Regiments and Soldiers

Daniel Scott Smith

Death is the final event in the life of a person, but what structures its timing is not just the characteristics of the individual. Until the last few decades, studies of socioeconomic differentials in mortality depended on data collected for populations located in geographic units. Thus when nineteenth-century English investigators commented on the high mortality of the poor, they had to rely on correlations among registration districts in the incidence of the poor and the death rate. A skeptic might charge that this conclusion rested on an ecological fallacy because the evidence did not reveal who actually died within each district.

Although based on necessity and dependent on published data, this approach is conceptually not entirely fallacious. Family reconstitution studies of early modern village populations suggest that socioeconomic differences in mortality of people living in an area tended to be small or nonexistent, whereas differences between areas, particularly cities and rural areas, tended to be very large (Smith 1982). The risk of death faced by individuals in the past was one that they partially shared with their neighbors. In a mortality regime dominated by infectious diseases, dangers lurking in the food, water, and air threatened people living in proximity. On the other hand, such influences shared by neighbors are certainly not the entire story. Over and over again, for example, demographers have shown that death rates vary systematically with age.

Data sets constructed recently, such as the one detailing the experiences of Union Army enlisted men serving in the Civil War and after (Fogel 2000), represent a major advance beyond studies constrained by published tabulations. First, multiple and overlapping factors associated with the inci-

Daniel Scott Smith is professor of history at the University of Illinois at Chicago.

dence of death can be assessed simultaneously. Second, variation in the risk of death can be examined over time.

Paradoxically, the pioneering analyst of disease mortality of individual soldiers that is recorded in this unique data set found that factors beyond the individual were important. Variations between urban and rural areas and between rural farmers and nonfarmers, indexes interpreted as tapping the incidence of prior exposure to disease, were major determinants of the risk of acquiring and dying from disease in the army. Childhood nutrition and health, inferred from height, did not matter. Economic resources, indexed by property wealth recorded in the federal census of 1860, may have had an influence only for diseases related to nutrition among residents of metropolitan counties (Lee 1997, and ch. 3 in this volume). It was not just the economists who might or should be surprised by these results. Historical demographers are confident that death rates for adults steadily increase with age, even among young men who served in the army. Yet this routinely observed pattern appears only for nonfarmers and for men enlisting in metropolitan counties (Lee's ch. 3 in this volume).

These results contain three paradoxes. First, the healthier, the wealthier, and large groups of the younger were not unambiguously more likely to live than the less healthy, poorer, and older. Second, the analysis of a unique individual-level data set uncovered the importance of a factor—prior exposure to disease—whose source was collective. Third, the orientation of the discipline of epidemiology (or sociology) seems to be more relevant for understanding these results than those of other disciplines.

4.1   Exposure to Risk at Place of Origin: Urbanization and Mortality

Given the importance of the definition, scope, and functioning of disease environments, more needs to be known about them. Building on Lee's work, this paper combines both individual- and aggregate-level data and attempts to specify several of the correlates of disease mortality at a finer level of detail. An investigation of the incidence and timing of disease mortality among Union Army enlisted men in companies from New York state is placed in the context of a parallel study of mortality of regiments and other units of army volunteers that were organized in the Empire State.

New York is the focus primarily because of a uniquely detailed published tabulation of outcomes of military service by regiments and other units. Its author was Frederick Phisterer (1912, vol. 1, 288–303), a pioneering statistician of the Northern military effort during the Civil War (1907).[1] For offic-

---

1. Born in Germany in 1836, Phisterer served in the regular army, entering as a private in the artillery in 1855 and leaving as a sergeant in 1861. Reenlisting in the U.S. Army in July 1861, he was discharged as captain in 1870. From 1877 onward he was active in the National Guard, rising to the rank of Brevet Major-General and the position of Adjutant-General of the New York National Guard. Living in Albany, between 1890 and 1908, he published three editions of a five-volume survey totaling 4,499 pages on the New York men and units who fought in the Civil War.

ers and enlisted men, he reported the numbers who were killed in action, who died of or recovered from wounds received in action, who died of disease, and who died of six other known causes (and one unknown cause) that were less frequent. He also tabulated these data separately for those who became prisoners of war and those who were never captured. Contemporaries and historians of the Civil War have highlighted the horrendous conditions and high death rates in prisoner-of-war camps. Since the fraction of a regiment that fell into enemy hands varied considerably depending on circumstances (the median percentage was 5.35 while the mean was 7.96 and the standard deviation 11.38), this adjustment is useful.

Among the 267 New York volunteer organizations, there were 183 regiments of infantry, 33 of cavalry, and 3 of engineers, and 48 regiments, battalions, or batteries of artillery. Unlike most of the compilers of other state reports, Phisterer provides an approximation of the population at risk. However, the column headed by the phrase "the number of men in organization among whom losses occurred" misleads. The heading in the recapitulation replaces "men" with "enlistments," indicating that those who reenlisted were counted more than once. In any case, the available proxy for the population at risk does not take account of other causes of attrition—transfer, desertion, discharge, etc.[2] Finally, Phisterer provides a detailed summary of the history of the unit, including the dates it was mustered in and out and places where it served. The former allows the calculation of death indexes by duration, and the latter information can be mapped onto regional disease environments.

In the nineteenth century, urbanization dramatically increased mortality (Haines 2001). Although less well documented, it also was related to health and morbidity. Contemporaries certainly believed as much. A medical examiner of draftees and recruits for a New York City district noted, among other comments, that "congestive diseases, as apoplexy, delirium tremens, &c, dependent on causes too palpably incident to a large, crowded, immoral, and ill-cleaned city to need specification, are numerously met with" (Roberts 1865, 264). Another city medical examiner, Dr. W. H. Thompson, reported on the unhealthy conditions in his district, especially for the Irish. He was also "struck with number of persons among the better classes, and native Americans, with weak constitution, deficient girth of chest, and slender physique, especially among the younger men. The contrast, in this respect, with what I had noted in American country-recruits in 1862 is so marked that I have been led to consider city-life in New York as exerting an unfavorable influence on physical development, especially in children" (Thompson 1865, 252).

There were towns and cities in the state outside of New York City. Further, factors other than urbanization, such as residence along transporta-

2. Since the population at risk cannot be precisely captured, these measures are referred to as death indexes rather than rates.

tion routes such as the Erie Canal, could be associated with exposure to disease (Haines, Craig, and Weiss forthcoming, table 3). Data from New York state allow a subtler isolation of ecological variables that theoretically are associated with the extent of prior exposure to disease than is possible by merely characterizing counties as urban or rural. Two sources were used to index the disease environment among counties within the state of New York. Three censuses—the 1850 federal and the 1845 and 1855 state returns—yielded a relative index, however underestimated, of the crude death rate in each county. Township-level data from the 1845 census were also used to calculate the proportion in each county who resided in places with populations of 2,500 and larger and of 5,000 and larger.

Although men in regiments and especially companies were recruited locally, they did not all come from the same county. A rather elaborate procedure was used to index the disease environment of recruits in the various military units. Based on reports from families, the 1865 state census tabulated, for each regiment or other unit, the number of living New York–resident soldiers who were from each county (New York Secretary of State 1867, 637–48). The four counties with the largest share of troops in the 278 units included, on average, 74 percent of the men. In the 192 infantry regiments, the figure was 77 percent. The estimated death and urbanization index for each regiment was the average, weighted by the share of each county and the residual in the totals of living soldiers reported for each unit, of crude death rates and urbanization rates in these four counties and the residual.

The data from the New York state census of 1845 indicate (see table 4.1) that the urbanization effect on mortality is continuous rather than dichotomous. Crude death rates increased from a rate of 11.4 per 1,000 in townships under 1,000 in population to a rate of 15.7 per 1,000 for places between 7,500 and 60,000 in population. The rate for New York City was even

Table 4.1   Township Population Size and Census Crude Death Rate, New York 1845

Population of Township	Crude Death Rate	Town Population		Number of Townships
		Total	Percent	
Under 1,000	11.4	60,792	2.3	94
1,000–1,499	12.5	159,255	6.1	124
1,500–1,999	12.5	325,197	12.5	184
2,000–2,499	12.9	343,542	13.2	153
2,500–4,999	13.1	825,108	31.7	247
5,000–7,499	14.2	231,129	8.9	39
7,500–19,999	15.6	107,478	4.1	10
20,000–60,000	15.8	177,460	6.8	5
New York City	16.9	371,223	14.3	1
Total	13.86	2,601,184	—	857

Source: Calculated from New York Secretary of State (1846).

higher—16.9 per 1,000.[3] However, the extent of urbanization in a county, measured by the share of its population living in places over 5,000, bore no relationship to the crude death rate in the 812 towns under 5,000 in population. There was no spillover of higher urban mortality to the nonurban areas of a county. However, the crude death rate of a town was positively related to the death rate in the rest of the county. For the analysis in this article, practical considerations limited my refinement of the urbanization effect to the level of the county.

The published results of examinations for military service during the last half of the war provided estimates of the fraction of draftees, and of recruits and substitutes rejected for service of those presumably examined medically (Baxter 1875, vol. 1, pp. 637–767; Fry 1866, 165–213).[4] Since recruits and substitutes sought to join the army, their rejection rate is more likely than that for draftees to reflect actual health status (Smith 2000b).[5] These data are reported for thirty-one registration districts whose boundaries were those of congressional districts. The rate for each registration district was assigned to each county it included, with the nine districts in New York County merged into one. As before, the rate for the regiment is imputed by the weights derived from the distribution of soldiers among counties reported in the 1865 state census.

As table 4.2 shows, the imputed background urbanization and death rates for regiments and other units correlate with the deaths from disease during the Civil War. Regiments whose recruits came from counties that were more rural and that had lower crude death rates experienced higher mortality during the war. Regiments whose men were from counties that were part of congressional districts where fewer recruits and substitutes failed their medical examinations in the final two years of the war also had higher disease mortality during the war.

The relationship between imputed county-of-origin characteristics to mortality during the war is not as linear or continuous as the relationship between town size and the crude death rate in 1845 (table 4.1). Further, there was substantial variation not accounted for by the different classifications (see the eta-squared statistics in table 4.2). The plan to develop a background mortality index that would complement the urbanization effect

3. In his studies, Lee operationalized the effect of prior exposure to disease with a rural-urban dichotomy, based on having a city over 10,000 in Ohio, or in a metropolitan area in 1860 for troops from the entire North. Six counties—Albany, Erie, Kings, New York, Richmond, Rensselaer—of the sixty in New York in 1860 were classified as urban. It is quite plausible that men who enlisted in the fifty-four nonurban counties had not, on average, been exposed to disease to the extent of those joining in the six urban counties.

4. These estimates assume that draftees rejected for nonmedical reasons were never medically examined and that recruits and substitutes rejected because they were too old or too young were also not examined (Smith 2000).

5. In the calculation, those excluded because they were under- or overage were excluded from the denominator, as it was assumed that they never had a medical examination.

Table 4.2   Correlates of Disease Death Indexes for New York Regiments

Classification and Category	Disease Death Index	Number of Regiments
Inferred crude death rate in 1845	69.4	258
Under 11 per 1,000	94.8	7
12 per 1,000	82.3	52
13 per 1,000	80.9	86
14 per 1,000	55.1	69
15 per 1,000 and higher	51.6	64
η^2 and F-value	.023	1.50
Inferred crude death rate in 1855	69.4	258
Under 11 per 1,000	105.1	72
12 per 1,000	65.3	43
13 per 1,000	60.2	53
14 per 1,000	46.9	37
15 per 1,000 and higher	49.0	53
η^2 and F-value	.058	3.90**
Inferred share of population over 5,000 in 1845	69.4	258
Under 20%	98.8	48
20–30%	89.8	72
30–50%	50.3	64
50–70%	47.4	44
70% and higher	46.3	30
η^2 and F-value	.056	3.74**
Inferred share of population over 2,500 in 1845	69.4	258
Under 60%	105.8	73
60–70%	60.1	74
70–80%	53.5	54
80% and higher	50.1	57
η^2 and F-value	.058	5.19**
Inferred recruit medical rejection rate, 1863–65	69.4	258
Under 215 per 1,000 examined	106.2	61
215–300 per 1,000	67.9	97
300–350 per 1,000	45.6	35
350 and above per 1,000	49.9	65
η^2 and F-value	.054	4.81**
Actual region of organization of regiment	69.5	257
New York County	47.8	81
County contiguous to New York County	53.9	30
County on Erie Canal	71.7	60
Elsewhere in state	93.8	86
η^2 and F-value	.039	3.59*

Sources: New York Secretary of State (1846, 1857); Phisterer (1907, 80–91 and 288–303); Dyer (1959); Baxter (1875, vol. 2, pp. 637–767).
**Significant at the 1 percent level.
*Significant at the 5 percent level.

failed. Instead, a methodological mountain has yielded something of a substantive mole hill. Since the background urbanization and mortality indexes were highly correlated (0.7 to 0.9), only one can be employed as a predictor of the wartime disease mortality index.

4.2 Disease Mortality and Shared versus Distinct Disease Environments of Men and Regiments

In addition to throwing men together from diverse disease environments, soldiering during the Civil War sent men into regions of the country with a range and variable intensity of disease patterns. The aggregated results tabulated by Phisterer permit some insight into the scope of disease environments in the Union Army. Usually ten companies, originally composed of approximately 100 men each, comprised an army infantry regiment. Although companies were sometimes detached from their regiments for special service, usually they were not. Companies in regiments in which the other companies had higher disease death indexes also suffered a higher incidence of fatalities from disease. A 1 percent increase in the disease death index of the men in all other companies in the regiment is associated with nearly a 1 percent increase in death index for companies in the New York regiments that experienced a high rate of combat-related deaths (Fox 1974, 183–241).[6] While common regional origin within New York is also relevant, the regression equation below also points to an effect from the region of service during the war.[7]

Company Disease Index $= 7.87 + (0.881)$

$$\times \text{ (Other Men in Regiment Disease Index)}$$

Officers who led army companies obviously shared geographic locales with the men they led. Each company typically had three officers—a captain, a first lieutenant, and a second lieutenant—and thus each regiment typically included only thirty line officers and nine staff officers (Shannon 1928, vol. 2, 270). As the size of companies and regiments shrank through attrition, officers were more likely to be replaced than were men. The best estimate is that just over 5 percent of men in New York units in the Union Army were officers.[8] In just over a quarter of the regiments, no officers died

6. Included in this analysis are the thirty-nine "fighting regiments" that had more than 130 men killed or died from wounds or, if in a smaller unit, had a high percentage of such combat deaths.

7. The F-value for the equation is 233.3, with a standard error of the slope of 0.058 and an adjusted R-squared of 0.346; there were 433 companies in the analysis. This relationship could be spurious to the extent that the compiler William Fox had more complete coverage of either the deaths or the numbers enrolled in a unit.

8. In his detailed assessment, Phisterer (1907, 186), estimated that there were 16,000 officers and 294,000 enlisted men in New York volunteer units. Officers thus comprised 5.16 percent of the total strength, the figure used in dividing the figure for the total in the organization.

from disease outside of prison, and nearly 80 percent of the regiments had two or fewer disease deaths among officers. Given the small numbers in the base population of officers, it is not surprising that the correlation of the disease death index of officers and men within regiments is weak. On average, a 1 percent increment in the disease index for enlisted men increased the officer index by only a sixth of 1 percent.

Officer Disease Index $= 10.35 + (0.172) \times$ (Enlisted Men Disease Index)

The F-value is 21.46, the standard error of the slope is 0.037, and the adjusted R-squared is 0.083. There were 228 regiments in the analysis.

Any novelty in destination of service could be dangerous, as hinted by the disease death rates of two exceptional units that stayed home. The 925 men in the 20th and 28th artillery batteries, organized in late 1862 in New York City, served throughout the entire course of the war in Fort Schuyler and Fort Columbus, which guarded New York harbor. Only twelve of these men died of disease, giving them a death index of 5 per 1,000 man-years, a mere fifth of the overall average for soldiers from the state.

Most New York regiments served only in the eastern theater of operations and there mostly in the ninety miles between Richmond, Virginia, and Washington, D.C. Categorizing the units by a distinctive other region of service, table 4.3 suggests that being sent to Louisiana or along the Gulf of Mexico was the most hazardous. The lower Mississippi lived up to its reputation as a deadly region. From July 1861 to June 1865, disease death rates for Union soldiers in the Department of the Gulf were 26 percent higher than for the army as a whole (U.S. Surgeon General 1990, vol. 1).[9] However, experience in North or South Carolina, which was limited to the coastal area until the very end of the war, did not yield remarkably higher mortality indexes.

There was, however, marked variation in the incidence of disease within regions.[10] This variability is to be expected. At some point, as the incidence of sickness increases, a "tipping point" may be reached after which the number of cases and fatalities accelerates in a way not predictable by objective conditions. Such an epidemic occurred in the five regiments of the Vermont brigade in the fall of 1861, units whose living and sanitary conditions were, according to investigators, no more miserable than regiments in which the incidence of sickness was quite low (Benedict 1886, 237–40). Even without such an accelerant, clustering of deaths within particular companies and regiments is to be expected. These units encountered particular circumstances or their members had special characteristics that are not known or knowable to an investigator nearly a century and a half later.

9. Deaths occurring in general hospitals are excluded in this comparison.
10. Many of the regiments that had some experience outside of the eastern theater also spent time within that area. Employing analysis of variance for both four- and five-category regional classifications shows that the difference between regions was significant only at the 0.1 level.

Table 4.3   **Disease Death Indexes for New York Regiments and Other Units by Rank, Cause, and Distinctive Region of Service, for Prisoners and Nonprisoners**

Region of Service of Regiment or Other Unit	Disease Death Indexes Per 1,000 Man-Years	Disease Death Indexes Per 1,000 Men	N Men	N Units
Totals for region of service	24.7	64.0	303,662	249
Only in eastern theater	22.1	54.0	204,239	164
Only in New York	5.0	13.0	925	2
Ever in Louisiana or Gulf region	41.8	110.5	30,229	28
Ever in the Carolinas	24.2	71.3	48,924	38
Ever in western theater	27.0	77.4	20,270	19
With Sherman to the sea	32.7	90.7	13,220	12
Not with Sherman	16.2	52.3	7,050	7
By military rank		63.2	317,340	264
Enlisted men		65.4	288,719	264
Officers		23.0	15,713	264
After being wounded		123.2	55,442	267
Enlisted men		122.2	52,245	267
Officers		136.1	3,197	267
Prisoners of war (disease)		153.0	31,066	267
Enlisted men		156.6	30,112	267
Officers		39.8	954	267
Prisoners of war (wounds and other)		32.3	31,066	267
Enlisted men		32.7	954	267
Officers		19.9	30,112	267

Notes: The denominator of the index based on man-years is the "number of men in organization among whom losses occurred" multiplied by the difference between date the regiment or other unit was mustered in and the date it was mustered out. Ideally, the denominator should be the average number of men in the unit over the duration of its service.

Sources: Phisterer (1907, 80–91 and 288–303); Dyer (1959).

Officers and men in the same regiment may have advanced (or failed to advance) through the South together, but they did not share entirely the smaller disease milieu of the camp. Phisterer's tabulations are especially valuable here in suggesting the boundaries of disease environments. Overall, enlisted men were three times as likely to die from disease as were officers (see table 4.3). While the Center for Population Economics (CPE) sample is restricted to enlisted men, limited evidence indicates that officers were taller, more likely to be native-born, and more frequently drawn from the ranks of the middle class than were enlisted men. As noted, these attributes are not associated with a lower death rate from disease. Whether officers were more likely to come from cities and larger towns than enlisted men is uncertain.

Officers and enlisted men did not live in immediate proximity. According to regulations, privates in an army camp were grouped by company with a street in between. At one end, perpendicular to the street of enlisted men, were rows: first, noncommissioned officers, then the commissioned officers of the companies, and finally the staff and commander of the regiment, who were located in front of the baggage train. Behind the baggage train were the latrines for the officers, while the soldiers relieved themselves in latrines at the opposite end of the camp (Wiley 1952, pp. 55 and 373n. 45). Officers and men also ate at separate messes, and officers used their own funds to purchase food. The leaders and the led shared geographically defined disease environments (e.g., malarial regions) but not what might be called the micro-microbe-disease space.

The fourfold ratio of the mortality indexes between officers and enlisted men incarcerated in POW camps also illustrates the importance of the environment in which those in the Union Army served. With rare exceptions, Union officers were imprisoned in camps apart from captured enlisted men (Marvel 1994, 293). Imprisoned officers died more frequently than those who were never captured (and at much higher rate if duration of exposure could be calculated), but conditions for captured officers sometimes were not harsh (Mitchell 1988, 221n. 64). Nearly one in six captured New York enlisted men died in Confederate prisons compared to one in twenty-five officers.

A common circumstance—being wounded in action—yielded quite similar mortality outcomes for officers and enlisted men. Indeed, a slightly higher percentage of wounded officers died (13.6 percent) than wounded men (12.2 percent). Possible explanations of this similarity are that the distribution of severity of the wounds was not radically different for men and officers and that postwound infections were a great leveler. All else equal, officers should have had a lower wound case fatality rate. Because they were salaried and paid for their food, wounded officers were not hospitalized with enlisted men. If the wounds were minor, they were cared for in their own quarters by an orderly. Other options for wounded officers included care in a private hospital or sick-leave at home (Adams 1952, 171–72). The smaller disparity between the mortality indexes among officer and enlisted POWs due to wounds and other causes (19.5 and 32.7 per 1,000) compared to disease (39.8 and 156.6) leads to the speculation that officers were, on average, more severely wounded than men.

4.3 Measuring Length of Observation and Deaths of Individual Enlisted Men in New York Sampled Companies

Key to demographic analysis is the concept of population at risk. The rich detail in the sample of Union Army enlisted men can be exploited to capture when men first came under observation and when they no longer were. To do so required a variety of assumptions. In the version of the CPE data set used in this paper, there were 7,617 enlisted men in companies organized by New York state. For 208 (2.73 percent), there were no dates except those for enlistment recorded on the descriptive roll of the company, the original source of the data. With the assumption that no military service record could be located, these men were dropped from the analysis; the implicit assumption here is that their mortality experience in the army was identical to those whose entry and exit dates could be determined.

Accepting the enlistment date provided in the descriptive rolls as the appropriate date of entry into observation was the most critical assumption. Other sources, presumably the military service records, provided up to three separate enlistment dates. Of these, some 7.5 percent came six or more months before the enlistment date on the descriptive roll and 5.4 percent came a year or more earlier. In all, 13.6 percent had earlier dates of enlistment, but very short intervals can be attributed to slight variants in recording the same date or as the result of men who served previously for three months under Lincoln's original call of 15 April 1861 for 75,000 men. New York provided 13,906 men in this instance. The longer intervals may be attributed to those enlisting in a sampled company after serving two years under the second call of 1861 in another company or regiment. New York provided the only troops (30,950) enlisting for two years under this call (Phisterer 1907, 3–4). Whatever the reason for the discrepancy between the enlistment date recorded on the descriptive roll and the enlistment dates appearing on other records, the former must be correct from a demographic perspective. The soldier is not at risk to die before joining one of the companies that were sampled at the beginning of the project. However, for 2.7 percent of the cases missing information on the date of enlistment in the descriptive roll, an enlistment date from other records was taken as the date of entry into observation.

Some ambiguity exists with respect to the date the soldier was last under observation during the war. On the assumption that the date of death was an important and definitive event, and given that there are no variant records of this date, it was accepted as correct. Of those who died of disease before 1866, 6.9 percent had some other occurrence in their lives recorded as taking place after they had died. For 3.5 percent of these deaths this unnatural event occurred more than three months after they had died. Since the timing of this postmortem event was found by computing the maximum date among all of the many events recorded by date in the data—discharge, military court action, release from hospital, etc.—the procedure is sensitive to errors in the original records or in the data entry.

If no death during the war era was recorded, the men were regarded as being under continuous observation in the first period until the date of the latest event recorded unless there was a definitive break of more than 0.25 years between a seeming date of departure and a subsequent date of reentry. The working assumption here was that a soldier was really under continuous observation until proven otherwise, a conjecture that by expanding the period at risk tends to minimize the measured mortality rate. For example, someone who deserted but later returned was treated as never having left. It would be possible to make better judgments, on a case-by-case basis, as to whether someone was really under observation at every point. Using assumptions that maximized the apparent length of the first period that the soldier was under continuous scrutiny, the goal was to minimize the complexity of the data set. Only if there was a gap of more than 0.25 years between a date of discharge and a date of reenlistment was the first period terminated by the discharge date. In this chapter, the relatively few second and ever-fewer subsequent observation spells that began with reenlistments were excluded from the analysis.

Limiting this study to soldiers from one state, even one as large as New York, sharply reduces the number of events to be analyzed. To maximize that number, 619 deaths from all specified noncombat causes are included. While death from disease was around four times higher than that experienced by young adult men in civilian life in the mid-nineteenth century, only 8.3 percent of sampled soldiers died from these causes. Almost half of the deaths were due to two causes: diarrhea (27.5 percent) and typhoid (22.3 percent). Other relatively numerous killers were fevers of various types (6.8 percent), dysentery (4.5 percent), tuberculosis (3.7 percent), pneumonia (3.2 percent), scurvy (2.6 percent), and starvation (2.6 percent). A handful of deaths probably incident to wounds (gangrene, erysipelas, and possibly some of the unspecified diseases) are included.

4.4   Seasoning and the Effect of Duration of Service

Seasoning—the elevation of disease and death from disease that occurred as a consequence of movement—is a pervasive phenomenon in the literature of historical demography. Whether moving to cities in the early modern era, to the Chesapeake region from Great Britain in the seventeenth century, or into the Union Army from rural Ohio, arrivals did poorly during their initial exposure to the new disease environment. As table 4.4 demonstrates for enlisted infantrymen in units organized in New York state, death from disease declined with the length of time served (Lee 1997, 42). The overall death rate from disease was 46.0 per 1,000 man-years. In the first year of observation the rate was 55.6 compared to 41.8 for the second year. For those under observation longer than two years, the rate was 34.8 per 1,000 from then until the end of military service.

As was the case for Ohio troops studied by Lee, the chances of death from disease peaked well into the first year of service. In New York, the death rate for the first six months was lower (45.2 per 1,000 man-years) than in the second six months (69.2). Given the predominance of infectious diseases, this delay in the seasoning peak is surprising. Only 11 percent of those whom

Table 4.4   **Death Rates by Duration of Exposure, New York Union Army
                  Enlisted Men**

Period of Exposure	Death Rate per 1,000	Number of Deaths	Man-Years at Risk	Starting Cohort Size
Enlistment until exit	46.0	613	13,325	7,548
Enlistment to end year 1	55.6	330	5,928	7,548
Start year 2 to end year 2	41.8	147	3,514	4,338
Start year 3 until exit	34.8	136	3,883	2,721
First six months	45.2	151	3,343	
Second six months	69.2	179	2,585	
Third six months	47.7	94	1,968	
Fourth six months	34.2	53	1,545	
Fifth six months	50.3	62	1,232	
After 2.5 years to exit	27.9	74	2,652	2,283

Source: Fogel (2000).

the 1850 census (DeBow 1855, 23) reported dying from such diseases, classified then as zymotic, were sick longer than a month. The apparent delay in seasoning is consistent with the substantial increase in disease mortality in the Union Army during the first year and a half of the war (Elliott 1862; Olmstead 1866). Death rates from disease more than doubled between the third quarter of 1861 and the first quarter of 1862 and then rose by an additional 30 percent by the final quarter of 1862 (U.S. Surgeon General 1990, vol. 1).

Data collected in an innovative quantitative investigation of camp conditions are suggestive about the delay in peak seasoning mortality until the second half of the year of first service. Investigators from the U.S. Sanitary Commission, a nongovernmental organization, evaluated various aspects of the camps that they considered relevant to the incidence of sickness. The agency then coded the responses to questions about camp sites, tents, cleanliness, rations, discipline, water supply, medical services, etc., for 450 units that were surveyed between August and early December 1861. Conditions were ranked from 1 ("extremely bad") through 5 ("indifferent") to 10 ("perfect"); scores above 7 ("very good") were rarely awarded. In December 1861, Frederick Law Olmstead (1866, 34), the commission's executive director, reported on a tabulation of these scores for 200 regiments surveyed prior to 1 November 1861 and gave his impressions of the army's medical problems. Olmstead and his fellow commission directors, however, relied on prior beliefs and tabulations of each variable separately to support policy recommendations made in a letter to President Abraham Lincoln on 21 July 1861. They charged that "the careless and superficial medical inspection of recruits made at least 25 per cent of the volunteer army raised last year not only utterly useless, but a positive incumbrance and embarrassment, filling our hospitals with invalids" (U.S. War Department 1899, 235). Using the microfilm edition of the original returns (Scholarly Resources 1999, microfilm roll 27, frames 268–1197, and roll 28, frames 8–28), conditions relevant to disease can be related to the rate of sickness a regiment experienced during a month.

Over a quarter of the 450 regiments whose conditions were quantified after being surveyed by the Sanitary Commission inspectors were from New York. On average, nearly four months (119 days) had passed between mustering in and inspection. The influences on sickness early in the war were not those that can be related to mortality from disease during the first year of service. Neither the overall sickness rate (57 per 1,000) nor its components—sick in quarters, in the regimental hospital, or in the general hospital—bore any relationship to the extent of urbanization or the crude death rates of the counties where the units had been recruited. Perhaps surprisingly, none of the conditions in the camps had an impact on the rate of sickness.[11] The only indicator that predicted significantly more sickness was the report that the initial medical examination had been inadequate. On average, the sickness rate in the twenty-seven regiments that had a thorough examination upon entering the army was only 33.0 per 1,000 strong compared to the overall rate of 56.6, a finding that supported one of the main prescriptions of the Sanitary Commission for reform.

There is suggestive evidence that the theory of the Sanitary Commission as to what mattered shaped how their investigators assessed the evidence. That is, the retrospective conclusion about the thoroughness of the initial medical inspection, presumably learned in conversation with the regimental surgeons (whose training was almost always favorably evaluated by the man from the Sanitary Commission), was not independent of knowledge of the monthly sickness rate.

In a regiment with a lot of sickness, what or who was to be blamed? Thirty-five of the 117 New York regiments were inspected on more than one occasion during the five-month period. The investigators reported the same evaluation of the initial medical examination for only twenty-two of the regiments. In thirteen cases, the inspectors differed on whether the examination upon entering the army had been adequate. For eight regiments, the scoring of the initial medical examination as inadequate was associated with a much higher rate of sickness (36 per 1,000 on average) than that experienced during the month that the inspector reported a thorough initial exam. For the five remaining anomalous regiments, a more favorable assessment of the initial examination with a smaller increase in the sickness rate (5 per 1,000).

---

11. This was not true in the data that included all of the inspections. Regiments from regions (the Midwest and northern New England) that had greater disease mortality during the war also experienced a higher incidence of early sickness.

Table 4.5   **Death Rates by Geographic Location of Service**

Region of Service	Death Rate per 1,000	Number of Deaths	Man-Years at Risk
First service region total	50.0	458	9,152
Eastern theater	49.8	365	7,325
Louisiana and Gulf	71.2	61	856
Carolinas	26.6	24	903
Western theater	119.4	8	67
For second geographic region of service			
First service region total	36.8	154	4,186
Eastern theater	32.2	95	2,947
Louisiana and Gulf	43.6	21	481
Carolinas	45.2	28	620
Western theater	71.9	10	139
For both first and second geographic regions			
First service region total	45.9	612	13,338
Eastern theater	44.8	460	10,272
Louisiana and Gulf	65.9	82	1,337
Carolinas	34.1	52	1,523
Western theater	87.4	18	206

Sources: Fogel (2000); Dyer (1959).

The risk of death from disease continued to decrease after the first year of service. Possibly due to the small sample of deaths in later six-month intervals, the decrease was not monotonic. Lee also found a second peak toward the end of the second year of service in his analysis of Ohio troops.

The seasoning effect is intertwined with the destination of service. If most of the service in a region were concentrated into the first segment of a company's tour of duty, then the apparent effect of serving in that region would be exaggerated. Table 4.5 divides the sample into the first and all other subsequent geographic locations of service. The results concur with the finding in the regimental-level data (table 4.3) that service in Louisiana and the Gulf region was most hazardous to life. However, these data, tabulated throughout by the region of first service, suggest that the apparent higher mortality in Louisiana and the Gulf is elevated because of the high rate of New York men sent there at the beginning of their time in the army. Initial service in the Carolinas was not less deadly than soldiering elsewhere.[12]

Many factors contributed to the incidence of death from disease among New York enlisted infantrymen. For each of these variables, column (2) of table 4.6 reports the index per 1,000 men of dying from disease while they

12. Figures tabulated at the conclusion of the war indicate that Union soldiers in coastal South Carolina—the Department of the South—experienced higher disease mortality than the rest of the army in the first and last years of the war but lower mortality in the middle half (U.S. Surgeon General 1990, vol. 1).

Table 4.6   Logistic Regression of Longitudinal Disease Mortality Index by Timing of Death

| | Bivariate Results | | Entire-Sample Odds Ratio | Death-in-First-Year Odds Ratio | Death-after-First-Year Odds Ratio |
| | Percent | Index | | | |
Variable and Category	(1)	(2)	(3)	(4)	(5)
Height****			Group (n.s.)	Group (n.s.)	Group (n.s.)
Under 65"	16.3	71	1.02	0.97	1.07
65–66"	27.6	66	0.76*	0.69*	0.87
67–68"	28.7	88	Ref.	Ref.	Ref.
69" or taller	27.4	104	1.05	1.01	1.14
Inferred previous enlistment					
(before date in descriptive roll)**			Group**	Group*	Group (n.s.)
No discrepancy	87.6	85	Ref.	Ref.	Ref.
Gap under one year	8.3	96	1.02	1.10	0.92
Gap greater than one year	4.1	25	0.26***	0.31**	0.12*
Region of county of enlistment****			Group (n.s.)	Group*	Group (n.s.)
New York County	26.5	60	0.79	0.57**	1.04
Contiguous to New York	13.7	57	0.75	0.54*	1.07
On Erie Canal	20.0	85	0.84	0.72	0.98
Elsewhere in state	39.8	108	Ref.	Ref.	Ref.
Occupational group****			Group**	Group**	Group (n.s.)
Professionals and proprietors	7.9	50	0.79	0.55	1.13
Unclassified and missing	3.6	65	0.96	0.73	1.24
Farmers	31.2	120	1.43**	1.42*	1.26
Workers	57.3	70	Ref.	Ref.	Ref.
Country of birth****			Group**	Group (n.s.)	Group (n.s.)
United States	53.5	103	Ref.	Ref.	Ref.
Canada	7.0	61	0.62*	0.70	0.58
England	4.4	71	0.84	0.82	0.90
Ireland	19.4	66	0.74*	0.65*	0.80
Germany	10.7	48	0.55**	0.62	0.57
Other foreign country	5.0	59	0.63	0.58	0.68

			Group* / Group**** / Group (n.s.)	Group****	Group (n.s.)
Year of enlistment****	100.0	83.6	Group*	Group****	Group (n.s.)
1861	26.4	83	1.02	0.52**	1.50
1862	32.5	107	1.08	0.63*	1.58
1863	9.7	99	Ref.	Ref.	Ref.
1864	20.6	72	1.04	1.32	0.75
1865	10.8	23	0.42**	0.60	0.04
Birth cohort****			Group****	Group****	Group****
Before 1830	20.6	124	1.98****	1.80***	2.42****
1830–39	35.3	71	0.96	0.88	1.11
1840 and after	44.1	75	Ref.	Ref.	Ref.
Location of first distant service in field****			Group**	Group*	Group**
Eastern theater	78.0	80	Ref.	Ref.	Ref.
Louisiana or Gulf	8.9	133	1.72***	1.25	1.98***
Carolinas	11.1	61	1.07	0.51	1.42
Western theater	2.0	133	1.52	1.30	0.93
Ever a prisoner of war?****			Group****	Group****	Group****
Yes	3.0	332	6.23****	2.54***	8.14****
No	97.0	76	Ref.	Ref.	Ref.
Length of term***			Group (n.s.)	Group (n.s.)	Group (n.s.)
Under three years	14.5	54	0.81	0.92	0.31
Three years or more	85.8	89	Ref.	Ref.	Ref.
Intercept			-2.45	-2.49	-3.49
Standard error			(.21)****	(.27)****	(.32)****
Initial -2 log-likelihood			3,900.0	2,469.9	1,934.8
Improvement with model			306.0****	168.1****	161.3****
Base-sample size			6,784	6,785	3,886
Number of disease deaths			567	302	265

Source: Fogel (2000).

Notes: Ref. = Reference category; n.s. = not significant.

****Significant at the .01 percent level.

***Significant at the .1 percent level.

**Significant at the 1 percent level.

*Significant at the 5 percent level.

were in the Union Army. (The percentage of men in each category appears in column [1]). Overall, 8.36 percent of those who enlisted died from disease while they were in the army.

Three variables—year of enlistment, term of service, and birth cohort—should be regarded as controls. These indicators have statistical but not substantive relevance. The first two affect the proportion every dying of disease by altering the potential period at risk. It is not surprising, for example, that only 2.3 percent enlisting in 1865 died of disease while in the army. Age, of course, bears a substantive relationship to the risk of death, but this relationship is so well known that it lacks interest here. That only the oldest age group—those born before 1830—had a higher fraction die of disease may be attributed mostly to the fact that men born before 1830 were much older than the birth cohort of the 1830s. They were 38.6 years old at the time of enlistment compared to 26.6 for those born in the 1830s and 19.8 for those born in 1840 or after. Depending on location or status, infantrymen differed in average age. For example, natives were three years younger than the foreign-born, those enlisting in New York City were 1.1 years older and farmers were 1.3 years younger than the overall average. Such differences in age distribution potentially can obscure or distort the relationships that are of more genuine interpretive interest. Hence age is included as a separate variable in the analysis.

Three of the indicators reflect different wartime circumstances. Not surprisingly, ever being a prisoner of war of the Confederates was particularly deadly. No less than one-third of captured New York infantrymen in the CPE sample died of disease. In addition, first serving beyond the Atlantic coast—either in the western theater or in the Louisiana–Gulf of Mexico region—elevated the disease death index.

Of particular interest are those attributes characterizing the soldiers at or before the time of enlistment in one of the sampled companies. Those who had not previously served in the army (8.6 percent), farmers (12.0 percent), the native-born (10.3 percent), those who enlisted in upstate New York outside of the areas of New York City and the Erie Canal (10.8 percent), and those who were of more than 69 inches in height (10.4 percent) were more likely to die from disease in the army.

Additionally, men who enlisted in counties that had lower rates of medical rejections for service of recruits and substitutes in the last two years of the war ($r = -0.07$), that were less urban in 1845 ($r = -0.07$), and that had lower crude death rates in 1855 ($r = -0.08$) were also modestly (but statistically significantly) more likely to die from disease in the Union Army. As was shown by Lee (1997, and ch. 3 in the present volume), seemingly healthier men from apparently healthier environments were particularly likely to succumb to disease during the war.

To deal with the influence of a range of interrelated variables requires, of course, a multivariate approach. Taking a relatively simple approach to complexity, table 4.6 uses logistic regression analysis to estimate the odds of death from disease over the entire period the soldier was in observation (column [3]).[13] Since the categorical and interval-level aggregate variables statistically overlap, the latter are omitted from table 4.6. Not unexpectedly, the statistical significance of some of the remaining variables wanes in this assessment, including height and the variable detailing the geographic region of enlistment within the state. Everything considered, farmers were more likely—and those born in Canada and Germany among the foreign-born were less likely—to die from disease. Interpretation should follow the Seussian objection to identifying specific importance of any variable with how many "stars upon thars," i.e., *** attached to standard errors to indicate the extent of statistical significance.[14] The level of statistical significance depends on how validly each variable was defined and how reliably each was measured, and on the number of covarying indicators included in the analysis. Recall that table 4.1 suggested that a continuous relationship existed between the size of a town and the crude death rate. The county of enlistment is, of course, larger than the town of enlistment. Further, soldiers tended to enlist in central places—towns and cities that were larger than the places where they actually lived. Given the rates of geographic mobility in nineteenth-century America, an enlistee's town of residence could often differ from the place he spent his childhood and youth. A safe conclusion is that, all else considered, prior exposure to disease did increase one's risk of death from disease while serving in the Union Army, rather than that it was a farm background that *really* mattered (also see Lee's ch. 3 in this volume).

To isolate the impact of seasoning, separate logistic regression analyses were undertaken of disease mortality during the first year (column [4] of table 4.6) and the interval following the conclusion of the initial year of service (column [5]). The logic here is that the background factors associated with prior exposure to disease should be much stronger in the first year than thereafter. That logic of the source of seasoning mortality is confirmed, most suggestively by the importance of region of enlistment during the first year of service and the nearly complete absence of its impact thereafter. Similarly, variation in the risk of death wanes after the first year of service among soldiers whose prewar occupations differed.[15] Two of the factors re-

13. Again, this index differs from a true cohort death probability since it does not account for varying lengths of time that the soldier was in the army before exiting via death from combat, desertion, discharge, etc.

14. As told by Dr. Seuss (Geisel 1961, 3–4), the Plain Belly Sneeches had "none upon thars": "But, because they had stars, all the Star-Belly Sneetches / Would brag, We're the best kind of Sneetch on the beaches."

15. It should be noted that the shrinkage of the sample contributes the decline in the indicators of statistical significance. In the first year, some 302 disease deaths occurred to an original 6,786 enlistments. After the first year, there were only 265 deaths caused by disease among the 3,887 soldiers who were still in the army at the beginning of the second year of service. Thus, some of the odds ratios diverge after the first year, even though they are less likely to pass a test of statistical significance.

lated to wartime experience—being a prisoner of war, and the region of first service—increase in importance after the first year. During the first two years of the Civil War, prisoners were generally exchanged or paroled after relatively brief incarceration. Later in the conflict, prisoner exchanges between the Union and Confederate forces broke down.

Even after taking into account both background and wartime factors, an indicator that relates to the sharing of more particular mortality environments or the process of contagion also must be incorporated into the analysis. This indicator—the percentage of other men who died from disease in a sampled company—represents an attempt to operationalize the concentration of mortality experience associated with soldiering together than cannot be attributed to the areas of origin within New York state or to broad geographic regions of service while in the army.[16] In order to isolate this factor, which taps otherwise unmeasured aggregate influences on mortality, on seasoning, the analysis in table 4.7 divides company-mortality incidence into periods during (column [2]), and after (column [3]) the first year of service as well as overall (column [2]).

Overall, its inclusion resulted in a 9.3 percent improvement of the model. An absolute increment of 10 percent in the disease death index of the other men in a company increased the death index for the individual soldier by 5.4 percent. Its effect on the other variables shows up markedly in the attenuation of the impact of location of first service. This outcome is not surprising, since both service location and the intracompany concentration of death are indicators measured at the aggregate level. However, it had almost no impact on the other company-level indicator—where the unit was organized within New York state. Effects on individual-level characteristics such as nativity and occupation are barely noticeable. This bunching of death within companies in a regiment is an independent dimension of the structuring of disease mortality.[17]

This paper has demonstrated that a multiplicity of factors must be considered to understand variation in death from disease of soldiers from New York during the Civil War. Background factors such as occupation and type of residence, sensibly viewed as related to the extent of prior exposure to disease, mattered. Once in the army, the risk of death varied depending on how long the soldier had served and whether he had prior military service. The background factors mattered to any great extent only during the initial year of experience in the military. After a year of service, seasoning having

16. For example, consider a company with 100 infantrymen that experienced eight deaths from disease. In this case, the clustering index for a soldier who died of wartime disease was 7/99 and 8/99 for a man who did not. If two or more companies from the same regiment were included in the CPE sample, the base of the index is the entire number sampled from the regiment.

17. Without the addition of other variables, the ordinary least squares estimate is that an increase of 10.0 per 1,000 in the death index of other men in a company would increase the individual index by 5.6 per 1,000.

Table 4.7   **Logistic Regression of Longitudinal Disease Mortality Index by Timing of Death with Company-Disease Mortality Included**

Variable and Category	Entire-Sample Odds Ratio (1)	Death-in-First-Year Odds Ratio (2)	Death-after-First-Year Odds Ratio (3)
Height	Group (n.s.)	Group (n.s.)	Group (n.s.)
Under 65″	1.02	0.99	1.03
65–66″	0.76*	0.70*	0.85
67–68″	Ref.	Ref.	Ref.
69″ or taller	1.04	1.00	1.12
Inferred previous enlistment			
(before date in descriptive roll)	Group**	Group*	Group (n.s.)
No discrepancy	Ref.	Ref.	Ref.
Gap under one year	1.01	1.04	0.96
Gap greater than one year	0.28**	0.33**	0.13*
Region of county of enlistment	Group (n.s.)	Group*	Group (n.s.)
New York County	0.86	0.58**	1.00
Contiguous to New York	0.83	0.60*	0.98
On Erie Canal	0.88	0.76	0.90
Elsewhere in state	Ref.	Ref.	Ref.
Occupational group	Group*	Group*	Group (n.s.)
Professionals and proprietors	0.79	0.55	1.11
Unclassified and missing	0.94	0.71	1.24
Farmers	1.37**	1.34*	1.26
Workers	Ref.	Ref.	Ref.
Country of birth	Group**	Group (n.s.)	Group (n.s.)
United States	Ref.	Ref.	Ref.
Canada	0.62*	0.72	0.54
England	0.87	0.83	0.93
Ireland	0.74*	0.64*	0.74
Germany	0.62*	0.71	0.63
Other foreign country	0.68	0.64	0.69
Year of enlistment	Group*	Group***	Group (n.s.)
1861	1.03	0.59*	1.36
1862	0.94	0.62*	1.22
1863	Ref.	Ref.	Ref.
1864	1.04	1.38	0.75
1865	0.47*	0.74	0.04
Birth cohort	Group****	Group****	Group****
Before 1830	1.95****	1.82***	2.36****
1830–39	0.96	0.89	1.10
1840 and after	Ref.	Ref.	Ref.
Location of first distant service	Group (n.s.)	Group (n.s.)	Group (n.s.)
Eastern theater	Ref.	Ref.	Ref.
Louisiana or Gulf	1.35*	1.23	1.55*
Carolinas	1.06	0.58	1.33
Western theater	1.10	0.76	0.93
Ever a prisoner of war?	Group****	Group**	Group****
Yes	5.52****	2.11**	7.98****
No	Ref.	Ref.	Ref.

(*continued*)

Table 4.7   (continued)

Variable and Category	Entire-Sample Odds Ratio (1)	Death-in-First-Year Odds Ratio (2)	Death-after-First-Year Odds Ratio (3)
Length of term	Group (n.s.)	Group (n.s.)	Group (n.s.)
Under three years	0.80	0.86	0.35
Three years or more	Ref.	Ref.	Ref.
CPE Company Disease Mortality			
Index (%)[a]	1.0539****	1.0867****	1.0661****
Intercept	−2.89	−2.99	−3.70
Standard error	(.23)****	(.23)*****	(.32)****
Initial −2 log-likelihood	3,900.0	2,469.9	1,934.8
Improvement with model	334.4****	189.3****	179.5****
Base-sample size	6,784	6,785	3,886
Number of disease deaths	567	302	265

Source: Fogel (2000).
Notes: Ref. = Reference category; n.s. = not significant.
[a]Company disease mortality based on each duration specified.
****Significant at the .01 percent level.
***Significant at the .1 percent level.
**Significant at the 1 percent level.
*Significant at the 5 percent level.

been accomplished, soldiers recruited from upstate New York died from disease at a rate identical to that of soldiers enlisted in New York County, in contiguous counties, or counties the Erie Canal traversed. Experience in the army also helped to determine disease mortality. If the soldier found himself in a more dangerous disease environment—along the lower Mississippi or the Gulf of Mexico, or, most drastically, in a POW camp—he was more likely to die from disease. Finally, the soldier shared mortality risks with those men with whom he was in close contact—the other enlisted men in his company and regiment. With the troops, but not intermingled with them and the microorganisms they embodied, officers were much less likely to succumb to disease.

Why did so many Union Army soldiers die of disease during the Civil War? Perhaps because the sources of mortality were so diverse.

References

Adams, G. W. 1952. *Doctors in blue: The medical history of the Union Army in the Civil War.* New York: Henry Schuman.
Baxter, J. H. 1875. *Statistics, medical and anthropological of the Provost-Marshal-*

General's Bureau derived from records of the examination for military service in the armies of the United States during the late War of the Rebellion of over a million recruits, drafted men, substitutes, and enrolled men. 2 vols. Washington, D.C.: GPO.

Benedict, G. G. 1866–88. *Vermont in the Civil War: A history of the part taken by the Vermont soldiers and sailors in the war for the Union, 1861–5.* Burlington, Vt.: Free Press.

DeBow, J. D. B. 1855. *Mortality statistics of the seventh Census of the United States, 1850.* Washington: A. O. P. Nicholson.

Dyer, F. H. 1959. *A compendium of the War of the Rebellion.* 3 vols. New York: Thomas Yoselloff. Original edition 1909. Cedar Rapids, Iowa: Torch Press.

Elliott, E. G. 1862. Preliminary report on the mortality and sickness of the volunteer forces of the United States government during the present war. Sanitary Commission Report no. 46. New York: W. M. C. Bryant.

Fogel, R. W. 2000. *Public use tape on the aging of veterans of the Union Army: Military, pension, and medical records, 1860–1940.* Version M-5. Chicago: University of Chicago, Graduate School of Business, Center for Population Economics.

Fox, W. F. 1974. *Regimental losses in the American Civil War 1861–1865.* New York: Morningside Bookshop. Original edition 1898. Albany, N.Y.: Albany Publishing Company.

Fry, J. B. 1866. *Final report made to the Secretary of War, by the Provost Marshal General.* 39th Cong., 1st sess. H. Exec. Doc., serial 1252, vol. 4, pt. 1. Washington, D.C.: GPO.

Geisel, T. S. 1961. *The Sneetches and other stories.* New York: Random House.

Haines, M. R. 2001. The urban mortality transition in the United States, 1800–1940. *Annales de Demographie Historique* 2001 (1): 33–64.

Haines, M. R., L. A. Craig, and T. Weiss. Forthcoming. The short and the dead: Mortality, nutrition, and the "antebellum paradox" in the United States. *Journal of Economic History.*

Lee, C. 1997. Socioeconomic background, disease, and mortality among Union Army recruits: Implications for economic and demographic history. *Explorations in Economic History* 34:27–55.

Marvel, W. 1994. *Andersonville: The last depot.* Chapel Hill: University of North Carolina Press.

Mitchell, Reid. 1988. *Civil War soldiers.* New York: Viking.

New York Secretary of State. 1846. *Census of the state of New York, for 1845.* Albany: Carroll and Cook.

———. 1857. *Census of the state of New York, for 1855.* Albany: C. Van Benthuysen and Sons.

———. 1867. *Census of the state of New York, for 1865.* Albany: C. Van Benthuysen and Sons.

Olmstead, F. L. 1866. A report to the Secretary of War of the operations of the Sanitary Commission, and upon the sanitary condition of the volunteer army, medical staff, hospitals, and hospital supplies, December 1861. Documents of the U.S. Sanitary Commission, no. 40. New York: U.S. Sanitary Commission.

Phisterer, F. 1907. *Statistical record of the armies of the United States.* New York: Scribner. Original edition 1883. New York: Scribner.

———. 1912. *New York in the War of the Rebellion, 1861 to 1865.* 3rd ed. 6 vols. Albany: Adjutant-General of the State of New York.

Roberts, W. C. 1865. Extracts from report of Surgeon Board of Enrollment Eighth District of New York. In *Statistics, medical and anthropological.* Vol. 1, ed. J. H. Baxter, 246–52. Washington, D.C.: GPO.

Scholarly Resources. 1999. *United States Sanitary Commission records: Guide to the Scholarly Resources microfilm edition.* Wilmington, Del.: Scholarly Resources.

Shannon, F. A. 1928. *The organization and administration of the Union Army, 1861–1865.* 2 vols. Cleveland: Arthur H. Clark.

Smith, D. S. 1982. Differential mortality in the United States before 1900. *Journal of Interdisciplinary History* 13:267–91.

———. 2000a. Dimensions of non-combat mortality among Union Army forces: A survey of patterns in aggregated data. Unpublished paper prepared for the NBER Conference on Health and Work over the Life Cycle.

———. 2000b. A reconstruction of examinations for service in the Union military, 1863–1865. Department of History, University of Illinois, Chicago. Unpublished paper.

Thompson, W. H. 1865. Extracts from report of Surgeon Board of Enrollment Ninth District of New York. In *Statistics, medical and anthropological.* Vol. 1, ed. J. H. Baxter, 252–55. Washington, D.C.: GPO.

U.S. Surgeon General. 1990. *The medical and surgical history of the Civil War.* 11 vols. Wilmington, N.C.: Broadview. Original edition titled *The medical and surgical history of the War of the Rebellion (1861–65),* Washington, D.C.: GPO, 1875–83.

U.S. War Department. 1899. *The War of the Rebellion: A compilation of the official records of the Union and Confederate armies.* Series 3, vol. 2. Washington, D.C.: GPO.

Wiley, B. I. 1952. *The life of Billy Yank: The common soldier of the Union.* Indianapolis: Bobbs-Merrill.

The Height of Union Army Recruits
Family and Community Influences

Sven E. Wilson and Clayne L. Pope

5.1 Introduction

In the past two decades we have seen the birth and flourishing of a new line of inquiry among economic historians who have used physical stature (primarily height) as an indicator of the welfare of historical populations.[1] This line of research has highlighted the dramatic variability in the mean height of numerous populations across both time and place, including, quite surprisingly, some periods of moderate decline in the early stages of industrialization in both Europe and the United States.

Given the nature of the available data, there has been a tendency in most studies to make a strict dichotomy between genetic and environmental factors affecting height. We suggest that as better data become available, an understanding of the factors affecting human growth and development will necessitate a richer categorization and investigation of those factors typically lumped together in the environmental category. An obvious place to begin developing an expanded classification is by making a distinction between community-level and family-level influences on health. Family background may influence child health and welfare through a number of chan-

Sven E. Wilson is assistant professor of political science and adjunct assistant professor of economics at Brigham Young University. Clayne L. Pope is professor of economics and dean of the College of Family, Home, and Social Sciences at Brigham Young University, and a research associate of the National Bureau of Economic Research.

Financial support for this research was provided by the National Institute on Aging (AG10120) and Brigham Young University. Damon Cann, Lauren Cundick, Ben Howell, and Shawn Waddoups provided excellent research assistance.

1. Several excellent volumes and survey articles covering anthropometric history as it relates to both human biology and economic development have been written by leading scholars in recent years. See, for example, Steckel (1995), Floud, Wachter, and Gregory (1990), Komlos (1994), and Steckel and Floud (1997).

nels that are related to, but distinct from, community-level factors. In the case of socioeconomic variables, it is likely that the community level of economic development and the distribution of income are both important in explaining height. In modern populations, for instance, income distribution may matter less if social programs exist that augment the nutrition and health care of poor children in the community. Furthermore, parents make investments in the physical and intellectual human capital of their children that include nutrition, schooling, and labor requirements. Their investments will be a function of their own stock of human capital and the resource constraints that are present both within the household and at the community level. There are surely family-specific determinants of height that are neither genetic nor observable in aggregate statistics.

In this study we investigate family and community influences on adult height using newly collected data on Union Army recruits. Data on a sample of 35,570 Union Army recruits has recently been linked to almost 11,500 census records from the 1850 U.S. Census manuscripts. Furthermore, we have matched these census records to the county-level published data to investigate county-level economic and demographic data with the household-level variables present in the early lives of the recruits, including occupation, wealth, nativity, migration, school attendance, literacy, and family size.

Our analysis is an extension of important papers that used earlier versions of the same data source. Fogel (1986) drew attention to the similar patterns of decline in height and mortality for the antebellum period in the United States when gross domestic product (GDP) and GDP per capita were growing vigorously. He drew on the analysis of Margo and Steckel (1983), which used the same Union Army sample before it had been linked to the census manuscripts, and on unpublished work by Steckel using the National Guard.[2] From the enlistment records they were able to identify the recruit's height, occupation, and place of residence, but they lacked the early-life influences present in the census data. Costa (1993) was able to link the recruits to the census records, but her sample was much smaller in size and was limited almost exclusively to the states of New York and Ohio.

In addition to providing new estimates for family and community influences on adult height using ordinary least squares (OLS), we complement the analysis by employing a variety of alternative specifications. We explore potential differences between urban and rural populations and across occupational categories. We also estimate the model using county-level fixed effects and compare these results to the OLS equations. Finally, we estimate our main specification using quantile regression, a technique that has received increasing recognition over the past decade as a method of exploring the impact of covariates on the entire conditional distribution of the de-

---

2. Later published in Steckel and Haurin (1994).

pendent variable (in our case, height), rather than simply estimating the conditional mean, which is what OLS achieves.

This paper follows a somewhat different path than a similar analysis by Haines, Craig, and Weiss (2000). They use recruit information combined with previously unexploited county-level variables (such as aggregate calorie production and access to rail and waterways), but lack household-level data from the census. An important distinction, however, is that even though we use many of the same county variables, Haines, Craig, and Weiss use the 1850 aggregates from the county of birth, whereas we use the 1850 aggregates from the county in which the recruits were living in 1850. In short, we extend the county-level characteristics employed by Haines, Craig, and Weiss by emphasizing the early life household information from the 1850 census manuscripts.

5.2 Background

5.2.1 Height and History

Height is now widely accepted as a net measure of the cumulative nutritional history of an individual. The consensus is that while variation *within* a population is largely determined by genetics, variation *between* populations is seen as primarily determined by environmental factors. Height is a useful mirror of a society's well-being because it is thought to capture both the nutritional inputs available for growth and the energy demands upon those nutrients.

Heights were first used systematically by economic historians to gather evidence on the standard of living of slaves in the antebellum South (Steckel 1979; Margo and Steckel 1982; Fogel 1989). The use of heights gathered from coastwise manifests of ships transporting slaves and from records of ex-slave recruits into the Union Army were useful as evidence of the net nutritional status of slaves and, hence, their standard of living. This use of heights in the study of slavery quickly led to interest in using military records, which routinely recorded height to study trends in the standard of living of the broader population. When systematic trends in height were gathered for both Europe and the United States, the most striking findings were the declines in height during the early periods of industrialization. Margo and Steckel (1983) and Fogel (1986) find a downturn in heights for the United States in the antebellum period of industrialization, while Floud, Wachter, and Gregory (1990) find that height grew in early industrialization but declined in the mid-nineteenth century. Komlos (1994) found similar results on the continent of Europe. The decline in heights in the United States during the antebellum period is particularly puzzling because of the impressive growth in GDP and GDP per capita during that period (Gallman and Wallis 1992). Normally, one would expect decreases in height to be associated with increases in mortality and morbidity and with declines in productivity, as argued by Fogel (1994). Thus, this antebellum period of declining heights and increasing economic growth as conventionally measured is particularly anomalous.

Alternative explanations for the antebellum decline in heights have been suggested. Fogel (1986) emphasizes immigration and its effect on the infectious disease environment. Steckel (1995) suggests a number of possible explanations, including migration and urbanization. He also argues that an increase in the inequality of per capita income could offset the growth in income. In addition to citing changes in the distribution of income, Komlos (1998) suggests that sectoral shifts out of agriculture may have influenced height through a variety of mechanisms, including increases in the relative price of food, more cyclicality in income, and larger numbers of consumers per farmer. Costa and Steckel (1997) emphasize deterioration in height because of greater exposure to infectious disease due to international immigration, urbanization, and changes in workplace environment.[3] Finally, Margo (2000) suggests that short-term declines in real wages may have contributed to some of the decline in height, although this cannot be a dominant part of the explanation since real wages were generally rising, he notes, from 1820 to 1850.

5.2.2   The Impact of Environmental Variables

The dramatic secular increase in height over the past 150 years around the globe is evidence that environmental variables in general, and economic modernization in particular, are the driving forces behind improvements in health. Fogel (2000) has written extensively on what he terms the "techno-physio evolution" that has occurred over recent centuries. This evolution is likely still proceeding, since socioeconomic differentials in height (as well as all other common measures of health) persist today, both across and within countries. Class and income differences are more pronounced within poorer countries than in the developed world, but they exist even in the United States and Western Europe (Eveleth and Tanner 1990).

In both modern and historical times, differentials in child health are driven both by the distribution of material resources available to individual families and by community-level factors. Many variables thought to affect health have both family and community counterparts. For instance, the occupation of individuals may matter because it affects wages, living conditions, and the extent of interaction with other people and, therefore, the family's nutritional intake and their infectious disease risk. But the same

---

3. Komlos argues that the height decline could not be exclusively caused by deterioration in the disease environment because there were periods where physical stature rose as population density, urbanization, and commercialization also increased (which would likely have worsened the disease environment), he concludes that the decline in heights could not be caused exclusively by a deterioration in the disease environment.

forces are at work at the community level. Growth in manufacturing, for instance, may raise wages, but it may also concentrate individuals in a fashion that facilitates the spread of disease—even to those who are not directly involved in manufacturing. Similarly, an individual's place of birth (particularly the nation of birth) may be a strong indicator of the childhood nutritional and disease environment, but living where there is a high concentration of foreign-born may have health consequences as well, even for the native-born. In short, a family's health risks, particularly in terms of infectious diseases, are a function of both the factors within the family and the larger disease environment.

5.3 Data

5.3.1 The Union Army Data Collection

The process of sample creation consisted of selection of Civil War companies, attachment of military, pension, and medical records to recruits in those companies, and finally, linkage of household entries from the census manuscripts for the recruit and his family in the censuses of 1850, 1860, 1900, and 1910. In 1850, and probably in 1860, the recruit was likely to be a son in the household of his parents. The sample consists of a random selection of 301 companies, which were part of the U.S. Army during the Civil War, excluding cavalry and companies composed of regular army professionals. The random sample of companies was chosen, in place of a random sample of individuals, to reduce the costs of collection to a manageable level. The collection of companies achieved good geographical balance across the Northern states. Analysis to date suggests that the base sample is a random sample of recruits into the U.S. Army during the Civil War. The most obvious differences between the Civil War recruit sample and the population of those same birth cohorts are the absence of women and African American men and severe underrepresentation of Southern-born men from the sample. Consequently, results should be interpreted as being confined to Northern, white males born between 1815 and 1847.

The analysis conducted here requires that the military and pension records of the recruit be linked to the census manuscript of his pre–Civil War family. Thus, biases may be introduced if the probability of linkage is correlated with the variables under consideration here. For example, it is possible that families who migrate will be more difficult to find in the census because of moves between 1850 and year of enlistment. Or it is possible that it is easier to link to households living in rural or farming counties than to households in larger urban areas. Such biases will imply that the rates or prevalence of various characteristics cannot be accurately measured from the sample. But the statistical purposes of this paper are served if we have sufficient observations to have the full range of characteristics, even if some characteristics, such as rural residence, are overrepresented in the sample relative to the population.

In general, linkage rates from the pension record to the antebellum censuses do exhibit some systematic variation, although rates do not vary widely by socioeconomic characteristics. Clearly, rural households are easier to link than urban households, with households in larger cities being the most difficult to link. However, census indices reduce the disparity between linkage rates for urban and rural households. Foreign-born recruits are less likely to be found in the census, especially the 1850 census. Rates of immigration were high between 1845 and 1857. Those migrating after 1850 are obviously not going to be linked to the census. Even the children of the foreign-born will have lower linkage rates because of the increased tendency for the foreign-born to migrate within the United States as they searched for economic opportunities. One would also expect a slightly lower rate of linkage for native households in migration near the census year since the process of movement was time consuming in the nineteenth century. Large families are easier to find in the census than small families because large families are less likely to be living in multiple-family households. There is no evidence that wealthier households are easier to link although the teenage children of poorer households may be more likely to have left home to work and supplement the income of their parents.

This variation in linkage rates will bias the mean height of the sample of recruits linked to the census above the mean height of the recruit sample as a whole. This bias is primarily due to the lower linkage rates for urban and foreign-born recruits. However, this variation in linkage rates does not necessarily bias the analysis of what follows. Here, the interest is in the effect of socioeconomic characteristics both at the household- and county-level on height. Hence, bias in estimates would require that linkage rates for households with a given characteristic were correlated with height (e.g., tall recruits of farm households are more likely to be linked to the census than short recruits, thereby overstating the effect of a farming occupation on height). Such biases could be conjectured, but they have not been investigated to date.

5.3.2   The Height Variable

An attractive feature of the Union Army data is that height is collected at the time of enlistment for 98.8 percent of the recruits in the sample.[4] Other heights are sometimes available in the data, most of which come either from a second enlistment date or from occasional comments in pension files. Although it would be possible to incorporate height from later observations to get a better measure of maximum adult height, this would introduce a

---

4. This figure is after a handful of extreme heights (those less than 48 or greater than 84 inches) were excluded. The range of heights in the sample actually used in the analysis, after linking to the Census records and applying age restrictions, is 52 to 81 inches. It is likely that almost all the extreme heights were inputting errors. Many of the shorter ones are even too small for young children who may have served.

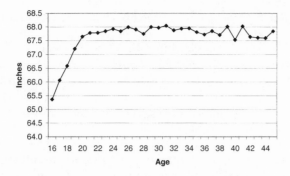

Fig. 5.1   Mean height, by age (16–45)

bias where those who enter into the pension system are systematically taller than those who have no pension files. We, therefore, restrict our attention to the first recorded enlistment height.

Enlistment height does, however, pose an important challenge to the analysis in that a significant portion of the recruits enlist at ages during which males are still growing. It is widely known that males can continue growing well into their twenties. Figure 5.1 shows mean height by age for the recruits in the sample aged sixteen to forty-nine. This graph shows relatively steep growth between ages sixteen to twenty-one in the Union Army sample. Note, however, that this figure incorporates the impact of both age and birth cohort.

Some studies have addressed this problem by restricting their analysis to older ages. For instance, Margo and Steckel (1983) drop cases below age twenty-five, and Costa (1993) looks only at those age twenty-three and older. We, on the other hand, restrict our sample to those over age sixteen and attempt to control for the significant growth between sixteen and twenty-one with age-specific dummy variables. A potential downfall of our approach is that the probability of growing significantly in late adolescence may not be random, but may be correlated with the other variables in the model, such as socioeconomic status. If this is the case, then a portion of the impact of other correlates will be captured by the age variables.

The primary reason for including the younger ages is that we are able to greatly increase sample size. Height is a variable that is primarily due to genetic variation. Furthermore, there is a likelihood of serious measurement error due to problems such as clumping and rounding. Since, even under the best of circumstances, environmental variables are going to explain only a small portion of the variance in height, if any reasonable degree of precision in estimating is desired, large sample size is a necessity.[5] Moreover, a higher

5. Increasing the minimum age restriction to twenty-three, for instance, lowers the sample size by over 70 percent. Exploratory analysis with this restricted data confirm the expectation of extremely large standard errors on almost all covariates and, for those few variables measured more precisely, little difference with the larger sample.

age restriction introduces another potential bias. Recruits who were, for instance, age twenty in 1861 and enlisted in the army at age twenty-three in 1864 would be included in the sample with a higher minimum age, but that same twenty year old who enlists in 1861 to 1863 would be excluded. Thus a higher minimum age restriction systematically excludes younger men who enlist early in the war, while including those who wait until the end of the war to enlist. Evidence presented later suggests that those who wait until the end of the war to enlist are significantly shorter than earlier entrants.

Linkage to the census, as discussed above, also creates a set of bias issues. Figure 5.2 provides a distribution of adult heights (twenty-one to forty-nine) for the full recruit sample and for those linked to the census. The full sample (aged twenty-one to forty-nine) has an average height of 67.9 in., while the census-linked group average 68.3 in. Note that the center of the distribution is the same for both samples (68 in.), but the census-linked cases are heavy on the right, and the full sample is heavier to the left. In the census-linked sample, 5.7 percent of recruits are 54 in. or shorter, while 8.4 percent of the full sample fall in this extreme. In the upper tail, 3.8 percent of recruits in the census-linked sample are taller than 72 in., compared to 5.1 percent of the full sample.

Clearly the census-linked sample is taller than the full recruit sample. This is likely because census matching is more successful among rural, native families than among urban, migrant families, categories which are also correlated with height. However, both distributions appear normally distributed, with no obvious truncation in either sample, and figure 5.2 suggests a more or less parallel shift in the distribution of heights as a result of the census linkage. Unfortunately, methods of controlling for selection bias

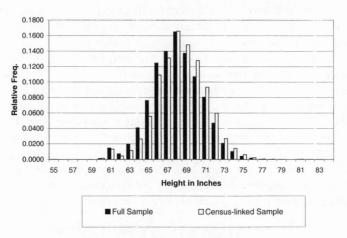

Fig. 5.2   Height distribution for full and linked samples

in this sample cannot be easily implemented, since variables that determine census linkage are also those that determine height.

5.3.3   Explanatory Variables

Linkage to the 1850 census allows the inclusion of a number of characteristics that affected the recruit's early life. These include the father's occupation, place of birth, literacy, and real estate wealth. Additionally, the place of birth of the recruit and the size of the recruit's family can be measured. Because county is known on all the census records, it is relatively simple to incorporate county-level variables from the published summary tables of the 1850 census.[6] Data available at the county level includes population, number of foreign-born, literacy rate, number of children in school, average family size, and number of deaths, as well as the detailed age distribution of the county.

At the family level, the most obvious candidates for variables that might influence height are the occupation of the family head and his real estate wealth. A problem with both these important variables is missing data. Roughly half of households report no real estate wealth. Since values of zero were not recorded on the census manuscripts, it is typically assumed that unreported cases are those where little or no wealth existed, but there is no known way to verify this assumption in individual cases. We create, therefore, five wealth classifications: (a) $1–100; (b) $101–500; (c) $501–1,000; (d) $1,001+; and (e) no reported wealth. Many occupations are, likewise, unknown. In fact, unknown is the most common occupation following farmer. We use occupation codes—provided in the data and found in the data documentation—to identify four classes of occupation: (a) farmers; (b) professionals and proprietors (codes 2 and 3); (c) artisans; and (d) laborers.

In addition to incomplete values, a limitation of this data set is that we only have real estate wealth and not personal wealth. An option would be to include the personal wealth variable in the 1860 census. While the 1860 values may prove fruitful in future analyses, we have not included them in this analysis for two reasons. First, linking the recruits to those who have nonmissing values in the 1860 census would further decrease the sample size, which is already relatively small given the nature of the question we are addressing. And second, by 1860 we are no longer talking about early life effects for most recruits, who are approaching adulthood by this point. While the 1860 wealth may be highly correlated with previous levels of wealth, a large number of recruits have already left their childhood homes by 1860, and information on their fathers is no longer available in the Union Army data.

---

6. We used the corrected and expanded version of ICPSR #3 created by Michael Haines (see Haines, Craig, and Weiss 2000), and we extend our appreciation to Professor Haines for graciously offering the use of the data.

Another important group of family-level variables are created from place of birth data. For each household member, the state or country of birth is almost always known, although city and county are often missing. Therefore, we classify both the recruit and his father as either native, an interstate migrant (meaning born in a different state than his 1850 residence), or foreign-born. We then interact the recruit and father's variables. This allows us to see the effect of migration holding constant the nativity of the father. It may be that interstate migration among the children of the foreign-born has different impacts on height than migration among children of native-born fathers. Of course, comparing 1850 residence to place of birth is a crude measure of internal migration, as is the absence of information on county-to-county and city-to-city moves within a state.

The final family variables we can get from the data are number of children and the literacy of parents. We expect that the effect of family size will vary by occupation. For farmers, children are an important labor input that can increase the economic well-being of the family. Fertility, consequently, is higher in farm families. Among other occupations, children are likely more of a drain on resources. Of course, with family size it is hard to determine the direction of causality, since family size (particularly in areas with high child mortality) is both a cause and a consequence of the family's economic condition. For literacy, we incorporate the mother's literacy, which is highly correlated with the father's literacy.

At the community level (and we use county as proxy for community), there are several variables that may influence height. We follow most other researchers in this area by hypothesizing that height is significantly affected by population and urbanization. There are potential positive aspects of urbanization—higher wages and closer access to agricultural markets—but we expect that the dominant effect is negative, likely because of increased exposure to infectious disease.

For our county-level variables we employ most of the variables used in Haines, Craig, and Weiss (2000). The most important is the percentage of the county that is urbanized, which is measured here as the percent of county residents living in towns of over 25,000 residents. We also employ the measure developed in Haines, Craig, and Weiss that indicates whether the county was served by rail or water transport (almost all the variation in this variable occurs, of course, in nonurbanized counties, since almost all urbanized communities had access to rail or water in 1850). Another variable strongly associated with urbanization is the percentage of the county that was foreign-born. Other important county-level variables reflect both urbanization and the economic vitality of the county, including the value of capital invested in manufacturing and agriculture; the "surplus" per capita calories produced in the county; the crude death rate; the school attendance rate; the illiteracy rate; and, finally, the average family size.

Mean height and 95 percent confidence intervals are given in table 5.1 for

Table 5.1 **Mean Height, by Major Demographic Category**

	N	Mean	Standard Deviation	95% Confidence Interval
All	5,758	67.74	2.66	(67.67, 67.81)
Region				
New England	858	67.67	2.66	(67.49, 67.84)
Mid-Atlantic	1,819	67.24	2.63	(67.11, 67.36)
South	530	68.26	2.79	(68.03, 68.50)
West	2,477	68.02	2.60	(67.92, 68.12)
County-level variables				
Percent Urban				
0	3,955	67.92	2.68	(67.84, 68.01)
1–24%	1,085	67.38	2.55	(67.23, 67.53)
25–49%	429	67.54	2.60	(67.29, 67.79)
50–100%	315	66.94	2.61	(66.64, 67.23)
County population				
0–4.9K	330	68.39	2.85	(68.09, 68.70)
5–9K	608	68.05	2.65	(67.84, 68.26)
10–24K	2,155	67.93	2.63	(67.82, 68.04)
25–49K	1,620	67.68	2.61	(67.56, 67.81)
50K+	1,045	67.05	2.63	(66.89, 67.21)
Percent foreign-born				
0–10%	3,795	67.88	2.63	(67.79, 67.96)
10–24%	1,436	67.54	2.66	(67.40, 67.68)
25+%	527	67.29	2.66	(67.06, 67.52)
Household-level variables				
Father and recruit native	2,630	67.65	2.66	(67.55, 67.75)
Father: interstate migrant				
Recruit: native	1,993	67.92	2.69	(67.80, 68.04)
Recruit: interstate migrant	522	68.02	2.63	(67.79, 68.24)
Father: foreign-born				
Recruit: native	406	67.22	2.55	(66.97, 67.46)
Recruit: interstate migrant	54	68.30	2.64	(67.57, 69.02)
Recruit: foreign-born	118	67.12	2.65	(66.64, 67.60)
Occupation				
Farmer	2,605	68.02	2.56	(67.92, 68.12)
Professional/proprietor	327	67.24	2.53	(66.96, 67.51)
Artisan	888	67.20	2.70	(67.02, 67.38)
Laborer	662	67.04	2.60	(66.84, 67.24)
Unknown	1,276	68.05	2.76	(67.90, 68.20)
Father's wealth				
$1–100	120	67.50	2.64	(67.02, 67.98)
$101–500	1,000	67.85	2.69	(67.68, 68.02)
$501–1000	931	67.96	2.65	(67.79, 68.13)
$1001+	1,516	67.94	2.60	(67.81, 68.07)
Unreported	2,191	67.47	2.68	(67.36, 67.58)
Number of children				
1–3	1,880	67.55	2.66	(67.43, 67.67)
4–6	3,185	67.77	2.64	(67.67, 67.86)
7+	693	68.13	2.76	(67.92, 68.33)

the major demographic variables discussed above. This table gives us our first look at how height varies according to the family-level and community-level variables we have identified. Although there are several significant differences between categories, we postpone a discussion of the patterns found in table 5.1 to the analysis of the OLS regression results. In brief, table 5.1 reveals the strong and significant differences for urbanization and population and for occupation, variables that prove to be important in the regression results of the next section.

Before proceeding further with the analysis, it is wise to point out two additional limitations of the variable definitions used above. First, county is a crude proxy for community. Any notion of community (and we shall not enter the quagmire of defining the term) is certainly smaller than a county. Neighborhood data would be much more desirable. Second, given the wide age range under study, the family-level and county-level variables in 1850 affect the sample individuals at very different points in the developmental process—some are in early childhood, and others are adolescents. What we know about the growth process indicates that certain time periods (particularly the first three years and the adolescent growth spurt) are particularly sensitive periods. Though unfortunate, this is an inescapable feature of using data where environmental variables were collected only at particular points in time.

An alternative to our approach would be to use information from the county of birth rather than the county of residence in 1850. Unfortunately, close to half the recruits in the Union Army sample do not have county of birth identified (although state is almost always present). We feel that linking the recruits to both county of birth and to the 1850 census reduces the sample size to such a degree that meaningful analysis is not possible and would hinder our primary objective of testing the effect of family variables on the determination of height.

5.4   Results

5.4.1   OLS Regression Results

Table 5.2 provides information relevant to the distribution of the independent variables used in the regression analysis, while table 5.3 presents our main results. In addition to estimates for the sample as a whole, we divide the sample into two parts, according to urbanization, and estimate the model for rural and urban counties separately (a county is defined as urban if it contains any communities with more than 25,000 residents, including towns that cross over county lines).[7] Table 5.4 further divides the sample

---

7. Margo and Steckel employed a similar technique, but they used population of the city or town, rather than county population. Their cutoff was at 2,500 persons.

Table 5.2   **Means and Frequencies of Independent Variables**

	Frequency (%)	Mean	Standard Deviation
Region			
New England	14.9		
Mid-Atlantic	31.6		
South	9.2		
West	44.3		
County-level variables			
Percent urban		0.094	0.187
Agricultural capital per capita		191.434	83.080
Manufacturing capital per capita			
Surplus calories (in thousands)		2.212	1.478
Percent foreign-born		9.758	9.562
Rail or water connection		0.745	0.436
Crude death rate		12.831	5.693
School attendance rate		0.045	0.043
Illiteracy rate		0.628	0.164
Average family size		5.613	0.326
Household-level variables			
Father and recruit native	45.7		
Father: migrant			
Recruit: native	34.6		
Recruit: interstate migrant	9.1		
Father: foreign-born			
Recruit: native	7.1		
Recruit: interstate migrant	0.9		
Recruit: foreign-born	2.0		
Occupation			
Farmer	45.2		
Professional/proprietor	5.7		
Artisan	15.4		
Laborer	11.5		
Unknown	22.2		
Father's wealth			
Excluding unreported		1759.84	3338.05
Assuming unreported = 0		1090.19	2762.63
$1–100	2.1		
$101–500	17.4		
$501–1000	16.2		
$1000+	26.3		
Unreported	38.1		
Mother literate	8.0		
Mother illiterate	92.0		
Number of children		4.39	1.78
1–3	32.7		
4–6	55.3		
7+	12.0		

(*continued*)

Table 5.2   (continued)

	Frequency (%)	Mean	Standard Deviation
	Enlistment variables		
Enlistment year			
1861	22.7		
1862	36.6		
1863	6.2		
1864	25.5		
1865	9.0		
Enlistment age		20.955	3.135
16	1.0		
17	2.5		
18	25.4		
19	13.3		
20	10.0		
21	12.0		
22	8.4		
23	6.8		
24	6.0		
25+	14.7		
N	5,758		

along a different dimension: occupation. Excluding those cases with occupation unknown, we divide the sample according to whether or not the recruit's father was a farmer in 1850. The unknown group are excluded since it is probably the case that a large share of them are farmers and inclusion of them in the nonfarmer category would mask the differences that might exist between farmers and nonfarmers. While we rely primarily on the full sample results, the estimation of the model across urban/rural and farm/nonfarm groups should be considered exploratory, since the reduced sample sizes significantly reduce the statistical power of our estimation.

We turn first to a discussion of the regional and county-level influences on height. Previously, table 5.1 showed noticeable differences in height across regions. The tallest recruits come from the South, followed in descending order by the West, New England, and the Mid-Atlantic States. More than an inch separates the South from the Mid-Atlantic.[8] The regression results, however, find smaller differences across regions, except for the Mid-Atlantic, which has significantly lower heights (by half an inch) than the other regions. The tallest recruits are from the West, which is particularly true in urban counties, indicating a substantial difference between Western and non-Western urban areas.

The regressions in table 5.3 and table 5.4 confirm that height is inversely

8. Recall that since the sample is drawn from the Union Army, the sample does not contain a representative sample of Southerners.

Table 5.3 OLS Regressions

	Full Sample			Rural Counties			Urban Counties		
	Mean or Frequency	Coefficient	T-statistic	Mean or Frequency	Coefficient	T-statistic	Mean or Frequency	Coefficient	T-statistic
Dependent variable = enlistment height (in.)	67.74			67.92			67.34		
Region									
Mid-Atlantic	.32			.26			.44		
New England	.15	.392	2.51	.10	.355	1.54	.26	.406	1.73
South	.09	.559	2.98	.12	.453	2.08	.03	.550	1.14
West	.44	.551	4.00	.52	.434	2.31	.27	.823	3.82
County-level variables (1850)									
Percent urban	.09	-.899	-2.83				.30	-.391	-.73
Rail or water connection	.75	-.281	-2.72	.63	-.295	-2.85	.99	-.313	-.48
Agricultural capital per capita	169.44	-.002	-2.57	163.87	-.002	-2.62	181.50	.000	-.18
Manufacturing capital per capita	21.99	.000	.06	13.80	-.002	-.48	39.73	.002	.40
Surplus calories (in thousands)	2.21	-.023	-.62	2.52	-.010	-.26	1.55	-.085	-1.12
Percent foreign-born (× 100)	9.76	-.009	-1.59	7.32	-.006	-.85	15.04	-.015	-1.28
Crude death rate (per 1,000)	12.83	0.15	1.99	11.87	.014	1.77	14.90	.013	.70
School attendance rate (× 100)	62.91	-.003	-.72	61.77	-.003	-.73	65.38	.001	.12
Illiteracy rate (× 100)	4.13	-.036	-3.00	4.78	-.042	-3.31	2.73	.014	.34
Average family size	5.61	.596	3.14	5.66	.559	2.61	5.52	.680	1.76

(*continued*)

Table 5.3   (continued)

	Full Sample			Rural Counties			Urban Counties		
	Mean or Frequency	Coefficient	T-statistic	Mean or Frequency	Coefficient	T-statistic	Mean or Frequency	Coefficient	T-statistic
Household-level variables (1850)									
Father and son native	.46			.42			.55		
Father: interstate migrant									
Recruit: native	.35	-.101	-.96	.40	-.126	-.99	.23	-.109	-.54
Recruit: interstate migrant	.09	-.255	-1.81	.11	-.446	-2.61	.05	.422	1.61
Father: foreign-born									
Recruit: native	.07	-.195	-1.40	.05	-.193	-.98	.12	-.117	-.58
Recruit: interstate migrant	.01	.193	.55	.01	-.052	-.11	.01	.585	1.08
Recruit: foreign-born	.02	-.432	-1.51	.01	-.819	-2.06	.04	-.005	-.01
Occupation									
Farmer	.45	-.391	-2.94	.51	-.341	-1.75	.33	-.475	-2.47
Professional/proprietor	.06	-.438	-3.94	.04	-.494	-3.35	.10	-.434	-2.39
Artisan	.15	-.433	-3.47	.12	-.335	-2.02	.23	-.582	-2.86
Laborer	.11	-.066	-.56	.09	.002	.02	.17	-.247	-1.26
Unknown	.22			.25			.16		
Father's wealth									
$1–100	.02			.02			.01		
$101–500	.17	.191	.73	.20	.217	.72	.12	.066	.13
$501–1000	.16	.318	1.25	.17	.343	1.17	.14	.195	.37
$1000+	.26	.273	1.07	.26	.346	1.18	.28	.026	.05
Unknown	.38	.179	.70	.35	.228	.78	.45	-.027	-.05
Mother illiterate	.08	-.096	-.74	.10	-.003	-.02	.04	-.636	-2.24
Number of children									
1–3	.33			.30			.38		
4–6	.55	-.017	-.21	.57	.009	.09	.52	-.073	-.57
7+	.12	.190	1.46	.13	.136	.89	.10	.280	1.11

Enlistment variables

	Model 1			Model 2			Model 3		
Enlistment year									
1861	.23			.22			.25		
1862	.37	.040	.37	.37	.039	.29	.35	.033	.20
1863	.06	−.336	−1.95	.06	−.371	−.171	.06	−.236	−.88
1864	.26	−.319	−2.91	.24	−.382	−2.73	.28	−.241	−1.45
1865	.09	−.642	−4.82	.11	−.703	−4.37	.06	−.453	−1.89
Enlistment age									
16	.01	−3.190	−9.75	.01	−3.062	−7.68	.01	−3.268	−5.83
17	.03	−1.960	−8.09	.03	−1.861	−6.33	.02	−2.322	−5.85
18	.25	−1.535	−12.74	.26	−1.555	−10.49	.24	−1.496	−7.06
19	.13	−.795	−6.61	.13	−.752	−4.86	.15	−.869	−4.57
20	.10	−.380	−2.83	.10	−.340	−2.06	.10	−.543	−2.30
21	.12	−.181	−1.35	.12	−.115	−.71	.13	−.330	−1.39
22	.08	−.286	−1.95	.09	−.270	−1.53	.08	−.331	−1.23
23	.07	−.277	−1.83	.07	−.162	−.90	.07	−.527	−1.84
24	.06	−.141	−.86	.06	−.110	−.54	.06	−.259	−.89
25+	.15			.14			.16		
Intercept		65.7465	54.89		66.10801	48.42		64.83274	26.46
Sample size		5,758			3,939			1,819	
R^2		.119			.115			.114	

Notes: Urban counties are those with at least one town of over 25,000 (including towns that cross over county lines). See text for other variable definitions. *T*-statistics are based on robust (heteroscedasticity-consistent) standard errors clustered at the county level.

Table 5.4   OLS Regressions, by Farming Status

	Full Sample			Farmers			Non-Farmers		
	Mean or Frequency	Coefficient	T-statistic	Mean or Frequency	Coefficient	T-statistic	Mean or Frequency	Coefficient	T-statistic
Dependent variable = enlistment height (in.)	67.74			68.02			67.15		
Region									
Mid-Atlantic	.32			.26			.46		
New England	.15	.392	2.51	.16	.560	2.63	.21	.143	.62
South	.09	.559	2.98	.03	.849	2.47	.02	.259	.47
West	.44	.551	4.00	.56	.406	2.15	.31	.766	3.60
County-level variables (1850)									
Percent urban	.09	-.899	-2.83	.05	-.705	-1.37	.17	-.175	-.39
Rail or water connection	.75	-.281	-2.72	.71	-.305	-2.22	.88	-.328	-1.42
Agricultural capital per capita	169.44	-.002	-2.57	167.54	-.002	-2.00	180.80	.000	.27
Manufacturing capital per capita	21.99	.000	.06	17.54	.001	.27	31.94	.000	.04
Surplus calories (in thousands)	2.21	-.023	-.62	2.40	.009	.22	1.78	-.153	-1.66
Percent foreign-born (× 100)	9.76	-.009	-1.59	9.31	-.009	-1.20	12.33	-.015	-1.70
Crude death rate (per 1,000)	12.83	0.15	1.99	12.62	.016	2.23	13.36	-.013	-.83
School attendance rate (× 100)	62.91	-.003	-.72	66.68	-.005	-.90	65.95	-.003	-.38
Illiteracy rate (× 100)	4.13	-.036	-3.00	3.78	-.044	-2.72	3.20	-.026	-.97
Average family size	5.61	.596	3.14	5.60	.482	1.72	5.54	.602	2.08
Household-level variables (1850)									
Father and son native	.46			.42			.52		
Father: interstate migrant									
Recruit: native	.35	-.101	-.96	.41	.025	.18	.25	-.232	-1.26
Recruit: interstate migrant	.09	-.255	-1.81	.10	-.139	-.72	.07	-.045	-.19
Father: foreign-born									
Recruit: native	.07	-.195	-1.40	.05	.126	.62	.11	-.525	-2.68
Recruit: interstate migrant	.01	.193	.55	.01	.368	.79	.01	1.144	1.73
Recruit: foreign-born	.02	-.432	-1.51	.01	-.832	-1.79	.04	-.283	-.75
Occupation									
Farmer	.45								
Professional/proprietor	.06	-.391	-2.94				.17	.026	.16

Artisan	.15	-.438	-3.94				.47	-.049	-.33
Laborer	.11	-.433	-3.47				.35		
Unknown	.22	-.066	-.56						
Father's wealth									
$1–100	.02			.02			.02		
$101–500	.17	.191	.73	.18	-.031	-.07	.16	.655	1.51
$501–1000	.16	.318	1.25	.18	.263	.58	.13	.497	1.13
$1000+	.26	.273	1.07	.37	.257	.59	.15	.393	.90
Unknown	.38	.179	.70	.25	.314	.70	.53	.287	.67
Mother illiterate	.08	-.096	-.74	.07	-.037	-.19	.06	-.154	-.59
Number of children									
1–3	.33			.31			.39		
4–6	.55	-.017	-.21	.56	-.033	-.28	.52	-.002	-.02
7+	.12	.190	1.46	.13	.279	1.64	.08	-.082	-.30
Enlistment variables									
Enlistment year									
1861	.23			.19			.25		
1862	.37	.040	.37	.40	-.156	-.95	.34	.123	.71
1863	.06	-.336	-1.95	.06	-1.012	-4.18	.06	-.015	-.05
1864	.26	-.319	-2.91	.24	-.526	-3.18	.27	-.342	-1.83
1865	.09	-.642	-4.82	.11	-.703	-3.47	.09	-.737	-3.24
Enlistment age									
16	.01	-3.190	-9.75	.01	-2.453	-6.13	.01	-3.081	-5.82
17	.03	-1.960	-8.09	.02	-1.667	-3.84	.03	-1.841	-4.51
18	.25	-1.535	-12.74	.24	-1.296	-8.02	.28	-1.433	-7.20
19	.13	-.795	-6.61	.12	-.806	-4.22	.15	-.625	-2.93
20	.10	-.380	-2.83	.10	-.353	-1.79	.09	-.374	-1.37
21	.12	-.181	-1.35	.12	-.170	-.91	.12	-.327	-1.38
22	.08	-.286	-1.95	.09	-.444	-2.00	.08	-.032	-.12
23	.07	-.277	-1.83	.07	-.249	-1.26	.06	-.216	-.71
24	.06	-.141	-.86	.06	.003	.01	.06	-.306	-.93
25+	.15			.17			.12		
Intercept		65.831	55.95		66.5387	37.45		65.27195	34.32
Sample size		5,758			2,605			1,877	
R^2		.119			.086			0.103	

Notes: Individuals with father's occupation unknown are excluded from both the farmer and nonfarmer groups. See text for other variable definitions. *T*-statistics are based on robust (heteroscedasticity-consistent) standard errors clustered at the county level.

related to urbanization. However, it appears that the greatest effect is between rural counties and counties with at least some urbanization. The regression in the urban group shows that little variation in height can be explained by the level of urbanization. Furthermore, table 5.4 shows that the urbanization effect is stronger among farmers than nonfarmers. All the results presented here are consistent with a farming advantage in terms of height, but closer examination reveals that farmers are further advantaged by living in rural locations.

Other county-level variables are also important. Access to transportation (primarily an issue in rural counties) has a significant negative effect. The aggregate level of capital is significant for agricultural capital, but negligible for manufacturing capital. Furthermore, the effect of capital in agriculture is concentrated almost solely in rural counties. Thus even though agricultural capital may raise farm output, it is negatively associated with height in rural areas. We speculate that this is because agricultural capital is indicative of access to centers of trade and commerce, which would also raise exposure to infectious disease, though we have not tested this argument directly.

The percent foreign-born is also a negative indicator (although not statistically significant), and, surprisingly, the illiteracy rate of the county has a statistically significant negative impact, though the magnitude of the effect is small and only exists in rural counties. Finally, average family size in the county turns out to be an important predictor of the variation in height (a 1 standard deviation increase in average family size raises height by 0.2 in.).

It should be noted that we find a few sharp differences between our results and those of Haines, Craig, and Weiss (2000). They find that surplus calories and the crude death rate are both negative, while we find essentially no effect of surplus calories and a positive correlation with the crude death rate. We also try their measure of protein and find similar results. Furthermore, we have not found that deleting other variables from the model changes these effects. The obvious difference between our two approaches is that we are looking at the county of residence in 1850 and they are looking at the 1850 values for the county of birth, but we have not reconciled these contrary findings.

Turning to family-level variables, clearly the most important and robust finding is the impact of occupation, almost all of which appears to be a farmer advantage. Professionals and proprietors do a little better than artisans and laborers, but the difference is not statistically significant. Furthermore, the farmer advantage exists in both rural and urban counties and, in fact, is slightly higher in the urban counties. This effect must be considered in association with the earlier result that population had greater effects among farmers than among nonfarmers. Taken together they imply that the farmer advantage is augmented by living in a rural setting, but significant advantages for farmers exist in urban counties as well.

The impact of father's wealth is somewhat ambiguous. The coefficient estimates in the full sample show that wealth in the $101 to $500 category increases height by 0.191 in. (relative to $1 to $100) and by 0.318 in. in the $501 to $1,000 range, with no further increases for the highest wealth category (0.273 in.). These magnitudes are nontrivial, but the estimates are not statistically significant. Interestingly, the estimates of wealth effects are much higher for nonfarmers than farmers, but they are virtually nonexistent for residents of urban counties in general. Because the effect of wealth may be nonlinear, occurring primarily at very low values, and because of our relatively small sample, we have found that it is infeasible to test for further interactions of wealth with other covariates, either through interacting wealth directly with other variables or by estimating the sample on selected subsets of the overall sample.

The migratory history of recruits and their parents is associated with very large differences in height, though individual coefficients tend to fall short of statistical significance at the 0.05 level. Overall, foreign-born recruits are in the worst situation. Foreign-born recruits in rural counties are 0.819 in. shorter than their native counterparts, and, similarly, the foreign-born who are farmers are 0.823 in. shorter than native-born farmers (note that these statistically significant effects are some of the largest presented here and are substantially larger than, for instance, the marginal effects of region, urbanization, or occupation). Another striking pattern is that effect of recruits who migrate across state lines. Movers who are the sons of native-born are somewhat shorter than nonmovers (though movers into urban counties are taller than natives of urban counties). However, movers whose fathers are foreign-born are taller than the nonmigrating recruits. This is especially true among the urban group and nonfarmers. In all cases there is a clear distinction between the sons of foreign-born who have moved and those who have not. The extreme case is among the nonfarming population: Among the sons of foreign-born fathers in this group, recruits who have moved are 1.67 in. taller than nonmovers. While moving can be traumatic, it is likely the case that movers are systematically more robust than nonmovers, especially among immigrants, since it was difficult and costly to move inland from the port cities to which they often settle upon first arriving in America.

Finally, the mother's literacy has little impact on height for the sample as a whole. A notable exception to this is the large and statistically significant impact of mother's illiteracy among those in urbanized counties. Indeed, among urban residents, the mother's literacy may be a more important marker of socioeconomic status than either the father's real estate wealth or occupation, since we do not have a measure in 1850 of personal wealth. Finally, recruits from households with seven or more children in 1850 were 0.19 in. taller than others, though the effect is predominantly concentrated within the farming group.

Finally, controls for age and year of enlistment are included. The age variables indicate that young men of this cohort tended to grow about three inches between age sixteen and age twenty-five, which, incidentally, is significantly higher than the rate of late growth in modern populations of males (U.S. Department of Health and Human Services 1987, 23), suggesting that "catch-up" growth is occurring for part of the recruit population. We also find that enlistment year is an important indicator of height, particularly in the rural counties. Recruits enlisting in 1863 to 1864 were about 0.33 in. shorter than earlier enlistees, whereas those enlisting in 1865 were 0.64 in. shorter. Apparently, early enlistees were healthier than later ones.[9]

5.4.2 Fixed Effects

An alternative way to control for county-level effects is to allow each county to have an unrestricted impact on height through the specification of a fixed effects model. If we index individuals by i and counties by j, we can specify the following model:

$$H_{ij} = a_j + B(X_{ij}) + u_{ij}$$

Here H_{ij} is the height of the individual, X_{ij} is the vector of regressors, and a_j is the county-specific error term. The error terms are assumed to be independent across individuals and counties, as well as uncorrelated with the X_{ij}. In this analysis there are 726 counties. The minimum number of persons per county is one, and the maximum is seventy-six. There are on average 7.9 recruits per county. Overall, the county-level fixed effects explain 32.5 percent of the variation in height, though not too much should be made of this result, given the low number of recruits per county.[10]

Table 5.5 repeats the earlier OLS results for the full model and compares them with a model with no county variables and one with county fixed effects. The primary differences between the regressions with no county variables and the "full model" are that the occupational differences are stronger without the county variables (more of a farmer advantage) as are the migration effects. These differences indicate that the occupation differences in height depend on the characteristics of the county. Likewise, moving across state lines would appear to have a strong positive effect on height if the county variables are excluded, but this is not found when the charac-

9. The enlistment year effects are remarkably similar in pattern and magnitude to those found by Margo and Steckel (1983); they even find that the year effects are stronger in rural areas than in urban ones, as do we.

10. In fixed effects models, as the number of individuals per groups falls, the variance of the dependent variable explained by variation across groups will automatically rise.

Table 5.5   **Fixed Effects Estimates**

	Mean or Frequency	Full Model		No County Variables		Fixed Effects	
		Coefficient	T-statistic	Coefficient	T-statistic	Coefficient	T-statistic
Dependent variable = enlistment height (in.)	67.74						
Region							
Mid-Atlantic	.32	.392	2.51				
New England	.15	.559	2.98				
South	.09	.551	4.00				
West	.44						
		County-level variables (1850)					
Percent urban	.09	−.899	−2.83				
Rail or water connection	.75	−.281	−2.72				
Agricultural capital per capita	169.44	−.002	−2.57				
Manufacturing capital per capita	21.99	.000	.06				
Surplus calories (in thousands)	2212.23	.000	−.62				
Percent foreign-born ($\times$ 100)	9.76	−.009	−1.59				
Crude death rate (per 1,000)	12.83	0.15	1.99				
School attendance rate ($\times$ 100)	62.91	−.003	−.72				
Illiteracy rate ($\times$ 100)	4.13	−.036	−3.00				
Average family size	5.61	.596	3.14				
(continued)							

Table 5.5 (continued)

	Mean or Frequency	Full Model		No County Variables		Fixed Effects	
		Coefficient	T-statistic	Coefficient	T-statistic	Coefficient	T-statistic
		Household-level variables (1850)					
Father and son native	.46						
Father: interstate migrant							
Recruit: native	.35	–.101	–.96	.235	2.44	–.096	–.91
Recruit: interstate migrant	.09	–.255	–1.81	.160	1.24	–.241	–1.53
Father: foreign-born							
Recruit: native	.07	–.195	–1.40	–.281	–2.22	–.166	–1.09
Recruit: interstate migrant	.01	.193	.55	.450	1.29	.503	1.32
Recruit: foreign-born	.02	–.432	–1.51	–.478	–1.74	–.332	–1.26
Occupation							
Farmer	.45						
Professional/proprietor	.06	–.391	–2.94	–.605	–4.34	–.403	–2.52
Artisan	.15	–.438	–3.94	–.667	–6.21	–.453	–4.06
Laborer	.11	–.433	–3.47	–.672	–5.41	–.413	–3.17
Unknown	.22	–.066	–.56	.061	.54	.021	.15
Father's wealth							
$1–100	.02						
$101–500	.17	.191	.73	.182	.69	.043	.16
$501–1000	.16	.318	1.25	.248	.97	.204	.75
$1000+	.26	.273	1.07	.080	.32	.132	.49
Unknown	.38	.179	.70	–.005	–.02	.071	.27
Mother illiterate	.08	–.096	–.74	.010	.08	–.087	–.60
Number of children							
1–3	.33						
4–6	.55	–.017	–.21	.055	.67	–.133	–1.68
7+	.12	.190	1.46	.300	2.27	.115	.94

Enlistment variables

Enlistment year							
1861	.23						
1862	.37	.040	.37	-.017	-.14	-.083	-.73
1863	.06	-.336	-1.95	-.253	-1.36	-.378	-2.08
1864	.26	-.319	-2.91	-.353	-3.25	-.452	-3.72
1865	.09	-.642	-4.82	-.598	-4.41	-.692	-4.23
Enlistment age							
16	.01	-3.190	-9.75	-2.992	-9.03	-3.378	-8.66
17	.03	-1.960	-8.09	-1.802	-7.52	-1.871	-7.56
18	.25	-1.535	-12.74	-1.440	-11.87	-1.469	-12.56
19	.13	-.795	-6.61	-.748	-6.18	-.734	-5.52
20	.10	-.380	-2.83	-.339	-2.50	-.348	-2.42
21	.12	-.181	-1.35	-.157	-1.16	-.083	-.61
22	.08	-.286	-1.95	-.234	-1.59	-.303	-2.01
23	.07	-.277	-1.83	-.247	-1.60	-.297	-1.82
24	.06	-.141	-.86	-.119	-.71	-.137	-.81
25+	.15						
Intercept		65.74645	54.89	65.746	54.89	68.789	232.07
Sample size		5,758		5,758		5,758	
R^2		.119		0.095		0.081	

Notes: See text for other variable definitions. T-statistics are based on robust (heteroscedasticity-consistent) standard errors clustered at the county level. The R-squared for the fixed effects model is the "within-groups" R-squared, which is the regression obtained from subtracting county-level means from the dependent and independent variables. The OLS regression values are taken from table 5.3.

teristics of the county of destination are controlled for. Both of these implications make intuitive sense.

In contrast, very little difference exists within the coefficients between the OLS and the fixed effects models. An important exception is that wealth is even less important in the fixed effects model than in the OLS framework. This is possibly attributed to a relationship between individual wealth and county, which might cause some of the wealth effect to be attributed to the county-specific error terms. Additionally, the effect of interstate migration is more pronounced in the fixed effects model than in the OLS case.

5.4.3   Quantile Regressions

The final alternative specification to be explored in this analysis is quantile regression. In estimating the effects of environmental variables on height, the principal assumption is that the body is deprived of the nutrients it needs during the growth process. Implicit in the OLS model is that contributing factors have a uniform effect across the distribution of heights. In other words, if factor X lowers height by 1 in., then a person who would be 72 in. tall will be 71 in., a person who would otherwise be 68 in. will end up at 67 in., and so on for each height. But what would it imply if the impact of a particular growth factor has nonuniform effects across the distribution of heights?[11] It is usually assumed that the distribution of heights is normal. But in conditions where growth is suppressed for some reason, such as due to disease or to nutritional deprivation, it is not clear a priori that the effect of such deprivation will be constant across the distribution of heights.

Quantile regression is a technique that has seen increased use in the past decade as a method of estimating the effects of covariates at different points in the conditional distribution of the dependent variable.[12] Estimates are derived by minimizing the sum of the absolute deviations around a designated point in the conditional distribution. Median regression is the simplest case, but any point can be estimated, such as the first quartile (the 25th percentile) or the first decile (10th percentile), and so on. In practical terms, this amounts to solving, as shown by Koenker and Bassett (1978), the following minimization problem

$$\min(B) \sum_{y \geq XB} \theta |h_i - X_i B| + \sum_{y < XB} (1 - \theta)|h_i - X_i B|$$

where θ is the quantile to be estimated, and the other notation is the same as used previously. As can be seen from the formula above, the values of the dependent variable to the left of θ are given more weight when $\theta < 0.5$ and

11. We should be clear that we are not talking here about the possible nonlinear effects of covariates; those can be accommodated in a straightforward fashion in the OLS framework or by nonlinear least squares.

12. Important examples in recent years include the study of wage distributions (Buchinsky 1994), intergenerational earnings transmissions (Eide and Showalter 1999), and wealth and economic mobility in the nineteenth century (Conley and Galenson 1998).

those to the right are given more weight when $\theta > 0.5$. Naturally, the weight given to extreme values of h_i increases as θ approaches the extremes of 0 and 1, making the estimation of very low or high values of θ potentially sensitive to some types of measurement error or other causes of outliers. In the case of heights, it is surely the case that a portion of those veterans with a height of 5'0", 5'1", and 5'2" are, in reality, 6'0", 6'1", and 6'2", but were entered incorrectly. In general, quantile regression is more robust in these cases since the absolute deviation is being modeled, rather than the squared deviation, as is the case with OLS.

It should be noted that, assuming an uncensored distribution of heights, quantile regression is not "right" and OLS "wrong." OLS has numerous desirable properties, not the least of which are small and large sample properties that are well known. The small sample properties of quantile regression, on the other hand, are not known. But quantile regression provides a method of investigating the complete conditional distribution of heights. At the very least, it is a useful comparison of the OLS results.

Table 5.6 presents quantile estimates for $\theta = 0.1, 0.5, 0.9$. Standard errors are calculated using the formula of Koenker and Bassett (1982) and Rogers (1992). The first column presents the OLS coefficients presented earlier. Though some of the variables in the model have relatively uniform effects across the quantiles estimated in table 5.3, there are several important exceptions. For instance, the effect of urbanization is much greater in the right tail of the distribution than in the center or at the first decile. It is in the left tail of the conditional distribution, however, that other county-level variables are the most important. Indeed, only the transportation and family size variables have any impact at the 0.9 quantile, whereas all the county-level variables other than urbanization and transportation have significant effects at the 0.1 quantile. The median effects are roughly equivalent to the OLS estimates.

The effects of other variables also differ across the conditional distribution of heights. Perhaps most important is the variation in occupational effects. In the left tail we find the first evidence that occupational variation among nonfarmers may be important, since the effect of being a laborer is nearly three times as large as the professional/proprietor effect (which is not statistically significant from farmers). The opposite occupational pattern holds, however, in the upper tail of the distribution. And again, the median results are qualitatively similar to the OLS results.

Estimating quantiles near zero is essentially a procedure that identifies those factors which best explain very low heights, while estimates of upper quantiles point to factors leading to great height. The key variable for identifying high heights is urbanization, while a variety of other county-level variables explain the low heights. We have not yet developed a theory to explain the pronounced nonuniformity of the effects at the extreme ends of the distribution, but the results suggest an important nonlinearity of effects,

Table 5.6   Quantile Regressions

	OLS		Quantile = .1		Quantile = .5		Quantile = .9	
	Coefficient	T-statistic	Coefficient	T-statistic	Coefficient	T-statistic	Coefficient	T-statistic
Dependent variable = enlistment height (in.)								
Region								
Mid-Atlantic								
New England	.392	2.51	.453	2.20	.499	2.61	.169	.87
South	.559	2.98	.336	1.35	.484	2.03	.953	4.01
West	.551	4.00	.589	3.63	.451	2.78	.665	3.80
			County-level variables (1850)					
Percent urban	-.899	-2.83	.074	.19	.499	2.61	-1.906	-4.56
Rail or water connection	-.281	-2.72	-.186	-1.45	.484	2.03	-.320	-2.41
Agricultural capital per capita	-.002	-2.57	-.003	-2.99	.451	2.78	-.002	-2.35
Manufacturing capital per capita	.000	.06	-.007	-1.85	.000	-.02	.010	2.64
Surplus calories (in thousands)	-.023	-.62	-.088	-2.07	-.028	-.64	.007	.15
Percent foreign-born (× 100)	-.009	-1.59	-.025	-3.16	-.008	-1.13	-.004	-.52
Crude death rate (per 1,000)	.015	1.99	.022	2.35	.008	.82	.011	1.14
School attendance rate (× 100)	-.003	-.72	-.009	-1.99	.001	.26	.000	.03
Illiteracy rate (× 100)	-.036	-3.00	-.052	-3.23	-.034	-2.14	-.030	-1.83
Average family size	.596	3.14	.499	2.26	.718	3.76	.564	2.95
			Household-level variables (1850)					
Father and son native								
Father: interstate migrant								
Recruit: native	-.101	-.96	-.240	-1.84	-.080	-.61	.055	.40
Recruit: interstate migrant	-.255	-1.81	-.262	-1.31	-.263	-1.36	-.236	-1.14
Father: foreign-born								
Recruit: native	-.195	-1.40	.004	.02	-.369	-1.82	-.560	-2.64
Recruit: interstate migrant	.193	.55	.356	.77	.087	.18	.369	.71
Recruit: foreign-born	-.432	-1.51	-.726	-1.98	-.534	-1.52	-.557	-1.63
Occupation								
Farmer								
Professional/proprietor	-.391	-2.94	-.296	-1.32	-.400	-1.86	-.251	-1.11
Artisan	-.438	-3.94	-.569	-3.76	-.500	-3.40	-.257	-1.69
Laborer	-.433	-3.47	-.635	-3.54	-.459	-2.68	-.201	-1.11
Unknown	-.066	-.56	-.372	-2.64	-.076	-.54	-.007	-.04

Father's wealth								
$1–100	.191	.73	.252	.69	.493	1.44	.423	1.16
$101–500	.318	1.25	.425	1.16	.504	1.46	.566	1.54
$501–1000	.273	1.07	.338	.93	.499	1.46	.245	.67
$1000+	.179	.70	.281	.79	.398	1.19	.363	1.02
Unknown	-.096	-.74	.211	1.12	-.161	-.88	-.228	-1.18
Mother illiterate								
Number of children								
1–3								
4–6	-.017	-.21	-.005	-.04	.024	.23	-.011	-.10
7+	.190	1.46	.005	.03	.355	2.20	.276	1.66
Enlistment variables								
Enlistment year								
1861								
1862	.040	.37	.232	1.77	-.112	-.88	.024	.18
1863	-.336	-1.95	-.753	-3.44	-.447	-2.08	-.411	-1.87
1864	-.319	-2.91	-.021	.15	-.427	-3.06	-.576	-3.96
1865	-.642	-4.82	-.520	-2.61	-.611	-3.22	-.858	-4.34
Enlistment age								
16	-3.190	-9.75	-3.544	-7.25	-3.152	-6.51	-3.067	-6.26
17	-1.960	-8.09	-2.018	-5.94	-2.072	-6.39	-1.522	-4.44
18	-1.535	-12.74	-1.380	-8.53	-1.648	-10.55	-1.631	-10.05
19	-.795	-6.61	-.688	-3.67	-.930	-5.20	-.833	-4.44
20	-.380	-2.83	-.114	-.56	-.455	-2.35	-.465	-2.31
21	-.181	-1.35	-.240	-1.27	-.265	-1.44	-.203	-1.05
22	-.286	-1.95	-.166	-.78	-.410	-2.00	-.308	-1.44
23	-.277	-1.83	-.010	-.04	-.214	-.98	-.371	-1.65
24	-.141	-.86	-.572	-2.43	0.35	.16	-.146	-.62
25+								
Intercept	65.831	55.95	63.914	45.27	64.800	52.24	68.527	55.22
Sample size	5,758							
R^2	.119		.075		.069		.059	

Notes: See text for other variable definitions. *R*-squared for the quantile regressions are "pseudo *R*-squared" values. The OLS regression values are taken from table 5.3.

likely associated with urbanization, that is not captured in the OLS framework. The quantile results for urbanization mirror the earlier results that variation in urbanization had a greater effect on height among farmers than upon nonfarmers, since farmers are likely to dominate in the upper tail of the conditional distribution. Further exploration of these nonlinearities and potential is certainly warranted.

5.5   Conclusions

Our results confirm and extend many of the previous findings related to height in antebellum America. In particular, we find significant effects for region and for various measures of urbanization. Although we do not know with certainty why urbanization matters, the most compelling explanation to date is the role of infectious disease. Though we have certainly not ruled out the importance of the quantity and quality of food in urban populations, it is notable that the effects of urbanization are strongest among farmers, where we would expect access to high-quality food to be less important. In addition to population density, which is proxied (though far from perfectly) by the percentage of the county living in urban areas, access to rail and water transport is important for rural counties. This fact further stresses the importance of infectious disease. We don't find, in contrast to Haines, Craig, and Weiss (2000), that calories produced within the county are important.

Our main intention here has been to explore the possibility that early life, family-level variation in socioeconomic status might have affected health and nutrition of the recruits in the sample. Previous studies have been limited to information available at the time of enlistment and to county-level aggregates. If there is a smoking gun here, it is occupation. The farming advantage exists even after controlling for urbanization, whether through the urbanization index or through estimating the equations separately for urban and rural counties. Furthermore, other investigations (not shown here) indicate that the farmers are at a distinct advantage in even sparsely populated counties. A lingering question in the field's current understanding of the health advantages accrued to the farming class is whether the story is one of access to food or remoteness from population centers and, hence, exposure to communicable disease. The analysis here points to the importance of *both* explanations, though the overall advantage of farming is likely due to several factors.

Other variables suggest the importance of individual characteristics. The descriptive statistics of table 5.1 reveal a positive relationship between wealth and height, but this occurs primarily at low levels of wealth. The regression results show a similar pattern, but the estimates are not statistically significant. The effects of the mother's literacy (in urban counties) and the large differences in effects of migratory history also suggest the importance of the family-specific variables. For instance, the sharp differences between the movers and nonmovers among the sons of the foreign-born point directly to family-specific influences on health and nutrition. The positive effect of geographic mobility (which is likely an indicator for a variety of unobserved family-specific characteristics) of the recruits with foreign-born parents is more than strong enough to offset the negative impact of foreign nativity on the height of the children.

We have attempted to confirm the robustness of the central results by using different estimation techniques, including a county-level fixed effects regression, which revealed no notable differences from the OLS results, and quantile regression. The quantile regressions demonstrate that even though many of the county and household variables simply shift the conditional distribution of height upward or downward, many other variables have sharply different effects at different points in the conditional distribution. The most important is that the effect of variation in urbanization is highly concentrated in the upper tail of the distribution. We conjecture that those in the lower end of the conditional distribution already have had so many insults to their health and nutrition that additional variation in urbanization does not matter significantly. In a sense, the quantile regressions can be interpreted as a diagnostic tool of the basic linear specification of the full OLS model. They reveal that the effects of urbanization are not constant across subgroups of the population—which is the same thing that is shown in making comparisons between urban and rural counties (table 5.3) and between farmers and nonfarmers (table 5.4).[13]

These results leave open many avenues for future research, including understanding why farmers (whether living in urban or rural counties) enjoyed a significant height advantage; what explains the regional variations in height; and what, in general, are the relative contributions of gross nutrition and infectious disease on height. We expect the progress will be made both in the exploitation of additional data and through implementing new empirical specifications and techniques of estimation. The results to date suggest that there is no single socioeconomic mechanism working in concert with genetics to determine height. Rather, variation in height is the result of an interplay of genetics, location specific characteristics and family characteristics.

References

Buchinsky, Moshe. 1994. Changes in the U.S. wage structure 1963–1987: Application of quantile regression. *Econometrica* 62 (March): 405–58.

13. In exploratory work, not presented here, we have explored a variety of interactive effects, where we interacted urbanization, wealth, and occupation. We found no compelling results in this exercise, and we note again that interacting variables often results in cell sizes that are much to small to estimate reliably given the size of our data set.

Conley, Timothy G., and David W. Galenson. 1998. Nativity and wealth in mid-nineteenth-century cities. *Journal of Economic History* 58 (June): 468–93.

Costa, Dora L. 1993. Height, wealth, and disease among the native born in the rural antebellum North. *Social Science History* 17 (Fall): 355–83.

Costa, Dora L., and Richard Steckel. 1997. Long-term trends in health, welfare, and economic growth in the United States. In *Health and welfare during industrialization*, ed. Richard H. Steckel and Roderick Floud, 47–90. Chicago: University of Chicago Press.

Eide, Eric, and Mark H. Showalter. 1999. Factors affecting the transmission of earnings across generations: A quantile regression approach. *Journal of Human Resources* 34:253–67.

Eveleth, P. B., and J. M. Tanner. 1990. *Worldwide variation in human growth.* 2nd ed. Cambridge: Cambridge University Press.

Floud, Roderick, Kenneth W. Wachter, and Annabel Gregory. 1990. *Height, health, and history: Nutritional status in the United Kingdom, 1750–1890.* Cambridge: Cambridge University Press.

Fogel, Robert W. 1986. Nutrition and the decline in mortality: Some preliminary findings. In *Long-term factors in American economic growth,* ed. Stanley L. Engerman and Robert E. Gallman, 439–555. Chicago: University of Chicago Press.

———. 1989. *Without consent or contract: The rise and fall of American slavery.* New York: Norton.

———. 1994. Economic growth, population theory, and physiology: The bearing of long-term processes on the making of economic policy. *American Economic Review* 84 (June): 369–95.

———. 2000. *The fourth great awakening and the future of egalitarianism.* Chicago: University of Chicago Press.

Gallman, Robert E., and John J. Wallis. 1992. *American economic growth and standards of living before the Civil War.* Chicago: University of Chicago Press.

Haines, Michael R., Lee A. Craig, and Thomas Weiss. 2000. Development, health, nutrition, and mortality: The case of the "antebellum puzzle" in the United States. NBER Working Paper no. H0130. Cambridge, Mass.: National Bureau of Economic Research, October.

Koenker, Roger, and Gilbert Bassett Jr. 1978. Regression quantiles. *Econometrica* 46:33–50.

Komlos, John. 1994. *Stature, living standards, and economic development: Essays in anthropometric history.* Chicago: University of Chicago Press.

———. 1998. Shrinking in a growing economy? The mystery of physical stature during the Industrial Revolution. *Journal of Economic History* 58 (September): 779–802.

Margo, Robert A. 2000. *Wages and labor markets in the United States: 1820–1850.* Chicago: University of Chicago Press.

Margo, Robert A., and Richard H. Steckel. 1982. The heights of American slaves: New evidence on slave nutrition and health. *Social Science History* 6 (Fall): 516–38.

———. 1983. Heights of native-born whites during the antebellum period. *Journal of Economic History* 43 (1): 167–74.

Rogers, W. H. 1992. sg11: Quantile regression standard errors. *Stata Technical Bulletin* 9:16–19.

Steckel, Richard H. 1979. Slave height profiles from coastwise manifests. *Explorations in Economic History* 16 (Fall): 363–80.

———. 1995. Stature and the standard of living. *Journal of Economic Literature* 33 (December): 1903–40.

Steckel, Richard H., and Roderick Floud, eds. 1997. *Health and welfare during industrialization.* Chicago: University of Chicago Press.

Steckel, Richard H., and Donald Haurin. 1994. Health and nutrition in the American Midwest: Evidence from the height of Ohio National Guardsmen, 1850–1990. In *Stature, living standards, and economic development,* ed. John Komlos, 117–28. Chicago: University of Chicago Press.

U.S. Department of Health and Human Services. 1987. Anthropometric reference data and prevalence of overweight, United States, 1976–1980. Publication no. 87-1688. Washington, D.C.: DHHS, October.

6

The Prevalence of Chronic Respiratory Disease in the Industrial Era
The United States, 1895–1910

Sven E. Wilson

6.1 Introduction

A typical Union Army soldier returning home from the war in 1865 returned to a world that was still largely rural, agrarian, and unmechanized. Over three-quarters of the population lived either in sparsely populated areas or in towns and villages populated by fewer than 2,500 people. Those veterans who lived to old age were to see dramatic changes over the course of their lives. The modern world, with its new conveniences, crowded living conditions, and accelerated pace, descended rapidly as the twentieth century dawned in America. The growth of manufacturing and commerce in the several decades after the Civil War laid the economic foundations for tremendous improvements in standard of living over the twentieth century. These improvements included not only material gains, but also dramatic increases in life expectancy and general health at all points in the life course.[1]

A largely unresolved question, however, is what was happening to health during the period these changes were taking place. Most inferences on health in the nineteenth century come from trends in adult height, which is a comprehensive measure of the cumulative nutritional intake and disease environment present in childhood. In the mid-nineteenth century, a signifi-

Sven E. Wilson is assistant professor of political science and adjunct assistant professor of economics at Brigham Young University.

Financial support for this research was provided by the National Institute on Aging (AG10120) and Brigham Young University. Damon Cann, Lauren Cundick, Ben Howell, and Shawn Waddoups provided excellent research assistance. Special thanks are due to Dr. Louis Nguyen for suggestions on disease classification issues.

1. Life expectancy at birth (all races, both sexes) increased from 47.3 in 1900 to 76.5 in 1997 (NCHS 1999). Evidence is emerging, as well, that age-specific prevalence rates have fallen since the early-twentieth century for a variety of chronic illnesses (Fogel and Costa 1997; Costa 2000).

cant decline occurred in mean height, beginning with the cohorts born after 1830 and bottoming out with the cohorts born in the 1880s.[2] Height among birth cohorts born after the Civil War increased steadily, but did not fully recover until into the twentieth century. Fogel (1986) and Pope (1992) demonstrated a similar pattern in life expectancy. These trends together imply that although life expectancy rose over the latter part of the century and deaths from infectious diseases such as tuberculosis were falling (Leavitt and Numbers 1985), the elderly at the turn of the century had a particularly poor nutritional history and many of them had suffered the ravages of the Civil War, including the associated exposure to an infectious disease. Costa (2000) has shown recently that early life exposure to chronic illness had significant impacts on having a variety of chronic illnesses at the turn of the century.

Data on specific conditions and disabilities did not begin to be collected systematically in the United States until the 1950s, with the onset of the National Health Interview Surveys. However, new historical data have recently been collected from the pension records of Civil War veterans that can be used to perform epidemiological analyses of a rich variety of specific health conditions around the turn of the century. These data come from a randomly drawn sample of the Union Army that follows over 35,000 Union Army recruits from early childhood until death, by linking the recruits to census manuscripts and to the pension files that were maintained by the pension bureau. In these files are over 87,000 detailed medical examination certificates of board-certified physicians who determined the veteran's medical eligibility for pension assistance.[3]

One body system that may have been particularly sensitive to the demographic and economic trends in the latter nineteenth century is the respiratory system. In this paper, I provide a detailed (although by no means comprehensive) analysis of the medical data on the respiratory system covering the period from 1895 to 1910. I explore the variety of respiratory conditions that the examining physicians identified and how the distribution of conditions varied by age, occupation, population, and place of birth at four points in time: 1895, 1900, 1905, and 1910. A system-based approach is very practical when using the pension data, since the examining physicians typically recorded their observations system by system and recommended financial compensation by body system as well.

6.2   The Historical Setting

From 1870 to 1910, the United States experienced a dramatic continuation of the trend toward heavy industry and population concentration in

2. This trend was initially identified by Margo and Steckel (1983) and Steckel and Haurin in 1982 (but published only in 1994) and documented later by Fogel (1986), Komlos (1987), and Steckel (1992), among others.
3. All data used in this study come from Fogel (1999).

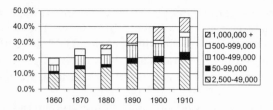

Fig. 6.1   Percent of U.S. population living in urban areas, 1860–1910
Source: U.S. Bureau of the Census (1976).

large cities. Since a primary reason for living in the large cities was access to manufacturing jobs, industry and population growth tended to go hand in hand. Figure 6.1 highlights growth in urbanization. From the end of the Civil War to 1910, the percentage of the population living in urban areas (over 2,500 residents) doubled. Even more striking is that most of this growth occurred in cities of over 50,000 residents.

Urbanization and industrialization both may have increased the odds of respiratory disease. Surely the filthy, crowded conditions of the large cities served to spread infectious agents, which may have contributed to the development of chronic respiratory problems. More likely still is that the tremendous growth of coal-burning industries led to dramatic declines in air quality. In 1870, the United States consumed about 21 million tons of dirty, bituminous coal and about 20 million tons of cleaner-burning anthracite coal. By 1910, consumption had increased to 81 million tons of anthracite coal and a whopping 406 million tons of bituminous coal.[4] Stradling (1999) documents that although some extolled the supposed virtues of smoke and soot, by the turn of the century vigorous antismoke efforts had begun, although it wouldn't be until the post–World War II period that significant gains in pollution control would be made.

Unfortunately, direct air quality measures from cities in this period are not available, although extensive descriptions of the heavy black clouds that hung over many cities have been given (Stradling 1999). Coal burning was a particular problem in cities such as Pittsburgh, where the surrounding hills worked to create air inversions that effectively trapped the smoke in the valleys, and most of the coal used was bituminous.

Industrial toxins affected urban residents not only through the air they breathed, but also on the factory floor. In modern times a wide variety of industrial pollutants affect respiratory health; these include coal dust, silica dust (from stone and other dry materials), asbestos, and other industrial chemicals in detergents, glues, paints, and other materials. In the 1920s, a public health report noted the high rates of respiratory disease (acute and chronic bronchitis, emphysema, asthma, and tuberculosis) in such indus-

4. Shurr and Netschert (1960), as cited in Stradling (1999).

tries as garment, cigar, and foundry where exposure to dust from fibers, vegetable materials, and metals was high (Britten and Thompson 1926). Of course, organic materials such as animal waste and dander, cotton dust, and dust from wheat and other grains are also sources of respiratory disease. Thus the nonfarmers, as a whole, are not necessarily at greater risk for respiratory illness than farmers.

Respiratory disease may have been rising at the turn of the century for another reason: the dramatic upturn in smoking during the latter part of the nineteenth century. In modern epidemiological studies, the dominant risk factor for respiratory diseases, such as emphysema and chronic bronchitis, is cigarette smoking. In the mid-nineteenth century, however, the cigarette in America was little more than a curio, although tobacco had long been consumed in other forms. But by the end of the century, the situation had changed. In 1839, the curing process for tobacco was revolutionized in North Carolina, giving birth to the "Bright Leaf" tobacco, which had the effect of making the smoke much easier to inhale than the dark leaf varieties found in cigar and pipe smoke. During the Civil War, tobacco use of all types spread among soldiers in America, just as it had earlier during the Crimean War in Europe. In 1884, Buck Duke, shortly to become the undisputed king of the tobacco industry, started to employ on a full-time basis the revolutionary machinery patented by James Bonsack in 1880. The Bonsack machine allowed, for the first time, the mass production of cigarettes at a fraction of the cost it took to hire North Carolina girls and women to roll them by hand.[5]

The new technology, coupled with vigorous marketing campaigns by Duke and his competitors, introduced to the modernizing country a stylish, clean, cheap, and very efficient method of delivering tobacco smoke deep into the lungs, where it could pass directly into the bloodstream. While there are no data that I know of that reveal specific consumption patterns of tobacco (who smoked it, when, and how often), from U.S. government statistics, we can calculate per capita production of cigarettes going back to 1870. Figure 6.2 displays the tenfold increase that occurred in per capita cigarette production between 1880 and the end of the century.[6] While the upward trend in cigarette production is striking, two features of figure 6.2 need to be noted. First, the rise in production after 1910, not shown in the figure, is even more profound, with per capita production rising from about 100 per year in 1910 to 1,000 by 1930 and 2,500 by the end of World War II. Though part of this growth can be attributed to increased exports, it is clear

5. This paragraph constitutes a much-condensed version of Kluger's (1997) fascinating history of the tobacco industry.

6. Tobacco production numbers are my calculations from the published government statistics (U.S. Bureau of the Census 1976). These numbers do not count for either exports or imports of cigarettes, nor changes in the composition of smokers, such as increases in the rate of smoking by women. Also, a large number of people still rolled their own cigarettes, but these numbers are not included in figure 6.1.

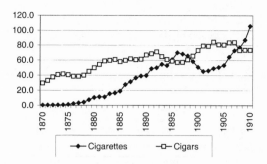

Fig. 6.2   Per capita U.S. production of cigarettes and cigars, 1870–1910
Source: U.S. Bureau of the Census (1976).

that post-1910 consumption was dramatically higher than pre-1910 levels. Second, there is a notable downswing that occurs in cigarette production between 1895 and 1905, although an upswing in cigar production compensates for this lull. This movement is likely due to the vigorous actions of social reformers who, convinced that cigarettes were either unhealthy, immoral, or both, successfully stigmatized cigarette smoking and succeeded in banning their sale in some states for a time (Kluger 1997).

Other public health reforms pushed ahead during the latter part of the century may have had significant impacts on chronic disease incidence and prevalence. Garbage was being picked up, water supplies began to be protected, and the general consciousness about the spread of disease increased. For instance, when Koch identified the bacteria responsible for tuberculosis in 1882, the annual death rate from tuberculosis was about 300 cases per 100,000 persons. By the time streptomycin (the first effective treatment) became available in the 1940s, the death rate had already fallen to below fifty cases, with about half the decline occurring before 1910. This decline illustrates dramatically the effectiveness of the public health movement.[7] (Leavitt and Numbers 1985)

In summary, although the years surrounding the turn of the century were characterized by important reforms in public health, it was still a time of rapid population movements to the big city, both from the countryside and from abroad, and it was a heyday of manufacturing, unhampered by modern pollution controls or workplace safety regulations. It was also a few years after the dawn of an extremely important new health risk: the mass-produced cigarette. Furthermore, the elderly people most at risk for chronic disease had a nutritional history which, as measured by their heights, declined across successive birth cohorts.[8] Thus, several factors were present

7. Other measures indicate the effectiveness of public health advances, such as the halving of the infant mortality rate between 1880 and 1910.

8. For example, the cohort aged sixty to sixty-five in 1890 had a better nutritional history, as measured by height, than cohorts entering the same age range in 1895, 1900, 1905, and 1910.

which could have caused the prevalence of respiratory disease to be either rising or falling at the turn of the century.

6.3 Classification of Respiratory Disease

6.3.1 The Modern Conception

Respiratory diseases are a diverse group of disorders. They are characterized by various symptoms, attributed to numerous causative factors— most poorly understood—and diagnosed with a variety of tools. It is convenient for the purpose at hand to make a distinction between upper respiratory (UR) conditions, including diseases of the nasal passages, sinuses, larynx, and pharynx, and lower respiratory (LR) conditions, which include diseases of the bronchi and the lungs. An additional useful classification is provided by the ninth version of the *International Classification of Disease* (ICD-9), which differentiates among the following major groupings:

1. Acute respiratory infections (460–69)[9]
2. Other diseases of the upper respiratory tract (470–78);
3. Pneumonia and influenza (480–87);
4. Chronic obstructive pulmonary disease and allied conditions (490–96);
5. Pneumoconiosis and other lung diseases due to external agents (500–08);
6. Other diseases of the respiratory system (510–19).

Although UR diseases are usually acute in nature and caused by bacterial or viral infection, chronic inflammation does occur. Indeed, the most commonly reported chronic condition in the National Health Interview Surveys is chronic sinusitis (sinus inflammation), with a prevalence of 13.6 percent among the general U.S. population in 1990 to 1992. Slightly less prominent is hay fever, or allergic rhinitis, which has a prevalence of 9.7 percent.[10] In addition to chronic sinusitis (473) and allergic rhinitis (477), chronic UR conditions include deviated nasal septum (470) and nasal polyps (471), as well as diseases of the nose and pharynx (472), tonsils and adenoids (474), and the larynx and trachea (476).

Upper respiratory conditions have a high degree of overlap. Oftentimes, for instance, inflammation of the nasal passages is associated with sinus inflammation. A common cause of UR inflammation is the presence of

9. In the ICD-9 classification system, the three-digit codes (indicated in parentheses) are usually further differentiated with fourth or even fifth digit classifications. For example, 493 refers to asthma, which is further differentiated as extrinsic asthma (493.0), intrinsic asthma (493.1), chronic obstructive asthma (493.2), and asthma, unspecified (493.9).

10. Prevalence rates are from Collins (1997).

allergens. Seasonal, regional, and climactic variation in allergens, as well as other organic and inorganic particles, is thought to influence the prevalence of chronic UR disease. In the late-twentieth-century United States, the regional variation in common UR conditions is readily apparent, especially in the case of chronic sinusitis. While the self-reported prevalence of chronic sinusitis is 17.5 percent in the South and 15.7 percent in the Midwest, in the Northeast it is only 9.4 percent, and in the West it is merely 8.8 percent (just over half the rate in the South). It is the West, however, that faces the highest rate of allergic rhinitis (11.7 percent), followed by the South (10.2 percent), the Northeast (8.5 percent) and the Midwest (8.2 percent). The South, therefore, has a relatively high prevalence for both sinusitis and rhinitis, while the Northeast has relatively low rates for both conditions. The West, probably because of its relatively arid climate, is prone to rhinitis but not sinusitis, while the situation is reversed in the Midwest.[11] In a recent important study, Ponikau et al. (1999) argue that the dominant cause of chronic sinusitis is not an allergic reaction at all, but an immune system response to fungus. Further study may attribute the importance of region to the presence of the fungus.

Table 6.1 below lists definitions of the most important chronic LR conditions. Goldring, James, and Anderson (1998) note that clinicians use a great variety of terms to define specific combinations of symptoms. Among the LR conditions, the most prominent are those conditions usually associated with obstruction of the airways. These include chronic bronchitis, emphysema, and asthma. Chronic obstructive pulmonary disease (COPD) is often used clinically as a nonspecific, catch-all term to describe chronic respiratory disease. Following the above authors, I will define the term COPD to include either chronic bronchitis or emphysema. A common classification is represented in the schema given in figure 6.3, which is adapted from Snider's characterization of the definitions put forward by the American Thoracic Society (1998). Diseases not allied with pulmonary obstruction include a variety of occupational lung diseases (pneumoconiosis) and other diseases, such as emphysema (510) and pleurisy (511).

The causes of lung disease are varied and not fully understood. COPD is generally believed to result from exposure of lung tissue to environmental agents, primarily tobacco smoke. According to the Surgeon General, almost 90 percent of COPD is attributable to cigarette smoking (U.S. Department of Health and Human Services 1994).[12] Asthma is typically classified as either allergic (extrinsic) or nonallergic (intrinsic). Allergic asthma

11. Prevalence rates cited here are from Collins (1997). Data come from self-reported conditions in the National Health Interview Surveys, 1990 to 1992. Rates are not adjusted for age or other factors.

12. A small number of persons with COPD have a genetically determined deficiency of the protein alpha 1-antitrypsin, a trait present in approximately 7 percent of the population (Snider 1998).

Table 6.1   **Definitions of Specific Chronic Lung Diseases**

Disease Group	ICD-9 Codes	Description
Cystic fibrosis	277.00, 277.01	Genetic disease with exocrine gland dysfunction resulting in pancreatic insufficiency, chronic progressive lung disease, and elevated sweat chloride concentration
Chronic bronchitis	490–491	Excessive tracheobronchial mucus production associated with narrowing of the bronchial airways and cough
Chronic obstructive bronchitis	491.2	Same as chronic bronchitis with involvement of smaller airways associated with airflow abnormalities
Emphysema	492	Alveolar destruction and associated airspace enlargement
Asthma	493	Reversible airway obstruction with airway inflammation and increased airways responsiveness to a variety of stimuli
Bronchiectasis	494	Destruction of bronchial wall
Allergic alveolitis	495	Immunologically induced inflammation of the lung parenchyma
Chronic airway obstruction	496	Generalized airway obstruction not classifiable as chronic bronchitis or chronic obstructive bronchitis
Other externally induced pneumoconioses	500–504, 506.4, 507.1, 507.8, 515, 516.3	Dust-, fume-, or mist-induced pneumoconioses or lung injury, nonimmunologically mediated
Sleep apnea	780.51, 780.53, 780.57	Repetitive cessation of breathing during sleep.

Source: Goldring, James, and Anderson (1998).

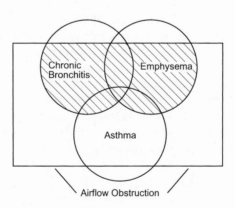

Fig. 6.3   Chronic lung diseases (COPD in shaded area)
Source: Adapted from Snider (1998).

is dominant in children, while adults have both allergic and nonallergic asthma in about equal numbers (Goldring, James, and Anderson 1998). Given that a family history of asthma is a significant risk factor, asthma may be, in part, genetically determined. In children, chronic exposure to allergens (primarily indoors) is associated with increased risk of asthma. The identified risk factors associated with adult onset of asthma are largely unknown, although occupational dust is a known cause (a condition usually classified as occupational asthma). Other occupational lung diseases, such as silicosis, asbestosis and coal-workers pneumoconiosis, are also the result of numerous environmental agents. Finally, interstitial lung diseases[13] have largely unidentified risk factors, though smoking and environmental agents are suspected causes.[14]

6.3.2   The Historical Record

A central concern in using the Union Army data, which cannot be fully resolved within the scope of this project, is whether or not the diagnoses of examining physicians in the late-nineteenth and early-twentieth centuries were valid and reliable. Physicians could visually observe UR conditions, but LR conditions would have been more challenging, although simple physical exam techniques can reveal much about the general conditions of the lung. Certainly the nineteenth-century physicians lacked a variety of modern diagnostic techniques, such as spirometry (which measures the expired volume as function of time), various tests for lung capacity, x-ray, biopsy of lung tissue, arterial blood gas measurements, and CT scanning of the chest (Snider 1998). However, patient-reported symptoms and history, which were available historically, still play a dominant role in diagnosing respiratory diseases today.

Although legitimate concerns remain about diagnostic competency and, in particular, the physicians' ability to differentiate between specific diagnoses, the historical classification of disease was not far removed from what exists today. In 1892, William Osler published what was quickly to become the most important medical text of the day. He classified both chronic and acute diseases of the UR system, including the nose, larynx, and pharynx. He also gave detailed discussions of diseases of the bronchi and lungs. Chronic bronchitis is characterized by a general inflammation of the bronchi indicated by chronic shortness of breath. Osler differentiates asthma from chronic bronchitis by the tendency of asthmatics to have severe attacks: "One of its most striking peculiarities is the bizarre and extraordinary variety of circumstances which at times induce a paroxysm"

---

13. Interstitial disease is that which occurs in the spaces between different tissues in the lung. These diseases are described generally as pulmonary fibrosis, alveolitis, and pneumonitis.

14. The preceding paragraph summarizes, again, the discussion of Goldring, James, and Anderson (1998).

(1892). Although emphysema could not have been confidently diagnosed prior to autopsy, Osler notes that the condition led to "enlargement of the lungs, due to distension of the cells and atrophy of their walls, and clinically by imperfect aeration of the blood and more or less marked dyspnoea" (1892).

The classification system used by Osler is remarkably similar in many respects to what we use today. Although autopsy allows a greater understanding of conditions than physicians could have been able to diagnose with living patients, the physicians of the day reported a wide variety of both upper- and lower-respiratory conditions that correlate closely with modern categories of respiratory diseases. The analysis that follows takes these physicians at their word. Since much more research is necessary to make confident comparisons between historical rates of respiratory disease, I will make such comparisons only in passing. The central intent here is to explore the variation in these physician-diagnosed conditions across important variables and across the period of study.

6.4 Methods

6.4.1 The Pension System and Surgeons' Certificates

The Civil War pension system began in 1862 as a means of providing financial support for soldiers disabled in battle. From this early date throughout the life of the system, applicants for assistance appeared before a board of examining physicians who conducted a detailed physical exam and forwarded their findings, noted on what was typically called a Surgeons' Certificate, to the pension board. These medical exams provide the essential data used in this study. Of the 35,570 Union Army veterans in the sample, 17,721 were examined at least once during their lives. A total of 87,271 examination records exist on these veterans, with an average of 4.9 exams (median = 4) per veteran.[15]

Changes in the pension laws fundamentally affected the number of medical exams available for analysis. For several years, the pension system was available only to people who could prove that their disability was somehow related to service in the military. This greatly limited the number of pensioners, although in practice, a wide variety of conditions, such as rheumatism or heart disease, were commonly ascribed to military service. In 1890, however, the system was changed dramatically, and any disabled veteran was eligible for coverage as long as he had served a period of at least ninety

15. The 35,570 recruits constitute 89 percent of the original random sample drawn from the Union Army regimental records. The original sample consisted of 331 randomly selected companies. To date, only 303 companies have been collected due to budgetary reasons. However, the uncollected companies come almost entirely from the Midwest, an area that was somewhat overrepresented in the original sample.

Annual Examination Rate

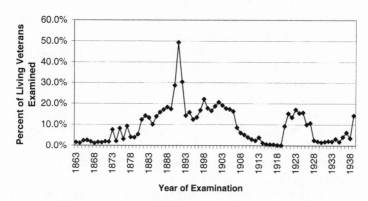

Fig. 6.4   **Annual examination rate among current and future Civil War pensioners**

days in the war. In 1904, Teddy Roosevelt issued an executive order that further expanded coverage, classifying old age as an infirmity, and Congress changed the law in 1907 making the pension system officially age-based. However, under the 1890 law, veterans who were aged sixty-five or older received a minimum pension unless they were "unusually vigorous." Thus any veteran over age sixty-two became eligible for a pension.[16]

These legal changes significantly affected the number of veterans getting a physical exam in any given year. Furthermore, as the veterans aged, they naturally acquired new conditions that made them eligible for new and increased support, which would often lead to a new examination. Figure 6.4 illustrates the annual rate of examination. The figure graphs the number of recruits examined in each year as a percentage of all veterans, who would at some point be in the system and who were known to be alive during the year indicated. The figure reveals the dramatic influx of exams following the implementation of the 1890 law. In 1891, half the veterans in the sample were examined.

Although the role of the physician was to provide a basis for granting or rejecting the claimant's petition, eligibility for the pension was not determined by the physician, but by the pension board. The physician's duty was to investigate the conditions made in the claimant's statement and to provide a systematic physical exam that was spelled out in a set of standardized instructions. The physician would typically go through the body systems one by one (usually starting with the cardiovascular system, followed by the respiratory system) and note any findings, whether positive or negative. Thus many conditions could be recorded, whether or not they were reported by the claimant, and whether or not they were pensionable.

16. See the discussion of the pension laws in Fogel (1999).

6.4.2   Disease Categories

The respiratory findings the physicians report are extensive, and the classification scheme used at the time was remarkably similar to the one we have today. The collection of this data into electronic form was designed to organize the data as much as possible without losing any of the detail present in the exams, thereby precluding future researchers from developing their own classification system. Consequently, in the data-inputting process, exam findings are entered chiefly in open-ended form. To facilitate the inputting process, the data collection team developed specially designed computer "screens," which correspond to each major body system.

This research exploits three central variables on the respiratory screen. First, a field exists for the description of any UR inflammation. Data are entered into this field essentially as written on the examination certificate. In all, there are over 18,000 unique phrases in the data that indicate the presence (or lack) of an UR inflammation, such as rhinitis, tonsilitis, or pharyngitis. Oftentimes, there are several UR comments on a given exam. Since the overwhelming majority of these inflammations are likely due to acute infections, UR inflammations are considered here only if the certificate explicitly states that the condition is chronic.

Second, specific LR conditions are also noted, although sometimes in very unspecific terms, such as "disease of the lung." There are, however, relatively frequent observations of the three main types of chronic lung diseases outlined above: emphysema, chronic bronchitis, and asthma. Tuberculosis is also present, but since tuberculosis is usually not classified with other respiratory conditions, it is not included here. Observations that are chronic in nature, but where no mention of the above specific conditions are made, are included in the "other" category. Other LR observations are considered acute unless they are specifically designated chronic by the physician.[17]

Third, as part of the examination process, physicians would often designate particular conditions as deserving of compensation. These physician ratings are an indicator of chronicity, since only chronic conditions were eligible for pension assistance. Oftentimes, the rating is the only piece of information present on a particular body system. Although the ratings some-

17. Findings assumed to be chronic include adhesion, allergy, anthracosis, atrophy, bronchiectasis, cavity, empyema, fibrosis, pleuritis, and pneumonitis. The findings assumed to be acute, unless specifically indicated to be chronic, are abscess, atelectasis, bronchitis, edema, effusion, hemoptysis, pneumonia, pneumothorax, tracheitis, and diseases of the lungs not further specified. The conditions mentioned here are actually standardizations of a wide variety of synonyms. The scheme for standardizing these synonyms was developed by Dr. Louis Nguyen, in consultation with the other physicians involved in the collection of the Surgeons' Certificates. Dr. Nguyen also recommended which findings to classify as chronic. I performed the actual coding of the data, and all mistakes are, consequently, my responsibility.

times lack specificity, they provide a valuable source of summary information on whether the physician viewed the claimant as having respiratory disease severe enough to warrant disability compensation.[18]

Other information related to the respiratory screen—such as dyspnea, respiratory sounds, cough descriptions, and indications of pulmonary dullness—may prove useful in making further diagnoses. I have confined this analysis, however, to specific diagnoses made by the examining physicians. Future research may be served by exploitation of these additional variables. Given the variable descriptions and caveats noted above, I present in the next section prevalence rates for chronic respiratory disease in six categories:

1. Chronic disease of the UR system
2. Chronic disease of the LR system
3. Chronic disease in either the UR or LR system
4. Any diagnosed or rated (DOR) respiratory disease
5. Asthma
6. COPD

These categories, therefore, represent both system-level classification of chronic illness as well as two important specific chronic diseases: asthma and COPD. The DOR category is the most general and indicates the presence of either a specifically designated chronic LR or UR condition or a physician rating. Due to the nonspecific nature of many of the exams, the DOR category is useful for measuring the prevalence of respiratory disease in general.

6.4.3   Prevalence Estimation

Strictly speaking, the estimates provided are not point prevalence rates for each disease category. Because of the irregular and sometimes infrequent examinations, the outcome to be measured is the percentage ever diagnosed. Given the chronicity of the conditions under study and the lack of effective treatment, this measure is a suitable proxy for the actual prevalence and has been used in other studies with the same data (Costa 2000). In order to minimize the underenumeration of conditions in those cases where a recent examination has not been conducted, only those individuals who have been examined in the five years prior to the prevalence date are included.

An examination of figure 6.3 reveals an obvious time period for examining the prevalence of disease in general, namely the period following the

18. Determining whether a rating was given is actually a rather involved process that requires sifting through the respiratory rating variables (p_rat*) as well as at the related diseases variables (p_rel*), which often contain indications that lung diseases are rated with another nonrespiratory condition.

rapid influx of veterans into the system after the liberalization of the law in 1890. For the next several years, a relatively high annual rate of examination exists which remains well over 15 percent through 1906. In 1907, the rate falls precipitously and examinations virtually disappear over the next decade.[19] Given the time pattern of examinations reflected in figure 6.4, I calculate prevalence at four dates: January 1 of 1895, 1900, 1905, and 1910. In each case, only those cases known to be alive[20] on that date and examined in the previous five years are included in the denominator. The decline in the examination rate from 1907 to 1909 will likely cause prevalence in 1910 to be underestimated relative to the other years.

This approach presents some potential biases. Because we must accumulate exams over a five-year period, there will be a tendency to understate prevalence because a portion of the population will have acquired respiratory conditions since their most recent exam. A potential bias in the other direction is that it may be that those applying for additional assistance are, in general, less healthy than those who do not get examined. Related to this second bias is potential variation in the health of the examined population during different time periods. As noted earlier there was a rush of examinees in 1890 and 1891, which might imply a healthier group of people got examined in those years. But many of these new examinees were severely ill people who were denied pension assistance prior to 1890 because their ailments could not be attributed to the war.

It is not clear, therefore, what the net effect of the 1890 liberalization would have been in terms of the health of a typical examinee. Increases in prevalence between 1900 and 1910 are even harder to attribute to changes in law. In fact, by the same reasoning assumed above, we would expect that as the de facto pension awards for age became more common, people who were eligible for pension due to age would be more likely to apply, thus successive cohorts of examinees would, on average, be increasingly healthier. This trend would cause disease rates to decline.

Finally, it is important to note that all the estimates presented here are for the population that lived long enough to be eligible for the pension after the liberalization of the pension system in 1890. Thus the prevalence rates presented in the next section are only valid, generally, for those fifty and older. There may be important features of the epidemiology of respiratory disease that would be uncovered by examining younger individuals, but the data at hand do not lend themselves to such an analysis.

19. On 6 February 1907 Congress passed the Service and Age Pension Act which introduced a new age-based system, although it is not clear if this was the reason why physical exams disappeared. In 1917, 1918, and 1920 further amendments were made to the laws (Sanders 2000). The administrative policies that may have been associated with these acts, including a reappearance of regular exams following 1920 (although by this time, all Civil War veterans qualified for age-based assistance) have not been investigated.

20. This is either from a death date recorded in the pension files (the majority of cases) or from the existence of a subsequent exam.

6.5   Results

This section presents an array of results concerning the distribution of respiratory disease in the population over the fifteen-year period under study. In order to simplify the presentation, confidence intervals are not reported for the descriptive statistics. As a general rule, the differences between years are statistically significant, while the differences across categories are not. Significance levels are reported for the probit regression results that follow the discussion of the descriptive statistics.

6.5.1   Age and Date

Table 6.2 below presents age breakdowns for each of the nonexclusive disease categories noted above. Sample sizes for each cell are given in the lower right corner of the table.[21] Note that changes from 1895 to 1910 in the age-specific rates can be observed by following the same age group horizontally across the columns. Within-cohort changes over time are seen by tracking the cohort diagonally in a southeasterly direction. The prevalence of disease among the oldest age groups, however, should be interpreted cautiously, given the small sample sizes in those cohorts.

Not surprisingly, the within-cohort prevalence increases for almost all cohorts and almost all categories.[22] More remarkable, however, is that age-specific disease rates are rising significantly over time for all categories. The biggest jump is generally between 1895 and 1900, but increases continue through 1910. Across the board categories of LR and UR disease, the prevalence rates double or triple in the period across age groups. Regarding specific conditions, asthma also rises significantly between 1900 and 1910 (except for the seventy-five to seventy-nine and eighty to eighty-four groups), while COPD increases are generally more modest, except for the sharp jump among the seventy-five- to seventy-nine-year-olds.

Table 6.2 also reveals important differences between the experiences of successive cohorts. If we look at the summary measure of all chronic respiratory conditions (which include physician ratings of disease that is not specifically identified as occurring in either the UR or LR system), we see that in 1895 the younger cohorts start out with significantly higher prevalence than older cohorts. This cross-sectional distribution may be due to two factors, both of which merit considerable further research. First, the overall force of mortality was high, which may have led to a declining preva-

21. Also, among those who were forty-five to forty-nine in 1895, most were in the forty-eight to forty-nine age group, since few people in the forty-five to forty-seven group were young enough to have served in the military.
22. The cohort that is age seventy to seventy-four in 1900 experiences a modest decline in prevalence between 1900 and 1905 for both LR and UR conditions as well as for asthma. The prevalence increases, however, for the category of COPD and the broad category of physician-rated respiratory disease.

Table 6.2   **Physician-Diagnosed Chronic Respiratory Conditions, by Age (percent of living pensioners ever diagnosed)**

Age	1895	1900	1905	1910
		Lower respiratory		
45–49	5.7			
50–54	6.4	8.1		
55–59	6.0	9.0	9.5	
60–64	6.0	9.3	10.7	11.3
65–69	5.4	7.9	10.6	12.2
70–74	5.4	8.8	11.6	14.3
75–79		7.1	7.7	18.1
80–84			10.9	4.2
		Upper respiratory		
45–49	8.0			
50–54	7.6	13.9		
55–59	6.4	12.6	16.3	
60–64	6.1	10.3	14.1	20.3
65–69	7.2	9.2	13.8	14.1
70–74	6.5	11.1	12.1	14.6
75–79		7.1	10.9	13.0
80–84			9.4	15.5
		Upper or lower		
45–49	12.6			
50–54	12.9	20.0		
55–59	11.7	19.4	23.6	
60–64	11.4	17.8	22.3	27.9
65–69	12.0	15.7	21.6	23.1
70–74	10.9	18.6	21.6	25.1
75–79		13.5	17.3	28.8
80–84			17.2	18.3
		Diagnosed or rated		
45–49	30.5			
50–54	30.4	40.7		
55–59	26.7	41.2	44.7	
60–64	25.1	37.8	45.1	47.4
65–69	24.9	34.9	42.7	46.2
70–74	21.4	37.6	41.5	46.7
75–79		34.0	40.1	49.2
80–84			34.4	45.1
		Asthma		
45–49	2.4			
50–54	2.4	3.9		
55–59	2.3	3.6	4.2	
60–64	2.3	3.8	4.2	5.0
65–69	2.7	2.5	4.5	4.7
70–74	3.6	4.1	4.9	6.6
75–79		2.8	3.2	2.8
80–84			6.3	0.0

Table 6.2 (continued)

Age	1895	1900	1905	1910
	Chronic Obstructive Pulmonary Disorder			
45–49	1.4			
50–54	1.7	2.4		
55–59	1.8	2.6	2.0	
60–64	1.8	3.4	3.0	2.3
65–69	1.7	3.3	3.6	4.2
70–74	1.7	2.9	3.6	4.1
75–79		2.8	4.0	8.5
80–84			2.5	1.4
	Sample size			
45–49	1,821			
50–54	4,239	1,166		
55–59	2,625	2,531	990	
60–64	1,761	1,497	2,228	666
65–69	1,031	958	1,298	1,319
70–74	477	441	708	610
75–79		141	284	177
80–84			64	71

Notes: Percentages are calculated only for those cases where the veteran was examined in the five years prior to the date indicated. See text for definitions of disease categories. All years represent the percentage as of 1 January.

lence across age groups at a point in time. Second, recent research referred to earlier on the antebellum patterns in adult heights suggests that these younger cohorts were shorter than the older groups, indicating a harsher nutritional and disease history. Thus, the later occurrence of disease may be linked to the early nutritional experience of the recruits.

Even though the younger groups have higher rates of disease in 1895, it is the older groups who see the sharpest increase in disease rates over the next fifteen-year period, and by 1910 the age profile has flattened considerably. It is particularly notable that over this time period there is a sharp divergence between UR and LR conditions with respect to the age pattern. Whereas an inverse relationship between age and prevalence exists for UR conditions in 1910, there is a positive association between age and the prevalence of LR conditions. Further analysis may attribute this trend to other influences, but it may be the case that older cohorts are starting to see the effects of increased long-term exposure to environmental agents, such as cigarette smoke and industrial pollutants.[23]

23. The glaring exception to the trend in LR disease is the sharp decline in prevalence for the oldest group shown in table 6.2, although the small sample size at these old ages makes it hard to interpret this outcome.

6.5.2   Occupation

The most obvious potential link between occupation and respiratory disease is through the presence of pollutants and fine particulates associated with particular industries. Important occupation-specific diseases include pneumoconiosis (black lung), which strikes coal workers, and silicosis, which strikes workers who are exposed to concentrations of silica dust, such as stone cutters. In modern times more than 200 causative agents have been associated with occupational asthma. These agents include a variety of diverse sets of materials coming from plants and animals, grains, metals, chemicals, and drugs (Goldring, James, and Anderson 1998). In the nineteenth century we might posit an even greater role for industrial-based diseases, given the general lack of pollution control and worker protection that existed at the time.

Occupation is also associated with a number of other factors that may be associated with respiratory health. Low wages in some occupations may lead to poor nutrition and residency in crowded environments where exposure to infectious disease is more likely, as is exposure to pollution. Differences in the physical demands of labor across occupations may also play a role. Additionally, some have recently argued that relative position in the social hierarchy is associated with health.[24] Thus, individuals in lower-status occupations would be under more stress and, consequently, more prone to disease. Finally, in modern times, occupation is often a proxy for knowledge of health and access to medical care, although it is not clear that knowledge of health or health care were effective enough to have made a significant impact upon disease in the nineteenth century at the individual level.

The occupation of Union Army veterans is reported at several points during the recruit's lifetime. The recruit reported his occupation as part of the military enlistment record, and those who were linked to the 1850 and 1860 censuses may also have an occupation listed, if they were old enough to be employed at the time. Occupation was also reported as the recruit applied for a pension, either in the application or on the official certificate of the examining physician. Finally, occupation in later life is found on the census manuscripts for those recruits who were successfully linked to the 1900 and 1910 censuses. Although several reports of occupation are found in the data, a central weakness is that occupational information is seldom present between the end of the Civil War and the time when the recruit entered the pension system—usually several decades later.

Occupational categories are defined as follows. First, individuals are classified as high-risk if they ever report an occupation or industry where persistent exposure to smoke, dust, or fumes is likely. This includes occupa-

---

24. See Wilkinson (1996), for example.

tions such as miners, masons, smiths, painters and finishers, printers, tenders of fires and furnaces, and workers at foundries and mills. Managers and clerks who worked in these industries are also reported at high-risk. General factory work is not reported as high-risk. Other occupational classifications are determined by either the occupation on the Surgeon's Certificate or the most recently reported occupation prior to the year under investigation. For those who are retired, their most recent known occupation is used. Additional occupational categories include farmers (including farm laborers); white-collar occupations, which include all types of professionals, proprietors, clerks, and salesmen; and skilled and unskilled labor.[25]

Table 6.3 reports prevalence of respiratory conditions according to the occupational classifications previously defined. In general, the occupational differences are not large. High risk occupations seem to have the greatest effect, as we would expect, on LR conditions, including COPD and asthma, to a lesser extent. Farmers have roughly equivalent rates with the high risk categories, while skilled workers have notably lower prevalence. White-collar and unskilled labor generally fall in the middle.

Patterns found in the descriptive statistics are suggestive of the importance of occupation, but they are not conclusive due to the limited scope of this analysis. The difference in prevalence between the high-risk group and skilled laborers gives some justification for the classification scheme used and shows the impact of occupation more than any other pattern in the data. Unskilled labor is also high, but this group has such a high percentage of workers where so little is known about the nature of their work that it is not meaningful to make direct comparisons to other groups. Farmers also have high rates of both LR and UR conditions. Of course farmers are exposed to a variety of organic materials that can lead to farmer's lung and other respiratory conditions, such as occupational asthma.[26] An additional explanation for the higher rate among farmers is that all-cause mortality was lower for farmers than for other groups. An unresolved puzzle is the high rate of respiratory illness amongst the white-collar group. Possibly, it is long periods of working indoors or the tendency to work in smoky and congested central cities that raises the prevalence among this group.

The classification scheme used in this analysis is, by necessity, crude and preliminary. It should be noted that thousands of individual occupational titles exist in the data, and collapsing these to five categories is sure to sacrifice important details. Further explorations of occupational health generally, and respiratory health specifically, are certainly warranted. The lack of

25. Any type of trade or craft, such as carpentry or carriage making, was classified as skilled labor, as were those who reported the manufacture of specific items. Unskilled laborers were those who reported themselves as "laborer," "worker," or "helper" in any industry (other than those classified as high-risk).

26. Operators of threshing machines and grain elevators were classified as high-risk, although the harvesting and storing of grain would be a common activity for most farmers.

Table 6.3 **Physician-Diagnosed Chronic Respiratory Conditions, by Occupation (percent of living pensioners ever diagnosed)**

Occupation	1895	1900	1905	1910
Lower respiratory				
Farmer	6.1	9.0	11.5	13.8
High-risk	7.0	8.7	10.1	12.8
White-collar	6.3	8.3	9.1	12.4
Skilled	4.7	7.8	8.5	8.3
Unskilled	5.9	8.7	9.8	11.9
Upper respiratory				
Farmer	7.7	12.2	14.4	16.8
High-risk	6.5	12.0	13.6	15.4
White-collar	7.4	13.2	14.7	15.5
Skilled	5.9	10.4	12.3	13.3
Unskilled	6.1	9.2	13.7	14.2
Upper or lower				
Farmer	12.8	19.3	23.3	26.6
High-risk	12.6	18.6	21.5	25.2
White-collar	12.2	19.0	20.3	23.8
Skilled	10.0	16.3	19.4	19.4
Unskilled	11.3	16.5	21.9	24.0
Diagnosed or rated				
Farmer	30.5	41.4	46.0	48.2
High-risk	26.2	36.8	42.1	46.6
White-collar	28.1	38.2	41.9	45.5
Skilled	22.5	35.0	38.9	43.2
Unskilled	24.4	36.0	43.1	45.3
Asthma				
Farmer	2.3	3.4	4.5	5.0
High-risk	3.0	3.6	4.7	5.4
White-collar	2.0	2.8	4.0	5.6
Skilled	2.5	3.2	3.2	2.5
Unskilled	2.9	4.6	4.5	5.6
Chronic Obstructive Pulmonary Disorder				
Farmer	1.6	2.8	3.4	4.6
High-risk	2.0	3.6	3.0	5.2
White-collar	2.2	2.4	2.9	4.0
Skilled	1.7	3.4	2.7	1.9
Unskilled	1.3	2.5	2.7	2.1
Sample size				
Farmer	6,626	3,650	2,561	1,315
High-risk	1,181	769	843	461
White-collar	907	532	627	323
Skilled	1,498	805	661	324
Unskilled	1,704	967	863	430

Notes: Percentages are calculated only for those cases where the veteran was examined in the five years prior to the date indicated. See text for definitions of disease categories. All years represent the percentage as of 1 January. The high-risk category includes workers of any type who have a history of employment in industries at risk for respiratory disease (see text). White-collar workers include professionals, proprietors, clerical workers, and salespersons. A small number of cases with no known occupational history are excluded.

complete occupational histories is also a potential source of bias, since no controls for time spent in specific occupations are undertaken here. Of particular concern is that some individuals may change occupations because of their health, which would cause overestimates of the prevalence rates in the occupations that unhealthy people transitioned to.

6.5.3   Region and Population

As is the case with other variables, such as occupation, place of residence is typically not known for the decades between the war and the initial pension application. However, when the veterans apply for a pension, their residency is known with great detail (street addresses, in many instances) and with a high rate of completion. As before, the convention is followed of assigning the last known place of residence if the residence is not given in the examination record. In all cases, cities are categorized using the population in 1900.

As noted earlier, the prevalence of UR conditions varies significantly by region in the modern United States. Regional variation for UR conditions is also apparent among the Union Army veterans. Table 6.4 reveals that in 1910 the rate of UR disease is about 10 percent in the New England and Mid-Atlantic regions, 16 to 18 percent in the North Central regions, 18.3 percent in the South and border states, and 20.3 percent in the West. Interestingly, these differences are much less pronounced in earlier years of the period, although the pattern exists in 1895 for respiratory conditions in general. Also notable is that LR conditions follow the same pattern (though the range is much smaller), with the striking exception of a dramatically low rate of LR disease in the South and border states.

Given the rapid shift of the nineteenth century population to the nation's large cities, which are widely viewed as teeming with filth and disease, we might expect that the large cities would be characterized by high rates of respiratory illness. The patterns present in table 6.5 reveal that no direct relationship between population and the prevalence of respiratory disease exists. On the contrary, the relationship is not monotonic at all. The largest cities and smaller cities between 25,000 and 99,000 have the lowest rates, while cities between 100,000 and 500,000 and locales under 25,000 have the highest rates of illness.

Numerous features of urbanization at the turn of the century need to be explored to make sense of these results. Here I make just brief mention of factors that may affect the variation in respiratory health across regions and population. First, public health programs that began in the late-nineteenth century had little impact outside of the cities, which may explain part of the high rates for the rural areas. Preston and Haines (1991, 91), for example, show that the child mortality rate in 1900 was lower in the 10 largest cities than it was in other cities 25,000 and over. However, Preston and Haines also note that most of the advances in public health were in the area of water and sewage, not air quality. Third, this analysis lumps together all locales under

Table 6.4   **Physician-Diagnosed Chronic Respiratory Conditions, by Region**
(percent of living pensioners ever diagnosed)

Region	1895	1900	1905	1910
Lower respiratory				
New England	5.3	6.7	7.2	10.2
Mid-Atlantic	4.8	7.5	10.2	10.7
East North Central	6.4	9.3	11.0	13.7
West North Central	7.1	9.9	10.0	13.2
South/border state	3.9	6.8	9.4	5.4
West	6.7	9.6	10.6	15.8
Upper respiratory				
New England	6.0	7.9	9.3	10.2
Mid-Atlantic	6.1	9.1	10.9	10.3
East North Central	7.5	12.8	15.5	16.5
West North Central	7.7	12.9	14.9	18.1
South/border state	8.2	13.1	16.6	18.3
West	5.6	11.3	13.3	20.3
Upper or lower respiratory				
New England	10.7	13.3	15.6	19.1
Mid-Atlantic	10.5	15.3	19.1	19.3
East North Central	12.8	19.9	23.7	26.2
West North Central	13.6	20.6	22.4	27.9
South/border state	11.9	18.2	24.1	22.0
West	10.7	18.7	21.5	29.7
Diagnosed or rated				
New England	20.1	25.1	31.5	38.2
Mid-Atlantic	23.2	35.0	38.3	40.3
East North Central	31.4	42.5	47.2	49.5
West North Central	29.0	39.8	45.2	50.4
South/border state	31.3	43.6	49.9	45.2
West	23.0	36.7	37.6	43.0
Asthma				
New England	2.1	3.0	3.3	4.5
Mid-Atlantic	2.2	3.6	5.3	5.6
East North Central	2.7	3.7	4.5	5.0
West North Central	2.4	3.5	3.7	4.8
South/border state	1.5	3.0	3.0	2.2
West	2.5	3.2	3.3	3.8
Chronic Obstructive Pulmonary Disorder				
New England	1.2	2.7	2.4	3.2
Mid-Atlantic	1.1	2.6	2.5	2.4
East North Central	2.2	3.5	3.6	5.1
West North Central	1.7	2.6	2.5	3.2
South/border state	1.1	1.9	2.8	1.1
West	1.8	1.3	2.1	5.1

Table 6.4   (continued)

Region	1895	1900	1905	1910
		Sample size		
New England	768	406	333	157
Mid-Atlantic	2,493	1,403	1,141	534
East North Central	4,548	2,638	2,194	1,235
West North Central	2,593	1,377	1,085	524
South/border state	852	473	361	186
West	447	311	330	158

Notes: Percentages are calculated only for those cases where the veteran was examined in the five years prior to the date indicated. See text for definitions of disease categories. All years represent the percentage as of 1 January.

25,000 persons, although there is considerable heterogeneity within this group that needs to be further explored. Fourth, it is mostly UR conditions that have low prevalence in the great cities, with only relatively modest differences in LR conditions across city size. Fifth, the fact that the heavily industrial regions of New England and the Mid-Atlantic had much lower rates of UR disease would have reinforced the lack of UR conditions in the big cities. Sixth, the great cities of the East—New York, Boston, and Philadelphia—burned a much higher percentage of cleaner, anthracite coal and are believed to have much better air quality than many smaller industrial cities further west (Stradling 1999). Finally, and probably most importantly, the high all-cause mortality rates in cities may have suppressed prevalence rates. It is also conceivable that respiratory disease survival was shorter in the cities, thus driving prevalence downward relative to the rural areas.[27]

6.5.4   Probit Regression Results

This section further explores demographic patterns in chronic respiratory disease by simultaneously controlling for the variables outlined above in a regression context. Probit equations will be estimated, one for each of the four prevalence dates under examination: 1895, 1900, 1905, and 1910. It should be emphasized that this analysis is exploratory and not designed to confirm the causality of any factors involved. The occurrence of disease is a function of a variety of processes over the life cycle, while the regression equations account only for the variation in contemporaneous variables at a point in time. This exploratory analysis, however, is useful in that it allows us to gauge the relative importance of different factors and identify potentially important variables for future research.

Table 6.6 contains regression results from twelve probit regressions, while table 6.7 gives the relative frequency of the explanatory variables. Each of

27. Evidence that survival with respiratory disease is shorter in large cities is found in Costa (2003).

Table 6.5   Physician-Diagnosed Chronic Respiratory Conditions, by Population (percent of living pensioners ever diagnosed)

City Population (1900)	1895	1900	1905	1910
Lower respiratory				
500,000+	4.1	6.9	8.1	11.0
100–499,000	5.0	8.0	8.1	10.3
25–99,000	4.9	6.6	7.1	7.0
0–24,000 (nonfarmer)	6.2	8.7	10.0	12.6
0–24,000 (farmer)	6.3	9.2	11.8	13.9
Upper respiratory				
500,000+	2.2	5.2	9.1	7.7
100–499,000	7.3	12.0	14.4	15.1
25–99,000	6.0	9.3	12.3	17.1
0–24,000 (nonfarmer)	6.8	11.5	13.9	14.9
0–24,000 (farmer)	7.7	12.4	14.6	16.9
Upper or lower respiratory				
500,000+	6.1	11.3	15.7	16.5
100–499,000	12.2	18.0	20.4	22.6
25–99,000	10.4	14.5	16.8	19.8
0–24,000 (nonfarmer)	12.0	18.2	21.9	24.8
0–24,000 (farmer)	13.0	19.7	23.6	26.8
Diagnosed or rated				
500,000+	14.3	28.2	28.3	29.7
100–499,000	30.3	41.3	46.3	45.2
25–99,000	23.2	33.4	34.2	39.6
0–24,000 (nonfarmer)	26.1	37.1	43.3	47.8
0–24,000 (farmer)	30.8	41.8	46.4	48.5
Asthma				
500,000+	1.5	3.2	4.5	4.4
100–499,000	2.9	4.3	5.6	6.8
25–99,000	1.8	2.7	3.4	2.1
0–24,000 (nonfarmer)	2.6	3.7	4.1	5.0
0–24,000 (farmer)	2.4	3.5	4.6	5.2
Chronic Obstructive Pulmonary Disorder				
500,000+	1.5	3.2	2.5	2.2
100–499,000	1.4	3.0	1.1	2.1
25–99,000	1.5	2.7	0.9	2.1
0–24,000 (nonfarmer)	1.8	2.9	3.2	3.8
0–24,000 (farmer)	1.7	2.9	3.4	4.7
Sample size				
500,000+	413	248	198	91
100–499,000	558	300	270	146
25–99,000	715	407	351	187
1–24,000 (nonfarmer)	3,917	2,332	2,281	1,165
0–24,000 (farmer)	6,158	3,413	2,442	1,258

Notes: Percentages are calculated only for those cases where the veteran was examined in the five years prior to the date indicated. See text for definitions of disease categories. All years represent the percentage as of 1 January. The nonfarmer designation includes a small number of cases where occupational category is unknown. Cities are categorized based on their population in 1900.

Table 6.6   **Sample Characteristics, by Year (percent)**

	1895	1900	1905	1910
Age				
45–49	15.2			
50–54	35.5	17.3		
55–59	22.0	37.6	17.8	
60–64	14.7	22.2	40.0	23.3
65–69	8.6	14.2	23.3	46.2
70–74	4.0	6.5	12.7	21.3
75–79	100.0	2.1	5.1	6.2
80–84		100.0	1.1	2.5
85–89			100.0	0.5
				100.0
City population				
500,000+	3.5	3.7	3.6	3.2
100–499,000	4.7	4.5	4.8	5.1
25–100,000	6.0	6.0	6.3	6.5
0–24,000	84.3	85.3	84.8	84.8
Unknown	1.6	0.5	0.5	0.4
	100.0	100.0	100.0	100.0
Region				
New England	6.4	6.0	6.0	5.5
Mid-Atlantic	20.9	20.8	20.5	18.7
East North Central	38.0	39.2	39.4	43.2
West North Central	21.7	20.4	19.5	18.3
South/border state	7.1	7.0	6.5	6.5
West	3.7	4.6	5.9	5.5
Foreign/unknown	2.1	1.9	2.3	2.2
	100.0	100.0	100.0	100.0
Occupation				
Farmer	55.4	54.2	46.0	46.0
High-risk	9.9	11.4	15.1	16.1
White-collar	7.6	7.9	11.3	11.3
Artisans	12.5	12.0	11.9	11.3
Laborers	14.3	14.4	15.5	15.0
Unknown	0.3	0.2	0.3	0.2
	100.0	100.0	100.0	100.0
Wartime disease				
Tuberculosis	1.7	1.9	1.9	1.8
Pneumonia	4.4	4.3	4.7	4.6
Other respiratory	6.7	7.1	6.9	7.2
Measles	4.9	5.2	5.9	6.6
Typhoid	6.0	6.1	6.4	7.3
Malaria	3.6	3.8	3.6	4.1
Small Pox	1.2	1.3	1.3	1.4
Scurvy	1.8	2.0	1.8	2.1
Diarrhea	8.9	9.6	9.5	9.6
Fever	15.7	16.3	16.4	18.0
Enlistment height				
differential (inches)	0.17	0.17	0.18	0.27

Notes: Sample includes only cases where the veteran was examined in the five years prior to the date indicated. Height is measured as the deviation from age-specific averages at enlistment. Cities are categorized based on their populations in 1900. Individuals often have more than one wartime disease. The standard deviation of height is 2.50 inches.

the four years is investigated for three general categories: any diagnosed LR condition; any diagnosed UR condition; and any DOR condition. These are the same categories as used above, and the same definitions apply to both the dependent and independent variables. Regression coefficients are represented as changes in the estimated probability of disease, which occurs from changing the given explanatory variable from zero to one while holding all other variables constant at their mean values. Asterisks represent levels of statistical significance (see table 6.7 notes) based on robust, heteroskedasticity-consistent standard errors.

In addition to the variables previously discussed, I have included data on health-related variables from the veterans' early life and war time experience. From the medical records kept during the war, it is possible to identify the occurrence of important infectious diseases that the recruits had during their military service. Of primary importance are diseases affecting the respiratory system. These are tuberculosis, pneumonia, and other lung diseases, which include any illness of the lungs or bronchi (exclusive of tuberculosis and pneumonia). Measles is another infectious disease that can sometimes have serious respiratory consequences. Costa (2000) cites evidence that measles leads to pneumonia, bronchilar obstruction, distension of airways, and thickening of the peribronchial walls. Among soldiers in the Civil War, others have found that measles was often followed by chronic bronchitis, pneumonia, pleurisy, chronic diarrhea, and general debility (Cliff, Haggett, and Smallman-Raynor 1994, 105). Other common infectious diseases in the military records are typhoid, malaria, and small pox. Diarrhea and scurvy can also be indicators of nutritional deficiencies. Finally, any mention of fever that is exclusive of the above diseases is also included as a separate category.[28]

The final variable is the recruit's height at enlistment. This height is measured as the deviation from the age-specific mean height, since many recruits enlisted at young ages and grew several inches during the war. Height has been used widely as a measure that summarizes the health and nutritional history of an individual.

Among DOR conditions, a relatively strong age-pattern exists in all four years, whereby age is inversely related to the prevalence of disease, as expected. This same pattern was found in the descriptive statistics. The earlier time periods show a stronger relationship than later years, but the pattern persists. It would be interesting to know the composition of UR and LR conditions among the physician-rated conditions that are not further specified, since the age patterns prevalent in modern data show varying age profiles. In the early 1990s, the prevalence of allergic rhinitis peaks in early adulthood (11.7 percent among males aged eighteen to forty-four) and de-

---

28. These disease classifications are a modification and extension of those developed by Chulhee Lee.

Table 6.7   Marginal Effects for Probits

	Any Lower Respiratory Condition				Any Upper Respiratory Condition				Any Diagnosed or Rated Condition			
	1895	1900	1905	1910	1895	1900	1905	1910	1895	1900	1905	1910
Age												
45–49	−.004				.015*				0.29**			
50–54	.001	−.015			.010	.033**			.026**	.018		
55–59		−.006	−.013			.019*	0.21			.024	.016	
60–64	.000	−.002	−.002	−.030*	−.001		−.001	.057***	−.015		.021	.001
65–69	−.005	−.011	.010	−.023	.012	−.011	−.017	−.007	−.014	−.026	−.010	−.012
70–74	−.001	−.007	−.032*		.006	.005	−.031		−.043	−.006	−.031	
75–79		−.011	.010	.025		−.034	−.039	−.024		−.026	−.083	.008
80–84				−.095**				.007				−.036
85–89				.016				−.005				−.121
City population												
500,000+	−.011	−.009	−.016	.000	−.046***	−.061***	−.041	−.065	−.120***	−.098***	−.137***	−.159***
100–499,000	−.010	−.014	−.020	−.030	.002	−.008	−.002	−.013	.025	.011	.024	−.030
25–100,000	−.009	−.017	−.030*	−.053**	−.009	−.025	−.018	.023	−.039**	−.051	−.091***	−.067*
0–24,000												
Unknown	−.018	−.008	−.055		−.011	−.033	−.017		−.101***	−.117	−.159*	
Region												
New England												
Mid-Atlantic	.005	−.011	−.031*	.005	−.005	−.024	−.029	−.014	−.047***	−.118***	−.081**	−.032
East North Central	.015**	.014	.003	.024	.005	.029**	.041***	.056***	.053**	.045***	.070***	.069
West North Central	.020***	.022	−.010	.015	.007	.030**	.037**	.079***	.024*	.017	.046**	.080**
South/border state	−.012	−.013	−.017	−.061**	.015	.036*	.055	.084**	.064***	.051*	.098***	.042**
West	.016	.019	.001	.063	−.013	.011	.017	.099***	−.035	−.012	−.029	.009
Unknown	.050**	−.005	.065**	.132**	−.014	−.025	.014	.058	.061*	.042	.096*	.119*

Table 6.7   (continued)

	Any Lower Respiratory Condition				Any Upper Respiratory Condition				Any Diagnosed or Rated Condition			
	1895	1900	1905	1910	1895	1900	1905	1910	1895	1900	1905	1910
Occupation												
Farmer												
High-risk	.017**	.006	−.006	.001	−.001	.016	.005	.000	−.011	−.014	−.007	.011
White-collar	.012	−.001	−.012	.004	.010	.030*	.012	−.009	.018	.006	−.008	.014
Artisans	−.007	−.001	−.019	−.042**	−.006	.005	−.007	−.021	−.041***	−.021	−.034	−.014
Laborers	.008	.010	−.010	−.004	−.006	−.013	.002	−.009	−.026**	−.020	.004	.013
Unknown	.047	.339	.090	.334	−.002		−.069		−.014	−.043	−.078	.246
Wartime disease												
Tuberculosis	.045**	.115***	.141***	.160**	.021	.076*	.052	−.064	.168***	.226***	.177***	.207**
Pneumonia	.076***	.110***	.148***	.119***	.022*	.041*	−.003	.007	.165***	.168***	.135***	.164***
Other respiratory	.040**	.064**	.115***	.061	.015	.117**	.068	.003	.108***	.228***	.146**	.062
Measles	.030***	.025*	.030*	.044*	.057***	.051**	.051***	.080***	.144***	.158***	.128***	.198***
Typhoid	.003	−.002	.006	−.018	.007	.016	−.010	.017	.026	.047*	.033	.025
Malaria	−.001	.034*	−.011	.008	−.001	.030	.036	−.007	−.020	−.003	−.015	.007
Small Pox	.002	.009	.015	.047	.023	.012	.068	.135**	.002	−.013	.065	.124
Scurvy	−0.21	−.004	−.014	−.063	.019	−.034	.015	.049	.053*	.029	.095*	.013
Diarrhea	.043**	.040	.007	.062	.026	−.019	.039	.112*	.108***	−.006	.047	.149*
Fever	.005	.008	−.002	.000	.005	.032**	.039***	.033*	.013	.043**	.027	.044*
Enlistment height (inches)	−.001	−.001	−.003*	−.006**	.001	.000	−.001	−.001	.000	.000	−.003	−.008**
Dependent variable mean	.060	.088	.104	.127	.071	.116	.139	.156	.280	.390	.436	.468
Sample size	11,877	6,693	5,553	2,839	11,877	6,693	5,553	2,839	11,877	6,693	5,553	2,839
Pseudo-R^2	.042	.039	.040	.059	.018	.024	.021	.033	.041	.031	.029	.037

Notes: The marginal effects are calculated as the change in probability resulting from a discrete change in the dummy variable from 0 to 1, holding all other variables constant at their sample means. *P*-values are based on robust standard errors.

***$P < .01$.

**$P < .05$.

clines thereafter (6.6 percent at age seventy-five and older). Sinusitis, on the other hand, peaks in the forty-five to sixty-four age group and then declines. LR conditions rise much more sharply with age, but COPD prevalence falls in the seventy-five plus age group, whereas asthma stays relatively flat across age groups (Collins 1997). What we see with the UR and LR categories is broadly consistent with the modern age-patterns, particularly the sharp decline in LR conditions in the latter ages in 1905 and 1910, and the generally negative relationship between age and UR disease prevalence.

Among the other covariates estimated, region is again the most pronounced, and the regional patterns highlighted earlier remain prominent when controlling for other factors. Relative to the Mid-Atlantic and Western states, the New England region has sharply lower prevalence, as measured with DOR, while the North Central and Southern regions have much higher prevalence. It is apparent that much of the regional variation is due to UR conditions. There is some variation in LR conditions, however. In 1895, LR condition prevalence is significantly higher in the North Central regions, though the magnitude of the differences are not large. The final region on table 6.7, which includes veterans living in foreign countries or cases where the residence is not available from the surgeons' certificates, has notably higher rates of respiratory disease, especially in the latter periods, although no obvious explanation exists for this occurrence.

Table 6.7 reiterates the patterns shown in the descriptive statistics for population. For DOR conditions, rural locations (the omitted group) have higher rates of illness than do either small cities or large cities. The only group comparable to the rural areas is the mid-size cities of 100,000 to 499,000. Again, the largest effects seem to be in terms of UR conditions. If we look only at cities, the prevalence of LR conditions rises with city size across all years.

The wartime disease variables, particularly diseases affecting the respiratory system, prove to be strong predictors of respiratory disease in later life, particularly LR conditions. As we might expect, tuberculosis, pneumonia, other lung conditions, and measles have very large and statistically significant positive impacts on the probability of having LR conditions (recall that tuberculosis is not included as a LR condition in this analysis). Indeed, these wartime conditions essentially double the probability of having LR disease diagnosed later in life. Interestingly, the wartime diseases have a much smaller and generally statistically insignificant impact on UR conditions (pneumonia has essentially no effect). The exception is measles, which has a powerful impact on both LR and UR disease. Other infectious diseases generally increase the odds of both LR and UR conditions, although often not at significant levels. In sum, the importance of infectious disease as a predictor of respiratory disease in later life is striking not only in the magnitude of their effects but also because we have the early life health history for only a narrow interval of time—the years they served in the war.

Furthermore, many of the conditions reported (such as other respiratory disease, diarrhea and fever) may have been relatively minor viruses that we would not expect to have long-term consequences, making their effects all the more surprising.

One hypothesis for why the disease prevalence rates may have been increasing with successive cohorts is long-term effects of childhood nutrition. The height variable is supposed to proxy for both childhood nutrition and health. Height does have a negative effect on LR disease, but this is only significant in later years. However, a 2–standard deviation increase in height would lower the probability of LR disease by 3 percentage points in 1910. This is nontrivial, given that the mean LR prevalence in that year was only 12.7 percent. Enlistment height has essentially no effect on UR disease.

Finally, all the covariates discussed in table 6.7 must be interpreted in light of the fact that data are available only for those who survived until at least 1895. Since we have little data on either the Union Army cohort prior to 1890, and no data on subsequent cohorts, the analysis can say nothing about the correlates of disease at younger ages.

6.6 Conclusions

This research explores demographic patterns associated with different categories of chronic respiratory disease for the period 1895 to 1910. A central finding is that the age-specific prevalence of respiratory disease (as measured by the percent of the sample ever diagnosed) among the veterans of the Civil War increased sharply between 1895 and 1910. This trend holds true both for UR and LR conditions and for the specific conditions of asthma and COPD. The sharpest period of increase was between 1895 and 1900, but steady increases occurred after 1900 as well. For instance, the prevalence of the most general category, DOR, increased over the 1900 to 1910 interval from 37.8 percent to 47.4 percent among the sixty- to sixty-four-year-old group, from 34.9 percent to 46.2 percent for those sixty-five to sixty-nine, from 37.6 percent to 46.7 percent for those seventy to seventy-four, and from 34.0 percent to 49.2 percent for the seventy-five- to seventy-nine-year-olds.

Earlier I identified four factors that suggest increasing prevalence of respiratory disease (in particular LR conditions) over this time period. These factors are (a) increased exposure to infectious disease due to rapid urbanization (though public health programs likely mitigated the effect of population growth); (b) decreased indoor and outdoor air quality rising from a booming and unregulated manufacturing sector; (c) the rise of mass-produced cigarettes in the 1880s; (d) a deterioration in childhood health and nutrition as reflected in the declining heights of successive cohorts within this study. The first three factors are, at this point, merely conjectures since I do not have direct evidence on cigarette consumption or air quality. The final point finds some limited support, but only for LR conditions.

Exploratory analysis of the primary demographic variables present in the Surgeons' Certifications does reveal a few significant patterns. Regional variation in UR disease reflects roughly the same pattern as found today. New England states had significantly lower prevalence than other groups, while the Southern, Western, and Midwestern rates were significantly higher. This same general pattern was found for LR conditions as well, with the exception of the Southern and border states, where the rate was much lower.

The results for population and occupation suggest that we need to probe much deeper into the relationship between rapid urbanization/industrialization and the health of the population. The story is nowhere as simple as urban and industrial centers are unhealthy, and rural areas are healthy. Indeed, in the cross sections examined here, it is the rural residents, farmers in particular, who have the highest rates of respiratory disease—equally as high as high-risk occupations, such as coal mining and stonecutting. Residents of the largest cities actually have lower prevalence of respiratory conditions than any other population group.

Another way of interpreting these results is to conclude that neither population nor broad occupational categories adequately capture the effects of urbanization and industrialization during this period. A clear direction in future research is to conduct more city-specific analyses of respiratory disease. The development of estimates of air quality (as proxied by type and amount of coal consumption) and estimates of differences in the industrial mix of different cities may prove very fruitful. Similarly, more detailed analysis of respiratory disease among farmers might include incorporation of the geographical variation in climate, the types of crops grown in different areas, and trends in agricultural methods.[29] Agricultural differences may explain some of the strong regional effects that have been detected here.

As far as occupational classification goes, much more detail can be incorporated from the present data to study occupational health more generally, with respiratory health a particular focus. It is highly plausible that the lack of significant occupational variation in respiratory disease reflects not the lack of importance of occupation, but instead, the ubiquity of respiratory disease agents across a wide swath of occupations.

The strongest predictors of respiratory disease in this study are, perhaps surprisingly, the presence of respiratory diseases during the Civil War.[30] They had consistently stronger effects on respiratory health later in life than

29. Consumption of commercial fertilizer, for instance, increased from 164,000 tons in 1860 to 2,730,000 tons in 1900 (U.S. Bureau of the Census 1976).

30. Costa (2000), who examined a narrower set of respiratory indicators, also found strong effects of wartime infectious disease.

any other variable in the analysis (although, it should be noted, the overall fit of the probit equations is low). These results indicate the importance of looking at respiratory health in a life-cycle context. Although the data employed here have significant shortcomings, they are advantageous in that they contain data over the course of life—a feature that is frequently missing from modern data sets.

Although the patterns presented here are puzzling in many respects, it bears repeating that the estimates reported are for *prevalence*. A given prevalence rate can be consistent with a variety of incidence and mortality trends. Indeed, the uncertain impact of differential mortality across demographic subgroups is an example of the fact that this analysis raises far more questions than it answers. While there are some inherent data constraints, such as a lack of air quality measures, there is still an abundance of data in the massive Aging Veterans of the Union Army (AVUA) collection that remains to be exploited. The wartime disease variables suggest the importance of incorporating additional disease history in order to understand the etiology of respiratory disease. Clearly a next step is a detailed longitudinal analysis of all these potential risk factors for respiratory illness. The classifications of respiratory disease developed here should provide a useful starting point in this endeavor.

The results presented here will hopefully spur further research investigating the epidemiology of chronic illness during this critical time in American history. Recent research has highlighted the decline in chronic illnesses over the twentieth century. This study suggests that, at least in the case of respiratory disease, any decline in age-specific prevalence rates must have begun to occur some time after 1910, since the evidence presented here suggests a sharp rise in the years prior to 1910. Fogel's work in recent decades has emphasized the secular improvements in health over recent centuries. This study suggests the importance of reference points when making these long-term comparisons. Previous research on the decline in chronic illness over the past century has typically used 1910 as a reference point.[31] In the case of respiratory disease, the reported declines would be much more modest if an earlier reference point, say 1895 or 1900, had been used rather than 1910. And given the trends in smoking, urbanization, and industrialization discussed earlier, it is likely that the cohorts coming of age after the Civil War would have experienced even higher incidence and prevalence of respiratory disease than that experienced by the Union Army cohort in the 1895 to 1910 period.

At the very least, the research presented here reflects both the challenges and the importance of understanding the relationship between economic development and health. Respiratory disease, in both acute and chronic forms, remains a significant public health concern today. The past decade

31. See Fogel and Costa (1997), for example.

has seen a sharp rise in the prevalence of asthma, and epidemiological research has linked even minute particulates in the air to respiratory disease, causing a vigorous public debate over the Environmental Protection Agency's air pollution standards concerning fine particulates. Furthermore, researchers have still not completely disentangled the effects of smoking from the numerous social, economic, and environmental factors which also can lead to respiratory disease. Further investigation of respiratory illness in this dynamic period of American economic history promises to illuminate the relationships between health and economic activity.

References

Britten, Rollo H., and L. R. Thompson. 1926. A health study of ten thousand male industrial workers: Statistical analysis of surveys in ten industries. Public Health Bulletin no. 162. Washington, D.C.: GPO.

Cliff, Andrew, Peter Haggett, and Matthew Smallman-Raynor. 1994. *Measles: An historical geography of a major human viral disease from global expansion to local retreat, 1840–1990*. Oxford: Basil Blackwell.

Collins, John G. 1997. *Prevalence of selected chronic conditions: United States, 1990–1992*. Vital and health statistics, series 10, no. 194. Hyattsville, MD: U.S. Department of Health and Human Services, Centers for Disease Control and Prevention, National Center for Health Statistics.

Costa, Dora L. 2000. Understanding the twentieth-century decline in chronic conditions among older men. *Demography* 37 (1): 53–72.

———. 2003. Understanding mid-life and older age mortality declines: Evidence from Union Army veterans. *Journal of Econometrics* 112 (1): 175–92.

Fogel, Robert W. 1986. Nutrition and the decline in mortality since 1700: Some preliminary findings. In *Long-term factors in American economic growth*, ed. S. L. Engerman and R. E. Gallman, 439–555. Chicago: University of Chicago Press.

———. 1999. *Public use tape on the aging of veterans of the Union Army: Surgeon's certificates, 1860–1940*. version S-1 unstandardized. Chicago: University of Chicago, Graduate School of Business, Center for Population Economics.

Fogel, Robert W., and Dora L. Costa. 1997. A theory of technophysio evolution, with some implications for forecasting population, health care costs, and pension costs. *Demography* 34 (1): 49–66.

Goldring, Jay M., David S. James, and Henry A. Anderson. 1998. Chronic lung diseases. In *Chronic disease epidemiology and control*. 2nd edition, ed. Ross C. Brownson, Patrick L. Remington, and James R. Davis, 375–420. Washington, D.C.: American Public Health Association.

Kluger, Richard. 1997. *Ashes to ashes: America's hundred-year cigarette war, the public health, and the unabashed triumph of Phillip Morris*. New York: Vintage Books.

Komlos, John. 1987. The height and weight of West Point cadets: Dietary change in antebellum America. *Journal of Economic History* 47 (4): 897–927.

Leavitt, Judith W., and Ronald L. Numbers. 1985. Sickness and health in America: An overview. In *Sickness and health in America: Readings in the history of medicine and public health*. 2nd ed., rev., 3–11. Madison: University of Wisconsin Press.

Margo, Robert A., and Richard H. Steckel. 1983. Heights of native-born whites during the antebellum period. *Journal of Economic History* 43 (1): 167–74.

National Center for Health Care Statistics. 1999. *National vital statistics report* 47 (28).

Osler, William. 1892. *Principles and practices of medicine.* New York: Appleton.

Ponikau, Jens U., et al. 1999. The diagnosis and incidence of allergic fungal sinusitis. *Mayo Clinic Proceedings* 74:877–84.

Pope, Clayne L. 1992. Adult mortality in America before 1900: A view from family histories. In *Strategic factors in nineteenth century American economic history: A volume to honor Robert W. Fogel,* ed. C. Golding and H. Rockoff, 267–96. Chicago: University of Chicago Press.

Preston, Samuel H., and Michael R. Haines. 1991. *Fatal years: Child mortality in late nineteenth-century America.* Princeton, N.J.: Princeton University Press.

Sanders, Matthew. 2000. History of the Civil War pension laws. In *Data user's manual: Military, pension, and medical records 1820–1940.* Version M-5, ed. Robert W. Fogel, 323–42. Chicago: University of Chicago, Center for Population Economics.

Schurr, Sam H., and Bruce C. Netschert. 1960. *Energy in the American economy.* Baltimore: Johns Hopkins University Press.

Snider, Gordon L. 1998. Chronic obstructive pulmonary disease. In *Internal medicine,* 5th ed., ed. J. H. Stein, 437–47. St. Louis, MO: Mosby.

Steckel, Richard H. 1992. Stature and living standards in the United States. In *American economic growth and standards of living before the Civil War,* ed. R. E. Gallman and J. J. Wallis, 265–310. Chicago: University of Chicago Press.

Steckel, Richard H., and Donald Haurin. 1994. Health and nutrition in the American Midwest: Evidence from the height of Ohio National Guardsmen, 1850–1990. In *Stature, living standards, and economic development,* ed. J. Komlos, 117–28. Chicago: University of Chicago Press.

Stradling, David. 1999. *Smokestacks and progressives: Environmentalists, engineers, and air quality in America, 1881–1951.* Baltimore: Johns Hopkins University Press.

U.S. Bureau of the Census. 1976. *Historical statistics of the United States, colonial times to 1970.* Bicentennial ed. Washington, D.C.: GPO.

U.S. Department of Health and Human Services. 1994. *The health consequences of smoking. Chronic obstructive lung disease: A report of the surgeon general.* Publication PHS 84-50205. Washington, D.C.: DHHS.

Wilkinson, Richard G. 1996. *Unhealthy societies: The afflictions of inequality.* London: Routledge.

7

The Significance of Lead Water Mains in American Cities
Some Historical Evidence

Werner Troesken and Patricia E. Beeson

7.1 Introduction

By the turn of the twentieth century, cities throughout the United States were using lead service mains to distribute water. For example, in 1900 the nation's five largest cities—New York, Chicago, Philadelphia, Saint Louis, and Boston—all used lead services to varying degrees (Baker 1897, 42, 89, 170, 373, 501). Despite the fact that many of these mains are still in use and that up to 20 percent of all lead exposure in young children comes from drinking water, the significance of lead service mains is poorly understood and there exists little scientific evidence that would allow us to precisely measure their effects on human health (U.S. Environmental Protection Agency 2000).

The dearth of information and scientific study on lead services is unfortunate. It is well known that ingesting even small amounts of lead can adversely affect health and mental development, particularly among children (Needleman and Belinger 1991). Moreover, the Centers for Disease Control (1997) estimate that as many as 5 percent of all American children suffer from subclinical lead poisoning. There are, as a result, numerous studies exploring the health effects of exposure to lead through soil (Xintaras 1992), paint and house dust (Lanphear and Rogham 1997), industrial pollution (Trepka et al. 1997), leaded gasoline (Charney, Sayre, and Coulter 1980), and work environments (Sata et al. 1998). The importance of lead dissolved

Werner Troesken is associate professor of history and economics at the University of Pittsburgh. Patricia E. Beeson is professor of economics at the University of Pittsburgh.

We gratefully acknowledge helpful comments and advice from Dora Costa, Robert Fogel, Joel Tarr, Peter Viechnicki, and conference participants, and especially Rebecca Menes. The usual disclaimer applies.

from lead service mains has received much less attention, in part because over time oxidation has created a protective coating over the interior walls of lead pipes and limited the levels of lead ingested through drinking water (Wisconsin Department of Natural Resources 1993). Nonetheless, it would be useful to know just how widespread lead water mains are, and how they have affected human health both today and in the past.

Accordingly, our goals in this paper are twofold. First, we explore how many cities in the United States used lead services during the late nineteenth and early twentieth century and we examine what factors influenced the choice to use lead mains. The results indicate lead service mains were pervasive: 70 percent of all cities with populations greater than 30,000 in 1900 used lead service mains exclusively or in combination with some other type of main. As for the correlates of lead usage, the probability of using lead water mains was positively correlated with city size, a Midwestern location, and public ownership (publicly owned water companies used lead more often than did private water companies). Second, we explore how the use of lead service mains affected morbidity around the turn of the twentieth century. The evidence on morbidity is derived from a large sample of Union Army veterans whose health was assessed when they applied for pensions. Overall, our results suggest that the use of lead water mains probably did have some adverse effect on human health, but for the general population, these effects do not appear to have been very serious. For example, Union Army recruits living in cities that used lead service mains appear to have experienced more ailments associated with low levels of lead exposure, such as dizziness and hearing problems, but they did not suffer from more serious ailments associated with high levels of lead exposure, such as kidney problems.

Whatever implications these results might have for current policy, they should also interest historians and historical demographers. Some historians attribute the decline of Rome to the use of lead-lined water mains and lead-based vessels to distill alcohol and store water (Waldron and Stöfen 1974, 4–6). More recent studies have explored the possibility that prominent historical figures such as U.S. president Andrew Jackson (Deppisch et al. 1999) and the painter Francisco de Goya died of lead poisoning (Ravin and Ravin 1999). On a broader scale, several recent studies document tremendous improvements in human health and life expectancy over the past century and a half (e.g., Costa 2000; Fogel 1986; Fogel and Costa 1997). While the factors that contributed to this improvement are generally well known and include improved nutrition, investments in public water and sewer systems, the development of vaccines and antibiotics, etc., the relative and absolute importance of these various factors is much less clear. This paper helps to clarify the importance of one of these factors: the reduced risk of unhealthy levels of lead exposure.

7.2   The Use of Lead in Plumbing and Water Distribution Systems

In the late nineteenth- and early twentieth-century United States, lead was often used in the construction of water service mains. This section explains what service mains were, and some of the engineering concerns that prompted many cities to use lead services. Service mains were the pipes that connected individual homes and apartment buildings to street mains. The decision to install a service main was three dimensional, involving a choice about material, a choice about internal lining, and a choice about size. Services were made of iron, steel, or lead; if iron or steel, they were sometimes lined with lead or cement; and they typically ranged in size from three-quarters of an inch to one and one-quarter inches in diameter (Baker 1897).

The choices about material, lining, and size were influenced by the following five variables: cost of pipe; malleability; propensity for external corrosion; propensity for internal corrosion; and toxicity. Table 7.1 ranks the most common pipe types in terms of these variables. As for the first variable, the cost of materials, a small (three-quarter-inch) iron or steel pipe that was neither galvanized nor lined was the best choice. The primary drawback of this choice, however, was that small untreated iron pipes were subject to corrode sooner than other alternatives. Because replacing broken service mains often required digging up paved streets and working around other infrastructure such as gas and sewer mains, the costs of reduced main life often overwhelmed whatever savings were generated from reduced materials costs. As for the second variable, malleability, lead was a relatively soft and pliable metal and was the best choice. Malleability reduced labor costs by

Table 7.1   **The Costs and Benefits of Some Common Types of Service Main**

Main Characteristics	Cost of Material	Malleability	External Corrosion	Internal Corrosion	Toxicity
Material and lining					
Plain iron or steel[a]	1	3	3	5	2
Galvanized iron or steel[a]	2	4	2	4	1
Lead[a]	4	1	1	2	3
Iron: cement-lined[b]	3	3	2	1	2
Iron: lead-lined[c]	3	2	2	3	3
Size of pipe					
Small (3/4″ diameter)	1			3	
Medium (1″ diameter)	2			2	
Large (1 1/4″ diameter)	3			1	

Source: Engineering News, 28 September 1916, pp. 594–97.

[a]Unlined.

[b]Exterior of pipe, galvanized iron; interior of pipe, cement.

[c]Exterior of pipe, galvanized iron; interior of pipe, lead.

making it easier to bend the service main around existing infrastructure and obstructions (*Engineering News,* 28 September 1916, pp. 594–96).

As for the third variable, external corrosion, service mains were subject to corrosion from the outside, and mains laid in salt marsh, cinder fill, or clay experienced faster degradation than those laid in sand or gravel. Holding soil type constant, steel and iron services, whether plain or galvanized, experienced faster corrosion than lead services. If local authorities wanted to minimize the number of times services burst from external corrosion and required replacement, lead was the best choice (*Engineering News,* 28 September 1916, pp. 594–96).

As for the fourth variable, internal corrosion, service mains were subject to corrode from the inside as a result of contact with stagnant water. Interior corrosion was a concern because it weakened the pipe and increased the risk of a rupture, and because rust deposits built up and clogged the main. Before 1910, there was no effective technique for cleaning out rust-filled mains other than by digging them up and cleaning them out directly or by replacing the mains. Cement-lined service mains exhibited the least internal corrosion. Although not as resistant to internal corrosion as cement-lined pipes, lead services were subject to less corrosion than galvanized iron and steel. Another strategy for minimizing the problem of internal corrosion was to expand the size of the main, for the simple reason that the larger the diameter of the main the more rusted material necessary to clog the main.

It is important to note that the amount of internal corrosion depended not only on the type material used to construct the service pipe; it also depended on the corrosiveness of the water being distributed. As a general rule, water from underground wells and water that had been filtered was more corrosive than unfiltered water from above-ground sources. The corrosiveness of water also varied across regions: New England had particularly corrosive water (*Engineering News,* 28 September 1916, pp. 594–96).

As late as 1916, most engineers believed the benefits of using lead mains outweighed the potential costs. The *Engineering News,* a prominent trade journal, explained:[1]

> Lead is in many respects the most satisfactory material to use for service pipes. Its pliability and its comparative freedom from corrosive action make it almost ideal from a mechanical standpoint. The cost of lead pipe of sufficient thickness to safely withstand the pressure is more than the cost of many other materials used for services, but in a paved street the greater duration of life probably more than compensates for the extra cost, and in places where the streets are occupied by other pipes and con-

---

1. Beyond lead service mains, lead pipes were also used widely in household plumbing and in the solder used to connect iron pipes. The same features that made lead attractive for services also made it attractive for plumbing; lead was malleable and allowed plumbers to fit pipes around existing fixtures, and it did not corrode like iron.

duits the ease of getting over and under these obstructions with a flexible pipe is a great advantage. (16 September 1916, p. 595)

The same journal went on to confront, but then minimize, concerns about lead poisoning:

The most serious objection to the use of lead pipe for services is the possibility that the water may dissolve enough lead from the pipe to cause lead poisoning. It is certain that many cases of lead poisoning have been caused by the use of lead services. On the other hand, lead has always been used for services in most of the large places without any unfavorable effects. (28 September 1916, p. 595)

While it is true that most large cities did not incur substantial ill effects from the use of lead services, there were a handful of cases where the installation of lead service mains did have serious consequences. For example, after lead service mains were installed in Lowell and Milton, Massachusetts, around the turn of the twentieth century, several people died, and others suffered dementia and permanent nerve damage, because of lead ingested through drinking water. Following the poisonings in Lowell and Milton, the State Board of Health in Massachusetts began urging cities and towns in the state to avoid installing lead service mains. In addition, families of those injured by lead sued, and won, judgments against the cities and water companies that installed the lead services. Officials at the water companies in question later suggested that the use of lead services would not have had such deleterious effects had local water supplies not contained unusually large amounts of carbonic acid. Carbonic acid dissolved lead from the interior of service pipes and was introduced into the water partly by nature and partly through filtration and chlorination.[2]

7.3 Limiting Exposure to Lead through Lead Service Mains and Lead Plumbing

Today, the Environmental Protection Agency (EPA; 2000) recommends three steps to minimize the amount of lead in drinking water. First, households should flush their pipes before drinking the water. Because the amount of lead that dissolves into water is positively related to the time it sits in the pipes, running faucets for two minutes clears most lead-contaminated water. Second, households should use only cold water for drinking and cooking because hot tap water contains higher lead levels. Third, households should have their water tested to accurately measure its

2. See "Report of the Committee on Service Pipes" (1917, especially 354–59); and *Welsh v. Milton Water Company,* 200 Mass. 409 (1909). Also, at this point in our analysis, it is not clear to us which segments of society were most harmed by the installation of lead mains in these cities. In future work, we hope to identify the effects on different social groups such as children and the poor.

lead levels. According to the EPA, testing is especially important for individuals and families living in large apartment complexes, because flushing may not be effective in high-rise buildings with lead-soldered plumbing. It is not clear how many families at the turn of the century were aware of these simple preventive measures. Prominent engineering journals such as the *Engineering News* (28 September 1916, p. 595) argued that it was difficult to predict how much lead dissolved into water from water mains and recommended testing drinking water for lead content as the only safe guide to assessing levels of exposure:

> It seems practically impossible to determine definitely in advance what the effect of any water on lead pipe will be, as the laboratory results fail in many cases to show the action which will occur in actual practice. Tests of service pipes in use for a considerable period are the only safe guides.

Such lukewarm recommendations notwithstanding, it seems unlikely that most families would have been sufficiently concerned about lead in drinking water to motivate them to have had their water tested, or even to have flushed their pipes regularly. Recent studies suggest people were much more concerned about bacteriological pollution (e.g., typhoid) than they were about industrial and chemical pollution of water. Some experts even believed that a minimal level of industrial contaminants in water could be beneficial because it killed off otherwise harmful bacteria (Melosi 2000, 241–46). Moreover, it was not until the 1930s that states began passing laws regulating the amount of lead present in plumbing and water distribution systems, and it was not until 1986 that Congress banned the use of lead-based solder in plumbing (EPA 2000; Wisconsin Department of Natural Resources 1993). Finally, lead-based interior paints were marketed well into the mid-twentieth century (Markowitz and Rosner 2000).

7.4   The Frequency and Correlates of Lead Usage

At the turn of the twentieth century, the use of lead service mains was widespread, particularly in large cities. This can be seen in two independent samples of cities. In 1916, the New England Water-Works Association surveyed 304 cities and towns, largely in the New England area, and found that 95 (31 percent) of these cities used lead or lead-lined services exclusively (*Engineering News,* 28 September 1916, p. 594). Another sample, predicated on the sample of Union Army recruits described below (see also Fogel 2000), is more geographically diverse and includes 797 cities and towns observed in 1900 from all over the United States. Of these cities, 209 (26 percent) used lead or lead-lined services exclusively; 137 (17 percent) used lead or lead-lined services in conjunction with some other material type, such as galvanized iron or cement-lined iron; and 451 (57 percent) used no lead. Table 7.2, which breaks down the usage of lead service mains by city size,

Table 7.2   **City Size and Lead Usage in 1900**

City Size	Total Number of Cities	Number of Cities, by Service Main Type		
		Only Lead[a]	Lead and Other[b]	No Lead[c]
Population > 300,000	16	8 (50%)	7 (44%)	1 (6%)
30,000 < population < 300,000	107	55 (51%)	22 (21%)	30 (28%)
8,000 < population < 30,000	156	46 (29%)	36 (23%)	74 (47%)
Population < 8,000	518	100 (19%)	72 (14%)	346 (67%)
All towns and cities	797	209 (26%)	137 (17%)	451 (57%)

Sources: Data on services are from Baker (1897). The sample is restricted, however, to only cities and towns represented in the Union Army data. See Fogel (2000).
[a]Cities using lead or lead-lined service mains exclusively.
[b]Cities using lead or lead-lined service mains alongside services made of other materials such as galvanized iron or cement-lined.
[c]Cities using nonlead service mains exclusively.

suggests a strong positive correlation between lead usage and city size. For the largest cities, those with populations greater than 300,000, only 1 of 16 used no lead in its system of service mains. In contrast, for cities with populations less than 8,000, the majority (67 percent) used no lead whatsoever.

To more fully identify the correlates of using lead service mains, we estimate variants on the following ordered-probit model:

$$(1) \qquad L_i = \delta_0 + X_i\delta_1 + \varepsilon_i,$$

where L_i is an indicator variable that equals 2 if city i used lead service mains exclusively as of 1900, 1 if city i used lead services in conjunction with some other material, and 0 if it used no lead services; X_i is a vector of city characteristics that might have been correlated with main type, including city size, age of water system, region dummies, ownership of local water company (i.e., whether public or private), and measures of the development of other public infrastructure; and ε_i is a random error term. Equation (1) is estimated using data for all cities with populations greater than 30,000 as of 1902, and for which the relevant data are available. Data on service mains and ownership of local water systems are from Baker (1897); other data are from the U.S. census of 1900 and the *Statistics of Cities* (U.S. Department of Commerce and Labor, Bureau of Labor, 1902). We restrict the sample to cities with populations greater than 30,000 because data for these large cities are more easily acquired.

Table 7.3 presents descriptive statistics, predicted signs, and regression results. There are few notable descriptive statistics. Most cities (70 percent) with populations greater than 30,000 used lead exclusively (53 percent) or in combination with some other type of service main (17 percent); 74 percent of all large cities had public water companies; the typical large city con-

Table 7.3   The Correlates of Lead Usage in Large Cities (pop. > 30,000 in 1902)

| | | | Ordered Profit | Marginal Effects | |
Variable	μ (σ²)	Predicted Effect	Coefficient	Prob (L = 1)	Prob (L = 2)
				Dependent variable	
Water services (Lᵢ)					
2 if lead exclusively	.527				
1 if lead and other	.170				
0 if no lead	.303				
1 if public water company; 0 if private	.737	+	.671*	−.008	.340*
			(.30)	(.31)	(.12)
1 if built before 1860; 0 if after	.219		Omitted category	Omitted category	Omitted category
1 if built 1861–75; 0 otherwise	.365	±	.010	−.011	.004
			(.366)	(.02)	(.14)
1 if built 1876–90; 0 otherwise	.212	±	.394	.001	.155
			(.34)	(.01)	(.13)
1 if built after 1890; 0 otherwise	.182	±	−.004	.001	−.002
			(.80)	(.01)	(.31)
Miles of roads paved	113.3	+	−.002	.001	−.001
	(219)		(.01)	(.01)	(.01)
Miles of sewer mains	119.0	+	.004*	−.001	.002*
	(212)		(.002)	(.01)	(.001)
Miles of water mains	128.7	+	.005*	−.001	.002*
	(158)		(.003)	(.01)	(.001)
Area of city in thousands of acres	13.0	±	−.001	.001	−.001
	(23.1)		(.001)	(.01)	(.01)

Total population in 1900 (thousands)	139.3 (346)	±	−.004 (.003)	.001 (.01)	−.001 (.01)
1 if city in Northeast; 0 otherwise	.514	±	Omitted category	Omitted category	Omitted category
1 if city in Midwest; 0 otherwise	.272	±	.789* (.33)	No effect	No effect
1 if city in South; 0 otherwise	.175	±	.369 (.36)	No effect	No effect
1 if city in West; 0 otherwise	.039	±	−.411 (.82)	No effect	No effect
N	98		98		
Wald χ²			18.7	...	...
Pseudo-R^2			.101	...	...

Source: See text.

Notes: Coefficients, not marginal effects, are reported. Standard errors are in parentheses.

*Significant at the 5 percent level or higher.

structed its waterworks before 1875; and half of all large cities (51 percent) were located in the Northeast.

Predicted signs are as follows. The effect of public ownership should be positive. Because private water companies were often vulnerable to political expropriation, they would have been more reluctant than public companies to invest in lead service mains, which were more expensive and more durable than iron mains (Troesken 1997). We expect the coefficients on the "decade-of-construction" dummies to grow smaller over time. During the late eighteenth and early nineteenth centuries, doctors used lead acetate to treat bleeding and diarrhea; whiskey distilleries used lead tubing to distill alcohol; and households frequently used vessels with a high lead content to cook and store drinking water. By 1900, such dubious practices had grown much less common, although as noted in the previous section, they certainly had not disappeared (Aufderheide et al. 1981; Deppisch et al. 1999). Along the same lines, as people learned from events like those that occurred in Milton and Lowell, Massachusetts, the use of lead water mains would have grown less common over time.

After controlling for city size in terms of population and acreage, miles of paved roads, sewer mains, and water mains should be positively correlated with the use of lead because well-developed infrastructure makes malleability and durability more attractive—recall that on both of these characteristics lead (as opposed to iron or cement-lined) service mains ranked high (see table 7.1). For example, in a city where most roads were paved, it was costly to have a service pipe burst because replacing the service also would have required digging up the pavement. A city with few paved roads would not have confronted such costs. Finally, the attractiveness of lead would have varied depending on the city's climate, soil quality, and corrosiveness of water. These factors are captured by the regional dummies.

The coefficients on ordered-probit models are not easily interpreted. Accordingly, in addition to reporting the estimated coefficients in table 7.3, we also report the estimated marginal effects for two outcomes: some lead (1); and all lead (2). The estimates indicate the model does a poor job predicting the first outcome (i.e., when a city would have used lead in combination with some other type of main). The model does a better job predicting the use of lead exclusively. Consistent with predictions, cities with public water companies and cities with well-developed infrastructure in terms of miles of water and sewer mains installed were more likely than other cities to have used lead service mains exclusively. Aside from the large number of insignificant explanatory variables, there is one result that is particularly surprising: The estimated effect of population is small. The descriptive statistics in table 7.2 would have suggested otherwise: The table suggests a strong, positive correlation between city size and the use of lead mains.

There are two possible reasons we might find little correlation between city size and the use of lead in formal regression analysis. First, if city size were correlated with other variables, such as the development of urban infrastructure, controlling for those other variables would reduce the correlation between city size and lead usage. However, dropping the other explanatory variables from the regression model still does not strengthen the observed correlation in these data. A second explanation is that once a city's population reached 30,000, variation in population had little influence on its decision to use lead. (The sample used here is restricted to such cities.) This hypothesis is borne out by table 7.2, which shows that the use of lead drops off sharply only after population falls below 30,000.

7.5   The Health Effects of Lead

Lead affects multiple systems in the human body, including the central and peripheral nervous system, the gastrointestinal tract, the kidneys, and the hematological (blood) system. Although further study is required, recent studies suggest lead might also adversely affect the human immune system (e.g., Cohen et al. 1989; Fischbein et al. 1993; Sata et al. 1998). Which of these systems is affected and to what degree depends on how much lead is ingested and the overall size and health of the person exposed. Table 7.4 sum-

Table 7.4   **How Lead Affects Children and Adults**

	Effects	
Lead Level in Blood	Children	Adults
0–9 μg Pb/dl	Uncertain	Uncertain
10–19 μg Pb/dl	Decreased IQ, hearing, and growth; decreased vitamin D metabolism; EP[a]	Hypertension; EP[a] (women)
20–29 μg Pb/dl	Decreased nerve conduction velocity	EP[a] (men)
30–39 μg Pb/dl		Increased systolic blood pressure (men); decreased hearing acuity
40–49 μg Pb/dl	Decreased hemoglobin synthesis	Peripheral neuropathies;[b] infertility (men); nephropathy[c]
50–100 μg Pb/dl	Colic; frank anemia; nephropathy;[c] encyphalopathy[d]	Decreased hemoglobin synthesis; decreased longevity; frank anemia; encephalopathy[d]
> 100 μg Pb/dl	Death	Death

Sources: Perazella (1996); Ravin and Ravin (1999); Xintaras (1992).

[a]Erythocyte protoporphyrin (changes in the shape and size of red blood cells).

[b]Nerve disorders in the extremities. Historically, such disorders might have manifested themselves as complaints about "rheumatism" in the hands and feet; gout; and wrist and foot drop.

[c]Chronic or acute kidney failure.

[d]Any brain-related disorder. Historically, such disorders might have manifested themselves in violent mood swings, memory loss, and dementia.

marizes the effects of lead. At low levels of exposure (blood levels less than 20 μg Pb/dl), lead causes subtle changes in body chemistry and manifests itself in comparatively mild symptoms such as dizziness and hypertension in adults and developmental delays in children. At intermediate levels of exposure (blood levels between 20 and 40 μg Pb/dl), lead has more serious effects, including peripheral neuropathies, infertility in men, increased systolic blood pressure in adults, and reduced hemoglobin synthesis and vitamin D metabolism in children. At high levels of exposure (blood levels between 40 and 100 μg Pb/dl), lead causes nephropathy (chronic or acute kidney failure), frank anemia, and reduced hemoglobin synthesis in adults; and colic, nephropathy, and encephalopathy in children. At extremely high levels (blood levels exceeding 100 μg Pb/dl), lead will cause death.

Historically, it might have been difficult for doctors to accurately diagnose mild to moderate cases of lead poisoning. Deppisch et al. (1999) suggest that President Andrew Jackson's complaints of a severe and debilitating "rheumatism" in his right hand were consistent with peripheral neuropathy caused by lead poisoning. Because lead affects the gastrointestinal tract and can cause abdominal pain, anorexia, cramps, nausea, vomiting, and constipation, Jackson's many laments in this area also could have been related to exposure to toxic metals such as mercury or lead. Finally, it is possible that complaints about gout were related to plumbism (Ravin and Ravin 1999; Perazella 1996; Soliway et al. 1994).

7.6 How the Use of Lead Water Mains Affected the Health of Union Army Veterans

To assess the impact of lead service mains on human health we employ data from a large sample of Union Army recruits compiled by researchers affiliated with the University of Chicago (Fogel 2000). These data have been used in numerous published studies and readers unfamiliar with the data are directed to Fogel for a thorough description of the sample. There are only two significant differences between our study and previous work. First, it is necessary for us to supplement the Union Army data with information about the type of water mains used in the various towns where Union Army veterans resided. Data on the types of mains used (e.g., lead or galvanized iron) are from Baker (1897). Second, given the nature of the problem, we restrict the sample to Union Army recruits living in cities or towns with reliable information about their public water systems, and in particular, about the types of service mains used to distribute water. We use each recruit's address as of 1900 as his city of residence.[3]

3. This ignores the fact that many recruits moved. In future work, we will better control for this by including variables on years of exposure to lead.

After restricting the data this way, we are left with a sample of 2,215 recruits. The sample is geographically diverse, with recruits living in forty different states as of 1900, although the Midwest and the Northeast are overrepresented. Thirty-seven percent of the recruits lived in cities or towns using no lead water mains whatsoever; 27 percent lived in cities or towns using both lead and iron mains; and 36 percent lived in cities or towns using lead mains exclusively.

Given the discussion in section 7.4, one might expect Union Army recruits living in cities with lead water mains, compared to recruits in cities with iron mains, to exhibit more of the following symptoms: dizziness, ear problems; deafness; memory loss; kidney tenderness and pain; and kidney disease.[4] Accordingly, we estimate variants on the following logit model:

$$(2) \qquad X_i = \beta_0 + \beta_1 L1_i + \beta_2 L2_i + Z_i\beta_3 + \varepsilon_i$$

where X_i is an indicator variable equal to 1 if by 1910 the recruit reported a specific ailment related to lead poisoning (e.g., hearing or kidney problems), and zero otherwise; $L1_i$ is an indicator variable equal to 1 if the recruit resided in a city that used lead water mains in conjunction with other types of mains (e.g., iron) as of 1900, and zero otherwise (henceforth, we refer to this variable as the some-lead dummy); $L2_i$ is an indicator variable equal to 1 if the recruit resided in a city that used lead water mains exclusively as of 1900, and zero otherwise (henceforth, we refer to this variable as the all-lead dummy); Z_i is a vector of other related control variables, such as the recruit's occupation and health in 1900, his wartime regiment, the size of the city where the recruit resided in 1900, and the size of the city where the recruit had enlisted; and ε_i is an error term. The control variables included in Z_i are summarized in table 7.5, and for the most part, are identical to those employed in Costa (2000).

Table 7.6 reports the predicted effects of lead service mains under three conceivable hypotheses. The first hypothesis is that lead service mains had, at most, subclinical effects that did not manifest themselves in any ailments related to lead exposure and resulted in blood concentration levels less than 10 μg Pb/dl. Under this hypothesis, recruits living in cities with lead pipes as of 1900 would have experienced no more lead-related ailments than recruits living in cities without lead pipes, and the coefficients on lead water mains would be close to zero and statistically insignificant. One might expect results consistent with this hypothesis if people routinely flushed their pipes, used only cold tap water for cooking and drinking, and had their water tested. Results consistent with hypothesis 1 might also be obtained if the effects of lead service mains were overwhelmed by other sources of lead exposure we have not been able to fully control for, such as work-related ex-

---

4. It bears repeating that we are examining recruits that survived long enough to have been observed in 1910, and as a result, there is a concern about selection bias.

Table 7.5   List of Control Variables

	Individual Characteristics	City-Level Characteristics

At time of enlistment	Occupation
	  =1 if farmer
	  =1 if professional
	  =1 if artisan
	  =1 if laborer
	  =1 if skilled laborer
	  =1 if occupation unknown
	Physical condition
	  Height
	  Weight
		City size
		  =1 if < 4,000
		  =1 if > 4,000 and < 30,000
		  =1 if > 30,000

During wartime	Wounds, rank, etc.
	  =1 if gunshot wound
	  =1 if prisoner of war
	  =1 if dishonorable discharge
	  =1 if private
	  =1 if injured
	Illnesses
	  =1 if measles
	  =1 if diarrhea
	  =1 if respiratory
	  =1 if tuberculosis
	  =1 if typhoid
	  =1 if malaria
	  =1 if syphilis
	  =1 if rheumatism
		Regiment fixed effects

In 1900	Occupation
	  =1 if farmer
	  =1 if professional
	  =1 if artisan
	  =1 if laborer
	  =1 if skilled laborer
	  =1 if occupation unknown
	Age and marital status
	  Age
	  =1 if married
		City size
		  =1 if < 8,000
		  =1 if > 8,000 and < 30,000
		  =1 if > 30,000

posure, the use of lead-based solder and pipes in plumbing, or the use of lead-based paints.

The second hypothesis is that lead water mains had small but identifiable effects on human health, resulting in blood concentration levels between 10 and 40 μg Pb/dl and symptoms such as dizziness and reduced hearing acuity. Under this hypothesis, recruits living in cities with lead pipes as of 1900 would have experienced more ailments associated with low levels of lead exposure than recruits living in cities without lead pipes. The coefficients on lead water mains would be positive and statistically significant for dizziness and ear problems, but close to zero and statistically insignificant for more

Table 7.6   **Predicted Effects**

Variable	Dependent Variable (=1 if recruit reported)				
	Dizziness	Ear Problems	Deafness	Kidney Disease	Memory Loss
Hypothesis 1: Lead water mains had no effect (blood concentration < 10)					
Some lead (β_1)	0	0	0	0	0
All lead (β_2)	0	0	0	0	0
Relative effect					
Hypothesis 2: Lead water mains had small effect (blood concentration > 10 and < 40)					
Some lead (β_1)	+	+	0	0	0
All lead (β_2)	+	+	0	0	0
Relative effect	$\beta_1 < \beta_2$	$\beta_1 < \beta_2$			
Hypothesis 3: Lead water mains had large effect (blood concentration > 40)					
Some lead (β_1)	+	+	+	+	+
All lead (β_2)	+	+	+	+	+
Relative effect	$\beta_1 < \beta_2$	$\beta_1 < \beta_2$	$\beta_1 < \beta_2$	$\beta_1 < \beta_2$	$\beta_1 < \beta_2$

serious lead-related ailments such as kidney disease and memory loss. In addition, for dizziness and ear problems, we expect the coefficient on the some-lead dummy to be smaller than the coefficient on the all-lead dummy, because individuals living in cities that used lead mains in conjunction with iron mains would have been exposed to less lead on average than individuals living in cities that used lead mains exclusively. Results consistent with the second hypothesis would suggest that only small amounts of lead dissolved into water as a result of lead service pipes.

The third hypothesis is that lead water mains had large adverse effects on human health, resulting in blood concentration levels greater than 40 μg Pb/dl and symptoms such as kidney failure and memory loss. Under this hypothesis, recruits living in cities with lead pipes as of 1900 would have experienced more ailments associated with high levels of lead exposure than recruits living in cities without lead pipes. The coefficients on lead water mains would be positive and statistically significant for all of the lead-related ailments we consider—dizziness, ear problems, deafness, kidney disease, and memory loss. Again, we expect the coefficient on the some-lead dummy to be smaller than the coefficient on the all-lead dummy, because individuals living in cities that used lead mains in conjunction with iron mains would have been exposed to less lead on average than individuals living in cities that used lead mains exclusively. Results consistent with the third hypothesis would suggest that significant amounts of lead dissolved into water as a result of lead service pipes.

Of the three hypotheses, the third strikes us as the least plausible. If the use of lead services caused such serious and life-threatening conditions, city residents would have grown increasingly cognizant of the dangers of lead and lead mains and demanded that local and state governments take steps to eradicate lead service pipes. While these patterns are observable in Lowell and Milton, these towns appear to have been outliers and we generally do not observe political outcomes consistent with this. On the contrary, as noted above, all but a handful of the nation's largest cities (those with populations greater than 300,000) used, and continued to install, lead services well into the twentieth century, and as late as 1916, engineering journals were claiming that lead was the most attractive metal for service mains.

Table 7.7 reports some of the more important regression results for the variables of interest, $L1_i$ and $L2_i$. (Complete results for all coefficients are available upon request.) There are three notable findings. First, the explanatory power of these models is not high, and all of the pseudo–R-squareds are less 20 percent. This is consistent with other studies exploring the health of Union Army veterans. Second, overall, the results are most consistent with the second hypothesis: Lead water mains appear to have had a small but identifiable effect on the health of Union Army veterans. Only two mild ailments—dizziness and ear problems—show a robust and significant positive correlation with the use of lead mains. In the case of dizziness (ear problems), recruits living in cities with lead water mains were 50 to 100 percent (15 percent) more likely than recruits living in cities without lead mains to have reported dizziness. More serious symptoms and ailments such as memory loss show no significant correlation with the use of lead services. (Kidney disease shows a correlation in only one model.) Third, whenever we obtain statistically significant results, the estimated coefficient on the all-lead dummy is greater than the estimated coefficient on the some-lead dummy. Because recruits living in cities that used lead mains exclusively would have been exposed to more lead on average than recruits living in cities that used both lead and iron mains, we expect this pattern and view it as weak confirmation that we are estimating reasonable specifications.[5]

It is possible that veterans already in poor health were the most vulnerable to environmental insults, and therefore experienced more severe reactions to lead water mains. To explore this possibility, we restrict our sample to only those recruits who were privates throughout the Civil War on the assumption that they had poorer health than higher-ranking soldiers. Restricting the sample this way does not significantly alter our findings except that lead now appears to have had a much larger impact on the probability that the recruit reports dizziness (see table 7.8, which reports the important

5. Not reported in table 7.7 are our findings for deafness and kidney trouble. We find no statistically significant relationship between lead water mains and deafness, and between lead water mains and kidney tenderness and pain.

Table 7.7   **Regression Results: Full Sample**

							Dependent Variable (=1 if recruit reported)					
	Dizziness [.033]			Ear Problems [.420]			Kidney Disease [.012]			Memory Loss [.051]		
Variable	(1)	(2)	(3)	(4)	(5)	(6)	(7)	(8)	(9)	(10)	(11)	(12)
Some lead	.010	.012	.022	.021	.023	-.002	-.010	-.003	.002	-.004	-.006	-.004
	(.01)	(.01)	(.02)	(.04)	(.03)	(.03)	(.01)	(.50)	(.01)	(.01)	(.01)	(.02)
All lead	.017*	.017*	.031*	.052*	.056*	.058*	.001	-.081	.011*	-.001	-.001	.002
	(.01)	(.01)	(.017)	(.02)	(.03)	(.03)	(.01)	(.46)	(.01)	(.01)	(.01)	(.02)
					Table 7.5 controls							
Individual characteristics	no	yes	yes	no	yes	yes	no	yes	yes	no	yes	yes
Regiment fixed effects	no	no	yes	no	no	yes	no	no	yes	no	no	yes
City-level characteristics	no	no	yes	no	no	yes	no	no	yes	no	no	yes
Pseudo-R^2	.005	.060	.137	.002	.017	.069	.000	.084	.197	.000	.039	.107

Sources: see text.

Notes: All equations are estimated with a probit. Marginal effects are reported. Robust standard errors are reported in parentheses.

*Significant at the 10 percent level or higher.

Table 7.8 Regression Results: Privates Only

| | Dependent variable (=1 if recruit reported) | | | | | | | | | | | |
| Variable | Dizziness [.034] | | | Ear Problems [.424] | | | Kidney Disease [.011] | | | Memory Loss [.047] | | |
	(1)	(2)	(3)	(4)	(5)	(6)	(7)	(8)	(9)	(10)	(11)	(12)
Some lead	.030*	.033*	.118*	.019	.005	-.023	-.001	-.008	-.001	.001	-.005	.001
	(.02)	(.02)	(.05)	(.04)	(.04)	(.05)	(.01)	(.01)	(.01)	(.02)	(.01)	(.03)
All lead	.040*	.037*	.096*	.056*	.058*	.047	.003	.001	-.001	.002	.001	.008
	(.02)	(.01)	(.035)	(.04)	(.04)	(.04)	(.01)	(.01)	(.02)	(.02)	(.01)	(.03)
				Table 7.5 controls								
Individual characteristics	no	yes	yes	no	yes	yes	no	yes	yes	no	yes	yes
Regiment fixed effects	no	no	yes	no	no	yes	no	no	yes	no	no	yes
City-level characteristics	no	no	yes	no	no	yes	no	no	yes	no	no	yes
Pseudo-R^2	.023	.079	.198	.002	.025	.084	.021	.166	.453	.000	.057	.142

Sources: See text.

Notes: All equations are estimated with a probit. Marginal effects are reported. Robust standard errors are reported in parentheses.

*Significant at the 10 percent level or higher.

regression results). Complete results are available upon request. Finally, it is important to point out that to the extent that lead water mains affected children more than adults, the results reported in tables 7.7 and 7.8 will understate the adverse effects of lead water mains on the population as a whole.

7.7 Conclusions

The central conclusions of this paper are as follows. First, in 1900, lead water mains were pervasive, especially among large cities. In the sixteen largest cities in the United States, all but one used lead mains exclusively or in combination with some other type of main. According to the engineering literature, lead was attractive because it was pliable and easy to work with, and because it did not corrode as quickly as iron and steel. While engineers recognized the dangers of lead poisoning, they believed these benefits often outweighed the costs of using lead services. There were, however, isolated examples (e.g., Lowell and Milton, Massachusetts) where the use of lead services had disastrous consequences. Second, the use of lead service mains does not appear to have had serious effects on the health of Union Army veterans. Veterans living in cities with lead mains reported higher rates of dizziness and ear problems than veterans living in cities without lead, but they did not report higher levels of more serious lead-related ailments such as kidney failure.

In the future, we hope to pursue two related lines of research. First, we hope to quantify the economic costs of lead exposure through drinking water in terms of reduced labor force participation and early death. Second, because lead's effects can be especially serious for the young, it would be desirable to extend this analysis to explore how lead water mains affected the growth and development of children. A promising data set for this area of inquiry is the Intergenerational and Familial Aspects of Aging (ILAS) data compiled by researchers affiliated with the Center for Population Economics at the University of Chicago. Because the ILAS data, among other things, allow one to follow the life course of individuals from birth to death, we will be able to identify the effects of childhood exposure to lead through drinking water on development, morbidity, and premature death.

References

Aufderheide, A. C., F. D. Neiman, L. E. Wittmers, and G. Rapp. 1981. Lead in bone II: Skeletal-lead content as an indicator of lifetime lead ingestion and the social correlates in an archeological population. *American Journal of Physical Anthropology* 45:723–35.

Baker, M. N. 1897. *The manual of American water-works.* New York: Engineering News.

Centers for Disease Control and Prevention. 1997. Morbidity and mortality weekly report. May.

Charney, E., J. W. Sayre, and M. Coulter. 1980. Increased lead absorption in inner city children: Where does the lead come from? *Pediatrics* 65:226–31.

Cohen, N., D. Modai, A. Golik, J. Weissgarten, S. Peller, A. Katz, Z. Averbukh, and U. Shaked. 1989. Increased concanavalin A–induced suppressor cell activity in humans with occupational lead exposure. *Environmental Research* 48:1–6.

Costa, D. L. 2000. Understanding the twentieth-century decline in chronic conditions among older men. *Demography* 37:53–72.

Deppisch, L. M., J. A. Centeno, D. J. Gemmel, J. David, and N. L. Torres. 1999. Andrew Jackson's exposure to mercury and lead: Poisoned president? *Journal of the American Medical Association* 282:569–71.

Fischbein, A., P. Tsang, J. J. Luo, J. P. Roboz, J. P. Jiang, and J. G. Bekesi. 1993. The immune system as target for subclinical lead related toxicity. *British Journal of Industrial Medicine* 50:185–86.

Fogel, R. W. 1986. Nutrition and the decline in mortality since 1700: Some preliminary findings. In *Long-term factors in American economic growth,* eds. S. Engerman and R. E. Gallman, 439–555. Chicago: University of Chicago Press.

———. 2000. Public use tape on the aging of veterans of the Union Army: Military, pension, and medical records, 1860–1940. Version M-5. Chicago: University of Chicago, Graduate School of Business, Center for Population Economics.

Fogel, R. W., and D. L. Costa. 1997. A theory of technophysio evolution, with some implications for forecasting population, health care costs, and pension costs. *Demography* 34:49–66.

Lanphear, B., and K. J. Rogham. 1997. Pathways of lead exposure in urban children. *Environmental Research* 74:67–73.

Markowitz, G., and D. Rosner. 2000. "Cater to the children": The role of the lead industry in a public health tragedy, 1900–1955. *American Journal of Public Health* 90:36–46.

Melosi, Martin V. 2000. *The sanitary city: Urban infrastructure from colonial times to the present.* Baltimore: Johns Hopkins University Press.

Needleman, H. L., and D. Belinger. 1991. The health effects of low level exposure to lead. *Annual Review of Public Health* 40:111–40.

Perazella, M. A. 1996. Lead and the kidney: Nephropathy, hypertension, and gout. *Connecticut Medicine* 60:521–26.

Ravin, J. G., and T. B. Ravin. 1999. What ailed Goya? *Journal of Ophthalmology* 44:163–70.

Report of the Committee on Service Pipes. 1917. *Journal of the New England Water Works Association* 31 (3): 323–89.

Sata, F., S. Araki, T. Tanigawa, Y. Morita, S. Sukurai, A. Nakata, and N. Katsuno. 1998. Changes in T cell subpopulations in lead workers. *Environmental Research* 76:61–64.

Solliway, B. M., A. Schaffer, H. Pratt, and S. Yannai. 1994. A multidisciplinary study of lead-exposed subjects. *Environmental Research* 67:168–82.

Trepka, M. J., J. Heinrich, C. Krause, C. Schulz, U. Lippold, E. Meyer, and H. E. Wichman. 1997. The internal burden of lead among children in a smelter town: A small area analysis. *Environmental Research* 72:118–30.

Troesken, W. 1997. The sources of public ownership: Historical evidence from the gas industry. *Journal of Law, Economics, and Organization* 13:1–27.

U.S. Department of Commerce and Labor, Bureau of Labor. 1902. *Statistics of cities having a population greater than 30,000:1902.* Washington, D.C.: GPO.

U.S. Environmental Protection Agency, Office of Water. 2000. *Lead in your drinking water.* Available at [http://www.epa.gov/safewater/Pubs/lead1.html].

Waldron, H. A., and D. Stöfen. 1974. *Sub-clinical lead poisoning.* London: Academic Press.

Wisconsin Department of Natural Resources. 1993. *Lead in drinking water.* Available at [http://www.dnr.state.wi.us/org/water/dwg/lead.html].

Xintaras, C. 1992. *Impact of lead-contaminated soil on public health: An analysis paper.* Atlanta: U.S. Department of Health and Human Services, Agency for Toxic Substances and Disease Registry. Available at [http:www.atsdr.cdc.gov/exlead. html].

8

Internal Migration, Return Migration, and Mortality
Evidence from Panel Data on Union Army Veterans

Mario A. Sánchez

8.1 Introduction

The United States has traditionally had high rates of internal migration. In 1860, 27 percent of native-born Americans were living outside their state of birth. This measure of mobility decreased throughout the second half of the nineteenth century, reaching a low of 20 percent in 1900. Since then, this figure has increased and in 1990 was 31 percent.[1] Although we know that Americans were mobile, there are still many unanswered questions about nineteenth century migration. Who moved in nineteenth century America and how often? Was this move temporary or permanent? What factors determined whether this move was temporary or permanent? How costly was this move?

This paper examines the characteristics of intercounty migrants and estimates the hazard rate of changing county of residence within a year. It investigates whether return migration was common and the characteristics of return migrants. Finally, it examines the costs of migration, in terms of mortality. The paper is novel on two grounds. First, it uses a large longitudinal data set of residential histories for Union Army veterans, allowing me to investigate not just the migration decision through a richer specification than

At the time this research was conducted, Mario A. Sánchez was a Ph.D. candidate in economics at the University of Chicago, and a graduate research assistant at the Center for Population Economics, University of Chicago. He is currently affiliated with the Inter-American Development Bank.

I thank Joseph Ferrie, Steven Levitt, Robert Margo, Richard Steckel, and Peter Viechnicki for valuable suggestions. I am especially indebted to Dora Costa and Robert Fogel for their comments and guidance. Suggestions from participants of the Center for Population Economics weekly meetings are gratefully acknowledged. I am fully responsible for all errors.

1. Figures computed from the 1 percent 1860–1990 Integrated Public Use Microdata Samples (Ruggles & Sobek 1997).

previous researchers have been able to use, but also the return migration decision, which may be workers' optimal reaction to temporary economic shocks. Second, while previous research has mainly used aggregated or cross-sectional data, this paper uses these longitudinal microdata to study the relationship between migration and life expectancy. Because migration, particularly to urban areas, may have decreased the life expectancy of workers, a "mortality wage premium" may partly account for wage differentials between cities and rural areas.

8.1.1   Previous Literature: Mobility

Data availability has stymied past research on migration in nineteenth-century America. Previous researchers relied on aggregate decennial census data or data for small communities. For example, Kuznets and Thomas (1957) limited themselves to using census survival techniques to produce net migration estimates at the state level for the 1870–1950 period.[2] Gallaway and Vedder (1971) studied the effect of such state characteristics as per capita income, distance between states, number of jobs available, land availability, and similarity of climate and culture between states on net interstate migration flows. Because they had to define migrants as those whose state of residence at the time of the census differed from their state of birth, the time span over which migration could have occurred is very long, and death and undercounting bias their estimates.

Steckel (1989) was the first to use longitudinal microdata to present national estimates of mobility, geographical distribution, and distance traveled by migrants. He linked 1,600 families from the 1860 to the 1850 census, using the state of birth of children older than ten as a pointer to the residence of the family in 1850. Observing migration at the county level, and knowing that the movement occurred over a ten-year interval, he studied the effects of individual and household characteristics on the propensity to migrate, as well as on the distance and direction of the movement. Ferrie (1996) complemented Steckel's work by linking forward 4,938 families from the 1850 Public Use Sample of the Federal Census of Population to the 1860 federal census manuscripts. Using this data set, Ferrie (1999) analyzed the causes and consequences of migration to small towns and cities, and reexamined (Ferrie 1997) the theory that "the frontier" (90 degrees west longitude) served as a safety valve relieving pressure on urban labor markets in the east (Turner 1920).[3]

---

2. For a revision of Kuznets and Thomas's estimates using the state of birth–state of residence technique, see Lebergot (1970).

3. Steckel acknowledged that because of the "backwards" linkage technique, "the sample may not be representative of all families that had children, [and therefore] one must be cautious in interpreting the results. Inferences may apply only to that portion of the families" (191). Ferrie is in the process of linking approximately 7,000 families from the 1860 to the 1870 federal census manuscripts.

The outcome of these efforts to overcome data availability barriers is a more reliable picture of how mobile nineteenth-century Americans were, how far and where they decided to move, and the roles that national, regional, and individual characteristics played in shaping these decisions. However, the problems arising from making use of census manuscripts to assess how mobile Americans were still persist. In particular, mortality and census underenumeration, return migration, and the inability to observe more than one move within the ten-year interval potentially undermine the inferences made using samples linked across censuses.

This paper introduces the Union Army Migration Data set (UAMD), a panel data set consisting of postbellum residential histories for 17,017 Union Army veterans, with the intention of pushing forward this "data frontier." The Pension Board gathered the data from the recruit or his family, and they contain rich socioeconomic information on the recruit, his household, and his parents' household. Beyond serving as a basis to study the size of the bias of estimates of mobility for samples linked across decennial censuses of population, the use of UAMD should enhance our understanding of the circumstances under which these migration processes occurred.

8.1.2   Previous Literature: Migration and Life Expectancy

East-to-west migration and the movement from rural to urban areas were the two main sources that shaped geographical redistribution during the nineteenth century. As the century progressed, rural-to-urban migration became increasingly important (Haines 2000). Because urban areas had such high death rates from poor sanitation and overcrowding (Fogel 1986; Williamson 1990), it is reasonable to expect a decline in the life expectancy of movers to urban areas compared to individuals with similar characteristics who remained in or migrated to rural places. Curtin (1989, xiii) discussed this added cost to migration for the case of European soldiers migrating to other continents:

> From the beginning of European trade and conquest overseas, Europeans knew that strange "climates" could have fatal effects. Later, they came to understand that it was disease, not climate, that killed, but the fact remained that every trading voyage, every military expedition beyond Europe, had its price in European lives lost. For European soldiers in the tropics at the beginning of the nineteenth century, this added cost in deaths from disease—the "relocation cost"—meant a death rate at least twice that of soldiers who stayed home, and possibly much higher.

O'Rourke, Williamson, and Hatton (1994) presented evidence on the existence of an urban disamenities wage premium to migration. They studied the effect of such disamenities as population density, town size, and infant mortality on unskilled wage rates across British towns during 1834 and

1905. They concluded that these disamenities explained a good deal of the "bribe" that rural migrants had to be paid in order to move to urban places. They argued that high migration rates to cities indicate that workers were disposed to pay the disamenity costs of migration.

Fogel (1986) argued that both internal migration and immigration played important roles in explaining the sharp decline in life expectancy experienced by native-born Americans from the 1790s to the mid-nineteenth century, both in urban and rural places. Fogel referred to research that concluded that mortality rates were much higher in the immigrant wards than in the wards in which the native-born were preponderant, and that epidemics often began first in the foreign-born wards. Internal migration may have increased the spread of cholera, typhoid, typhus, malaria, dysentery, and other major killer diseases of the era in rural areas.[4]

The UAMD represents a unique opportunity to analyze the effect of the decision to migrate on the life expectancy of migrants. Its longitudinal structure allows me to estimate the impact of the migrant status on the length of the veteran's life span. This paper also investigates the effect of the characteristics of places of origin and destination on the number of years that recruits lived after the war and their causes of death. This will allow me to determine whether there was a mortality wage premium to migration.

8.2 The Data

The Center for Population Economics (CPE) at the University of Chicago collected military, socioeconomic, and medical information for 35,747 white males mustered into the Union Army during the Civil War.[5] This data set, collected as part of the Early Indicators of Later Work Levels, Disease, and Death (EI) project, contains information on the recruit, his household, and his parental household at numerous times during the recruit's life. They gathered the data by using the recruit's military-related information to link him to the 1850, 1860, 1900, and 1910 censuses of population[6] and to his pension records (PEN) and the medical examinations often included in them, and by using other historical documents as sources for ecological variables.

For those who survived the war and applied for a pension (either personally or through their legal heirs), EI is a rich source of residential information from the end of the war until the recruit's death. Postbellum residential information is abundant throughout PEN on pension claims, affidavits, correspondence with the Pension Board, envelopes retained in the pension

4. Fogel proposed an alternative approach to the bribery principle to compute the "mortality correction" to real wages due to a more rapid consumption of human capital in locations where disease was more prevalent.

5. For a discussion of sample design, data sources, and methodology see CPE (2000).

6. Linkage to the 1870 and 1880 censuses is in progress.

file, and vital statistics forms. These documents not only reveal the location of the recruit at the issuing time of the document, but often contain retrospective residential information provided by the recruit himself or, after his death, by his dependents. PEN also contains information on the date and location of a change in the recruit's marital status, of the birth of the recruit's children, and of the recruits' death.[7]

I combined the information in the pension documents to reconstruct the residential life history of the recruit after the Civil War; the final data set that I created is the UAMD. For a recruit linked to PEN, there are up to sixteen documents containing residential information, including death certificates or other communications to the Pension Board regarding the recruit's death. Although in some cases the city, county, and state of residence are recorded, it is more common to see the recruit at either the county or the city level. Because city and state of residence usually imply a unique county of residence, and not the other way around, UAMD contains residential histories recreated at the county level.

Of the 30,763 recruits in EI who survived the war, 20,674 provided information to the Pension Board. For 17,779 of these, information on residence and on dates of birth and death are provided. I omitted observations on recruits who were not born between 1820 and 1845 both to exclude unreasonable military ages and to exclude recruits in small cohorts. The final sample size of UAMD is 17,017.[8]

The next two subsections deal with the representativeness of UAMD and discuss the quality of the data.

8.2.1   Representativeness of the Sample

Fogel (1993) and Costa (1998) argued that white soldiers in EI constituted a representative cross section of their generation. A considerable proportion of white males of military age participated in the war[9] and soldiers' socioeconomic characteristics, life expectancies, and distribution of causes of death resembled those of the nonfighting population. As discussed in ap-

---

7. The following example of a pension document may clarify the type of information contained in PEN. On 16 April 1907 private James Dean declared in his first Declaration for Pension: "that his several places of residence since leaving the service have been as follows: Windsor, Conn., 1 year and 4 months; enlisted in regular service Nov. 21, 1867; returned to Windsor on December, 1870; reentered regular service March 21, 1871; discharged in 1876 and located in Bridgeport, Conn. until August, 1893; moved to Wallingford, Conn.; resided there until June 1885, returned to Bridgeport; have continued residing there until the present time." Thus, it is possible to reconstruct completely the residential life of a recruit up to the time when he or his heirs presented a pension application (or any other pension document), regardless of when and how many times they provided information.

8. See appendix A for a detailed discussion on the construction of UAMD.

9. From information provided by Dyer (1959), I computed that 40 percent of all Northern white men born between 1820 and 1845, 58 percent of those born between 1835 and 1845, and 80 percent of those who were born between 1840 and 1845 served in the Union Army during the Civil War.

pendix B in this chapter, being wounded in the war did not adversely affect soldiers' ability to move their place of residence. Mobility rates among veterans and nonveterans were similar. Sixty-three percent of Union veterans who survived to 1910 were living in a state other than their state of birth, compared to 67 percent of nonveterans who were either native-born or who, if foreign-born, migrated before the end of the war (figures computed from the 1 percent 1990 Integrated Public Use Microdata Sample).

Postbellum migration information is available only for those veterans in EI who applied directly for a pension or whose dependents applied for a pension.[10] However, while individual characteristics and military outcomes explained linkage to PEN, the most important factor explaining linkage failure was whether the recruit was dishonorably discharged (see appendix B). Because 90 percent of all soldiers were honorably discharged, the population in UAMD represents a large fraction of all soldiers.

8.2.2 Residential Information in UAMD

Figure 8.1 shows the number of recruits whose counties of residence are known from the end of the war until 1920[11] as a proportion of the total number of recruits alive at each year. Residential information is more abundant for those recruits who survived to later years, perhaps because as the number of widows' applications increased, so did the importance of collecting information to verify their claims. Because pretended widowhood was the most common way of filing a fraudulent claim (Glasson 1918), the recruit's residential history, as well as dates and places of birth of the veteran's children, were used to verify the validity of a widow's pension claim.

Figure 8.1 suggests a relationship between different pension regimes and the number of veterans with residential information for a particular year. I estimated a linear regression to explain the proportion of life after the war for which there is residential information for the recruit.[12] The variable with the most explanatory power was whether the veteran (or a dependent) submitted an application after 1907 (to have done so increases the proportion of life after the war with residential information by nearly 30 percent). Beginning in 1904, all pension forms (including widows' applications) explicitly asked for retrospective residential information. Figure 8.1 can therefore be explained by the evolution of the administrative procedures of the Pensions Board, rather than the behavior of the recruit seeking a pension.

---

10. Not all recruits linked to PEN entered the pension rolls. The recruits' legal heirs may have been the ones filing applications, and the Pension Board may have never accepted a claim as valid.

11. I chose 1920 as the last year of analysis, given that after that year residential information becomes increasingly scarce and the number of survivor veterans decreases rapidly.

12. The independent variables were as follows: number of applications recorded for the veteran, a set of dummy variables for pension regimes, age after the war, marital status, and an interaction term between admittance and year of entrance into the pension rolls.

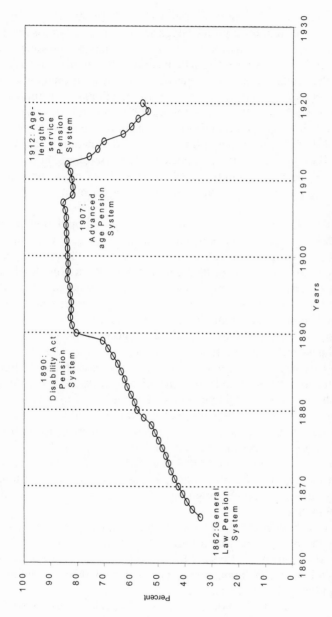

Fig. 8.1 Proportion of living recruits with residential information, 1866–1920

8.3   Empirical Framework and Methods

Models that serve as microfoundations to most of the research on migration can be classified in three broad categories: (a) models that assume that workers maximize their own expected discounted utility by choosing a geographical location and by investing in their capital, both human and physical (Sjaastad 1962; Todaro 1969); (b) models in which the decision units are not isolated individuals, but larger groups like couples, families, or households (Borjas 1994; Stark and Bloom 1985; Stark 1991); and (c) social networks models in which family and friends of the potential migrant, who have already established their residence at the location of destination, affect the migration decision by increasing the expected net returns of migration (Hugo 1981; Taylor 1986; Gurak and Caces 1992). The following is a summary of the implications of these three types of model that are relevant to this paper:

1. Migrants should be younger than the nonmigrant population because their longer life expectancy increases the discounted present value of their investment and because their physical costs of moving are lower. Migration of the young, however, may not be the best strategy for a household decisionmaker. For instance, a farm family faced with poor harvests may send its older, stronger son to work at another location, while the younger children stay to help with less strength-demanding tasks.

2. Married workers and those with children should move less often than single, childless ones because their moving costs are higher. However, at older ages, parents may move upon retirement to live with their children.

3. If there are differences in land availability or in location-specific economic conditions, people residing in less advantaged regions will be more likely to move to maximize their expected discounted wealth.

4. The sign of the correlation between wealth and the probability of changing locations is uncertain. Although relatively poorer individuals face a lower opportunity cost of migrating, financial constraints could prevent them from moving. On the other hand, a financially constrained household—or group—may decide to send one of its members to another location to accumulate assets.

5. Given the high correlation between wealth and type of job, it is not clear what the occupational distribution across the migrant population should be. After controlling for wealth, however, workers that depend more on their location-specific human or social capital should be less inclined to move out of their labor markets.

6. Healthier individuals endure better the physical and mental costs of migration. Thus, migrants could be positively self-selected in terms of their health. Migrants may also be healthier than nonmigrants because wage differentials across locations may be positively correlated with health. However, health itself may be a motive for migration. Workers and their families

may change their place of residence to escape from disease, and they may already be in poor health before moving. In this case, migrants would be negatively self-selected in terms of their health.

7. Individuals who have already experienced migration may be more prone to change locations, as they may belong to a social network that extends beyond their current place of residence. Lalonde and Topel (1997), for instance, showed that foreign-born immigrants tend to reside in ethnic enclaves, and that the locations that new waves of immigrants choose as their destination display a high concentration of ethnically similar individuals.

8.3.1   Estimation: Moving across Counties

Exploiting the yearly panel nature of the data, this paper studies the self-selection of migrants in terms of their observable characteristics—some of them time-varying—and their propensity to migrate over the life cycle, where the movements could have occurred within one year.

The probability that person i moves at the end of period t is modeled as a function of his possibly time-varying characteristics $X_{i,t}$, the characteristics of the location where i resides in period t, $Z_{i,t}$, and an error term $\mu_{i,t}$ that varies across individuals and time. Let $M_{i,t}$ be an indicator variable that takes a value of 1 if person i changes county of residence at t and a value of zero otherwise. Thus, this paper models the probability that at time t a person at risk of changing his place of residence will do so within the next year as

(1) $$\Pr(M_{i,t} = 1) = F(X_{i,t}, Z_{i,t}, \mu_{i,t}).$$

For empirical analysis, equation (1) takes the following form:

(2) $$P_{i,t} = \Pr(M_{i,t} = 1) = \Lambda(\alpha + \beta'X_{i,t} + \gamma'Z_{i,t} + \delta_t + \varepsilon_i)$$

where Λ represents the logistic cumulative distribution function and $\mu_{i,t}$ takes the form $\delta_t + \varepsilon_i$, where ε_i is a Gaussian term. The linearized version of equation (2) makes it easier to interpret the time coefficient δ_t:

(3) $$\log\left(\frac{P_{i,t}}{1 - P_{i,t}}\right) = \alpha + \beta'X_{i,t} + \gamma'Z_{i,t} + \delta_t + \varepsilon_i$$

The expected difference in the logarithm of the odds ratio of moving for two different persons i, j seen at times t and t' (respectively) is equal to

(4) $$E\left[\log\left(\frac{P_{i,t}}{1 - P_{i,t}}\right) - \log\left(\frac{P_{j,t'}}{1 - P_{j,t'}}\right)\right]$$
$$= \beta'(X_{i,t} - X_{j,t'}) + \gamma'(Z_{i,t} - Z_{j,t'}) + (\delta_t - \delta_{t'}).$$

If i and j shared the same individual and location characteristics at t and t' (respectively); the expected difference in their odds ratio would simply be $\delta_t - \delta_{t'}$: the difference in the logarithm of the odds of moving for two individuals who decide to migrate at different points in time, but are otherwise identical.

Years with missing residential information represent a complication when estimating the mobility of the UAMD population. Individuals with longer periods without location information recorded are at lower risk *to be seen* moving. Thus, defining as migrant someone with a recorded movement would produce a downward-biased estimate of the mobility of the sample.[13] To overcome this problem, I estimate the probability that the county of residence differs within two consecutive years, using for the estimation only the subsample of recruits who have nonmissing information for those two years. In other words, I impute the migration decision of an unobserved individual through the decision taken by a synthetically identical individual. This procedure implicitly assumes that after controlling for observable characteristics, there is no correlation between the probability of having residential information and the probability of changing locations for every pair of contiguous years.

8.3.2 Estimation: Return Migration

I examine return migration by estimating a logistic regression, where the dependent variable is a dichotomous indicator, taking a value of 1 if the recruit is a return migrant and a value of zero otherwise. The subsample under study is all veterans in UAMD who changed locations at least once, and who never left the country.

Let t_i represent the ith year at which a new county of residence is observed for the veteran after the end of the war, and let l_i be the location at time t_i. Thus, the requirement for a veteran to be included in the analysis is that a location l_2 exists. Using this notation, a veteran is a return migrant if there exists a time t_i^*, with $i \geq 3$, such that l_i^* is equal to $l_{i'}$ for $i' < i$. Let R be an indicator function that takes a value of 1 if t_i^* exists, and a value of zero otherwise. Let us define the probability of becoming a return migrant as

$$(5) \quad \Pr(R = 1) \equiv \Pr(\exists l_i^* \ s.t. \ l_i^* = l_{i'} \text{ for } i' < i) = \Lambda(\alpha + \beta' X_2 + \mu),$$

where X_2 is a row vector of individual characteristics of the recruit at the time of his first movement, and μ is a Gaussian term. Thus, in this paper, a return migrant is an individual with at least three different recorded locations and who returned to a location where he previously lived.[14]

Census-based estimators of mobility rates use the working assumption

---

13. Although 90 percent of the recruits in UAMD do not show "information gaps" larger than ten years, there is no available information on the literature that could give an idea on the size of the bias if I ignored this issue.

14. Some veterans returned to more than one location. However, this would be just a special case of equation (5), where the set of t_i^* such that $R = 1$ is not a singleton. Notice as well that this definition may underestimate the proportion of veterans who were returning migrants, as some of these return movements may not be observed.

that a person observed at the same location in two consecutive censuses did not move within the ten-year interval. Beyond acknowledging this caveat in their estimates, researchers have been unable to do much to measure the size of the return migration bias. Thanks to the panel nature of UAMD, it is possible, for the first time, to investigate the importance of return migration, and to describe the characteristics of the return migrants.[15]

8.3.3   Estimation: Migration and Life Expectancy

I study the effect of migrant status on life expectancy by estimating a time-varying covariates hazard model of mortality. Time until death is a function of a set $X_{i,t}$ of individual characteristics at time t, and a time-varying dichotomous variable $M_{i,t}$, which takes a value of zero if the recruit has not become a migrant by time t and a value of 1 otherwise. Let t^* be the year at which a veteran changes locations for the first time. Then, $M_{i,t} = 0$ for $t < t^*$, and $M_{i,t} = 1$ for $t \geq t^*$. For recruits who never acquire the status of migrant, $M_{i,t} = 0$ for all t.

It is important to model migrant status as a time-varying variable instead of just including a dummy variable M_i indicating whether the recruit ever changed locations. The coefficient on M_i is deceptive because recruits who died earlier were less likely to become migrants. A time-varying dummy, on the other hand, allows me to compare waiting times (the number of years that elapsed from the first year with information for the recruit to the year in which he actually moved) for recruits who were at risk of dying, with survival times for recruits who experienced events.

Following Cox (1984),[16] I model the hazard rate of dying as a function of time (represented by a fixed baseline function) and a function that depends on the covariates. Let T_i represent the year of i's death, and $h_i(t)$ be the probability i dies at $t + 1$ given that he has survived until t. Using this notation, the hazard rate of dying is

$$(6) \quad h_i(t) = \Pr\{T_i = t + 1 | T_i \geq t\} \equiv h(t; X_{i,t}) = h_0(t) \exp\beta' X_{i,t} + \delta M_{i,t}).$$

Under this framework, this paper tests the hypothesis that once the recruit changed his county of residence at time t his hazard rate of dying increased with respect to other comparable recruits who had not moved at time t.

There is an additional complication in the estimation of equation (6) for the UAMD sample. I mentioned in section 8.1 that survival times are right-censored for those recruits who lived beyond 1920. The likelihood function produced by equation (6) must take censoring into account in order to get unbiased estimates. Fortunately, the partial-likelihood method developed

---

15. See appendix C for a discussion on the biases of census-based estimations of mobility.
16. The expression for and development of the maximum-likelihood function for a discrete-time Cox model with time-variant covariates are quite cumbersome. I refer the interested reader to read Cox (1984).

Table 8.1   Distribution of the Number of Times Recruits in UAMD Changed
                   Locations after the War

Number of Times Recruit Changed Places of Residence	Number of Recruits	Percentage of Recruits
Never changed county of residence	10,015	58.9
Changed counties once	3,859	22.7
Changed counties twice	1,838	10.8
Changed counties three times	809	4.7
Changed counties four times	311	1.8
Changed counties five times or more	185	1.1
Total	17,017	

by Cox readily incorporates right-censoring, producing estimates that are consistent and asymptotically normal.[17]

I estimate a competing risks model to analyze how migration and the urban-rural status of both the location of origin and the hosting location affected the probability of dying of a particular type of disease. The procedure for estimating such models is simply to use time remaining to die from a particular type of disease as the dependent variable, while the life spans of people who died of other causes are treated as censored after the year of death. The only assumption behind this technique is that censoring is noninformative, that is, that conditional on the covariates, those who are at particularly high (or low) risk of dying of a particular type of disease are no more (or less) likely to die of any other type of disease.

8.4   Results

8.4.1   Results: Migration across Counties

Table 8.1 shows the distribution of the number of times recruits in UAMD changed county of residence. Approximately 41 percent of them migrated to another county at least once during the postbellum era.

Recall that I estimate mobility across counties using equation (3). Instead of running individual regressions (one for every pair of consecutive years), it is efficient to stack individual-time observations in a seemingly unrelated model (Greene 1997). Dummy variables for each year are included (omitting the dummy for 1867 to avoid perfect multicollinearity), and their slopes

17. Another issue in the Cox regression estimation is the existence of "tied data." The partial likelihood method assumes that it is possible to strictly order survival times. For the case of discrete data, it is common to find individuals who survived an equal number of years. In this case, it is not possible to strictly order the data. There are several methods proposed to handle such cases, and throughout this paper, I will be using a method called the *discrete method*, which was proposed by Cox (1984).

are interpreted as the effect of the state of external conditions during the year on the hazard rate of moving. Since residential information is missing for some individuals, I impute migration probabilities for synthetically identical individuals. This paper defines two individuals as synthetically identical if, for any given year, they were the same age, had the same marital status and number of children, lived in the same region, belonged to the same occupational group,[18] shared the same nativity, and had similar mobility and military pasts.

Table 8.2 shows the results for this stacked logistic regression. Younger, single, and rural recruits, who were foreign-born, had fewer children, resided in the Midwest, migrated before the war (as proxied by enlisting in a state different from state of birth), and had moved after the war[19] were at higher risk of moving next year. Surprisingly, occupational group does not significantly affect the propensity of veterans to move. Steckel (1989) found a similar result, and attributed it to the correlation between other variables in the regression and the occupational group.[20] Unexpectedly as well, people who were ill or wounded during the war were more mobile. It is possible that conditional on war survival, the average veteran's mobility was not seriously impeded.[21] Nevertheless, the reason the wounded were more mobile than the rest of the population remains as an interesting puzzle to be addressed in future research.

Figure 8.2 shows the hazard rate of movement across the life cycle, setting all time coefficients equal to zero (or equivalently assuming that veterans made all their moves—if any—in 1867) and all other variables at their means, and assuming that the mean veteran had not migrated during the postbellum period. Note that the propensity to move decreased continuously with age as the horizon over which individuals discounted the potential returns of moving decreased. Veterans were 62 percent more likely to migrate at age thirty compared to their propensity to move at age sixty.

How mobile were postbellum Americans? Let me rephrase this question as follows: How likely was a twenty-year-old recruit who lived until age seventy-five and who had the individual characteristics of the average veteran

18. I created the occupational-group dummy variables from the occupation of the recruit at enlistment time; therefore I am implicitly assuming that the veteran during his whole life kept the occupation he had at enlistment. It is possible to analyze the robustness of these results by linking UAMD to the several censuses of population available in EI. Moreover, for the segment of population linked to the censuses of population, wealth information is available and I could have incorporated it in the analysis for the linked sample. I did not do so, however, because that would have complicated the sample selection issues. See appendix A for a discussion on this matter.

19. As pointed out by Robert Margo in his referee report, the positive coefficients on migrant before and after the war could be evidence for state dependence or it could be evidence of a fixed effect.

20. However, he does not find a significant effect of family size.

21. In appendix B I make a case for this argument.

Table 8.2   Logistic Regression on the Probability of Moving Next Year, 1866–1920

Variable	Mean	Coefficient	Slope
Intercept		–2.53*	–0.0611
Age	52.51	–0.023*	
Age squared		0.00016**	
Married	0.8002	–0.3341*	–0.0082
Number of kids	2.7601	–0.0083**	–0.0002
Northeast region	0.2838	–0.4159*	–0.0100
South region	0.0557	–0.0869	–0.0021
West region	0.0445	–0.0823	–0.0022
Foreign-born	0.1679	0.1484*	0.0036
Migrant before the war	0.1699	0.0933***	0.0011
Migrant after the war	0.0477	0.5516*	0.0132
White-collar	0.0457	–0.0032	–0.0001
Manual worker	0.3227	–0.0121	–0.0003
Service worker	0.0°193	0.1053	0.0027
Urban	0.2061	–0.1147*	–0.0028
Ill or wounded during the war	0.2910	0.1296*	0.0034
Prisoner of war	0.0709	0.0563	0.0014
Time enlisted	622.00	0.0001	0.0000
1868	0.0146	0.1786***	0.0044
1869	0.0152	0.0992	0.0024
1870	0.0157	0.0983	0.0024
1871	0.0162	0.0397	0.0010
1872	0.0166	0.0709	0.0017
1873	0.0169	0.0793	0.0019
1874	0.0173	–0.0020	0.0000
1875	0.0177	0.2021***	0.0049
1876	0.0182	0.0669	0.0016
1877	0.0187	0.1266***	0.0031
1878	0.0190	0.1648***	0.0040
1879	0.0199	0.2196**	0.0054
1880	0.0208	0.3046*	0.0074
1881	0.0211	0.1981***	0.0048
1882	0.0215	0.2048***	0.0050
1883	0.0219	0.2011***	0.0049
1884	0.0222	0.2233**	0.0054
1885	0.0225	0.2233**	0.0054
1886	0.0228	0.2364**	0.0057
1887	0.0232	0.1723**	0.0041
1888	0.0237	0.1529***	0.0038
1889	0.0241	0.1697***	0.0041
1890	0.0264	0.1308***	0.0032
1891	0.0270	0.0104	0.0003
1892	0.0271	0.0150	0.0004
1893	0.0268	0.0619	0.0015
1894	0.0265	0.0352	0.0009
1895	0.0260	–0.0512	–0.0012
1896	0.0257	0.1542***	0.0038
1897	0.0252	0.0190	0.0005
1898	0.0246	0.1050	0.0026

Table 8.2   (continued)

Variable	Mean	Coefficient	Slope
1899	0.0241	0.1399***	0.0034
1900	0.0235	0.3782*	0.0092
1901	0.0229	0.3148*	0.0077
1902	0.0223	0.2413*	0.0059
1903	0.0216	0.1235***	0.0030
1904	0.0209	0.2585*	0.0063
1905	0.0202	0.2645*	0.0064
1906	0.0195	0.1214***	0.0030
1907	0.0179	0.1111	0.0027
1908	0.0171	0.3167	0.0077
1909	0.0162	0.8597	0.0210
1910	0.0155	0.0454	0.0011
1911	0.0147	−0.1644	−0.0040
1912	0.0125	−0.0167	−0.0004
1913	0.0112	−0.5345*	0.0130
1914	0.0099	−0.1185*	−0.0029
1915	0.0082	−0.2367*	−0.0058
1916	0.0071	−0.5567*	−0.0136
1917	0.0062	−1.149*	−0.0280
1918	0.0052	−1.0477*	−0.0255
1919	0.0045	−1.3930*	−0.0340
Number of observations	371,577		
−2 log-likelihood	45,691		
Max-rescaled R^2	0.0186		

Notes: Omitted variables are single, Midwest region, farmer, native-born, enlisted in state of birth, has not moved after the war, not ill or wounded during the war, not being a POW, rural, and 1867.
***Significant at the 10 percent level.
**Significant at the 5 percent level.
*Significant at the 1 percent level.

to change his county of residence during 1867? Integrating under the curve depicted in figure 8.2, the answer is approximately 59 percent.[22] Previous researchers could not address this kind of question at that level of specificity.

8.4.2   Results: Return Migration

Why do we observe return migration? Workers may move temporarily if an economic shock leads to a wage gap across locations. Liquidity constraints are another explanation. For instance, an unemployed migrant may return to his previous residence once he exhausted the financial and social

22. This is the first time such a figure is computed for this time period, and thus there is no comparison point to address whether the figure is larger or lower than expected. However, this figure is informative if we compare it with the 30 percent ten-year-period mobility rates estimated by other researchers.

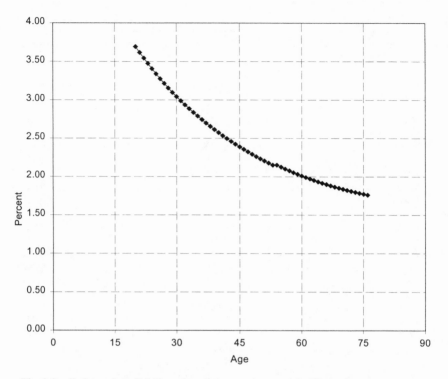

Fig. 8.2   Estimated probability of moving next year over the life cycle

Note: The graph is computed setting all time coefficients equal to zero and is computed at the sample mean for all other variables but age. The smoothness observed is the result of using a quadratic approximation.

capital that sustained him in the hosting location. Alternatively, he may accumulate assets while working at his new location and return home with these assets. Older migrants may retire to live with children who reside in a previous location. Finally, workers searching for the highest wages across locations may learn that they had already worked at the most attractive location available to them.

I study the characteristics of return migrants by examining recruits who moved at least once since the end of the Civil War until 1920 or their year of death, and who never left the country. Out of these 6,350 recruits, 992 (15.6 percent) returned to a previous county of residence, and the average time that elapsed for their return was 16.9 years.[23]

I estimate return migration probabilities using equation (5). The individual characteristics included as explanatory variables are age, marital status,

23. To provide an idea of the importance of return migration on census-based estimates of mobility, I computed the proportion of those return movements that occurred within a ten-year interval and found it to be equal to 3.5 percent (224 veterans), and significantly different from zero.

Table 8.3   Logistic Regression on the Probability of Returning to a Previous Location

Variable	Mean	Coefficient	Slope
Intercept	1.0000	0.8538*	0.1056
Age at first move	46.2814	−0.0348*	−0.0043
White-collar	0.0449	0.0368	0.0045
Manual worker	0.3041	0.1074	0.0133
Service worker	0.0236	0.1766	0.0218
Married at first move	0.7524	−0.2700*	−0.0334
Family size at first move	2.3387	0.0775*	0.0096
In Northeast after first move	0.1913	0.1421***	0.0176
In South after first move	0.0739	0.2898**	0.0358
In West after first move	0.0814	0.2396***	0.0296
In urban county after first move	0.1890	−0.0591	−0.0073
Logarithm of distance traveled	4.7421	−0.2309*	−0.0285
Number of observations	6,350		
−2 log-likelihood	2,646		
Max-rescaled R^2	0.0564		

Notes: Omitted variables are farmer and Midwest region.
***Significant at the 10 percent level.
**Significant at the 5 percent level.
*Significant at the 1 percent level.

and family size during the year the recruits first change county of residence. Additional explanatory variables are region and urban-rural status of the county in which they first lived as migrants, and the logarithm of the distance they traveled to their first new location.

Table 8.3 shows that return migrants were more likely to be younger, to be unmarried, to have bigger families, to have moved first to the South, and to have migrated only a short distance. As shown in the previous subsection, the young were more likely to migrate in the first place. The young are more financially constrained, face lower search costs, and have less information about various labor markets. If veterans left large families behind, then they may have been more likely to return to live with their children. Because migrating longer distances is more costly, those who traveled larger distances may have had characteristics that increased the likelihood of a successful first migration.

8.4.3 Results: Migration and Life Expectancy

Recall that I investigate the relationship between migration and life expectancy using the Cox regression model in equation (6). I restrict the sample to recruits with at least three years of residential information, with information on year of death, and who never left the country. The total sample size is 11,097.

Table 8.4 shows that once a recruit changed his county of residence, his

Table 8.4   Cox Regression on the Surviving Times of UAMD Veterans

Variable	Mean	Hazard Ratio	$Pr > \chi^2$
Age at first observation	37.96	1.126	0.0001
Age at first observation squared		1.000	0.0001
White-collar	0.05	1.109	0.0357
Manual worker	0.34	1.106	0.0001
Service worker	0.02	1.118	0.1319
Northeast at first observation	0.32	1.077	0.0029
South at first observation	0.06	0.976	0.6094
West at first observation	0.03	0.957	0.5256
Urban at first observation	0.17	1.173	0.0001
Foreign-born	0.18	1.066	0.0215
Migrant status (time-varying)		1.083	0.0005
Number of observations	11,097		
Censored observations	23,223		
Model χ^2 (Wald)	6,103.7 (p-value = 0.0001)		

Notes: Omitted variables are farmer, Midwesterner at first observation, rural at first observation, and native-born.

probability of dying within the next year was 1.08 times higher than that of his counterpart who did not migrate. As expected, recruits first seen in an urban county had a higher risk of dying than those first seen in a rural county. Farmers, Midwesterners, and the native-born were other groups with lower hazard rates of dying.

Migrants' life expectancies could be shorter either because of the environmental changes to which they were exposed or because migrants were a self-selected group.[24] Although self-selection cannot be ruled out, examining mortality among migrants in detail will help us understand some of the mechanisms through which migrations may have shortened life expectancy. Table 8.5 shows the distribution of recruits' causes of death using five classification groups: chronic, infectious (tuberculosis, venereal diseases, typhoid, cholera, dysentery, and other bacterial and viral diseases), acute respiratory, other diseases, and missing cause of death. I use these causes of death to estimate a competing-risks model of mortality.

Table 8.6 shows that migrants were more likely to die of infectious diseases than nonmigrants. Are these results solely attributable to the fact that they changed locations? Did it matter whether they moved to a rural or an urban place? Including a set of dummy variables for the urban-rural status of both the origin and final destination of migrants shows that conditional on being a migrant, migrants to rural counties had higher life expectancies (see table 8.7). Migrants to rural areas had lower life expectancies com-

24. For instance, migrants may have been poorer, and lower income may have been negatively correlated with a longer life span. On the other hand, migrants may have been taller, stronger, and in general healthier than those who did not move, and therefore longer-lived.

Table 8.5   Distribution of Causes of Death

Type of Disease	Frequency	Percentage
Chronic, not infectious	4,645	68.39
Neoplasm	389	5.73
Diseases of the blood	539	7.94
Circulatory system	1,571	23.13
Genitourinary	605	8.91
Other chronic, not infectious	1,541	22.69
Infectious	736	10.84
Tuberculosis	380	5.50
Venereal diseases	218	3.21
Other infectious	138	2.03
Acute respiratory	636	9.37
Other diseases	774	11.40

Notes: Percentages are computed based on the 6,791 recruits with nonmissing cause of death. Other chronic, not infectious includes allergies, diabetes, diseases of metabolic origin, uremia, and other chronic diseases of not-infectious origin affecting the nervous, digestive, genitourinary, cardiovascular, and gastrointestinal systems. Other infectious includes typhoid, cholera, dysentery, and other bacterial and viral diseases. Acute respiratory includes influenza, pneumonia, bronchitis, and acute laryngitis and tracheitis. Other diseases includes mental diseases, other acute diseases, accidents and violence, and malaria.

Table 8.6   Competing-Risks Regression for the Time Remaining to Die from Different Types of Diseases

	Hazard ratio				
Variable	Chronic, not Infectious, Diseases	Infectious Diseases	Acute Respiratory Diseases	Other Diseases	Unknown Causes of Death
Age at first observation	1.122**	1.082**	1.156**	1.116**	1.152**
Age at first observation squared	1.000**	0.999**	0.999**	1.000**	1.000**
White-collar	1.275**	0.861	1.266	1.334**	0.894
Manual worker	1.045	1.235**	0.981	1.278**	1.141**
Service worker	1.094	1.239	0.755	0.971	1.234**
Northeast at first observation	1.238**	1.048	1.094	1.043	0.910**
South at first observation	0.819**	1.298**	1.284	1.023	1.023
West at first observation	0.868	0.769	1.006	0.785	1.131
Urban at first observation	1.256**	1.511**	1.385**	1.229**	0.974
Foreign-born	1.073**	1.063	1.438**	1.199**	0.967
Migrant status (time-varying)	1.082**	1.151**	1.032	1.187**	1.064
Number of observations	11,097				
Model χ^2 (Wald)	3,298				
p-value	0.0001				

Notes: Omitted variables are farmer, Midwesterner at first observation, rural at first observation, and native-born.

**Significant at the 5 percent level.

Table 8.7   **Competing-Risks Regression for the Time Remaining to Die from Different Types of Diseases, for Migrants**

Variable	Any Cause of Death	Chronic, not Infectious Diseases	Infectious Diseases	Acute Respiratory Diseases	Other Diseases	Unknown Causes
	Hazard Rate					
Age at first observation	1.124**	1.112**	1.082*	1.181*	1.128*	1.141*
Age at first observation squared	1.000**	1.000	1.000	0.999	1.000	1.000
White-collar	1.096	1.104	1.164	1.611*	1.697*	0.876
Manual worker	1.087*	0.981	1.288*	1.144*	1.292*	1.134*
Service worker	1.272*	1.255	1.011	1.117*	1.516	1.342
Northeast at first observation	1.087*	1.247*	1.118	1.095	0.955	0.932
South at first observation	1.022	0.859	1.461*	1.633	0.851	1.07
West at first observation	0.912	0.938	1.153	1.133	0.618	0.903
Moved from urban to rural	0.892*	0.828	1.16	0.803*	0.680	1.009
Moved from rural to urban	0.864*	0.853	0.686	0.859	0.917	0.902
Moved from rural to rural	0.849*	0.739*	1.024	0.769	0.820	0.985
Foreign-born	1.059	1.047	0.913	1.316	0.970	1.082
Number of observations	5,010					
Model χ^2 (Wald)	1,451.5					
p-value	0.0001					

Notes: Omitted variables are farmer, Midwesterner at first observation, urban-urban migrant, and native-born.
**Significant at the 5 percent level.

pared to nonmigrants. Excluding migrants to urban counties, table 8.8 shows that even after controlling for the urban-rural status of the original location, changing locations had a negative effect on life expectancy.[25] Even migrants to rural places had a 2 percent higher risk of dying within the next year compared to rural nonmigrants.[26] These findings imply that there was a "pure" migration effect, perhaps related to the stress of moving to another location and the physical costs that these moves required.

25. Recall that in subsection 8.3.3 I mentioned that because individuals with longer life spans are at higher risk of moving, including a time-fixed dummy variable to indicate migrant status produces downward-biased estimates of the migration effect on life expectancy. Therefore, I cannot simply include dummies for rural nonmigrant and urban nonmigrant in the previous regression to make comparisons between movers and nonmovers.

26. As table 8.2 shows, a considerable number of recruits moved more than once. I estimated this competitive risks model using not the final, but the first destination as the relevant arrival location for migrants. The qualitative results hold.

Table 8.8   **Cox-Regression on the Survival Times of UAMD Veterans, Excluding Migrants to Urban Counties**

Variable	Mean	Hazard Ratio	$Pr > \chi^2$
Age at first observation	38.02	1.126	0.0001
Age at first observation squared		1.000	0.0001
White-collar	0.04	1.136	0.0177
Manual worker	0.34	1.107	0.0001
Service worker	0.02	1.093	0.2592
Northeast at first observation	0.31	1.063	0.0211
South at first observation	0.05	0.966	0.4931
West at first observation	0.02	0.969	0.6735
Urban at first observation	0.16	1.188	0.0001
Foreign-born	0.17	1.063	0.0384
Migrant status (time-varying)		1.026	0.0310
Number of observations	10,047		
Censored observations	2,076		
Model χ^2 (Wald)	5,474.5		
p-value	0.0001		

Notes: Omitted variables are farmer, Midwesterner at first observation, rural at first observation, and native-born.

8.5   Conclusions and Future Research

This paper used a new longitudinal data set to study migration in the postbellum United States and to examine the characteristics of migrants. The data allowed me not only to complement the work of previous researchers, but also to address questions that required longitudinal data. I estimated the hazard rate of changing county of residence within a year, arguing that this is a highly flexible specification for measuring mobility. This allowed me to investigate how the hazard rate of moving changed with age. I also showed that return migration was a common phenomenon during the second half of the nineteenth century. Younger, unmarried recruits who traveled shorter distances and who traveled to the South were more likely to return to a county where they previously resided. Migrants who left family behind were more likely to become return migrants. Migrant life expectancy was significantly shorter than that of counterparts who did not migrate because of migrants' higher probability of dying of infectious disease. Infectious diseases were particularly important in explaining the reduction in life expectancy for those who moved to urban counties. However, migrants across rural areas also suffered higher mortality rates relative to rural nonmovers.

The findings have implications for the extent of labor market integration in the postbellum United States. Price equalization across labor markets is achieved through migration. I found that workers were quite mobile, even at mature ages, and that many workers moved temporarily. These temporary moves suggest that workers responded to economic shocks even though migration reduced their life expectancies. Wage differentials between cities and rural areas (net of migration costs) may have been high because of reduced migrant life expectancy.

Appendix A
UAMD Variables

This section describes the variables in UAMD.

Year of birth. I imputed veterans' year of birth from date of and age at enlistment because these variables provide the most complete information on age.

Death year. This is generally known for all recruits linked to PEN. I assumed that all recruits without a wartime death date survived the war. This produced a wartime death rate of 12.8 percent, close to Dyer's (1959) estimate for the Union Army as a whole. Statewise comparisons of death rates yield equally consistent results.

Linkage to PEN. Any recruit with a pension application date, information on a Pension Board's resolution on claims made by him or his heirs, or with a pension certificate number was considered to be linked to PEN.

County of residence. After cleaning spelling errors, and inputting county from city of residence, I coded the county names using the ICPSR coding scheme created by Sechrist (1984). This coding scheme allows for changes in the names of counties through time, and I assigned a special code to the residences of recruits who reported having lived outside the United States during some part of their lives. Dates in which the veteran resided in a location accompany the location description. When two different sources reported conflicting information on the location of the recruit for a particular year (true in only 3 percent of all cases when two different documents are available), I coded the recruit's residence for that year as missing.

Occupation at enlistment. I coded the occupation of the recruit at enlistment using the 1950 census of population's four-digit classification scheme.

Urban-rural status. A county is considered urban if it contains a city with at least 25,000 inhabitants. I obtained the city population figures from the censuses of population. When two counties changed status from one census to another, I assumed exponential growth in population to impute the year in which the county's urban-rural status changed.

Number of children. Veterans and their dependents had to declare the number of children who were born alive and their dates of birth, as well as the dates of death of any of their children. If no death dates were given, I assumed that the veteran's children outlived their father.

Marital status. The Pension Board required veterans to inform them of any change in marital status. I assumed that if no death date was given for the wife that she outlived the veteran.

Distance traveled. Using Sechrist's (1984) data, I computed the distance (in miles) traveled by migrants from the county seats' longitude and latitude information.

Appendix B

Linkage Failure to PEN and the Effect of War-Related Wounds on the Mobility of Veterans

Veterans linked to PEN either applied claiming pensionable conditions or had legal heirs who claimed to be eligible pensioners. The definition of a pensionable condition changed constantly over time. Starting in 1862, as stated in the General Law of Pensions, pensions were granted to any honorably discharged veteran who served for more than ninety days and who had a war-related condition affecting his ability to perform manual labor. However, in 1890, with the Disability Act Pension Law System, veterans became eligible for pension if they suffered from any medical condition, war-related or not. By 1904, the federal government had equated older age and disability.[27]

Table 8B.1 presents the results of a logistic regression explaining linkage to PEN, where a value of 1 for the dependent variable indicates linkage and zero otherwise. The explanatory variables include individual characteristics, as well as variables for military outcomes, as these may have influenced the eligibility of the potential pensioner as well as the smoothness of the application process.[28]

Relatively older people, native-born veterans, farmers, people who enlisted in the Midwest, and people who were wounded or became prisoners during the war were more likely to be linked to PEN. Region of enlistment and occupation may predict linkage because pensions were an electoral weapon during the postbellum period (Costa 1998; Skocpol 1992). Political competition was highest in the Midwest and, as noted by Glasson (1918), farmers were overrepresented in the Grand Army of the Republic, the veterans' lobbying organization. Those who were honorably discharged (ap-

---

27. See Glasson (1918) for a detailed description of the main changes in the relevant pension legislation.

28. Only information recorded in military-time documents was used for this analysis. For some recruits, age, place of birth, occupation at enlistment, or time served during the Civil War is missing. When this is the case, a dummy variable indicating whether the information is missing for the recruit is included. Therefore, the coefficients for the nonmissing variables should be seen as interaction terms between having nonmissing information and the variable.

Table 8B.1   Logistic Regression on the Probability to be Linked to PEN

Variable	Mean	Logistic Coefficient	Slope
Intercept		0.0282*	0.0056
Age after the war	28.575	0.00938*	0.0529
Place of birth missing	0.03	−1.2942*	−0.0077
Foreign-born	0.286	−0.8129*	−0.0459
White-collar	0.061	−0.4854*	−0.0058
Service worker	0.008	−0.7414*	−0.0012
Manual worker	0.428	−0.3413*	−0.0288
Honorably discharged	0.82	1.1837*	0.1916
Prisoner of war	0.083	0.3473*	0.0057
Volunteer	0.246	0.0385	0.0019
Wounded during the war	0.265	1.3681*	0.0716
Time served	455.455	0.00021	0.0189
Enlisted in Northeast region	0.424	−0.2827*	−0.0237
Enlisted in South region	0.054	−0.1907*	−0.0020
Enlisted in West region	0.021	−1.6352*	−0.0068
N	30,763		
−2 log-likelihood	6593.127		
Max-rescaled R^2	0.2852		

Notes: Omitted variables are native-born, farmers and farm laborers, and enlisted in Midwest. The control variables include dummies indicating that age is missing, that place of birth is missing, that occupation is missing, that occupation is unclassifiable, and that time served is missing.
*Coefficient is significantly different from zero at least at the 1 percent level.

Table 8B.2   Distribution of Wounds Suffered during the War, by Severity

Wound Class	Frequency	Percent
Never had a wound examination	1,253	50.4
Examined for wounds, but given a zero rating	61	2.5
Wounds examined and granted a nonzero rating		
Equivalent to less than anchylosis of a wrist	566	22.8
Worse than above but less than third-degree	500	20.1
Worse than above but less than second-degree	82	3.3
Worse than above but less than first-degree	19	0.8
First-degree	5	0.2

Notes: Total number of recruits: 2,486. Third-degree was considered comparable to the loss of an arm below the elbow, second-degree to the loss of an arm above the elbow, and first-degree to the loss of an arm and a leg.

proximately 90 percent of all soldiers), had been prisoners of war, or were wounded during the war were also more likely to be pension recipients. Veterans who died at young ages were less likely to be linked, as they may not have developed any pensionable condition before dying.

Did being wounded in the war permanently affect recruits' capacity to relocate? Table 8B.2 shows the distribution of wounds suffered during the war by survivors who were wounded during the war and who were ever examined by a surgeon working for the Pension Bureau. Wounds are classified according to severity, where third degree is comparable to the loss of an arm below the elbow, second degree is equivalent to the loss of an arm above the elbow, and first degree is equivalent to the loss of an arm and a leg. This table shows that the majority of recruits in UAMD should not have been affected by their physical capacity to move. More than half did not suffer a permanent incapacity due to wounds suffered during the war. Nearly 30 percent of them were only mildly incapacitated. In fact, as shown in section 8.4.1, those recruits who were ill or wounded during the war were more mobile than those recruits who were neither ill nor wounded.

Appendix C

Size of Bias of Estimates of Mobility Relying on Samples Linked across Decennial Censuses of Population

Previous studies of nineteenth-century migration processes relied on estimates of mobility rates to answer the question "how mobile was this population?" Let P_t represent the number of persons who start period t at a different location with respect to the previous period, and who before t had not made a movement, and let N_{t1} be the total number of persons in the population of interest at $t1$. The mobility rate for the period $(t1, t2)$ is defined as

(A1)
$$M_{(t1,t2)} = \sum_{t1+1}^{t2} \frac{P_t}{N_{t1}}$$

Researchers relying on samples linked across censuses of population are confined to estimate the following version of equation (A1):

(A2)
$$M_{(t1,t1+10)} = \sum_{t1+1}^{t1+10} \frac{P_t}{N_{t1}}$$

Rather than observing P_t, the number of persons with a different location at $t1$ and $t1 + 10$ is used to estimate $\sum_{t1+1}^{t1+10} P_t$. Because people may have moved between census years and returned to their previous locations (return migration) within the same ten-year period, estimation of equation (A2) is downwardly biased.

Although N_{t1} can be observed, inference about moves can be made only for those who were observed and survived to N_{t11+10} (by construction), and therefore this population is taken as the base population. Whether this sample of survivors is representative of the base sample depends on whether the variables explaining census undercount and mortality are correlated to the propensity of individuals to move.

228 Mario A. Sánchez

The size of the return migration bias, and whether differences in life expectancy for migrants relative to nonmigrants exist, are issues that cannot be explored with decennial census data. My panel data enable me to explore more flexible specifications of the estimator for equation (A1) and to investigate return migration and the mortality of migrants.

References

Borjas, George J. 1994. The Economics of Immigration. *Journal of Economic Literature* 32 (4): 1667–1717.
Center for Population Economics. 2000. *Public use tape on the aging of veterans of the Union Army: Data user's manual.* Chicago: University of Chicago, Graduate School of Business, Center for Population Economics.
Costa, Dora L. 1998. *The evolution of retirement: An American economic history, 1880–1990.* Chicago: University of Chicago Press.
Cox, David R. 1984. *Analysis of survival data.* London: Chapman and Hall.
Curtin, Philip D. 1989. *Death by migration: Europe's encounter with the tropical world in the nineteenth century.* New York: Cambridge University Press.
Dyer, Frederick H. 1959. *A compendium of the War of the Rebellion.* Vol. 1. New York: Thomas Yoseloff.
Ferrie, Joseph P. 1996. A new sample of Americans linked from the 1850 public use sample of the federal census of population to the 1860 federal census manuscripts. *Historical Methods* 29 (4): 141–56.
———. 1997. Migration to the frontier in mid-nineteenth-century America: A reexamination of Turner's "safety valve." Northwestern University, Department of Economics. Unpublished manuscript.
———. 1999. How ya gonna keep 'em down on the farm (when they've seen Schenectady?): Rural-to-urban migration in the nineteenth-century America, 1850–70. Northwestern University, Department of Economics. Unpublished manuscript.
Fogel, Robert W. 1986. Nutrition and the decline in mortality since 1700: Some preliminary findings. In *Long-term factors in American economic growth,* ed. S. L. Engerman and R. E. Gallman, 439–555. Vol. 51 in Studies in Income and Wealth. Chicago: University of Chicago Press.
———. 1993. New sources and new techniques for the study of secular trends in nutritional status, health, mortality, and the process of aging. *Historical Methods* 26 (1): 5–43.
Gallaway, Lowell E., and Richard K. Vedder. 1971. Mobility of Native Americans. *Journal of Economic History* 31:3.
Glasson, William H. 1918. *Federal military pensions in the United States.* New York: Oxford University Press.
Greene, William H. 1997. *Econometric analysis.* 3rd ed. Upper Saddle River, N.J.: Prentice Hall.
Gurak, Douglas T., and Fe Caces. 1992. Migration networks and the shaping of migration systems. In *International migration systems: A global approach,* ed. Mary Kritz, Lin Lean Lim, and Hania Zlotnik, 150–76. Oxford, U.K.: Clarendon.
Haines, Michael R. 2000. The population of the United States, 1790–1920. In *The Cambridge economic history of the United States,* ed. Stanley L. Engerman and

Robert E. Gallman. Vol. 2, *The long nineteenth century,* 143–205. New York: Cambridge University Press.

Hugo, Graeme J. 1981. Village-community ties, village norms, and ethnic and social networks: A review of evidence from the third world. In *Migration decision making: Multidisciplinary approaches to microlevel studies in developed and developing countries,* ed. Gorden F. DeJong and Robert W. Gardner, 186–224. New York: Pergamon.

Kuznets, Simon and Dorothy Thomas. 1957. *Population redistribution and economic growth, United States, 1870–1950.* Philadelphia: American Philosophical Society.

Lalonde, Robert, and Robert Topel. 1997. Economic impact of international migration and the economic performance of migrants. In *Handbook of population and family economics,* eds. Mark R. Rosenzweig and Oded Stark, 799–850. Amsterdam: North–Holland.

Lebergott, Stanley. 1970. Migration within the U.S., 1800–1960: Some new estimates. *Journal of Economic History* 30:4.

O'Rourke, Kevin, Jeffrey Williamson, and Timothy Hatton. 1994. Mass migration, commodity market integration, and real wage convergence: The late-nineteenth-century Atlantic economy. In *Migration and the international labor market, 1850–1939,* ed. Timothy J. Hatton and Jeffrey G. Williamson, 203–20. London: Routledge.

Ruggles, Steven, and Matthew Sobek, et al. 1997. Integrated public use microdata series: Version 2.0. Minneapolis: Historical Census Projects, University of Minnesota, available at http://www.ipums.org.

Sechrist, Robert P. 1984. Basic geographic and historic data for interfacing ICPSR data sets, 1620–1983 (*United States*). ICPSR 8159. Baton Rouge, La.: Louisiana State University, and Ann Arbor, Mich.: Inter-university Consortium for Political and Social Research.

Sjaastad, Larry A. 1962. The costs and returns of human migration. *Journal of Political Economy* 70 (5): 80–93.

Skocpol, Theda. 1992. *Protecting mothers and soldiers: The political origins of social policy in the United States.* Cambridge: Harvard University Press.

Stark, Oded. 1991. *The migration of labor.* Cambridge, U.K.: Basil Backwell.

Stark, Oded and David Bloom. 1985. The new economics of labor migration. *American Economic Review* 75 (2): 173–78.

Steckel, Richard H. 1989. Household migration and rural settlement in the United States, 1850–1860. *Explorations in Economic History* 26 (2): 190–218.

Taylor, Edward J. 1986. Differential migration, networks, information and risk. In *Research in human capital and development,* vol. IV, ed. Oded Stark, 747–71. Greenwich, Conn.: JAI Press.

Todaro, Michael P. 1969. A model of labor migration and urban unemployment in less-developed countries. *American Economic Review* 59 (1): 138–48.

Turner, Frederick J. 1920. *The frontier in American history.* New York: Holt.

Williamson, Jeffrey G. 1990. *Coping with city growth during the British Industrial Revolution.* Cambridge: Cambridge University Press.

World Health Organization. 1949. *Manual of the international statistical classification of diseases, injuries, and causes of death.* 6th rev. of the *International lists of diseases and causes of death,* vol. 1. Geneva: World Health Organization.

9

Pensions and Labor Force Participation of Civil War Veterans

Tayatat Kanjanapipatkul

9.1 Retirement and Civil War Pension System

During the last century, retirement became an increasingly important aspect of the U.S. labor market. The retirement rate increased substantially, and more Americans began leaving the labor market at earlier ages, changing the ratio of retirees and workers. These changes coincided with the advent of the Social Security system and old age and disability benefits programs, which have grown significantly. The extent to which these benefits affect retirement not only is an interesting issue to analyze, but is also an important question to ask from the point of view of public policy. The desirability of these programs must be viewed in light of the reduction in the labor force they produced.

Several studies have attempted to empirically measure the change in labor force participation produced by nonlabor income from various programs. This paper will approach the issue by using Civil War pension data to identify the effect of pension income on the labor force participation of veterans. The original researcher in this area is Costa (1993, 1995b, and 1998a), who finds that a substantially lower participation rate of the Union Army veterans compared to the U.S. population at large resulted from the income effect of the federal pension system. In addition, comparisons over time reveal a declining elasticity of retirement with respect to income. Recently, the Center for Population Economics (CPE) at the University of Chicago and the Integrated Public Use Microdata Series (IPUMS) project

Tayatat Kanjanapipatkul received his Ph.D. in economics from the University of Chicago.

Valuable comments from Dora Costa, Robert Fogel, James Heckman, Peter Viechnicki, Todd Bridges, volume referees, participants at the NBER conference, and the Center for Population Economics are gratefully acknowledged.

at the University of Minnesota released new data sets that are suitable for this analysis. The availability of these new, larger, and more comprehensive data makes it sufficiently important to reexamine the earlier estimates of the impact of the Civil War pension on retirement rate among the Union veterans. This paper will also explore several ways to model the Civil War pension. Instead of using only the average monthly pension income, several measures of pension income such as the total lifetime amount and the inflation-adjusted amount will be employed in the regressions. In addition, this paper will try to identify the treatment effect of pensions by making a comparison between the Union and the Confederate veterans.

The Civil War pension program granted a large pension income to Union veterans. Over the decades that followed the war, there was a large expansion of the program both in its magnitude and scope. By the end of the nineteenth century, veterans were no longer required to prove that their disability was related to the military service in order to be eligible for a pension. Old age became the minimal eligibility requirement in the early years of the twentieth century. By 1910, more than 90 percent of Union Army veterans were receiving federal pensions. The average pension was $189.08 a year. This amount represents 74 percent of a farm laborer's average annual income, 51 percent of a laborer's average annual income, and 22 percent of a professional's average annual income.[1] The Report of the Commissioner of Pensions for 1917 stated that the total amount paid to the pensioners of the Civil War was over $4.9 billion, which is 70 times larger than the amount paid to pensioners of the War of the Revolution, 86 times larger than the War with Spain, 96 times larger than the Mexican War, and 107 times larger than the War of 1812.

Figure 9.1 plots the mean pension income per veteran.[2] To account for inflation, both the nominal value and the real value are plotted. The real value was computed by compounding or discounting the nominal value by an interest factor.[3] The base year in the computation is 1910. The interest factor for any year is the product of annual interest rate between that year and 1910. In contrast to the nominal pension profile, the real profile is relatively

1. The average annual income of farm laborers, laborers, and professionals are imputed annual incomes in 1900 calculated by Preston and Haines (1991).
2. The CPE data set records the amount of pension received for each pension application. For each application, the total pension amount is converted into the annual pension income. Then the pension profile is constructed by combining amounts in the same year from all applications together. Missing values in the ending date of the pension ruling are replaced by the beginning date of the next pension ruling. The fluctuation in the right tail of the plot occurs because of the small sample size.
3. The nominal interest rate used for the computation is the yield of the American railroads bond. The yield stops being published in 1937. After 1937, corporate bonds' yield (Moody's Aaa) is used. These numbers are obtained from Series X 476–477 in the U.S. Bureau of Census (1975). The computation of the real profile is as follows. Denote nominal pension income by A_t, and real interest rate by r_t. For any period t after 1910, the real value is $A_t / [\Pi_{i=1910}^{t}(1 + r_i)]$. For any period t before 1910, the value is $A_t \Pi_{i=t}^{1910}(1 + r_i)$.

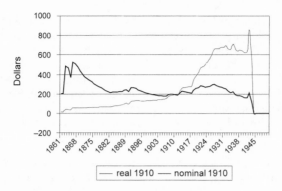

Fig. 9.1   Average annual pension income

flat, and is bounded within the range of $150 to $300 per year except for the years immediately following the war. Humps observed in the left tail of the discounted real profile are expected because the left tail is composed of veterans who received pensions immediately after the war at young ages. Most of these veterans could attribute their disabilities to the war, which allowed them to claim large pension incomes. After the revision of the pension law in 1890, veterans were not required to trace their health problems to the war. Hence, the pensioners after 1890 were composed more of veterans who developed health problems unrelated to their military service. The pension law provided a smaller amount of pension income to them.

Unlike most social insurance schemes, the federal pension was not a compensation for a loss of job, nor were the veterans required to stop working to be eligible for the pension. It did not produce a labor-leisure substitution effect. In general, the amount of the pension was granted based on rank, age, health conditions, the severity of disability (if any), and whether the disability was related to military service. The magnitudes of income and eligibility depend on which pension systems the veterans applied under. The Civil War pensions can be divided into two systems, the disability pension and the service pension system. The disability pension system, also known as the invalid pensions system and the General Law system, was created during the war. Its establishment was intended to attract voluntary enlistment by providing compensation to veterans who were injured during the war. Pensions were granted based on rank and the severity of the injury or disease contracted. According to Glasson,

> In passing the act of 1862, Congress founded what has been called in the Bureau of Pensions the "general law pension system." This was the only system of pension laws in force and applying to the Civil War until 1890. It provides pensions for soldiers who have incurred permanent bodily injury or disability in military service after March 4, 1861. The claimant must show that his disability was incurred as the direct consequence of

the performance of his military duty . . . from causes which can be directly traced to injuries received or disease contracted while in military service. . . . For disabilities caused by wounds received or disease contracted while in the service of the United States and in the line of duty, the act of 1862 granted pensions graded according to rank from thirty dollars to eight dollars per month in cases of total disability. . . . Proportionate pensions were to be given in each rank for partial disability. . . . In all cases invalid-pensions were to continue during the existence of the disability (1918, 125–26).

In contrast, the service pension system was created in 1890, and was intended to provide pensions to veterans who served the Union Army, whether or not they were injured during their service: "The Service Pension System provides pensions based on proof of the fact of military service in the Civil War for a period of ninety days or more and honorable discharge, coupled with the existence of a bodily disability not shown to be of service origin, or with the attainment of a certain age" (Glasson 1918, 125–26).

At the beginning of the service pension system, veterans were granted pension based on their health conditions alone. Old age was not pensionable until 1904 when the Roosevelt administration issued an executive order that allowed old age to be considered a health condition. The order became a part of the pension law in 1907:

[Order no. 78] provided that in the adjudication of claims under the act of 1890, as amended, "it shall be taken and considered as an evidential fact, . . . that, when a claimant has passed the age of sixty-two years he is disabled one-half in ability to perform manual labor and is entitled to be rated at six dollars a month; after sixty-five years at eight dollars a month; after sixty-eight years at ten dollars a month and after seventy years at twelve dollars a month. (Glasson 1918, 247)

The service pension system was a controversial plan. Many critics asserted that the plan was extraordinary liberal, and was made possible through the influence of the Union veterans in politics. On this issue, Glasson wrote,

The Disability Pension Act of 1890 . . . was really a service-pension law subject to a limitation—the existence in applicants of disabilities, regardless of origin . . . pensions were granted to ex-soldiers for incapacity to perform manual labor in such a degree as to render them unable to earn a support. . . . But a man might be in receipt of a comfortable of handsome income from his services as a skilled worker, salesman, clerk, lawyer, physician, public official, business man, or banker without thereby being ineligible for a pension. The law inquired only as to the ability of the applicant to perform crude manual labor, and rated in an arbitrary manner those physical and mental ills which, when of a permanent character, would hamper a man in performing such labor. . . .

Wealth, income, salary, ability to make a good living were ignored. (Glasson 1918, 236–37)

Union veterans could apply for pensions under both systems, the General Law system and the 1890 system. If both applications were approved, the veterans had to choose to receive their pension from only one system. This feature did not lead to a selection problem among the eligible. Many veterans switched from the disability pension system to the service pension system because, under the second system, the disabilities caused by the war as well as those unrelated to the war were pensionable. Only veterans with severe disabilities due to the military service, such as loss of sight, arms, or legs, chose to remain in the first system. For these types of veterans, the question about pension income and their labor force participation is not the main focus of this study. The analysis that follows will examine the pensioners under the service pension system and the selection problems that arise from the eligibility requirements of the pension law.

This paper is organized as follows. Section 9.2 discusses the estimation of the treatment effect by comparing the participation rates of Confederate and Union veterans. Section 9.3 attempts to identify the effect of pensions by using the variation in pension income among Union veterans to predict their participation status. Section 9.4 provides concluding remarks.

9.2 Eligibility Requirements, Selection, and Estimation of the Treatment Effect

The parameter of interest in evaluating the effect of pensions on labor force participation is the effect of the treatment on the treated, which reflects the reduction in the probability that a Union veteran would work compared to the probability he would have worked without receiving pension. The estimation of this parameter is complicated by the fact that there are no labor market data on the extent to which Union veterans would have worked if they were not granted the pensions, since most of them received the federal pension. Despite this problem, one way to estimate this parameter is to approximate the participation rate of the Union veterans not receiving pension by using the labor force participation of a control group whose characteristics are similar to those of the Union veterans, but who did not receive pension. Although it is possible to use the Northern population who did not fight in the war as a control group, the effect of war makes it unlikely that their physical health is comparable to that of the veterans. As a result, the following analysis will use the Confederate veterans as a control group.

This method will lead to an unbiased estimate of the treatment effect if pension status is exogenously determined so that the pensioners, Union veterans, were not selected in such a way that they received a larger or smaller pension income than the nonpensioners, Confederate veterans.[4] It may appear at first that the exogeneity assumption is valid for this analysis because the pension status is determined by the eligibility requirements of the pension law, and the pensioners do not have to retire from work to be eligible. However, the endogeneity problems can still arise if the pension law was created to benefit Union veterans through eligibility restrictions on their characteristics, which differ substantially from those of the Confederates, and by creating pensionable conditions on these characteristics. In this case, the Union veterans would receive larger pension income than the Confederates would have received if they were granted pension. As a result, it is not possible to identify the treatment effect with a regression that includes as independent variables only individual characteristics that directly determine retirement because, even after controlling for these individual characteristics, the correlation between pension income and the unobserved elements brought about by selection problems is not trivial. In order to correct this problem, the regression must include variables that determine eligibility of pension status in order to control for the endogenous selection even if they are not related to the retirement decision.

Consequently, when using Confederate veterans as a control group for Union veterans who did not receive pensions, factors determining the eligibility requirement need to be quantified so that the treatment group and the control group can be compared by individual characteristics directly determining retirement as well as the eligibility characteristics that entitle the Union veterans to larger pension than a hypothetical Confederate eligible for the pension. Neither the disability pension system nor the service pension system considered occupation, wealth, or other factors that differentiated the North and the South as pensionable conditions. If the Confederates were admitted to the federal pension system, the amount of pension income they would have received would be approximately the same based on this consideration alone. However, since the federal pensions' financing depended to a large extent on the greater incentives and greater lobbying power for a generous pension of the Union veterans, the regression needs to account for the characteristics of the Union veterans that enhance their ability to finance the federal pension system.

The Union veterans were well organized and exerted substantial political influence through the Grand Army of the Republic (GAR). The GAR was responsible for the passage of several bills that extended pension benefits under the disability pension system, and strongly lobbied for the service pension system. According to Glasson (1918), the service pension system was financed by the maintenance of high import tariffs in the Northern

---

4. Using the nonveterans in the Northern states as a comparison group will create selection based on health because only healthy recruits were admitted into the army.

economy. Since the Southern economy is very different from that of the North, it is unlikely that the Confederate veterans would be in a position to raise as much tariff revenue as the Union veterans—especially since there is far smaller industry in the South—or that they would be capable of lobbying to the same extent the GAR did. This suggests that the characteristics of the Northern economy, which can also be interpreted as a kind of eligibility requirement because they differentiate the North and the South, are correlated with the amount of pension income. As a result, state-level variables that summarize these economies need to be included in the regression of the veterans' labor force participation decisions.

Although various methods have been suggested, in the recent social program evaluation literature, for how to implement this regression and identify the treatment effect, the effectiveness of these estimators, when applied to historical data and the historical environments that generated them, is largely unknown. Most historical data available for statistical analysis lack sophisticated questionnaire designs, have small sample sizes, and contain limited numbers of variables. Application of many recently developed estimators will not always lead to better estimates of the treatment effect than the more traditional ones. The following analysis uses the matching method to control for the selection problem. The underlying assumption is that when the data are conditioned on economic characteristics of the Northern and Southern states, the problem will disappear, and the treatment effect can be recovered.

The analysis that follows is based on two sources of data. The first data set is cross-sectional data from the 1910 census obtained from IPUMS. It contains a 1 percent random sample of the 1910 census, which is the only census that asked whether the respondents were Civil War veterans and in which army the respondents served. The IPUMS data contain 617 Confederate veterans and 1,500 Union veterans. The second source of data is the life-cycle data of 4,528 Union veterans obtained from the CPE. This data set contains the variables from the 1910 census as well as the information from all of the veterans' federal pension applications, such as the amount of pension they received each year.[5]

Table 9.1 provides summary statistics for the two data sets.[6] The participation rate of Union veterans is 55 percent. This is lower than the participation rate of the entire population in the same cohort, 66 percent, and the participation rate of Confederate veterans, 71 percent. The mean age is 69. Confederates had larger families and were more likely to live in farm households and rural areas. Their literacy rate was approximately 6 percent lower

---

5. The IPUMS data can be downloaded from www.ipums.umn.edu. The Union veterans data can be downloaded from www.cpe.uchicago.edu.

6. Since the IPUMS Confederate and Union samples are drawn from the same source, all variables can be compared. However, only some variables from the CPE Union sample can be compared with the IPUMS variables.

Table 9.1   Summary Statistics for IPUMS Confederate, IPUMS Union, and CPE Union Samples

	IPUMS		CPE Union	
Variable	Confederate	Union	1910	1900
Number of observations	617	1,500	4,528	7,023
Participation rate	71%	55%	55%	93%
Age				
Mean	69.64	69.38	69.12	59.95
Standard deviation	6.09	5.30	5.33	6.09
Family size				
Mean	4.13	3.03		
Standard deviation	2.42	1.85		
Number of farm schedule				
Mean	1.64	1.27		
Standard deviation	0.55	0.47		
Literacy rate	88%	94%	94%	95%
Farm household	61%	27%	24%	40%
Head of household	79%	77%	84%	93%
Free of mortgage	61%	53%	51%	42%
Own house	70%	68%	64%	64%
Live in urban area	14%	36%		
Married	73%	71%	75%	86%

than that of Union veterans. The proportions of Confederate veterans who owned a house and of those who owned a house free of mortgage are higher than the corresponding proportions of Union veterans. Among the working veterans, more than 70 percent of Confederates were farmers,[7] while less than 50 percent of Union veterans were.

The matching procedure could be implemented on the data without making functional form assumptions by forming cells and comparing the participation rate in each cell. Unfortunately, the data do not allow detailed conditioning without violating the condition that each cell must contain both pensioners and nonpensioners. Hence, it is desirable to pursue the matching exercise through regression analysis as well. Matching by cells clearly demonstrates the importance of conditioning. The difference in the participation rates between the Confederate and the Union veterans is substantially reduced when the data are conditioned by variables related to farming. These variables include a dummy indicating whether a veteran lived in an urban or a rural county, a dummy indicating whether a veteran

7. Occupational classification is based on the 1950 classification. In this paper, the classification is grouped into the 1950 category into four broad occupations: professionals, clerks, laborers, and farmers. Professionals include professional, technical, and managers and proprietors. Clerks include clerical and kindred workers, craftsmen, and service workers. Laborers consist of sales workers, operative workers, and laborers. Farmers include farmers and farm laborers.

lived in a farm or nonfarm household,[8] and the number of farm schedules[9] (which indicates the number of farms the household operates). Table 9.2 shows that, when the veterans are compared by the number of farm schedules, the difference between the participation rates of Confederate and Union veterans is reduced substantially. When comparisons are made based on the urban county and farm household variables, the participation rate of the Confederate veterans lies between the participation rate of the IPUMS Union veterans and that of the CPE Union veterans. In addition, the participation rate of veterans who lived in farm households and rural counties are consistently higher than for those who lived in nonfarm households in all three samples.

The higher participation rates of the Confederate veterans in unconditional comparisons result from the fact that the labor force participation rate in the North is generally lower.[10] This pattern, geographically plotted in figure 9.2, probably reflects the self-employment nature of the agricultural occupations in the South.[11] This confirms that, in order to identify the treatment effect, it is necessary to compare (or match) participation rates of the Confederate and Union veterans by these characteristics because the pension law selected pensioners whose characteristics were systematically different from those of the general population in term of regional characteristics.

This can be implemented more effectively by imposing a functional form and estimating the regression equation. Denote the probability that each person participates in the labor force by P_1 if he is a pensioner, and P_0 if he is not. Let the value of U be 1 if he is a Union veteran and 0 if he is a Confederate veteran. The treatment effect can be expressed as

$$E(P_1 - P_0 \mid X, U = 1) = F_1(X) - F_0(X) + E(v_1 - v_0 \mid X, U = 1),$$

where F denotes a cumulative distribution function of labor force participation, which can be linear, logistic, or probit; X stands for individual char-

---

8. According to IPUMS, a household is classified as farm household if it is located on a tract of three or more acres used for any agricultural operations, regardless of the amount of labor or produce involved. Alternatively, a household is considered a farm household if it is located on a tract of fewer than three acres that either yielded above $250 in produce sales in the previous year, or employed at least one full-time farmer or agricultural laborer.

9. The number of farm schedules indicates how many farm schedules any member of the household received to be filled out for the agricultural census. It is a proxy for the number of farms the household member operated.

10. Most Union veterans were born in the northern states. Their pattern of residence had not changed much by 1910. The majority of Union veterans from both samples still lived in the East North Central (ENC), Middle Atlantic (MA), New England (NE), and Pacific (PC). The regional divisions are the same as census divisions.

11. Comparisons by head of household status, marital status, mortgage status, and home ownership status are also presented in table 9.1. The participation rate of the Confederate veterans is still significantly different from the participation rate of the Union veterans in both samples. The participation rate of Confederate veterans plotted by age and family size lies uniformly above that of Union veterans.

Table 9.2   Participation Rate in 1910 by Head of Household Status, Marital Status, Mortgage Status, Home Ownership Status, Farm Household, and Number of Farm Schedules

Value	IPUMS Confederate Participation Rate (%)	IPUMS Union Participation Rate (%)	χ^2	CPE Union Participation Rate (%)	χ^2
		Head of household status			
Head	81	62	57.43*	63	64.13*
Nonhead	33	28	0.87	28	1.51
		Marital status			
Married	79	60	48.26*	62	49.39*
Widowed	50	42	1.87	42	3.22***
		Mortgage status			
Mortgage	76	67	2.07	74	0.128
Free	76	56	41.47*	60	33.98
Missing	60	46	9.51*	46	11.774*
		Home ownership status			
Own	76	59	39.53*	63	29.31*
Rent	64	61	0.38	67	0.35
Missing	7	10	0.20	29	3.71***
		Farm household status			
Farm	84	80	2.12	89	4.52**
Nonfarm	50	45	1.85	52	0.40
		Number of farm schedules			
0	49	45	1.71		
1+	85	83	0.75		
		Urban county status			
Urban	54	52	0.07	55	0.04
Rural	73	56	45.61*	55	65.54*

Notes: The Chi-squared statistic tests whether the participation rate of IPUMS Confederate is larger than the participation rate of the corresponding CPE veterans.
***Significant at the 10 percent level.
**Significant at the 5 percent level.
*Significant at the 1 percent level.

acteristics; v is the unobserved elements; and the subscripts indicate the pensioners. By invoking the matching assumption, the treatment effect can be estimated in a regression with labor force participation as dependent variables. The estimation equation is $P = F_0(X) + UE(P_1 - P_0 \mid X, U = 1) + \varepsilon$, and the treatment effect can be computed from $F_1(X) - F_0(X)$. In this analysis, the linear and logistic models will be estimated. It is important to note that the treatment effect need not be a constant in these models because it represents both the shift in the entire participation equation and the inter-

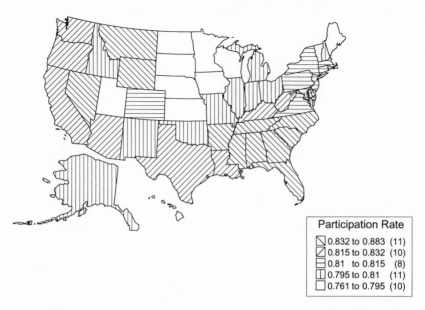

Fig. 9.2   Participation rate of male population over ten years of age in 1910
Source: U.S. Bureau of the Census (1912–14).

action of the shift with independent variables. To simplify the analysis it will be assumed that, with the exception of the intercept term, the coefficients of individual characteristics will be the same in both F_1 and F_0. With this assumption, the treatment effect in the linear model is the coefficient of the dummy variable indicating the Union veterans. For the logistic model, the treatment effect can be obtained by evaluating the difference between F_1 and F_0 at its own intercept, and the mean value of the explanatory variables.

The participation rate was regressed on the matching variables and some demographic variables that influence labor force participation decisions but do not affect selection, such as age, marital status, home ownership status, and head of household status. The matching variables were chosen to capture the differences in characteristics of the Union veterans, which are due mainly to regional differences. In the regression, these variables include a dummy variable indicating that the household received at least one farm schedule; a dummy for whether they lived in an urban county; a dummy for whether they were foreign-born; the state unemployment rate; the fraction of wage earners in their state; and the state's rank in manufacturing value-added, total manufacturing value, number of industrial establishments, and number of industries. Data for state characteristics were obtained from the 1910 census of manufacturing.

Table 9.3 reports the estimation results for the entire sample. It is not surprising to find that participation declines with age, nor that veterans who

Table 9.3   Coefficient Estimates, Marginal Effects, and Mean of the Matching Regression

Variable	OLS		Mean	Logistic			
	Estimate	Estimate		Estimate	Slope	Estimate	Slope
Intercept of nonpensioners	1.98*	2.36*		8.99*		9.71*	
Intercept of pensioner				8.66*		9.19*	
Dummy if Union veteran	-0.06***	-0.11*					
Age	-0.02*	-0.02*	69.45	-0.12*	-0.03	-0.11*	-0.02
Dummy if head of household	0.27*	0.24*	0.71	1.58*	0.37	1.09*	0.26
Dummy if widowed	-0.02	-0.02	0.78	-0.17	-0.04	-0.09	-0.02
Dummy if not married	0.06	0.03	0.23	0.47***	0.10	0.37	0.08
Dummy if rent house	0.09*	0.04	0.05	0.57*	0.12	0.20***	0.04
Dummy if ownership missing	-0.09***	-0.26*	0.24	-0.61***	-0.15	-2.07*	-0.47
Dummy if house mortgaged	0.07*	0.11*	0.08	0.44**	0.09	0.53*	0.11
Dummy if urban county	0.13*	-0.05***	0.14	0.61*	0.13	-0.27**	-0.06
Dummy if foreign-born	0.01	0.01	0.30	0.08	0.02	-0.00	0.00
Dummy if at least one farm schedule	0.41*		0.12	2.29*	0.43		
State unemployment rate	-2.16*	-2.38*	0.36	-12.90*	-2.87	-12.57*	-2.78
Percent of wage earner in state	0.01***	0.01	0.19	0.04**	0.01	0.01	0.00
State rank of manufacturing value	-0.01*	-0.01	6.62	-0.04*	-0.01	-0.01	0.00
State rank of manufacturing value added	0.01**	0.01	15.61	0.06*	0.01	0.03	0.01
State rank of number of industrial establishment	0.01***	0.01	15.84	0.02	0.00	0.02	0.00
State rank of number of industry	-0.01*	-0.01**	14.38	-0.04*	-0.01	-0.04**	-0.01
R^2	0.31	0.32		0.22		0.21	
Adjusted R^2	0.31	0.32					
Observations	2,117	2,117		2,117		2,117	

Notes: These regressions are based on the IPUMS sample. Statistical significance is based on the robust standard error. The slopes are evaluated at the mean value of the explanatory variables. In the linear model, the treatment effect is the coefficient of the dummy variable indicating the Union veterans. In the logistic model, the treatment effect must be computed from the difference of pensioner and nonpensioner logistic functions evaluated at its own intercept value.

***Significant at the 10 percent level.
**Significant at the 5 percent level.
*Significant at the 1 percent level.

were heads of household and rented a house, or owned a home not free of mortgage, have higher participation rates. In both the linear and logistic models, the matching variables are statistically significant except the dummy for foreign-born. They suggest that the states that were more manufacturing intensive tended to consist of the veterans with lower participation rates. Veterans who lived in states with a high fraction of wage earners, a high manufacturing value-added, and a high number of industrial establishments were less likely to work. The number of farm schedules and the state unemployment rate also control for the higher participation rate in the South due to regional factors discussed earlier. The estimate of the treatment effect in the linear model can be read directly from the coefficient of the dummy variable indicating Union veteran status, which is 5.6 percent with the standard error of about 0.03. For the logistic model, the estimate was computed by finding the difference of the probability of the participation of pensioners and nonpensioners evaluating the average value of the explanatory variables. This estimate is 8 percent.

The table also reports estimation results excluding the dummy variable for the number of farm schedules. The literature and the regression results based on Union veterans suggest that farmers who retire move away from their farms and do not operate any farms. The dummy variable for farm schedules might be picking up a retirement effect. Without the dummy variable, the treatment effect estimated from the linear model is 11 percent. The effect from the logistic model is 12 percent. It is interesting to note that the coefficient of the dummy for urban county became negative and significant. This probably reflects the effect of the farm schedule variable that was excluded.

When the sample was restricted only to the border states, the assumption that the veterans from both armies were similar is plausible. In this case, the border states restriction serves as a conditioning tool. The estimation results for the border states are reported in table 9.4. Age and head of household status remain significant predictors of participation rate. The estimate of the treatment effect is 6.2 percent from the linear model and 6.7 percent from the logistic model. The standard error is approximately 0.1.

9.3 Interaction Effects of Pension Income and Retirement

A major issue in the previous section is the endogeneity of pension status. The Civil War pension eligibility requirements produced systematic differences in the characteristics of the pensioners. Estimations of the treatment effect account for these factors by comparing participation rates conditional on the regional characteristics. Another technique to estimate the effect of pension is to use the pension income to predict participation status among the pensioners. This method is usually implemented by estimating a discrete choice model on a sample, which is restricted to veterans who

Table 9.4   Coefficient Estimates, Marginal Effects, and Mean of the Matching
                     Regression in the Border States

| | | Logistic | | |
Variable	OLS Estimate	Estimate	Slope	Mean
Intercept of nonpensioner	1.82*	6.84		
Intercept of pensioner		6.53*		
Dummy if Union veteran	–0.06			
Age	–0.02*	–0.10*	–0.02	69.56
Dummy if head of household	0.30*	1.35*	0.31	0.80
Dummy if widowed	–0.02	–0.13	–0.03	0.23
Dummy if not married	0.16	0.87	0.15	0.04
Dummy if rent house	–0.01	–0.11	–0.02	0.25
Dummy if ownership missing	–0.12	–0.69	–0.16	0.05
Dummy if house mortgaged	0.03	0.06	0.01	0.13
R^2	0.17			
Adjusted R^2	0.16			
Observations	506			

Notes: These regressions are based on the IPUMS sample. The slopes are evaluated at the mean value of the explanatory variables. In the linear model, the treatment effect is the coefficient of the dummy variable indicating the Union veterans. In the logistic model, the treatment effect must be computed from the difference of pensioner and nonpensioner logistic functions, evaluated at its own intercept value.

***Significant at the 10 percent level.

**Significant at the 5 percent level.

*Significant at the 1 percent level.

served in the Union Army and were eligible to receive a federal pension. This approach permits estimations of interaction effects, such as that between pension income and occupation. In addition, by including only pensioners in the regression, the estimation can use the more comprehensive data set available from the CPE. The pension effect is usually estimated by computing the change in the probability of participation between veterans who received larger amounts of pension and those with lower amounts. Denote the probability of being in the labor force by P and the pension income by I; following the notations from the last section, the effect of pensions on labor force participation can be written as $[\partial E(P \mid X, U = 1)]/\partial I$.

It is important to note that this parameter is different from the treatment effect. It reflects the interaction between pension status and pension income. The magnitude of the estimate measures the sensitivity of the probability of retirement of pensioners with respect to their pension income. Furthermore, this estimate applies only to the North. Since the CPE sample is a representative sample of the Northern white male population, estimation results based on the Union veterans alone will not suffer from selection problems. In the following discussion, the emphasis will not be on the selection issues that arise when comparing the Northern sample to the Southern sample, but on the estimation results within the CPE Union sample. The aims are to compare the results with Costa's (1998a) analysis based on a smaller sample of the current CPE data, known as the twenty-company sample, and to estimate other interaction effects from the larger data set.

Economic theory provides a general framework that leads to using variation in pension income to estimate pension effects by assuming that the objective of veterans was to maximize their utility, subject to their lifetime budget constraints. They will choose to retire if their reservation wage is greater than the market wage. Pension income thus affects retirement decisions by changing the reservation wage. The reservation wage of veterans is represented by the marginal rate of substitution between consumption and labor supply. The decision to retire depends crucially on the determinants of the marginal rate of substitution, which is the amount of consumption after retirement. Denoting the market wage rate by w_t, the consumption by c_t, the labor supply by l_t, and the utility function by U, we can write the probability of observing a veteran working in period t as

$$\text{prob(work at } t) = \text{prob}\left[-\frac{U_{l_t}(c_t, 0)}{U_{c_t}(c_t, 0)} \leq w_t \right].^{12}$$

Taking the first-order approximation of the marginal rate of substitution and market wage gives

$$-\frac{U_{l_t}(c_t, 0)}{U_{c_t}(c_t, 0)} = X\beta + bC + \varepsilon,$$

$$w_t = Z\varphi + \mu,$$

where C represents consumption, X stands for socioeconomic variables that affect reservation wage, Z stands for the proxy for wage, and ε and μ are residuals. The probability of working at time t is then

$$\text{prob(work at } t) = \text{prob}(\varepsilon - \mu \leq Z\varphi - X\beta - bC).$$

Depending on the assumption about ε and μ, the above probability statement can be estimated by a linear, logistic, or probit regression with the observed retirement decision as the dependent variable and the variables C, X, and Z as explanatory variables. The level of total consumption after retirement is determined by the veterans' full income after retirement, which depends upon total pension income and upon accumulated wealth.[13] To proxy total income, several measures of pension income, home ownership status, and mortgage status are used. Proxies for reservation wage are age, health,

---

12. This expression can be obtained from the utility maximization problem. The optimality condition is the equality of the marginal rate of substitution and the ratio of price of consumption to wage rate, $\forall t, -(U_{l_t}/U_{c_t}) \geq w_t (> \text{if } l_t = 0)$.

13. In symbols, the consumption must satisfy $\sum_{t=R}^{T} c_t/1 + r_t \leq A_0 + \sum_{t=R}^{T} A_t/1 + i_t$, where the summation is from the period in which the veterans retired to the period they died, and A_0 is the veterans' stock of wealth as of retirement.

and various socioeconomic characteristics. Proxies for health include body mass index (BMI), wound rating,[14] a dummy for whether the veteran was discharged from military service with a disability, the number of years the veteran lived after the census, and a dummy variable indicating whether the veteran served as a private. Body mass index was constructed by Song (2000). Both variables were created from the Surgeons' Certificates in the CPE data set. Other proxies for socioeconomic characteristics include marital status, a dummy for whether the veteran lived in a farm household, a dummy for whether the veteran was foreign-born, a dummy for whether the veteran lived in an urban county,[15] and the state unemployment rate. The proxy for wage is occupation, which is divided into four broad categories: professional, clerk, laborer, and farmer. Retirees were assigned the most recent occupations stated in their pension applications before they retired.

Logistic regressions were estimated for cross-sectional samples from the 1900 CPE and the 1910 CPE Union veterans. The estimation results are reported in table 9.5. The estimates of the coefficients of annual pension income are negative and statistically significant. Using four alternative measures of pension income yields the same results. Table 9.6 reports the marginal effect, elasticity, and average change in participation rate due to the pension income. The probability of participation in 1910 is lower by 0.00076 for every dollar of average monthly pension income. If veterans were granted the average monthly pension, which is $188.70, their participation rate would be lower by 14 percent (= –0.00076 · 188.70). Applying the same computation to other measures of pension income results in a reduction in participation rates between 6 and 14 percent. The estimated slope of the probability of retirement in 1910 from the twenty-company sample is 0.0112, and the average annual pension income is $171.90 (Costa, 1998a). If the veterans were given the average pension, their participation rate would be reduced by 19 percent (= 0.0112 · 16.94), which is larger than the figures computed above. For 1900, the estimation implies a reduction in participation rates between 1 and 3 percent.

The estimated elasticity of retirement varies substantially with the measure of pension income used to calculate it. The elasticity computed from lifetime pension or nominal measure of pension tends to be larger than that computed from annual or real measures.[16] In 1910, the maximum estimate (0.51) occurs when the monthly nominal pension income is used, and the

14. When veterans applied for pension, the federal Pension Board ordered them to take an examination conducted by a group of surgeons. The surgeons rated the veterans based on their overall health conditions as well as the specific conditions. The rating was then submitted to the Pension Board for approval (Glasson 1918). The wound ratings used in the regression are based on gunshot wounds or bodily injuries, most of which were due to the war. This variable is created by Mario Sanchez.

15. A county is defined as urban if it contains one or more cities with more than 25,000 inhabitants in 1910.

16. Refer to figure 9.1 and note 3 for the discussion of nominal and real pension income.

Table 9.5   **Logistic Estimation of Probability of Labor Force Participation with Participation Status as the Dependent Variable**

Variable	1910			1900		
	Estimate	Marginal Effect	Mean	Estimate	Marginal Effect	Mean
Intercept	7.0011*			8.5126*		
Monthly pension income	−0.0049*	−0.0008	188.6980	−0.0028**	−0.0002	166.5970
Dummy if professional	1.9761*	0.3719	0.1050	1.9406*	0.0384	0.1440
Dummy if clerk	2.0876*	0.4148	0.2040	1.5655*	0.0366	0.2010
Dummy if laborer	1.3795*	0.3045	0.2290	1.6471*	0.0397	0.2300
Interaction professional	0.0029**	0.0004	20.1860	0.0018	0.0001	25.0850
Interaction clerk	0.0005	0.0001	38.1940	0.0008**	0.0000	32.8600
Interaction laborer	0.0025*	0.0004	42.8460	0.0004	0.0000	37.3320
Age	−0.0889*	−0.0138	69.1160	−0.0525*	−0.0028	59.9460
Dummy if head of household	1.4477*	0.3436	0.8170	0.5707**	0.0240	0.9190
Dummy if not married	−0.1950	−0.0484	0.0570	0.2940	0.0087	0.0500
Dummy if widowed	−0.1894*	−0.0469	0.1900	−0.3653*	−0.0141	0.0920
Dummy if rent house	0.4485*	0.1073	0.1610	0.1920*	0.0062	0.2600
Dummy if ownership missing	−0.7244	−0.1791	0.2000	0.4167**	0.0120	0.1030
Dummy if house mortgaged	0.4058*	0.0971	0.1210	0.3746*	0.0113	0.1980
Dummy if nonfarm household	−3.4545*	−0.6757	0.5730	−3.4656*	−0.1421	0.5460
Dummy if nonfarm missing	−2.0043*	−0.4510	0.1920	−2.9067*	−0.3075	0.0920
Dummy if urban county	0.0992	0.0244	0.3140	−0.2621*	−0.0093	0.2650
State unemployment rate	−0.1721	−0.0267	0.2010	−5.9103**	−0.3150	0.2100
Dummy if foreign-born	−0.0896	−0.0221	0.1400	−0.1140	−0.0040	0.1490
Number of years lived after census	0.0631*	0.0098	9.6170	0.0257***	0.0014	15.5150
Dummy if BMI not missing	−2.8620***	−0.4947	0.8230	−3.8484*	−0.0622	0.8330
BMI	0.2108***	0.0327	19.0220	0.2958*	0.0158	19.2640
BMI^2	−0.0040***	−0.0006	450.1540	−0.0058*	−0.0003	455.5460
Dummy if discharged with disability	−0.0623	−0.0154	0.1880	−0.4072**	−0.0153	0.1940
Dummy if wound rating not missing	0.0202	0.0050	0.1230	0.2013	0.0063	0.1360
Wound rating	−0.0587	−0.0091	0.2050	−0.1345	−0.0072	0.2210
Dummy if not private	0.1324	0.0323	0.0940	0.1444	0.0046	0.1070
R^2	0.3436			0.0871		
Rescaled R^2	0.4634			0.2265		
Observations	4,540			7,007		

Notes: These regressions are based on the CPE sample. Statistical significance is based on the robust standard error. The slope reported here was computed by averaging the individual slope calculated from the predicted probability of each observation.

***Significant at the 10 percent level.

**Significant at the 5 percent level.

*Significant at the 1 percent level.

Table 9.6   Mean, Marginal Effect, and the Mean Pension Effect

Pension Income	Mean	Marginal Effect	Mean Pension Effect
1910 Census			
Average monthly pension	188.70	–7.61E-04	–0.1436
Average monthly real pension	223.85	–5.23E-04	–0.1171
Total pension	6,474.65	–1.97E-05	–0.1274
Total real pension	8,122.86	–9.29E-06	–0.0754
Annual pension in 1910	190.21	–2.94E-04	–0.0559
Total pension 1900–10	1,630.38	–3.81E-05	–0.0622
Total real pension 1900–10	1,962.90	–3.14E-05	–0.0616
1900 Census			
Average monthly pension	166.60	–1.51E-04	–0.0251
Average monthly real pension	149.75	–1.16E-04	–0.0174
Total pension	5,291.87	–3.78E-06	–0.0200
Total real pension	4,928.50	–2.26E-06	–0.0111
Annual pension in 1900	119.27	–1.31E-04	–0.0157
Total pension 1890–1900	1,133.59	–1.39E-05	–0.0157
Total real pension 1890–1900	1,382.77	–1.12E-05	–0.0155

Notes: This table is based on the CPE sample. The level of significance is computed relative to farmers' elasticity.
***Significant at the 10 percent level.
**Significant at the 5 percent level.
*Significant at the 1 percent level.

minimum estimate (0.18) occurs when the annual pension received in 1910 is used. The maximum elasticity from the 1900 sample (0.43) occurs when the monthly average pension is used, while the minimum (0.19) occurs when the lifetime real pension is used. Each estimate reflects a different behavioral aspect. The estimate of lifetime pension income reflects responses that include expectation of pension income in the future, while the estimate using pension income from 1900 or 1910 does not. Consequently, the estimates using lifetime or average measures tend to be larger. This result suggests that veterans reacted more toward the annuity feature of the federal pension than toward the amount of pension in a particular period. In addition, the lower estimates from real measures of pension income suggest that, to a large extent, the veterans simply considered the nominal monetary value of the pension income when making retirement decision.

Comparisons of the elasticity between 1910 and 1900 do not provide a clear trend as to whether elasticity is rising or falling. Elasticities computed from lifetime pension are rising from 1900 to 1910, while those computed from pension income received around 1910 and 1900 are falling. Nevertheless, all computed elasticities are significantly larger than zero, which confirms the hypothesis that, in contrast to findings from recent studies on social security, the income elasticity of retirement fell after 1910. The 1910 estimate from the twenty-company sample, 0.47, is very close to the current

Table 9.7   **Elasticity of Retirement with Respect to Pension Income by Occupation**

	Noninteracted	Farmer	Professionals	Laborers	Clerks
1910 Census					
Average monthly pension	−0.5123*	−0.4382	−0.2928***	−0.2515**	−0.5121
Average monthly real pension	−0.3894*	−0.3381	−0.7183	−0.3912	−0.2891
Total pension	−0.4544*	−0.4016	−0.5206	−0.2705**	−0.3640***
Total real pension	−0.2468*	−0.2186	−0.3591	−0.1778	−0.0935**
Annual pension in 1910	−0.1826**	−0.1622	−0.5197	−0.5139*	−0.0795
Total pension 1900–10	−0.2001*	−0.1810	−0.4324	−0.3777**	−0.2266
Total real pension 1900–10	−0.1982*	−0.1794	−0.4202	−0.3644**	−0.2221
1900 Census					
Average monthly pension	−0.4395*	−0.4389	−0.1721	−0.3716	−0.3153
Average monthly real pension	−0.3014*	−0.3033	−0.2380	−0.3923	−0.2057
Total pension	−0.3509*	−0.3671	−0.5220	−0.3172	−0.2852
Total real pension	−0.1925*	−0.2001	−0.2395	−0.2121	−0.0962
Annual pension in 1900	−0.2699*	−0.2809	−0.2887	−0.1086	−0.2217
Total pension 1890–1900	−0.2707*	−0.2856	−0.2702	−0.2205	−0.1744
Total real pension 1890–1900	−0.2661*	−0.2811	−0.2645	−0.2304	−0.1680

Notes: This table provides the elasticity from the regression based on the CPE sample. The level of significance is computed relative to farmers' elasticity.
***Significant at the 10 percent level.
**Significant at the 5 percent level.
*Significant at the 1 percent level.

estimate for the monthly nominal pension income, 0.51, and the lifetime nominal pension income, 0.45. However, the current 1900 estimate is lower than the estimate based on the twenty-company sample, 0.73.[17]

Table 9.7 shows that several of the pension-occupation interactions are statistically significant, although the magnitudes of the interaction effect vary with the measure of pension income used in the regression. In 1910, the majority of the estimates indicate that professionals are the most sensitive to pension income, followed by clerks. Farmers and laborers are the least sensitive. Professionals are also the most sensitive to pension in 1900, followed by laborers and clerks. The most radical difference is that the income elasticity of farmers had become almost as sensitive as that of professionals by 1900. Furthermore, the occupation dummies together with the farm dummy variables indicate that farmers who lived in farm households are the most likely to participate in the labor market, and farmers who live in nonfarm households are the least likely. The majority of the latter type of farmers were retired. This result confirms the findings in Costa (1995a) and Lee (1999), who found that liquidating farms was a strategy for financing retirement.

17. The difference might be related to the sample size. Costa's 1910 estimate is based on the twenty-company sample combined with a sample of veterans from Ohio, while her 1900 estimate is based on the twenty-company sample alone.

Most farmers exited the labor force either by transferring their farms to their children or by selling to outsiders. Ostergen (1981) found that the latter method was gaining popularity when land values increased between 1885 and 1915. High participation rates among farmers and the reduction in retirement elasticity from 1900 to 1910 may have resulted both from the increase in land values and from the self-employed nature of the occupation.

The regressions also suggest a considerable health effect. In both regressions, the number of years the veterans lived after the census and both the linear and quadratic BMI are statistically significant. The longer the veterans lived after the census, the less likely they were to retire. The estimated coefficients of BMI suggest that participation rates initially rose as BMI increased, but that after BMI reached 26.35 in 1910 and 25.59 in 1900, participation rates fell. Costa (1998a) also found an inverted U-shaped relationship between the retirement rate and BMI in the twenty-company sample. Furthermore, veterans who were discharged from military service with disabilities were less likely to participate in the labor market. This effect is statistically significant in the 1900 sample. The estimate for wound rating, which measures the severity of body wounds (mainly due to gunshots) during the war, is negative, as expected, but not significant. The veterans who served as nonprivates were more likely to participate in the labor force.

There is no conclusive evidence that different cohorts behaved differently. In general, participation rates decline with age, but the interaction term between pension income and age is not statistically significant. The 1910 regressions generate positive estimates, while the 1900 regressions generate negative estimates. Similarly, the interaction term between pension income and urban/rural status is not significant, although urban/rural status by itself is significant. In 1900, the estimate is negative, suggesting that veterans living in urban areas are more likely to retire. The estimate is positive but not significant in 1910. This result is consistent with the estimation based on the twenty-company sample, which produced the same pattern.

Other findings are as follows. A veteran who was head of household, rented a house, or had mortgage on an owned house was more likely to participate in the labor market. There is no evidence that foreign-born veterans behaved differently. Both widowed and single veterans were more likely to retire. Veterans who had missing values in the own/rent variables and farm household status were significantly less likely to participate. The estimates also suggest that veterans who rented their homes had a higher probability of labor force participation. Homeowners were likely to be more wealthy, allowing them to stay outside the labor market.

9.4 Concluding Remarks

This paper has examined the effect of the federal pension system on the labor force participation of Civil War veterans. The paper has made two major points. First of all, pension laws created systematic differences in characteristics of pensioners and nonpensioners through eligibility requirements. A substantial portion of the difference between the participation rates of Confederate and Union veterans is due to these differences. The identification of the treatment effect needs to account for this selection problem. The findings based on the matching methods suggest a strong impact of pensions on labor force participation. Second, variations in pension income among the Union veterans explain the differences in their participation rates by as much as 15 percent. The estimated effect depends on the measure of pension income used in the regression. The elasticity of retirement with respect to pension income also varies between occupations.

It is hoped that this study will encourage further research into long-term retirement patterns in America. By looking at the historical data, this research demonstrated the importance of military pension and farm liquidation as means to finance retirement. Although Social Security replaced these methods and became widely used, the continuous decline in labor force participation reflects a stable and persistent process that underlies the economics of retirement and remains to be examined further.

References

Costa, Dora L. 1993. *Health, income, and retirement: Evidence from nineteenth-century America.* Ph.D. diss. University of Chicago.
———. 1995a. Agricultural decline and the secular rise in male retirement rates. *Explorations in Economic History* 32 (4): 540–52.
———. 1995b. Pensions and retirement: Evidence from Union army veterans. *Quarterly Journal of Economics* 110 (2): 297–320.
———. 1998a. *The evolution of retirement: An American economic history.* Chicago: University of Chicago Press.
———. 1998b. The evolution of retirement: Summary of a research project. *American Economic Review* 88 (2): 232–36.
Fogel, R. W. 1998a. *Public use tape on the aging of veterans of the Union army: Military, pension, and medical records.* Version M-4. Chicago: University of Chicago, Graduate School of Business, Center for Population Economics.
———. 1998b. *Public use tape on the aging of veterans of the Union Army: U.S. federal census records.* Version C-2. Chicago: University of Chicago, Graduate School of Business, Center for Population Economics.
Glasson, William H. 1918. *Federal military pensions in the United States.* New York: Oxford University Press.
Heckman, James. 1997. Instrumental variables: A study of implicit behavioral assumptions in one widely used estimator. *Journal of Human Resources* 32 (3): 441–61.
Heckman, James, H. Ichimura, and P. Todd. 1997. Matching as an econometric evaluation estimator: Evidence from evaluating a job training program. *Review of Economic Studies* 64 (4): 605–54.

—————. 1998. Matching as an econometric evaluation estimator. *Review of Economic Studies* 65 (2): 261–94.

Lee, C. 1998. The rise of the welfare state and labor-force participation of older males: Evidence from the pre–social security era. *American Economic Review* 88 (2): 222–26.

—————. 1999. Farm value and retirement of farm owners in early-twentieth-century America. *Explorations in Economic History* 36 (4): 387–408.

—————. 2000. Labor market status of older males in early twentieth century America. University of Chicago. Working paper. Available at [http://www.cpe. uchicago.edu].

Ostergen, Robert. 1981. Land and family in rural immigrant communities. *Annals of the Association of American Geographers* 71 (3): 400–11.

Preston, Samuel, and Michael Haines. 1991. *Fatal years: Child mortality in late-nineteenth-century America.* Princeton, N.J.: Princeton University Press.

Ruggles, Steven, et al. 1997. *Integrated public use microdata series.* Version 2.0. Minneapolis: University of Minnesota Historical Census Projects.

Song, Chen. 2000. Cleaning of the height and weight variables in the Union Army Military and Surgeons' Certificates data sets. University of Chicago. Working paper. Available at [http://www.cpe.uchicago.edu].

U.S. Bureau of the Census. 1912–14. *Thirteenth census of the United States taken in the year 1910.* Washington, D.C.: GPO.

—————. 1975. *Historical statistics of the United States, colonial times to 1970.* Washington, D.C.: U.S. Bureau of the Census.

The Effect of Hernias on the Labor Force Participation of Union Army Veterans

Chen Song and Louis L. Nguyen

10.1 Introduction

The health status of the elderly and its impact on labor supply and on the quality of life before and after retirement is an empirical issue that may be best addressed by high-quality panel data, that is, data that contain comprehensive health and work information over time. One of the most frequently used contemporary data sets for research in this area is the Health and Retirement Study. Other popular contemporary data sets include the Retirement History Longitudinal Survey, the National Health Interview Survey, and the National Health and Nutrition Examination Survey.[1]

The health information recorded in many contemporary data sets suffers two major shortcomings. First, the overall measurement of health is a dichotomous indicator of self-assessed health status derived by classifying responses of "excellent," "very good," "good," "fair," and "poor." Second, the doctor-diagnosed conditions are coded as zero-one dummy variables, with

Chen Song is an economist at Resolution Economics, LLC, and a senior investigator at the Center for Population Economics at University of Chicago, Graduate School of Business. Louis L. Nguyen is a chief surgery resident with Barnes-Jewish Hospital at Washington University in St. Louis and a senior investigator for the Center for Population Economics.

We thank Robert Fogel, Max Henderson, Tayatat Kanjanapipatkul, Jibum Kim, Chulhee Lee, Mario Sánchez, Peter Viechnicki, and other conference participants for helpful comments. We owe special gratitude to Peter Blanck for being our discussant at the conference, and to Dora Costa for providing us with many insightful suggestions. We are responsible for all the errors in the paper.

1. See, for example, Blau and Gilleskie (2001), Bound et al. (1999), Chan and Stevens (2001), Coile and Gruber (2000a), Costa (2002), Dwyer and Mitchell (1999), Gustman and Steinmeier (2000), and Mitchell and Phillips (2000).

a one indicating the prevalence of a certain condition, and a zero indicating no such condition.[2]

Bound et al. (1999) identifies four potential problems with self-reported global health, the main problem being that the judgments are subjective and that responses may not be independent of the labor market outcomes an investigator hopes to explain, thereby introducing endogeneity into the explanatory variable. The zero-one condition dummies provide a more objective indicator of health status. However, those dummy variables do not account for the severity of the conditions experienced, so that all conditions are weighted equally. Comorbidity, or the prevalence of two or more conditions, does alleviate the lack of severity measure between conditions by purging away the correlation between any two of them, although severity within each condition is still left unmeasured.

This paper focuses on the labor supply implications of hernias, a specific chronic disability that can be extremely debilitating. We examine the retirement behavior of 3,406 older men. The Union Army (UA) health data in the Surgeons' Certificates (SC) file are longitudinal, because veterans could apply for the UA pension several times and be examined at different points in their lives. Compared to the contemporary health data, they are more comprehensive because symptoms of each disability are documented, which makes it possible for researchers to quantify severity.

A common approach taken by other projects that use the UA files is the inclusion of several zero-one disease indicators in the group of explanatory variables (e.g., Costa 2002). In comparison to those approaches, our investigation is more focused. We transcribe descriptions of hernia symptoms such as size, subtype, location, and morbidity into measures that we incorporate into a regression analysis. We study the labor participation implication using those measures, in addition to using the zero-one hernia dummy variable. Since data collection has become more sophisticated and precise over time, our methodology demonstrates one way of utilizing large-scale medical information. A more ambitious next step will be to construct a health composite index from all the available severity measures within each disability, as well as across all disabilities. This composite index will be superior to the traditional aggregate of zero-one disability dummy variables and will improve prediction of the role of health in economic behavior.

The organization of the rest of the paper is as follows: Section 10.2 provides a medical background for the history and the treatment of hernias; section 10.3 describes the UA sample; section 10.4 offers an empirical framework; section 10.5 analyzes the results; and section 10.6 concludes.

---

2. See, for example, Blau and Gilleskie (2001), Costa (2002, 2003), and Mitchell and Phillips (2000).

10.2   Medical Background

Although humans have been afflicted with groin hernias throughout history, a thorough understanding of the anatomy of the inguinal canal was not achieved until the early nineteenth century. During this time, cadaver dissections and clinical studies led to publication of anatomic atlases and treatises on the subject of groin hernias (Rutkow 1998). Despite the greater understanding of anatomy, surgical repair of hernias at the time was troubled by recurrence of the hernia. Thus, treatment of hernias was limited to the use of trusses, while surgery was performed in cases of hernia strangulation. Since then, improvements in anesthesia, surgical technique, sutures, and prosthetic materials have led to earlier surgical intervention and better clinical outcomes.

10.2.1   Prevalence

A hernia is an abnormal protrusion of organ or tissue out of the cavity in which it normally lies and into another space or potential space. Generally, the term refers to the more common groin or inguinal hernia, although other types exist and are described by their anatomic locations: epigastric, hiatal, obturator, umbilical, and ventral. Unfortunately, the epidemiology of groin hernias is not well defined. Historically, it was estimated that 4.6 percent of the entire population of the United States was afflicted with hernias (Iason 1941). A more recent survey based on clinical exams revealed that men aged twenty-five or older had a hernia prevalence rate (excluding repaired hernias) of 18 percent and a lifetime prevalence rate (inclusive of repaired hernias) of 24 percent (Abramson et al., 1978). In contrast, self-reported information from insurance enrollment questionnaires estimated the prevalence rate of men aged twenty-five to thirty-four to be 1 percent, but higher in men aged thirty-five to forty-four (1.8 percent), aged forty-five to fifty-four (2.2 percent), and aged fifty-five to sixty-four (3.9 percent; Rubenstein, Beck, and Lohr 1983). While some differences between the rates may be due to underestimation from self-reported surveys, the differences are large and representative of the disparity in the field.

10.2.2   Distribution

With respect to gender distribution, it is believed that the prevalence rate of groin hernias is higher in men than in women, although the exact ratio is not well known. An early-twentieth-century report from New York Hospital for Ruptured and Crippled reported at 3.1:1.0 male-to-female ratio (Coley, Keen, and DaCosta 1910). A more recent study from Henry Ford Hospital in Detroit showed a 12:1 male-female ratio (Ponka 1980). A review of the hernia repairs performed over the last fifty years at Shouldice Hospital in Toronto revealed a 21:1 male-female ratio (Welsh and Alexander 1993). The relative frequency of groin hernias compared to other hernias is also not well known. Representative data from the Henry Ford Hospital showed that in men, inguinal hernias comprised 81 percent of all hernias, while femoral (3 percent), combinations of inguinal/femoral (8 percent), umbilical (2 percent), incisional (4 percent), hiatal (2 percent), and epigastric (1 percent) comprised the rest. For women, the ratios were inguinal (35 percent), femoral (11 percent, combination inguinal/femoral (3 percent), umbilical (17 percent), incisional (18 percent), hiatal (15 percent), and epigastric (3 percent; Ponka 1980).

10.2.3   Natural history

Patients with hernias present a wide range of symptoms. Some patients are asymptomatic and have elective surgery to prevent future complications; others present with strangulated hernias and require emergency surgery. For most patients, a protuberant hernia is discomforting, but heavy lifting or straining can cause moderate or severe pain. This discomfort leads to avoidance of heavy labor and strenuous exercise unless the hernia can be retained with a truss or surgically corrected. Hernias also have a possibility of developing complications such as incarceration (inability to be reduced) or strangulation (in which vascular supply to herniated bowel is compromised).

10.2.4   Treatment

Although the anatomy of the human inguinal region was well demonstrated in the early nineteenth century by surgeons and anatomists such as Astley Cooper (1804, 1807), Franz Hesselbach (1806, 1814), and Antonio Scarpa (1809, 1821), surgical repair of hernias was complicated by frequent recurrence (Bull 1890). Thus, early remedies for hernias were nonsurgical and included the use of external binding bandages to prevent protrusion of hernias. Later refinements led to the use of trusses, which were formed binders capable of more direct pressure on the hernia site. Young patients could expect their hernias to be "cured" if the truss was worn regularly, whereas older patients could expect temporary relief and were dependent on the truss indefinitely (Cooper 1804). Most of the modern experience with trusses comes from the United Kingdom, where the access to surgery is reduced compared to other industrialized nations. Partial or complete control of the hernia was achieved in only 31 percent of patients (Law and Trapnell 1992). However, surveys have found that about 60 percent of truss wearers did not consult a physician before purchasing a truss (Cheek, Williams, and Farndon 1995). Furthermore, many trusses are poorly fitted, resulting in failure to hold the hernia or causing undue discomfort. Thus, the true efficacy of trusses has not been well defined.

In 1889, William Halsted and Edoardo Bassini (Halstead 1889; Bassini 1889) independently reported a hernia repair that reconstructed the inguinal floor by apposing the conjoined tendon with the posterior rim of Poupart's ligament. Both reported dramatically reduced recurrence rates (3 to 4 percent over four years) with their procedures compared to other methods available at the time. Later refinements in hernia repair by McVay (1948) and shouldice (Shearburn and Myers 1969) led to further improvements, yielding recurrence rates of less than 1 percent. The traditional dogma of hernia repair was revised when Lichtenstein published his experience with 6,321 cases of hernia repair. He believed that traditional repair methods using sutures were anatomically rigid, and instead supported the use of a prosthetic mesh to buttress the weak tissues. His patients had low recurrence rates (0.7 percent) and lower requirements for pain medications postoperatively (Lichenstein 1987). The recent development of laparoscopic hernia repair has allowed patients with bilateral hernias to have them fixed in one operation rather than two.

While the therapy for hernias has evolved, the method of diagnosis and natural history has not changed much since hernias were anatomically understood in the early nineteenth century. This characteristic of hernias permits us to study the effects of hernias on labor participation during a period when most hernias were not repaired electively. This unique look at the effects of hernias without intervention also provides insight into the beneficial effects of modern hernia therapy.

10.3   Data

The data used in this study were from Civil War records stored at the United States National Archives. A random sample of 39,616 white male recruits with enlistment papers (the Military Service Records file) was drawn from the National Archives, representing 331 companies mustered into the UA during the Civil War (Center for Population Economics [CPE] 1998). Approximately 85 percent of those recruits, or 33,674 men, were also linked to the Pension Bureau data set (the Pension Records file). At the time of this paper we were able to obtain records on 28,530 recruits from the Pension Records file.[3]

The bulk of the health information came from the Surgeons' Certificates file. This file stores details of the physical examinations of 16,713 pension applicants. The Pension Bureau surgeons conducted those examinations. An examination consisted of an inspection of the general organ systems as well as an investigation of active medical problems. Components of the handwritten exam entries were transcribed into "disease variables" that captured the essential information about the exam findings.

Table 10.1 presents the data availability under each variable of interest to

3. Data from Wisconsin, Indiana, New Mexico, and California were still being cleaned and were not included in the Military Records file. In addition to data from those four states, data from New Jersey were not included in the Pension Records file. Moreover, a prior pilot sample of twenty companies with the same geographical composition of recruits as the Military Records file was missing.

Table 10.1   **Variables and Data Sources**

Variable	Construction	Source	Number of Observations
		Cohort information	
Birth year	Enlistment year minus enlistment age	Military file	27,493 out of 28,530
Death year	Original data	Pension file Military file	27,493 out of 28,530, including deaths in the war and deaths recorded in pension applications
		Health information	
Hernia (kind, side, class, size, rating)	Cleaned hernia data	Surgeons' Certificates file	16,652 out of 16,713
		Socioeconomic information	
Birth state (native/foreign)	Original data	Military file	27,504 out of 28,530
Largest city population in 1900 residential county	Merged data	1900 census file	11,584 out of 11,606
1900 residential state	Original data	1900 census file	11,584 out of 11,606
1900 occupation	Original data	1900 census file	6,587 out of 11,606
1910 occupation	Original data	1910 census	4,092 out of 6,635
1900 literacy	Original data	1900 census	11,477 out of 11,606
1900 household relation	Original data	1900 census	11,306 out of 11,606
1900 marital status	Original data	1900 census	9,547 out of 11,606
Monthly pension amount in the year before but closest to 1910	Original data	Pension file	13,857 out of 28,530

our study. We group the variables into three categories pertaining to cohort, health, and socioeconomic status. While the cohort information is easy to obtain,[4] a fair amount of work is involved in the standardization of the hernia variable, as well as in the categorization of occupations. We provide a detailed explanation of how we construct hernia measures to fit the purpose of our study in the appendix. We give some examples in table 10.2 to illustrate the standardization process.

Table 10.3 summarizes the number of cases from the last step of transcription for 2,350 hernia patients and 6,395 patient-exam pairs in the Surgeons' Certificates file. The most common hernia subtype is hernia at the inguinal region, which covers 90 percent of the patients. The less usual, but representative subtypes are: ventral, where a hernia is abdominal incisional: umbilical, where a hernia protrudes through the abdominal wall under the skin at the umbilicus; and femoral, where a hernia passes through the femoral canal. Two rare subtypes are an epigastric hernia, which is a hernia protruding through the linea alba above the navel, and a hiatal hernia, which is a hernia of the stomach through the diaphragm.

Under the category "hernia morbidity and truss efficacy," truss effective refers to a hernia whose impact could be minimized by the wearing of a support, such as a truss. This group is considered the least morbid. The next morbid group was a reducible hernia, in which the contents of the protrusion could be returned to their normal location. Eighty-six percent of the patients had either truss-effective or reducible hernias. If wearing a truss did not have any effect at all, a hernia became more morbid than the previous two groups. A hernia is described as "inflamed" where there are in fact signs of inflammation. Furthermore, when a hernia is not irreducible, it is "incarcerated." An incarcerated hernia develops into a "strangulated" hernia if the circulation is compromised (Spraycar 1995, 788–90). A patient with a single hernia is less disabled than one with double hernias, and disability increases with the size of a hernia. Group proportions under each diagnostic category are comparable with those from other populations.

We use hernia ratings to estimate the overall degree of disability from having a hernia or hernias. The denominator of the rating variable is the maximum severity of hernias, and the numerator is the severity of hernias observed in a patient. Higher hernia ratings correspond to more severe hernias. Table 10.4 shows the distribution of surgeons' hernia ratings, ranging from 0.0000 to 1.0000. Out of the 6,395 hernia patient-exam pairs, we have ratings information for 5,026 of them. As a chronic condition, hernia was

---

4. When the year of birth (YOB) cannot be found from the Pension Records file, the year was inferred by subtracting the age at enlistment from the year of enlistment. Among records with YOB, age of birth, and year of enlistment, the distribution of the differential between the calculated YOB and the recorded YOB in the pension data centered at zero, with the majority of the mass clustered between –1 and 1 year (Song 1999). Year of death is useful, because many recruits still had several years to live after their last recorded medical exams.

Table 10.2   Examples of Transcription of Hernia Diagnoses

Original Description Appearing in Surgeons' Certificates	Transcribed Answer Classes (AC)	Transcribed Middle Modifiers (MM)
Hernia subtype		
2 complete hernias	Inguinal	Bilateral, complete
Right abdominal rupture	Ventral	Right
Directly above umbilicus	Umbilical	None
Complete right femoral hernia	Femoral	Right
Hernia linea alba	Epigastric	None
Rupture of stomach	Hiatal	None
Complete hernia	Nonspecified	None
Hernia morbidity and truss efficacy		
Left tumor descend into scrotum if not held by truss	Truss effective	Left
Left hernia requires more force than right to be reduced	Reducible	Bilateral
No bandage is of any use	Truss not effective	None
Inflamed	Inflamed	None
Adhesions prevent its full reducibility	Incarcerated	None
Left hernia strangulated	Strangulated	Left
Hernia is not inflamed	Nonspecified	None
Not aneurysm	Nonclassified	None
Hernia size		
Left three cent pieces	Less than 1″	Left
Man's two fingers	1″	None
Quail egg	2″	None
Right femoral 3 by 2 inches	3″	Right
Large grapefruit	4″	None
Pineapple	6″	None
Man's two fists	8″	None
Right very large	Nonspecified	Right
Veins 3 times normal	Nonclassified	None
Hernia location		
MM bilateral	Double	
MM right	Single	
MM left	Single	

given high ratings. The average rating is 0.4286, which is a little below half of total disability.[5] Over a third of the cases corresponded to at least half disability, and over a quarter of the cases corresponded to at least a quarter disability. In the sections that follow, we will refer to the hernia disability ratings as the major health indicator.

For those 28,530 recruits in the pension data, 9,114 were linked to the 1900 census, henceforth referred to as the 1900 census file, and 5,182 were

5. For purposes of the pension rating system, total disability was defined by the Pension Bureau as "a total disability for the performance of manual labor requiring severe and continuous exertion" (Glasson 1918, 131).

Table 10.3   **Hernia Severity (by diagnostic category) Where an Observation Is a Patient-Exam Pair**

Diagnostic Category	Number of Cases	Percentage of Total
Hernia subtype	5,440	
Inguinal	4,902	90.1
More unusual subtypes		
Ventral	226	4.2
Umbilical	146	2.7
Femoral	52	1.0
Epigastric	1	0.0
Hiatal	2	0.0
Nonspecified or nonclassified	111	2.0
Hernia morbidity and truss efficacy	4,610	
Truss effective	1,335	29.0
Reducible	2,609	56.6
Higher morbidity		
Truss not effective	319	6.9
Inflamed	2	0.0
Incarcerated	137	3.0
Strangulated	15	0.3
Nonspecified or nonclassified	193	4.1
Hernia location	4,942	
Single hernia		
Right hernia	2,437	49.3
Left hernia	1,642	33.2
Double hernias	594	12.0
Nonspecified or nonclassified	269	5.5
Hernia size	4,017	
Less than 1″	108	2.7
1–2″	577	14.4
2–3″	1,143	28.5
3–4″	746	18.6
4″ and up	800	19.9
Nonspecified or nonclassified	643	16.0

linked to the 1910 census, henceforth referred to as the 1910 census file.[6] We exclude veterans who were retired by 1900. This leaves us with 3,406 individuals. Out of those veterans, 1,848 men survive the data merge with the Surgeons' Certificates file, among which 1,796 have nonmissing information on monthly pension awards. By 1900, 257 had hernias. Ten years later, an additional eighty-nine men contracted this disability, making the total number of hernia patients 346 by 1910.

There are 1,558 men (3,406 – 1,848) without a surgeon's record. If they

6. The key to a successful link is the presence of "soundexes" for the census constructed by a commercial genealogist. The soundexes can map a recruit's name to a possible candidate in the census given the location of the recruit during the census year. Also, the Civil War enrollment lists may give addresses that would aid in the location of individuals not found through the soundexes.

Table 10.4   Hernia Severity (by ratings) where an Observation Is a
Patient-Exam Pair

Hernia Rating	Number of Cases	Percentage of Total	Cumulative (%)
0.0000	295	5.9	5.9
0.0556	4	0.1	5.9
0.1111	286	5.7	11.6
0.1250	6	0.1	11.8
0.1429	2	0.0	11.8
0.1667	29	0.6	12.4
0.2000	7	0.1	12.5
0.2222	632	12.6	25.1
0.2500	88	1.8	26.8
0.2778	10	0.2	27.0
0.3333	607	12.1	39.1
0.3750	3	0.1	39.2
0.3889	2	0.0	39.2
0.4286	1	0.0	39.2
0.4444	917	18.2	57.5
0.5000	310	6.2	63.6
0.5556	1,017	20.2	83.9
0.5882	1	0.0	83.9
0.6111	3	0.1	83.9
0.6250	7	0.1	84.1
0.6316	1	0.0	84.1
0.6667	424	8.4	92.5
0.7500	58	1.2	93.7
0.7778	235	4.7	98.4
0.8333	12	0.2	98.6
0.8824	1	0.0	98.6
0.8889	17	0.3	99.0
0.9444	39	0.8	99.7
1.000	12	0.2	100.0
Number of observations	5,026	100	100

were at risk to be linked, they fall into two categories: The first category consists of men who applied early because of severe war disabilities. The second category consists of men who applied late on the grounds of old age, and thus were never examined. On average, men who did not have a surgeon's record were in better health. Men who had a surgeon's record had at least one disability. A frequency of the application year by linkage to the Surgeons' Certificates file reveals that for those not linked, 617 of them had nonmissing application-year information: The mean application year is 1889, the earliest application year is 1863, and the latest application year is 1924. For those linked, 1,843 had nonmissing application-year information: The mean application year is 1885, the earliest is 1861, and the latest is 1912. Therefore, it is likely that men without surgeons' records were healthier and they tended to apply later.

We use two samples to study the effect of hernias on retirement. The first sample has 1,796 men with nonmissing pension award who are linked to the Surgeons' Certificates file. We compare retirement of men who had hernias with men who did not have hernias although they had some other disabilities. The second sample has 1,904 men. It combines 1,558 men not linked to the Surgeons' Certificates file with 346 hernia patients. We compare retirement of men who had hernias with that of men who were healthy. For men without surgeons' records, we do not have their health information. In addition, since many of them did not apply for pension, and since it is only men in the Pension Records file who were searched for in the 1900 and the 1910 censuses, we do not have demographic information for a substantial number of healthy recruits. Nonetheless, we include all 1,904 men in the second sample by creating a category of missing values for each demographic and health variable. The study, using the first sample, shows the effect of hernias relative to other disabilities on retirement, while using the second sample, it shows the effect of hernias relative to perfect health on retirement.

Three types of sample selection biases may exist. The first type relates to the representation of the UA men over the entire population of white males in the United States of similar birth and socioeconomic backgrounds. The second type of selection bias comes from the screening of potential recruits at enlistment.[7] The third type of selection bias comes from extracting the variables that are needed for our analysis from each file[8] of the UA sample and merging the resulting subsamples to create the final data set. Many recruits were dropped during this process because their records were not in all three UA files. By comparing the variable means in the final data set with those in each of the original UA file to detect whether the means have changed significantly after each merge, we conclude that the final data set we use for our analysis represents a random sample of the original UA files.[9]

10.4   Empirical Framework

In a standard intertemporal labor-supply model where an individual allocates his resources between consumption C_t and leisure L_t in each period,

---

7. Rejections were based on various grounds. For example, the army did not enlist recruits who were in their teens or who were over the age of forty-five. Also, wealthier men who were physically fit could buy substitutes to enlist for them (see Kemp 1990 for a discussion of controversy related to the practice of substitution and the commutation clause in the Enrollment Act and whether average laborers were overrepresented in the Union Army). Furthermore, there are medical disqualifications for military service in the United States. People with chronic diseases, such as abdominal and digestive-apparatus hernia, were exempted from military services in all situations (Baxter 1875, p. li of "Introduction"). Fogel (1993) estimates that 30 percent of the examinees in the UA were rejected for chronic diseases.

8. That is, the Military Records file, the 1900 census file, the 1910 census file, and the Surgeons' Certificates file.

9. We include all the recruits who survive the data-merge into our regressions, even though some of their records are incomplete, by creating dummy variables for missing values.

the first-order conditions for him to achieve the maximum amount of happiness U_t are

(1) $U_C(C_t, L_t) = \lambda_t,$

(2) $U_L(C_t, L_t) = \lambda_t W_t,$

where λ_t represents the marginal utility of wealth as of time t; $U_C(.)$ represents the marginal utility with respect to consumption; $U_L(.)$ represents the marginal utility with respect to leisure; and W_t represents the wage rate at time t.

In this framework,[10] if wages are exogenous and are not altered by individuals' decisions, declines in current health lower productivity and make working more painful. As a result, individuals work fewer hours. If wages are not exogenous but are dependent on human capital investment, then the more difficult it is to make such an investment, the more likely workers are to leave the work force when suffering health declines. For example, it is more difficult for a machine operator to acquire the skill of a clerk. Therefore, a machine operator is more likely to retire when his health deteriorates to the extent that heavy laboring becomes physically infeasible. Also, for example, it is difficult for older workers to acquire new skills. Therefore, the older workers, when suffering health declines, are more likely to retire, provided that those workers have equal nonwage income. For two workers both suffering from poor health, holding everything else equal, the one who has more nonwage income can more readily afford retirement.

Persistent future health declines affect current labor supply in this framework. Persistent future health declines can be expected to lower future wages and to raise future valuation of leisure. As a result, persistent future health declines raise the marginal valuation of wealth, which will tend to increase current labor supply. This is because individuals want to accumulate more wealth to compensate for fewer hours of work in the future and to avoid working in pain in the future. However, if individuals have been experiencing health declines for a while, they will not be able to increase current labor supply to prepare for the future, even if they want to do so.

Not only can current and future health declines affect the current labor supply, health history also matters. This is because both contemporary and past health conditions determine the future health condition. An individual who has been in poor health for a long time is less likely to recover than an individual who recently suffered a decline in health. In this case, the person who has been in poor health for a longer while will have worse expectations about the future than will the person who recently experienced a negative health shock.

Hernias were considered a persistent, chronic disability during the historical period of investigation, because no reliable treatment was available

---

10. See Bound et al. (1999) for a more sophisticated treatment of health status.

to offer a complete cure. Therefore, once a veteran developed a hernia, he had to cope with it for the rest of his life. We have identified three main factors that determine a worker's decision to exit or remain in the labor force: pain from working as a result of declining health, a wealth level to support fewer hours of work, and high switching costs because of human capital investment. We measure health by hernia screening (yes/no), severity of hernias indicated by hernia ratings, and how long ago a hernia patient had contracted hernias.

We also apply a quadratic function of body mass index (BMI, or weight in kilograms over the square of height in meters) as a control for general health (Costa 1996). We measure income by monthly pension awards granted in the year closest to, but before, 1910. We measure switching costs by the nature of a recruit's occupation in 1900. We assume that switching costs were higher for those individuals engaging in more manually demanding occupations where only physical strength mattered, and lower for those engaging in less manually demanding occupations where training and skills were required. Those with higher switching costs were more likely to retire once they became disabled due to the lack of alternatives.

We next assume that recruits had no hernias prior to enlistment, because hernias disqualified men for military service. Recruits contracted hernias either during the Civil War between 1861 and 1865, or after the war. The military pension for UA recruits started in 1862. Table 10.5 shows that the first major inflow of recruits who claimed a pension and were examined for conditions that occurred within a decade and a half after the Consolidation Act of 1873. By 1886, 46 percent of the veterans in the Surgeons' Certificates had been examined. There was another major inflow of new pension claimants within three years after the 1890 act.[11] By 1893, 92 percent of the recruits who would eventually have been examined went through their first round of examinations.

We have included about 80 percent of the final hernia patients, when 1900 is chosen as the base year, to study the labor force transition in the next decade. According to the last column of table 10.5, about a third of the recruits who would eventually contract hernias found out by 1890 that they had hernias. Between 1890 and 1900, an additional 44 percent of all eventual hernia patients claimed a pension under this disability. It is not clear whether the large hernia discovery rate between 1890 and 1900 was due to the influx of applicants taking advantage of the 1890 act, or to the rise in the risk of hernias as veterans started to reach older ages.[12] An important as-

---

11. This is because at the early stage of the development of the UA pension program, a recruit had to prove that the condition under his claim was war related. However, after the 1890 act, this constraint was relaxed, so that a veteran could be entitled to pension with any disability, although a war-related one received a higher rating that was transformed into a higher dollar amount.

12. An average recruit in the Surgeons' Certificates data would be sixty-five by 1900, and seventy-five by 1910.

Table 10.5   **Years of First Exams and Years When hernia First Found**

Exam Year	Number of Recruits Being Examined the First Time	% Recruits Eventually Examined[a]	Number of Recruits First Diagnosed with Hernias	% Recruits Eventually Diagnosed with Hernias[a]
1861–62	5	0.1	1	0
1863–70	36	0.3	0	0
1871–73	324	3.3	44	2.0
1874–86	4,021	40.3	407	19.2
		(44.0)		(21.2)
1887	364	3.6	45	2.1
1888	400	4.0	57	2.7
1889	421	4.2	48	2.3
1890	566	5.7	108	5.1
		(61.5)		(33.4)
1891	2,205	22.1	376	17.7
1892	709	7.1	184	8.6
1893	137	1.4	53	2.5
		(92.1)		(62.2)
1894–1900	521	5.2	372	17.4
		(97.3)		(79.6)
1901–06	235	2.4	261	12.3
1907–11	13	0.1	39	1.6
1912–29	19	0.2	133	6.1
Total	9,976	100	2,128	100

Notes: The Consolidation Act of 1873 established various grades of disability. The 1890 act marked the beginning of a universal disability and old age pension program under which the veteran's disability did not need to be related to military service. Legislation after 1912 consisted mainly of automatic increases in pension ratings for age and service. For a detailed description of the history of pension laws, see Costa (1998, appendix A).

[a]Cumulative percent in parentheses.

Table 10.6   **OLS Regression of 1910 Hernia Ratings on 1900 Hernia Ratings (369 recruits with nonmissing hernia ratings in both 1900 and 1910)**

	Coefficient Estimates	T-statistics
Intercept	0.1772***	7.81
1900 hernia ratings	0.6132***	11.69
Dependent variable (1910 Hernia Ratings) mean	0.43	
Independent variable (1900 Hernia Ratings) mean	0.39	
Adjusted R^2	0.2686	

***Significant at the 1 percent level.

pect for our study is that we have captured most of the hernia patients in our sample.

We argue that past (1900) and contemporaneous (1910) health status contributes to labor participation decisions. Table 10.6 presents the ordinary least squares (OLS) regression of hernia ratings in 1910 on a constant

Table 10.7   **Occupations Coded Using the 1950 Census of Population Index**

	Classification I	Classification II
(L) Less manually demanding	Professional, technical, and kindred workers Managers, officials, and proprietors Clerical and kindred workers Sales workers	Classification I, plus farmers and farm managers
(M) More manually demanding	Farmers and farm managers Craftsmen, foremen, and kindred workers Operatives and kindred workers Service workers Farm laborers and foremen Laborers, except farm and mine	Classification I, excluding farmers and farm managers
(R) Retirees[a]	—	—

[a]Following Lee (1998), we define retirees as those whose occupation was recorded as "retired," blank, "invalid or sick or disabled," "inmate or prisoner," "landlord," or "capitalist or gentlemen." To distinguish retirees from the unemployed, we define the latter as those whose occupation was recorded as "unemployed or without occupation."

term and on hernia ratings in 1900. If past health status possesses large predictive power over present health status, we would observe the adjusted R-squared to be close to 1, and the slope coefficient to be also close to 1 and to be statistically significant. Table 10.6 shows that past health partially predicts present health by explaining 27 percent of the variation in present health ($R^2 = 0.2686$). The intercept is 0.18, or about 45 percent of past hernia ratings (0.1772/0.39). The coefficient estimate is 0.61, which means that, on average, 61 percent of ratings in 1900 would contribute to our inference of ratings in 1910. Since the 1910 ratings contain new health information that is not captured by the 1900 ratings, we will use the 1900 ratings and the 1910 ratings to measure health.

If hernias were physically debilitating, we would expect workers in more manually demanding occupations to have higher retirement probabilities. Occupations are coded using the index in the 1950 census of population. We assign occupations into three categories:[13] less manually demanding, more manually demanding, and retired (see table 10.7). Out of 3,406 recruits in the 1900 labor force, 1,478 recruits were farmers and farm managers (43.39 percent). Obviously, one of the responsibilities of farmers and farm managers was management of farms, which probably required some skills and training. Also, many of them were owners of farms, so that they belonged

13. There are two possibilities as to why a recruit who was linked to a census failed to have an occupational record: (a) The recruit had a job but did not report it, or (b) the recruit was unemployed and did not report his usual occupation.

Table 10.8   Occupational Transition between 1900 and 1910 for Veterans in 1900
                    Labor Force (%)

	1910 Category		
1900 Category	Less Manually Demanding	More Manually Demanding	Retired
A. Farmers and farm managers classified as more manually demanding occupation			
Less manually demanding (718 veterans)	54.74	22.42	22.84
More manually demanding (2,688 veterans)	5.25	70.16	24.59
B. Farmers and farm managers classified as less manually demanding occupation			
Less manually demanding (2,196 veterans)	61.48	12.84	25.68
More manually demanding (1,210 veterans)	16.53	61.90	21.57

to a wealthier social class than farm laborers who only supplied physical labor for subsistence-level compensation. Because farmers and farm managers accounted for a high percentage of the labor force, and because their tasks included fieldwork (which was physically intensive) and general management (which was skill intensive), we group them using two classifications. In the first classification, farmers and farm managers are identified as more manually demanding occupations. In the second classification, they are identified as less manually demanding occupations.

Table 10.8 displays the occupational transition between 1900 and 1910 for those veterans who were in the labor force in 1900.[14] There were 3,406 veterans linked to both the 1900 and the 1910 census files. Panel A shows the transition under Classification I, where farmers and farm managers are classified as more manually demanding occupations. The more manually demanding category has a higher occupational persistence because 70 percent remained in the same category ten years later. In comparison, about half of the veterans who engaged in less manually demanding occupations in 1900 remained in the same category.

A fair proportion of veterans retired from their 1900 occupations in 1910. The percentage is slightly higher among more manually demanding occupations in 1900.[15] Few veterans in the more manually demanding category

14. Some of those veterans who were either retired or unemployed in 1900 could have returned to labor force in 1910. Lee (1998) detected persistence in the long-tern unemployment among older males. He found that for those men aged fifty or older in 1900, being unemployed in 1900 greatly increased the chances of retirement within the next ten years.

15. Costa found that, with the inclusion of retirement as a professional category, workers within the most physically demanding occupational categories (i.e., laborers and farmers) were the men most likely to retire (Costa 1998, 90, table 5.8). She used an earlier version of the 1900 and 1910 census data, which did not contain as many recruits as the current version. Margo (1993) used data from the 1900 census to study the proper labor force classification of older male Americans experiencing six months or more of unemployment (the long-term unemployed). He found that long-term unemployment was more prevalent among unskilled laborers and the building trades. The probability of long-term unemployment also rose with age, after controlling for occupation. Finally, the older an individual was on entering the state of

switched to the less manually demanding category. In contrast, occupational changes occurred four times as frequently for those in the less manually demanding category. This is consistent with the human capital argument that switching-costs were higher for those individuals engaging in occupations that required less human capital investment, and lower for those engaging in occupations where education and training were important.

Panel B shows the transition under the second classification, where farmers and farm managers are classified as less manually demanding occupations. Occupational persistence is the same between less manually demanding jobs (61.48 percent) and more manually demanding jobs (61.90 percent). Comparing panel A with panel B, we conclude that farmers and farm managers tended to remain in the same occupational category between 1900 and 1910. Including them in the less manually demanding group increases the persistence in that group from 54.7 percent to 61.48 percent. We also infer that some farm laborers and foremen might have acquired the farmland and become farmers and farm managers during the ten-year period. This is because the labor market mobility in the more manually demanding jobs increases from 5.25 percent in panel A, where farm owners and farm laborers are classified as being in the same occupational group, to 16.53 percent in B, where they are classified as being in different occupational groups and where moves between those groups are considered switching.

Classifications I and II represent a very crude measure of the extent of labor intensiveness of different occupations. Within the manually demanding occupational category, there can be a large variation in the degree of physical exertion required. Table 10.8 indicates that men in more manually demanding jobs in 1900 are unlikely to switch to less manually demanding jobs in 1910. However, for those who remained in the more manually demanding category in 1910, there could be switches from very physically intensive occupations to much less physically intensive occupations. For example, a factory worker might become a janitor if he contracted hernias and desired a less physically demanding occupation.

We extract a subsample of men whose occupations were classified as more manually demanding and code each occupation according to how physically intensive each occupation is: not much, somewhat, or very. Table 10.9 lists occupations under each group of physical intensity. Notice that in panel A of table 10.9, farm foremen and farm laborers are grouped under "very physically intensive," whereas farm owners and tenants are grouped under "not much physically intensive." We distinguish between physical in-

---

long-term unemployment, the greater the likelihood that he would leave the labor force in a short period of time. Our result that retirement is slightly higher among more manually demanding occupations circa 1900 is consistent with both Costa's and Margo's findings.

Table 10.9   **Degree of Intensity of Manually Demanding Occupations, Including Farmers and Farm Managers**

Degree of intensity	Occupation
	A. Degree of physical intensity
Not much physically intensive	Attendants, hospital and other institution
	Attendants, professional and personal service
	Barbers, beauticians, and manicurists
	Compositors and typesetters
	Conductor, bus and street railway
	Dressmakers and seamstresses except factory
	Farmers (owners and tenants)
	Jewelers, watchmakers, goldsmiths, and silversmiths
	Marshals and constables
	Milliners
	Policemen and detectives
	Service workers, except private household
	Sheriffs and bailiffs
	Tailors and tailoresses
	Taxicab drivers and chauffeurs
	Watchmen (crossing) and bridge tenders
Somewhat physically intensive	Bakers
	Bartenders
	Boarding and lodging-house keepers
	Bookbinders
	Charwomen and cleaners
	Cooks, except private household
	Decorators and window dressers
	Deliverymen and routemen
	Electricians
	Elevator operators
	Farm managers
	Furriers
	Guards, watchmen, and doorkeepers
	Housekeepers and stewards, except private household
	Housekeepers, private household
	Inspectors
	Inspectors, scalers, and graders, log and lumber
	Janitors and sextons
	Locomotive engineers
	Meat cutters, except slaughter and packing house
	Mechanics and repairmen
	Mechanics and repairmen, automobile
	Mechanics and repairmen, railroad and car shop
	Opticians and lends grinders and polishers
	Painters, except construction or maintenance
	Paperhangers
	Photoengravers and lithographers
	Piano and organ tuners and repairmen
	Plasterers
	Private household workers
	Shoemakers and shoe repairers, except factory

Table 10.9 (continued)

Degree of intensity	Occupation
	Stationary engineers
	Switchmen, railroad
	Teamsters
	Truck and tractor drivers
	Waiters and waitresses
	Weavers, textile
Very physically intensive	Apprentice bricklayers and masons
	Apprentices, metalworking trades
	Apprentices, other specified trades
	Blacksmiths
	Boatmen, canalmen, and lock keepers
	Boilermakers
	Brakemen, railroad
	Brickmasons, stonemasons, and tile setters
	Cabinetmakers
	Carpenters
	Craftsmen and kindred workers
	Dyers
	Engravers, except photoengravers
	Excavating, grading, and road machinery operators
	Farm foremen
	Farm laborers, wage workers
	Filers, grinders, and polishers, metal
	Firemen, fire protection
	Fishermen and oystermen
	Foremen
	Fruit, nut, and vegetable graders, and packers, except factory
	Furnacemen, smeltermen, and pourers
	Gardeners, except farm, and groundskeepers
	Glaziers
	Heat treaters, annealers, temperers
	Laborers
	Laundry and dry-cleaning operatives
	Locomotive firemen
	Longshoremen and stevedores
	Lumbermen, raftsmen, and woodchoppers
	Machinists
	Millers, grain, flour, feed, etc.
	Millwrights
	Mine operatives and laborers
	Molders, metal
	Motormen, mine, factory, logging camp, etc.
	Operative and kindred workers
	Painters, construction and maintenance
	Plumbers and pipe fitters
	Porters
	Rollers and roll hands, metal

(*continued*)

Table 10.9 (continued)

Degree of intensity	Occupation
	Sailors and deck hands
	Sawyers
	Stationary firemen
	Stone cutters and stone carvers
	Tinsmiths, coppersmiths, and sheet metal workers
	Tool makers, die makers, and setters
	Upholsterers

B. Degree of skill intensity

Degree of intensity	Occupation
Unskilled workers	Conductors, bus and street railway
	Taxicab drivers and chauffeurs
	Watchmen (crossing) and bridge tenders
	Bartenders
	Boarding and lodging house keepers
	Charwomen and cleaners
	Deliverymen and routemen
	Guards, watchmen, and doorkeepers
	Housekeepers and stewards, except private household
	Housekeepers, private household
	Janitors and sextons
	Elevator operators
	Private household workers
	Waiters and waitresses
	Apprentice bricklayers and masons
	Apprentices, metalworking trades
	Apprentices, other specified trades
	Farm laborers, wage workers
	Laborers
	Longshoremen and stevedores
	Lumbermen, raftsmen, and woodchoppers
	Mine operatives and laborers
	Painters, construction and maintenance
	Porters
	Sailors and deck hands
Skilled workers: artisans, managers, and skilled industrial workers	Attendants, hospital and other institution
	Attendants, professional and personal service
	Barbers, beauticians, and manicurists
	Compositors and typesetters
	Dressmakers and seamstresses except factory
	Farmers (owners and tenants)
	Jewelers, watchmakers, goldsmiths, and silversmiths
	Marshals and constables
	Milliners
	Policemen and detectives
	Painters, except construction or maintenance
	Service workers, except private household
	Sheriffs and bailiffs
	Tailors and tailoresses
	Bakers

Table 10.9 (continued)

Degree of intensity	Occupation
	Bookbinders
	Cooks, except private household
	Decorators and window dressers
	Electricians
	Farm managers
	Furriers
	Inspectors
	Inspectors, scalers, and graders, log and lumber
	Locomotive engineers
	Meat cutters, except slaughter and packing house
	Mechanics and repairmen
	Mechanics and repairmen, automobile
	Mechanics and repairmen, railroad and car shop
	Opticians and lens grinders and polishers
	Paperhangers
	Photoengravers and lithographers
	Piano and organ tuners and repairmen
	Plasterers
	Shoemakers and shoe repairers, except factory
	Stationary engineers
	Switchmen, railroad
	Teamsters
	Truck and tractor drivers
	Weavers, textile
	Blacksmiths
	Boatmen, canalmen, and lock keepers
	Boilermakers
	Brakemen, railroad
	Brickmasons, stonemasons, and tile setters
	Cabinetmakers
	Carpenters
	Craftsmen and kindred workers
	Dyers
	Engravers, except photoengravers
	Excavating, grading, and road machinery operators
	Farm foremen
	Filers, grinders, and polishers, metal
	Firemen, fire protection
	Fishermen and oystermen
	Foremen
	Fruit, nut, and vegetable graders, and packers, except factory
	Furnacemen, smeltermen, and pourers
	Gardeners, except farm, and groundskeepers
	Glaziers
	Heat treaters, annealers, temperers
	Laundry and dry-cleaning operatives
	Locomotive firemen

(*continued*)

Table 10.9   (continued)

Degree of intensity	Occupation
	Machinists
	Millers, grain, flour, feed, etc.
	Millwrights
	Molders, metal
	Motormen, mine, factory, logging camp, etc.
	Operative and kindred workers
	Plumbers and pipe fitters
	Rollers and roll hands, metal
	Sawyers
	Stationary firemen
	Stone cutters and stone carvers
	Tinsmiths, coppersmiths, and sheet metal workers
	Tool makers, die makers, and setters
	Upholsterers

tensity and skill intensity: The former measures the amount of effort exerted to perform manual labor, whereas the latter measures the level of human capital requirement. Having contracted hernias might stop an individual from remaining in occupations with high physical intensity, but might not hinder him in remaining in occupations with high skill intensity.

Even within the manually demanding occupational category, we observe a large skill variance in every job. For example, a bookbinder could not have taken on the tasks of a jeweler, or a carpenter could not have replaced a locomotive engineer. Ransom and Sutch (1986) argued that older men could extend their work lives by switching from skilled and semiskilled jobs to unskilled jobs. They call this phenomenon "downward occupational mobility." An implication of their finding is that workers in more-skilled and semiskilled jobs are less likely to retire than workers in unskilled jobs because of the option to switch. Panel B of table 10.9 reclassifies jobs in the more manually demanding occupations according to skill intensity, using the definition in Ransom and Sutch. Jobs considered very physically demanding in panel A could also be skill intensive in panel B. Some examples are machinists, locomotive firemen, brickmasons, and dyers.

Table 10.10, panel A, presents occupational transitions for veterans in more manually demanding occupations in 1900 when they are classified according to physical intensity. There are large numbers of farm owners and tenants, because when they are excluded from 1900 manually demanding occupations, the number of veterans in not much physically intensive jobs drop from 1,521 in panel A to 43 in panel B. In panel A, a negative relationship exists between the rate of retirement and the degree of labor intensiveness. Farm owners and tenants, who dominate this group, had a higher retirement rate. Veterans in more physically intensive occupations tended to stick to the same group (57.09 percent) and tended to have lower retire-

Table 10.10   **Occupational Transition between 1900 and 1910 for Veterans in 1900 More Manually Demanding Occupations (%)**

| | | 1910 Category | | | |
| | | More Manually Demanding | | | |
Number of Veterans in 1900 Category	Less Manually Demanding	Not Much Physically Intensive	Somewhat Physically Intensive	Very Physically Intensive	Retired
A. Farmers and farm managers classified as more manually demanding occupation, by physical intensity					
1,521 in not much physically intensive	3.22	58.57	1.77	9.47	26.96
175 in somewhat physically intensive	10.86	8.00	34.86	22.28	24.00
992 in very physically intensive	7.36	9.82	4.66	57.09	21.07
B. Farmers and farm managers classified as less manually demanding occupation, by physical intensity					
43 in not much physically intensive	18.60	25.58	9.30	23.26	23.26
175 in somewhat physically intensive	18.29	0.57	34.86	22.28	24.00
992 in very physically intensive	16.13	1.01	4.66	57.13	21.07

| | More Manually Demanding | | | |
	Less Manually Demanding	Unskilled	Skilled	Retired
C. Farmers and farm managers classified as more manually demanding occupation, by skill intensity				
522 unskilled veterans	6.90	42.08	25.74	25.29
2,166 skilled veterans	4.85	7.82	62.91	24.42
D. Farmers and farm managers classified as less manually demanding occupation, by skill intensity				
522 unskilled veterans	18.97	42.10	13.65	25.29
688 skilled veterans	14.68	9.78	56.79	18.75

ment probability (21.07 percent). It is more difficult for men in very physically intensive jobs to switch to other jobs within the manually demanding category due to the lack of job-specific knowledge. It is also more difficult for them to retire since the average income for this group is low. Table panels C and D of table 10.10 present occupational transitions for veterans in more manually demanding occupations in 1900 when they are classified according to skill intensity. As with panels A and B, the difference between panels C and D is that farm owners and managers who are considered skilled workers are included in the former but excluded in the latter. Retirement among the skilled was lower, although there was not much trickling down from skilled to unskilled occupations for those remaining in the labor force in more manually demanding occupations, because only 7.82 percent of the skilled veterans in 1900 switched to unskilled, manually demanding occupations in 1910, and that percentage was 9.78 percent in panel D.

Apart from switching costs, existing income is another crucial parameter in labor market decisions. The census file records three indicator variables that represent the wealth holdings of a household that a veteran belonged to: whether the household had a farm versus a house, whether the household owned the property or rented it, and whether there was a mortgage left to be paid. We decided not to incorporate those indicators because the value of a piece of land or property could be dramatically different from one area to another. It would be inappropriate to assume that two households were equally wealthy based on the information that they both owned property. The census file does not have other wealth data except in indicator forms. We decided to use the monthly amount of pension a veteran received from the Pension Bureau as an income measure.[16] This is because the average annual pension was a substantial portion of the average annual per capita national income. Pension awards, therefore, could have a significant impact on a veteran's incentive to retire.

Given that a recruit was in the labor force in 1900, define the probabilities of two outcomes as

(3) $p_r = \text{prob}(Y = 1 | L \text{ or } M) = \text{prob}(\text{retirement in } 1910 | L \text{ or } M)$

$1 - p_r = \text{prob}(Y = 0 | L \text{ or } M)$

$= \text{prob}(\text{remained in labor force in } 1910 | L \text{ or } M)$

We assume that recruit i's probability of each outcome can be approximated as a logistic function of health, pension income, switching costs, and other unobserved factors, ε_i, controlling for k-dimensional demographic characteristics in 1900, x_{ki}. Omit the recruit index i to simplify notation. We fit the logistic model

(4) $$\text{logit}(p_r) = \log\left(\frac{p_r}{1 - p_r}\right) = \alpha_1 + \beta' x.$$

Equation (4) can be reformulized as

(5) $$p_r = \frac{e^{\alpha_1 + \beta' x}}{1 + e^{\alpha_1 + \beta' x}}.$$

The slope of the logistic regression with respect to any explanatory variable x_k is

(6) $$\frac{\partial p_r}{\partial x_k} = p_r(1 - p_r)\beta_k.$$

Demographic characteristics x_{ki} include birth cohorts, nativity, residence, literacy, and household features. Original birthplaces were reported by recruits at enlistment and were stored in the Military Service Records file. At enlistment, 71 percent of the recruits were native-born. By the time of the pension, 90 percent of the pensioned veterans were native-born.

---

16. In an earlier version of the paper, we experimented with the household wealth indicators and found that none of them possess significant explanatory power over retirement. There are two explanations for this result: Nonliquid asset holdings do not have any impact on the labor participation of UA veterans, or zero-one property dummies are not accurate wealth measures.

Compared to the proportion of native-born veterans at enlistment, the proportion of native-born veterans who later entered the pension program was higher. Perhaps immigrants were at a disadvantage when they applied for pensions, because it was more difficult for them to provide the Pension Bureau with proof of identification and evidence of service.

Degree of urbanization of the 1900 residential county is also of interest to us because it approximates the residential population density.[17] Employment opportunities differ between urban and rural areas. Residents in urban areas were more likely to participate in the labor force and to engage in certain types of occupations. To a limited extent, literacy measures the intellectual capacity of a veteran. A veteran who could not read or write had limited employment opportunities. We realize, however, that literacy is a very crude proxy of basic education.[18] Finally, a veteran's marital status and head-of-household status could affect the resource allocation within the household, which could in turn affect labor participation.

10.5   Results

Table 10.11 compares health, pension income, household, and demographic characteristics of the 1900 samples of less manually demanding professions, more manually demanding professions, and recruits who were in the labor force overall. Farmers and farm managers are classified as more manually demanding occupations. The three samples are similar in terms of health and pension income. Because monthly pension award was based on the health condition of veterans, comparable means on health and pension-income variables indicate that pension was granted regardless of occupational classification. There is a slightly higher percentage of native-born and literate recruits in the less manually demanding jobs, because citizens enjoyed a social advantage over immigrants in the labor market, and because more educated individuals were better prepared to take on professional positions.[19]

Cohort and regional compositions in table 10.11 are notably different between the less versus the more manually demanding occupation samples. The proportion of veterans who were born between 1812 and 1839, or who were over the age of sixty by 1900, is higher in the more manually demanding category. This observation is rather counterintuitive, considering that physical strength, which was needed in this occupational category, normally declines during the aging process. But after we study the cohort composition in table 10.12, where farmers and farm managers are classified as less manually demanding occupations instead, we discover that the higher

17. A county is urban if it contains at least one city with a population of 25,000 or over. There are 165 urban counties in the 1900 census.
18. If a veteran could sign his name, he would be considered literate.
19. See Blanck and Song (2001) for a comparison of pension application experience between native and foreign-born recruits.

Table 10.11   Variable Means of 1,796 Recruits Who Were in Labor Force by 1900 (Sample I, Classification I)

	370 Veterans in Less Manually Demanding Professions	1,426 Veterans in More Manually Demanding Professions	Overall (both more and less manually demanding professions)
1900 in labor force, 1910 retired	24.32	25.39	25.17
Had hernias by 1900	13.51	14.24	14.09
Rated 0.0000	0.00	0.28	0.22
Rated 0.1111–0.1667	0.81	0.98	0.95
Rated 0.2222	1.89	1.75	1.78
Rated 0.2500–0.5000	4.59	4.00	4.12
Rated 0.5556–0.6250	1.62	2.24	2.12
Rated 0.6667–1.0000	0.81	1.05	1.00
Rating missing	3.78	3.93	3.90
Had hernias by 1910	19.19	18.72	18.82
Rated 0.0000	1.08	0.07	0.28
Rated 0.1111–0.1667	0.00	0.63	0.50
Rated 0.2222	0.81	0.98	0.95
Rated 0.2500–0.5000	1.62	1.47	1.50
Rated 0.5556–0.6250	0.81	1.96	1.73
Rated 0.6667–1.0000	0.54	0.91	0.84
Rating missing	14.32	12.69	13.03
Years having contracted hernias by 1900	1.59	1.59	1.59
BMI at first exam	23.32	22.87	22.97
Square of BMI at first exam	553.13	530.00	534.77
1812–34	5.41	9.05	8.30
1835–39	15.68	20.62	19.60
1840–44	50.81	46.21	47.16
1845–51	22.16	20.69	20.99
Birth year missing	5.95	3.44	3.95
1900 head of household	91.08	94.46	93.76
1900 household relationship missing	2.70	1.26	1.56
1900 number of residents in the household	3.02	3.28	3.23
1900 married	88.11	89.20	88.98
Native-born	90.27	87.66	88.20
Able to read	96.49	94.46	94.88
Literacy unknown	3.24	1.54	1.89
1900 residence			
Northeast region	30.27	40.60	38.47
South region	2.70	3.72	3.51
West region	5.14	3.02	3.45
Midwest region	59.46	51.47	53.12
Unknown	2.43	1.19	1.45
Urban county	32.43	21.32	23.61
Monthly pension aware before and closest to 1910	$14.92	$14.70	$14.75

Notes: Dummies in percentages. Sample I consists of men linked to surgeons' data. In Classification I, farmers and farm managers are classified as more manually demanding occupations. If a recruit did not have hernias by 1900, he had zero year of contracting hernias. If he was diagnosed of hernias in 1900, we assume that he had one year of contracting hernias. In general, for a hernia patient, years of contracting hernias are equal to the difference between 1901 and the exam year during which he was diagnosed of hernias for the first time. For the entire sample of 1,812 recruits, the average number of years recruits had hernias was 1.59 years. The average was small because many recruits who did not have hernias were assigned a value of zero for the length of period contracting hernias. The average length of period contracting hernias for 253 hernia patients (not shown in this table) is 11.32 years.

Table 10.12   **Variable Means of 1,796 Recruits Who Were in Labor Force by 1900 (Sample I, Classification II)**

	1,125 Veterans in Less Manually Demanding Professions in 1900	671 Veterans in More Manually Demanding Professions in 1900	Overall (both more and less manually demanding professions in 1900)
1900 in labor force, 1910 retired	27.73	20.86	25.17
Had hernias by 1900	13.33	15.35	14.09
Rated 0.0000	0.09	0.45	0.22
Rated 0.1111–0.1667	0.89	1.04	0.95
Rated 0.2222	1.96	1.49	1.78
Rated 0.2500–0.5000	4.53	3.43	4.12
Rated 0.5556–0.6250	1.87	2.53	2.12
Rated 0.6667–1.0000	0.98	1.04	1.00
Rating missing	3.02	5.37	3.90
Had hernias by 1910	17.42	21.16	18.82
Rated 0.0000	0.44	0	0.28
Rated 0.1111–0.1667	0.36	0.75	0.50
Rated 0.2222	1.24	0.45	0.95
Rated 0.2500–0.5000	1.33	1.79	1.50
Rated 0.5556–0.6250	1.42	2.24	1.73
Rated 0.6667–1.0000	0.80	0.89	0.84
Rating missing	11.82	15.05	13.03
Years having contracted hernias by 1900	1.46	1.83	1.59
BMI at first exam	23.03	22.85	22.97
Square of BMI at first exam	538.08	529.19	534.77
Birth year			
1812–34	8.62	7.75	8.30
1835–39	19.91	19.08	19.60
1840–44	47.38	46.80	47.16
1845–51	20.36	22.06	20.99
Birth year missing	3.73	4.32	3.95
1900 head of household	95.64	90.61	93.76
1900 household relationship missing	1.42	1.79	1.56
1900 number of residents in the household	3.26	3.17	3.23
1900 married	89.78	87.63	88.98
Native-born	89.87	85.39	88.20
Able to read	95.47	93.89	94.88
Literacy unknown	1.96	1.79	1.89
1900 residence			
Northeast region	30.31	52.16	38.47
South region	4.18	2.38	3.51
West region	3.29	3.73	3.45
Midwest region	60.80	40.24	53.12
Unknown	1.42	1.49	1.45
Urban county	17.51	33.83	23.61
Monthly pension aware before and closest to 1910	$14.90	$14.49	$14.75

Notes: Dummies in percent. Sample I consists of men linked to surgeons' data. In Classification II, farmers and farm managers are classified as less manually demanding occupations. If a recruit did not have hernias by 1900, he had zero year of contracting hernias. If he was diagnosed of hernias in 1900, we assume that he had one year of contracting hernias. In general, for a hernia patient, years of contracting hernias are equal to the difference between 1901 and the exam year during which he was diagnosed of hernias for the first time. For the entire sample of 1,812 recruits, the average number of years recruits had hernias was 1.59 years. The average was small because many recruits who did not have hernias were assigned a value of zero for the length of period contracting hernias. The average length of period contracting hernias for 253 hernia patients (not shown in this table) is 11.32 years.

percentage of the elderly in table 10.11 is due to the fact that farmers and farm managers are classified as more manually demanding occupations, and that they remained as caretakers of their farmland even after the normal retirement age. In fact, table 10.12 shows that the age composition is similar between the two occupational groups. The proportion of older veterans is slightly higher in the less manually demanding occupations, as one usually expects.

As demonstrated in both table 10.11 and table 10.12, there is a close link between occupation and region. A higher proportion of veterans in more manually demanding jobs resided in the industrialized Northeast, where operatives, kindred workers, service workers, and other nonfarm workers were in demand. In both occupational categories, a substantial number of recruits resided in the Midwest region. The proportion of Midwestern residents who were in the more manually demanding occupational group is higher in table 10.11 (51.47 percent) than in table 10.12 (40.24 percent), because farmers and farm managers who resided primarily in the Midwest are classified as the more manually demanding group in table 10.11, whereas they are not in table 10.12. We also notice that farmers and farm managers were not urban dwellers. This is because the occupational group to which they belong has a smaller percentage of individuals living in urban areas.

The effect of hernias on labor force transitions of veterans who were linked to surgeons' data is summarized in table 10.13 and table 10.14. Table 10.13 corresponds to the classification that includes farmers and farm managers in the more manually demanding group, and table 10.14 corresponds to the classification that excludes them from that group. In each table, the probability of retirement is explained by health, pension income, job-switching cost, cohort, nativity, literacy, and regional factors. We investigate four models. The first model treats health status as a combination of a general measure, BMI, and a specific measure, hernia screen. The second model replaces the zero-one hernia screen with a continuous hernia-ratings variable. The third model adds the length of period contracting hernias into the second model. Because the debilitating potential of hernias is at the core of our study, we want to test the robustness of our results by experimenting with various specifications in those three models. Finally, for the fourth model we add to the third model the interactions of the 1900 less manually demanding occupation dummy variable with regional dummies and with the hernia screen, and then the interaction of the hernia screen with pension income. Regional interaction terms act as controls for occupational differences resulting from labor specialization in certain geographical locations. Interactions with the hernia screen present an answer to the question of whether hernias affected individuals differently in less versus more manually demanding occupations, and whether wealthier hernia patients were more likely to retire.

Table 10.13 shows that hernias had a weak influence on retirement. In the

Table 10.13   Effect of Hernias on the Marginal Probability of Retirement (Sample I, Classification I)

	Hernia Yes/No and BMI $[\partial E(p_l)/\partial x_k]$	Hernia Ratings and BMI $[\partial E(p_{ml})/\partial x_k]$	Hernia Ratings, How Long, Had Hernias, and BMI $[\partial E(p_{ml})/\partial x_k]$	Hernia Ratings, How Long, BMI, and Interaction Terms $[\partial E(p_{ml})/\partial x_k]$
Intercept	−0.0289	−0.0040	−0.0072	−0.0356
Had hernias by 1900				
Rated 0.1111–0.1667	0.0961*	0.2811**	0.2550**	0.2510**
Rated 0.2222		−0.0098	−0.0353	−0.0458
Rated 0.5556–0.6250		0.0122	−0.0326	−0.0376
Rated 0.6667–1.0000		−0.0307	−0.0564	−0.0617
Rating missing		−0.0026	−0.0627	−0.0678
Had hernias by 1910				
Rated 0.0000	−0.0737	0.1801	0.1261	0.0917
Rated 0.1111–0.1667		−0.3543*	−0.3873*	−0.3893*
Rated 0.2222		0.0511	0.0215	0.0168
Rated 0.5550–0.6250		−0.0632	−0.0770	−0.0874
Rated 0.6667–1.0000		−0.0121	−0.0413	−0.0465
Rating missing		0.0156	0.0044	−0.0092
Years having contracted hernias by 1900			0.0052	0.0044
BMI at first exam	−0.0209	−0.0189	−0.0190	−0.0167
Square of BMI at first exam × 10^{-2}	0.0442	0.0390	0.0397	0.0347
Birth year				
1835–39	−0.0908**	−0.0915**	−0.0885**	−0.0877**
1840–44	−0.1577***	−0.1595***	−0.1572***	−0.1555***
1845–51	−0.2711***	−0.2741***	−0.2713***	−0.2688***
Birth year missing	−0.1594***	−0.1611***	−0.1619***	−0.1612***
1900 head of household	−0.0825*	−0.0781	−0.0787	−0.0778
1900 household relationship missing	0.0691	0.0747	0.0744	0.0754
1900 number of residents in the household	−0.0132**	−0.0129**	−0.0129**	−0.0126**

(*continued*)

Table 10.13 (continued)

	Hernia Yes/No and BMI $[\partial E(p_i)/\partial x_k]$	Hernia Ratings and BMI $[\partial E(p_{mi})/\partial x_k]$	Hernia Ratings, How Long Had Hernias, and BMI $[\partial E(p_{mi})/\partial x_k]$	Hernia Ratings, How Long, BMI, and Interaction Terms $[\partial E(p_{mi})/\partial x_k]$
1900 married	0.0091	0.0035	0.0036	0.0032
Native-born	0.0015	0.0010	0.0019	0.0028
Able to read	0.0816	0.0944	0.0922	0.0917
Literacy unknown	−0.0258	−0.0630	−0.0633	−0.0623
1900 residence				
South region	−0.0700	−0.0650	−0.0652	−0.0671
West region	0.2402***	0.2391***	0.2402***	0.2587***
Midwest region	0.1099***	0.1110***	0.1116***	0.1118***
Unknown	0.0037	0.0571	0.0526	0.0464
Urban county	−0.0321	−0.0316	−0.0307	−0.0393
Monthly pension aware before and closest to 1910	0.0091***	0.0094***	0.0094***	0.0095***
1900 occupation less manually demanding	−0.0186	−0.0239	−0.0243	−0.0287
And residence West				−0.0755
And residence Midwest				−0.0092
And residence urban				0.0309
And had hernias				0.0438
Interaction 1900 hernia and ruling amount × 10^{-2}				0.0815

Notes: Sample I consists of men linked to surgeons' data. In Classification I, farmers and farm managers are classified as more manually demanding occupations. The omitted hernias categories are 1900 hernia patients rated from 0.2500 to 0.5000, and 1910 hernia patients rated from 0.2500 to 0.5000. Other omitted categories are born between 1812 and 1834, and residence in the Northeast region in 1900. We did not include the dummy variable indicating a zero hernia rating in 1900. The number of observations in this category is so small that including this dummy variable in the regression would cause a convergence problem in the maximum likelihood estimation.

***Significant at the 1 percent level.
**Significant at the 5 percent level.
*Significant at the 10 percent level.

Table 10.14   Effect of Hernias on the Marginal Probability of Retirement (Sample I, Classification II)

	Hernia Yes/No and BMI $[\partial E(p_i)/\partial x_k]$	Hernia Ratings and BMI $[\partial E(p_{ml})/\partial x_k]$	Hernia Ratings, How Long Had Hernias, and BMI $[\partial E(p_{ml})/\partial x_k]$	Hernia Ratings, How Long, BMI, and Interaction Terms $[\partial E(p_{ml})/\partial x_k]$
Intercept	0.0175	−0.0133	−0.0157	−0.0649
Had hernias by 1900	0.0935			
Rated 0.1111–0.1667		0.2801**	0.2554**	0.2526**
Rated 0.2222		−0.0092	−0.0338	−0.0378
Rated 0.5556–0.6250		0.0118	−0.0303	−0.0369
Rated 0.6667–1.0000		−0.0311	−0.0557	−0.0645
Rating missing		0.0043	−0.0531	−0.0742
Had hernias by 1910	−0.0695			
Rated 0.0000		0.1437	0.0920	0.1162
Rated 0.1111–0.1667		−0.3401*	−0.3702*	−0.3795*
Rated 0.2222		0.0432	0.0152	0.0084
Rated 0.5550–0.6250		−0.0572	−0.0706	−0.0754
Rated 0.6667–1.0000		−0.0071	−0.0348	−0.0395
Rating missing		0.0160	−0.0033	−0.0091
Years having contracted hernias by 1900			0.0049	0.0050
BMI at first exam	−0.0201	−0.0183	−0.0184	−0.0089
Square of BMI at first exam $\times 10^{-2}$	0.0415	0.0367	0.0374	0.0191
Birth year				
1835–39	−0.0912**	−0.0921**	−0.0894**	−0.0858**
1840–44	−0.1583***	−0.1607***	−0.1585***	−0.1588***
1845–51	−0.2715***	−0.2751***	−0.2727***	−0.2758***
Birth year missing	−0.1614***	−0.1638***	−0.1646***	−0.1574***
1900 head of household	−0.0927*	−0.0870*	−0.0872*	−0.0890*
1900 household relationship missing	0.0724	0.0780	0.0778	0.0826
1900 number of residents in the household	−0.0134**	−0.0131**	−0.0130**	−0.0140**

(*continued*)

Table 10.14 (continued)

	Hernia Yes/No and BMI $[\partial E(p_i)/\partial x_k]$	Hernia Ratings and BMI $[\partial E(p_{mi})/\partial x_k]$	Hernia Ratings, How Long Long Had Hernias, and BMI $[\partial E(p_{mi})\partial x_k]$	Hernia Ratings, How Long, BMI, and Interaction Terms $[\partial E(p_{mi})/\partial x_k]$
1900 married	0.0124	0.0054	0.0054	0.0113
Native-born	-0.0028	-0.0033	-0.0025	-0.0046
Able to read	0.0724	0.0837	0.0816	0.0766
Literary unknown	-0.0421	-0.0733	-0.0737	-0.1025
1900 residence				
South region	-0.0786	-0.0738	-0.0737	-0.0535
West region	0.2352***	0.2338***	0.2348***	0.1141
Midwest region	0.1002***	0.1013***	0.1019***	0.0011
Unknown	-0.0097	0.0354	0.0317	0.0541
Urban county	-0.0273	-0.0274	-0.0267	-0.0732*
Monthly pension aware before and closest to 1910	0.0090***	0.0093***	0.0093***	0.0094***
1900 occupation less manually demanding	0.0476**	0.0464**	0.0457**	-0.0671*
And residence West				0.2064*
And residence Midwest				0.1615***
And residence urban				0.0715
And had hernias				-0.0050
Interaction 1900 hernia and ruling amount $\times 10^{-2}$				0.0881

Notes: Sample I consists of men linked to surgeons' data. In Classification II, farmers and farm managers are classified as less manually demanding occupations. The omitted hernias categories are 1900 hernia patients rated from 0.2500 to 0.5000, and 1910 hernia patients rated from 0.2500 to 0.5000. Other omitted categories are born between 1812 and 1834, and residence in the Northeast region in 1900. We did not include the dummy variable indicating a zero hernia rating in 1900. The number of observations in this category is so small that including this dummy variable in the regression would cause a convergence problem in the maximum likelihood estimation.

***Significant at the 1 percent level.
**Significant at the 5 percent level.
*Significant at the 10 percent level.

first model, where the zero-one past and contemporary hernia screens are considered, having hernias in 1900 increases the odds of retirement in 1910 by 10 percent. The coefficient has a marginal statistical significance. Because having hernias in 1900 positively correlates with having hernias in 1910, the coefficient estimate on the 1910 hernia screen variable is negative whenever the coefficient on the 1900 hernia screen variable is positive. In the second specification, where categorical dummies representing hernia ratings in 1900 and 1910 enter the regression, one group of hernia patients was influenced. Relative to those with median ratings (between 0.2500 and 0.5000) in 1900, patients having ratings of the least severe degree (between 0.1111 and 0.1667) in 1900 were 28 percent more likely to retire. Again, because of the positive correlation in ratings between 1900 and 1910, the coefficient estimate on the same group of patients (i.e., those having ratings of the least severe degree, between 0.1111 and 0.1667, in 1910) is negative. We get the same qualitative result of the weak explanatory power of hernias when we add years of contracting into the equation. Although patients with longer hernia disability histories were more likely to retire, the coefficient estimate is small and insignificant. The result remains the same even after we add interaction terms of the 1900 hernia screen with the 1900 less manually demanding job dummy variable and with monthly pension income. No difference in retirement probability exists for hernia patients regardless of their 1900 job category and regardless of their income.

Table 10.14 presents the same models as table 10.13, except that farmers and farm managers are classified as less manually demanding occupations. The two classifications result in almost the same implications on health. Hernias did not exert a strong influence on retirement, after we have controlled for general health measured by a quadratic function of BMI. We have previously reasoned that if hernias were physically debilitating, retirement probability ought to be higher for patients in more manually demanding occupations: If they were to remain in the same occupational category, they had to endure the pain while providing physical labor. If they chose to switch to the less manually demanding occupations, they had to incur human capital investment, which could be a difficult option especially as they grew older. We have also reasoned that retirement probability ought to be higher for patients with higher income. Both table 10.13 and table 10.14 show a weak relationship between the degree of severity of hernias and the propensity to retire. They show no evidence of higher probability for patients in the more physically intensive occupations, or for patients with larger pension income.

Why did hernias have little effect on retirement? One possibility is that hernias caused impairment but that the impairment was not significant enough to cause disability. As table 10.3 indicates, more than 90 percent of patients had the usual inguinal hernias, more than 85 percent of the veterans had less morbid hernias (29.0 percent truss effective and 56.6 percent reducible), more than 80 percent had a single hernia, and less than 40 percent had hernias of size three inches or up. Although the majority of the patients had hernias that were probably discomforting, they resorted to crude but effective methods to cope with the disability, such as wearing trusses or other supportable materials that they made themselves. These coping methods likely reflect a greater importance of income relative to comfort. Why did the least severe kind of hernias (rated between 0.1111 and 0.1667) result in a higher rate of retirement? If we assume that the majority of patients who developed hernias developed small hernias initially, then we can reason that perhaps those who were likely to retire, retired upon the initial development of a hernia, while those who were less likely to retire endured their hernias.

Table 10.13 and table 10.14 also give similar effects of age, income, and household characteristics on labor force transitions of veterans between 1900 and 1910. Age is a highly significant factor in the labor force participation of the Civil War veterans. Relative to the oldest veterans, those born in later cohorts are less likely to retire. Heads of households and recruits with larger families were less likely to retire because they had stronger financial obligations that kept them in the labor force. We have previously concluded that for hernia patients, there was no income effect in addition to the income effect that might have existed for all veterans. There did exist a strong income effect for all veterans: An increase of one dollar per month in the pension award increases the retirement probability by almost 1 percentage point.

Tables 10.10 and 10.13 show a strong regional effect on retirement in the first three models. Relative to those residing in the Northeast region, veterans from the West and the Midwest regions are more likely to retire. A large population of farm laborers and farm owners resided in the West and the Midwest regions. Compared to the industrial Northeast, where employment opportunities were ample, they might have fewer choices in the types of low-stress jobs that they could switch to. To investigate the possibility that the observed regional effect in the West and the Midwest was due to the lack of substitute occupations for farm-related work, we include interaction terms between the dummy variable of less manually demanding occupations with the West and the Midwest regional dummy variables and with the urban county dummy variable.

Table 10.13 shows that when farmers and farm managers are classified as more manually demanding occupations, coefficient estimates on regional interaction terms and on the urban interaction term are not statistically significant. This result indicates that under Classification I, regional effect did not originate from geographical distribution of occupations. However, under Classification II, where farmers and farm managers are classified as less manually demanding occupations, coefficient estimates in table 10.14 show that residing in the West or the Midwest per se did not have any impact on retirement probability. Instead, only those West or Midwest residents who belonged to the less manually demanding group were more likely to retire. Comparing the last model in table 10.14 with that in table 10.13, we conjecture that it was only the farmers and the farm managers in the West and the Midwest who had fewer occupational alternatives, because their knowledge was tied to the farm. As table 10.14 shows, once they left farming, they could not have easily acquired the skills of other less manually demanding jobs so that the only choice was to retire. In contrast, as table 10.13 shows, everything else being equal, farm laborers in the West and the Midwest had equal probability of retiring as others, because if they quit working on the farm, they could still engage in other physically intensive occupations.[20]

Finally, veterans in less manually demanding occupations were less likely to retire. This result was weak and insignificant when farmers and farm managers are grouped as more manually demanding jobs in table 10.13, but was strong and significant when they are grouped as less manually demanding jobs in table 10.14. This result confirms the argument that switching costs were higher for those individuals engaging in more manually demanding occupations because they had to invest in additional human capital.

We have studied retirement for a sample of men with hernias versus men with hernias but with other disabilities. An alternative sample of interest to us is that of men with hernias versus healthy men without any surgeons' records. Tables 10.15 through 10.18 present the effect of hernias on retirement using this alternative sample. Because more than half of the healthy men did not have any medical examination, we do not have information on health and demographic characteristics for them. Therefore, as the last column of tables 10.15 and 10.17 show, 56.51 percent of the sample has missing birth years, 54.57 percent of the sample has missing household relationships, marital status, literacy, and residence, and 54.94 percent of the sample has missing nativity.

Despite the lack of information for a large number of men, tables 10.16 and 10.18 demonstrate results that are comparable to those in tables 10.13 and 10.14 in both sign and magnitude. The yes/no hernia screen variable indicates that having hernias by 1900 increases the odds of retirement by about 10 percent. The ratings variables indicate that having hernias of the least severe kind has an influence on retirement. Overall, the effect of hernias on retirement is weak. Younger cohorts born between 1840 and 1851 were less likely to retire compared to older cohorts, as were men with larger numbers of household residents to support and men living in urban counties where there were plenty of job opportunities. Farmers in the Midwest

---

20. With regard to region, retirement may be defined differently for farm or business owners than for individuals who were not owners. It is possible that farm and business owners never really retired. Even though they passed their businesses to the next generation, they maintained advisory roles. I thank Peter Blanck for bringing up this point.

Table 10.15   Variable Means of 1,904 Recruits Who Were in Labor Force by 1900 (Sample II, Classification I)

	418 Veterans in Less Manually Demanding Professions	1,486 Veterans in More Manually Demanding Professions	Overall (both more and less manually demanding professions)
1900 in labor force, 1910 retired	22.25	23.89	23.53
Had hernias by 1900	12.20	13.86	13.50
Rated 0.0000	0	0.27	0.21
Rated 0.1111–0.1667	0.72	1.08	1.00
Rated 0.2222	1.91	1.68	1.73
Rated 0.2500–0.5000	3.83	3.90	3.89
Rated 0.5556–0.6250	1.67	0.22	2.10
Rated 0.6667–1.0000	0.72	1.08	1.00
Rating missing	3.35	3.63	3.57
Had hernias by 1910	17.70	18.30	18.17
Rated 0.0000	0.96	0.07	0.26
Rated 0.1111–0.1667	0	0.61	0.47
Rated 0.2222	0.72	0.94	0.89
Rated 0.2500–0.5000	1.67	1.41	1.47
Rated 0.5556–0.6250	0.72	1.82	1.58
Rated 0.6667–1.0000	0.48	0.94	0.84
Rating missing	13.16	12.52	12.66
Years having contracted hernias by 1900	1.42	1.54	1.51
Birth year			
1812–34	3.11	3.36	3.31
1835–39	6.70	9.08	8.56
1840–44	27.51	19.25	21.06
1845–51	11.48	10.30	10.56
Birth year missing	51.20	58.01	56.51
1900 head of household	47.61	41.52	42.86
1900 household relationship missing	48.56	56.26	54.57
1900 number of residents if number nonmissing	1.64	1.52	1.54
1900 married	46.65	38.43	40.23
1900 marital status missing	48.56	56.26	54.57
Native-born	45.93	38.90	40.44
Nativity missing	48.56	56.46	54.73
Able to read	51.43	41.92	44.01
Literacy unknown	48.56	56.26	54.57
1900 residence			
Northeast region	13.16	13.86	13.71
South region	0.96	1.82	1.63
West region	3.83	1.08	1.68
Midwest region	32.54	26.99	28.20
Unknown	48.56	56.26	54.57
Urban county	20.10	9.56	11.87
Urban county missing	49.76	56.39	54.94
Monthly pension award before and closest to 1910[a]	$7.38	$7.17	$7.22

Notes: Dummies in percentages. Sample II consists of 1,558 men linked to surgeons' data and 346 hernia patients. In Classification I, farmers and farm managers are classified as more manually demanding occupations.

[a]If a recruit did not apply for pension, or if he applied and did not get any pension, his monthly pension is zero. The average monthly pension award for 215 recruits in 1900 less manually demanding occupation who did get awarded is $14.36, for 713 recruits in 1900 more manually demanding occupation who did get awarded is $14.95, and for the overall 928 recruits who did get awarded is $14.81.

Table 10.16   Effect of Hernias on the Marginal Probability of Retirement (Sample II, Classification I)

	Hernia Yes/No $[\partial E(p_i)/\partial x_k]$	Hernia Ratings $[\partial E(p_m)/\partial x_k]$	Hernia Ratings, How Long Had Hernias $[\partial E(p_m)/\partial x_k]$	Hernia Ratings, How Long, and Interaction Terms $[\partial E(p_m)/\partial x_k]$
Intercept	-0.0133	-0.0301*	-0.0320	-0.0438
Had hernias by 1900	0.0966*			
Rated 0.1111–0.1667		0.1974*	0.1642*	0.1433
Rated 0.2222		-0.0095	-0.0399	-0.0803
Rated 0.5556–0.6250		0.0104	-0.0389	-0.0603
Rated 0.6667–1.0000		-0.0058	-0.0383	-0.0700
Rating missing		0.0253	-0.0455	-0.0648
Had hernias by 1910	-0.0453			
Rated 0.0000		0.1531	0.0900	0.0357
Rated 0.1111–0.1667		-0.2745	-0.3056	-0.3220*
Rated 0.2222		0.0412	0.0063	0.0002
Rated 0.5550–0.6250		-0.0021	-0.0178	-0.0591
Rated 0.6667–1.0000		-0.0096	-0.0469	-0.0755
Rating missing		0.0436	0.0223	0.0054
Years having contracted hernias by 1900			0.0061*	0.0034
Birth year				
1835–39	-0.0521	-0.0550	-0.0477	-0.0449
1840–44	-0.1013**	-0.1061**	-0.0996*	-0.0907*
1845–51	-0.2887***	-0.2980***	-0.2907***	-0.2820***
Birth year missing	-0.1870**	-0.1819***	-0.1796**	-0.1763*
1900 head of household	-0.0141	-0.0089	-0.0134	-0.0135
1900 number of residents in the household	-0.0202***	-0.0206***	-0.0204***	-0.0196***
1900 married	-0.0173	-0.0296	-0.0290	-0.0235
Native-born	0.0199	0.0192	0.0209	0.0253

(*continued*)

Table 10.16 (continued)

	Hernia Yes/No $[\partial E(p_t)/\partial x_k]$	Hernia Ratings $[\partial E(p_{mt})/\partial x_k]$	Hernia Ratings, How Long Had Hernias $[\partial E(p_{mt})/\partial x_k]$	Hernia Ratings, How Long, and Interaction Terms $[\partial E(p_{mt})/\partial x_k]$
Nativity missing	-0.0004	0.0117	0.0116	0.0204
Able to read	-0.0885	-0.0687	-0.0765	-0.0799
1900 residence				
South region	0.0593	0.0762	0.0782	0.0796
West region	0.0770	0.0728	0.0771	0.1390
Midwest region	0.0598*	0.0666*	0.0693*	0.0726*
Unknown	-0.1042***	-0.1060***	-0.1039***	-0.0932**
Monthly pension aware before and closest to 1910	0.0032*	0.0032*	0.0033*	0.0031*
1900 occupation less manually demanding	-0.0041	-0.0068	-0.0070	-0.0048
And residence West				-0.1412
And residence Midwest				-0.0205
And residence urban				-0.0334
And had hernias				0.0786
Interaction 1900 hernia and ruling amount $\times 10^{-2}$				0.0044

Notes: Sample II consists of 1,558 men linked to surgeons' data and 346 hernia patients. In Classification I, farmers and farm managers are classified as more manually demanding occupations. The omitted hernias categories are 1900 hernia patients rated from 0.2500 to 0.5000, and 1910 hernia patients rated from 0.2500 to 0.5000. Other omitted categories are born between 1812 and 1834, and residence in the Northeast region in 1900. We did not include the dummy variable indicating a zero hernia rating in 1900. The number of observations in this category is so small that including this dummy variable in the regression would cause a convergence problem in the maximum likelihood estimation. The variables 1900 marital status missing, residential region unknown, household relationship missing, urban county unknown, and literacy unknown are perfectly correlated with the variable nativity missing, and thus are omitted from the regression.

***Significant at the 1 percent level.

**Significant at the 5 percent level.

*Significant at the 10 percent level.

Table 10.17   Variable Means of 1,904 Recruits Who Were in Labor Force by 1900 (Sample II, Classification II)

	1,243 Veterans in Less Manually Demanding Professions	661 Veterans in More Manually Demanding Professions	Overall (both more and less manually demanding professions)
1900 in labor force, 1910 retired	24.22	22.24	23.53
Had hernias by 1900	12.63	15.13	13.50
Rated 0.0000	0.16	0.30	0.21
Rated 0.1111–0.1667	0.88	1.21	1.00
Rated 0.2222	1.85	1.51	1.73
Rated 0.2500–0.5000	4.10	3.48	3.89
Rated 0.5556–0.6250	1.85	2.57	2.10
Rated 0.6667–1.0000	0.97	1.06	1.00
Rating missing	2.82	4.99	3.57
Had hernias by 1910	16.65	21.03	18.17
Rated 0.0000	0.40	0	0.26
Rated 0.1111–0.1667	0.32	0.76	0.47
Rated 0.2222	1.13	0.45	0.89
Rated 0.2500–0.5000	1.29	1.82	1.47
Rated 0.5550–0.6250	1.29	2.12	1.58
Rated 0.6667–1.0000	0.80	0.91	0.84
Rating missing	11.42	14.98	12.66
Years having contracted hernias by 1900	1.37	1.78	1.51
Birth year			
1812–34	3.22	3.48	3.31
1835–39	7.88	9.83	8.56
1840–44	21.56	20.12	21.06
1845–51	9.41	12.71	10.56
Birth year missing	57.42	53.86	56.51
1900 head of household	42.00	44.48	42.86
1900 household relationship missing	56.40	51.13	54.57
1900 number of residents if number nonmissing	1.51	1.60	1.54
1900 married	39.90	40.85	40.23
1900 marital status missing	56.40	51.13	54.57
Native-born	39.58	42.06	40.44
Nativity missing	56.56	51.29	54.73
Able to read	42.88	46.14	44.01
Literacy unknown	56.40	51.13	54.57
1900 residence			
Northeast region	10.06	20.57	13.71
South region	1.77	1.36	1.63
West region	2.01	1.06	1.68
Midwest region	29.44	25.87	28.20
Unknown	56.40	51.13	54.57
Urban county	9.25	16.79	11.87
Urban county missing	56.88	51.29	54.94
Nonmissing monthly pension before and closest to 1910[a]	$7.06	$7.52	$7.22

Notes: Dummies in percentages. Sample II consists of 1,558 men linked to surgeons' data and 346 hernia patients. In Classification II, farmers and farm managers are classified as less manually demanding occupations.

[a]If a recruit did not apply for pension, or if he applied and did not get any pension, his monthly pension is zero. The average monthly pension award for 583 recruits in 1900 less manually demanding occupation who did get awarded is $15.04, for 345 recruits in 1900 more manually demanding occupation who did get awarded is $14.41, and for the overall 928 recruits who did get awarded is $14.81.

Table 10.18   Effect of Hernias on the Marginal Probability of Retirement (Sample II, Classification II)

	Hernia Yes/No $[\partial E(p_t)/\partial x_k]$	Hernia Ratings $[\partial E(p_{ml})/\partial x_k]$	Hernia Ratings, How Long Had Hernias $[\partial E(p_{ml})/\partial x_k]$	Hernia Ratings, How Long, and Interaction Terms $[\partial E(p_{ml})/\partial x_k]$
Intercept	-0.0138	-0.0310	-0.0330	-0.0491
Had hernias by 1900	0.0961*			
Rated 0.1111–0.1667		0.1979**	0.1648**	0.1440
Rated 0.2222		-0.0094	-0.0398	-0.0746
Rated 0.5556–0.6250		0.0108	-0.0381	-0.0595
Rated 0.6667–1.0000		-0.0053	-0.0377	-0.0796
Rating missing		0.0265	-0.0440	-0.0664
Had hernias by 1910	-0.0446			
Rated 0.0000		0.1448	0.0821	0.0744*
Rated 0.1111–0.1667		-0.2721	-0.3025	-0.3326
Rated 0.2222		0.0400	0.0054	0.0008
Rated 0.5550–0.6250		-0.0009	-0.0165	-0.0528
Rated 0.6667–1.0000		-0.0096	-0.0467	-0.0754
Rating missing		0.0437	0.0225	0.0092
Years having contracted hernias by 1900			0.0061*	0.0034
Birth year				
1835–39	-0.0514	-0.0540	-0.0468	-0.0416
1840–44	-0.1016**	-0.1064**	-0.0999*	-0.0911*
1845–51	-0.2877***	-0.2971***	-0.2899***	-0.2803***
Birth year missing	-0.1871**	-0.1823**	-0.1800**	-0.1741*
1900 head of household	-0.0146	-0.0088	-0.0131	-0.0083
1900 number of residents in the household	-0.0202***	-0.0205***	-0.0203***	-0.0196**
1900 married	-0.0189	-0.0313	-0.0307	-0.0270

Native-born	0.0190	0.0184	0.0201	0.0234
Nativity missing	-0.0068	0.0057	0.0059	0.0160
Able to read	-0.0917	-0.0726	-0.0803	-0.0835
1900 residence				
South region	0.0577	0.0748	0.0770	0.0785
West region	0.0733	0.0683	0.0727	0.1258
Midwest region	0.0583*	0.0649*	0.0677*	0.0654
Urban county	-0.1038***	-0.1059***	-0.1039***	-0.0979*
Monthly pension aware before and closest to 1910	0.0033*	0.0033*	0.0033*	0.0030*
1900 occupation less manually demanding	0.0092	0.0089	0.0083	0.0095
And residence West				-0.0582
And residence Midwest				0.0053
And residence urban				-0.0138
And had hernias				-0.0136
Interaction 1900 hernia and ruling amount $\times 10^{-2}$				0.0054

Notes: Sample II consists of 1,558 men linked to surgeons' data and 346 hernia patients. In Classification II, farmers and farm managers are classified as less manually demanding occupations. The omitted hernias categories are 1900 hernia patients rated from 0.2500 to 0.5000, and 1910 hernia patients rated from 0.2500 to 0.5000. Other omitted categories are born between 1812 and 1834, and residence in the Northeast region in 1900. We did not include the dummy variable indicating a zero hernia rating in 1900. The number of observations in this category is so small that including this dummy variable in the regression would cause a convergence problem in the maximum likelihood estimation. The variables 1900 marital status missing, residential region unknown, household relationship missing, urban county unknown, and literacy unknown are perfectly correlated with the variable nativity missing, and thus are omitted from the regression.

***Significant at the 1 percent level.

**Significant at the 5 percent level.

*Significant at the 10 percent level.

region were more likely to retire, as were men receiving higher monthly pension awards.

Yet another sample to test the robustness of the previous results is the sample containing only men in 1900 manually demanding occupations who had surgeons' records. As described before, we group men into three types of jobs according to physical intensity. Tables 10.19 through 10.22 show results pertaining to this sample. Comparing table 10.20 to tables 10.13 and 10.16, we notice two qualitative differences. First, the yes/no hernia screen variable ceases to be significant. The low explanatory power of hernia screen is likely due to the fact that the screen variable is only a very coarse measure of debilitation. When ratings are used instead, we get a result that is consistent with that from the other samples: Those in the lowest hernia ratings were significantly more likely to retire.

Second, with the interaction terms of physical intensity and other dummy variables, those in 1900 with very physically intensive jobs were more likely to retire, as panel A of table 10.20 indicates. Furthermore, panel B shows that veterans in the skilled occupations were less likely to retire. Those results are consistent with the theory by Ransom and Sutch (1986) of "downward occupational mobility" that predicts higher labor market exit rates for the unskilled. There is a significantly negative marginal effect on men engaging in physically intensive jobs and living in the West or the Midwest region. Those men were primary farm laborers who could not afford to retire and who were limited in alternative occupational choices. In contrast, there is a significantly positive marginal effect on skilled farm managers living in the West or the Midwest region.

Results in tables 10.21 and 10.22 relate to the investigation of 688 men who were a subsample of the 1,474 men in tables 10.19 and 10.20. Men excluded are farm owners and farm managers. The A panels of tables 10.22 and 10.20 are comparable, as are their B panels. A few variables such as regional dummies and interaction terms cease to be significant because of a much smaller sample size. Overall, using the sample of men in 1900 manually demanding occupations, we find a weak positive effect of hernia severity on retirement, positive age and income effects on retirement, and negative household-size and head-of-household effects on retirement.

10.6   Conclusions and Future Work

One of the challenging aspects in empirical studies on health and labor supply is the construction of an accurate measure of health status. Promising candidates for this measure include life expectancy, mortality rate, height, and BMI, and composite indicators of infectious diseases or chronic disabilities. As noted by Costa (1996, 64), "the difficulty in using life expectancy as a health measure is that life expectancies can be high and health poor if advances in medical technology have led to an increased burden

**Table 10.19   Variable Means of 1,474 Recruits in Labor Force by 1900
(Sample III, Classification I)**

Variable	Mean (dummies in %)
1900 in labor force, 1910 retired	25.44
Had hernias by 1900	13.98
Rated 0.0000	0.27
Rated 0.1111–0.1667	1.09
Rated 0.2222	1.70
Rated 0.2500–0.5000	3.93
Rated 0.5556–0.6250	2.24
Rated 0.6667–1.0000	1.09
Rating missing	3.66
Had hernias by 1910	18.45
Rated 0.0000	0.07
Rated 0.1111–0.1667	0.61
Rated 0.2222	0.95
Rated 0.2500–0.5000	1.42
Rated 0.5550–0.6250	1.83
Rated 0.6667–1.0000	0.95
Rating missing	12.62
Years having contracted hernias by 1900	1.55
BMI at first exam	22.87
Square of BMI at first exam	529.71
Birth year	
1812–34	8.68
1835–39	20.01
1840–44	44.84
1845–51	19.88
Birth year missing	6.58
1900 head of household	92.33
1900 household relationship missing	3.26
1900 number of residents in the household	3.22
1900 married	87.25
Native-born	84.53
Nativity missing	3.60
Able to read	92.47
Literacy unknown	3.26
1900 residence	
Northeast region	39.76
South region	3.60
West region	2.99
Midwest region	50.34
Unknown	3.26
Urban country	20.69
County unknown	3.32
1900 occupation	
Not Much Physically Intensive	54.82
Somewhat Physically Intensive	6.51
Very Physically Intensive	38.67
Unskilled	20.35
Skilled	79.65
Monthly pension award before and closest to 1910	$14.77

Notes: Sample III consists of men linked to surgeons' data who were in more manually demanding occupations in 1900. In Classification I, farmers and farm managers are classified as more manually demanding occupations.

Table 10.20   Effect of Hernias on the Marginal Probability of Retirement (Sample III, Classification I)

	Hernia Yes/No and BMI $[\partial E(p_l)/\partial x_k]$	Hernia Ratings and BMI $[\partial E(p_{ml})/\partial x_k]$	Hernia Ratings, How Long Had Hernias, and BMI $[\partial E(p_{ml})\partial x_k]$	Hernia Ratings, How Long, BMI, and Interaction Terms $[\partial E(p_{ml})/\partial x_k]$
	A. Controlling for physical intensity			
Intercept	-0.0824	-0.0779	-0.0814	-0.3492
Had hernias by 1900	0.0381			
Rated 0.1111–0.1667		0.2690**	0.2577**	0.2469**
Rated 0.2222		-0.0014	-0.0119	-0.0016
Rated 0.2500–0.5000				
Rated 0.5556–0.6250		-0.0239	-0.0455	-0.0355
Rated 0.6667–1.0000		-0.0568	-0.0701	-0.0387
Rating missing		-0.0002	-0.0258	-0.0374
Had hernias by 1910	-0.0300			
Rated 0.1111–0.1667	-0.3335*	-0.3477*	-0.3147	
Rated 0.2222		0.0811	0.0675	0.0720
Rated 0.2500–0.5000				
Rated 0.5550–0.6250		-0.0926	-0.0980	-0.0783
Rated 0.6667–1.0000		-0.0103	-0.0223	0.0135
Rating missing		0.0269	0.0182	0.0277
Years having contracted hernias by 1900			0.0023	0.0042
BMI at first exam	-0.0116	-0.0128	-0.0127	0.0033
Square of BMI at first exam $\times 10^{-2}$	0.0259	0.0273	0.0272	-0.0040
Birth year				
1835–39	-0.0662*	-0.0668*	-0.0657*	-0.0574
1840–44	-0.1161***	-0.1168***	-0.1156***	-0.1140***
1845–51	-0.2283***	-0.2286***	-0.2276***	-0.2272***
Birth year missing	-0.0942	-0.0894	-0.0909	-0.0691

1900 head of household	-0.1306**	-0.1252**	-0.1257**	-0.1303**
1900 number of residents in the household	-0.0139***	-0.0141**	-0.0140**	-0.0149***
1900 married	0.0270	0.0187	0.0187	0.0236
Native-born	0.0049	0.0070	0.0072	0.0068
Nativity missing	-0.0155	-0.0247	-0.0230	-0.0320
Able to read	0.0707	0.0780	0.0771	0.0765
1900 residence				
South region	-0.0432	-0.0392	-0.0392	-0.0121
West region	0.2509***	0.2574***	0.2582***	0.4404***
Midwest region	0.1045***	0.1050***	0.1050***	0.1839***
Urban county	-0.0195	-0.0198	-0.0199	-0.0262
Monthly pension award before and closest to 1910	0.0111***	0.0115***	0.0116***	0.0122***
1900 occupation				
Somewhat Physically Intensive	0.0004	0.0102	0.0102	0.1381
Very Physically Intensive	-0.0771***	0.0796***	-0.0792***	0.0390*
Somewhat Physically Intensive and residence West				-0.2680
Somewhat Physically Intensive and residence Midwest				-0.1520
Somewhat Physically Intensive and residence urban				-0.1042
Somewhat Physically Intensive and had hernias				-0.0926
Very Physically Intensive and residence West				-0.3768***
Very Physically Intensive and residence Midwest				-0.1799***
Very Physically Intensive and residence urban				-0.0850
Very Physically Intensive and had hernias				0.0516
Interaction 1900 hernia and ruling amount $\times 10^{-2}$				-0.0033

(*continued*)

Table 10.20   (continued)

	Hernia Yes/No and BMI $[\partial E(p_i)/\partial x_k]$	Hernia Ratings and BMI $[\partial E(p_{mi})/\partial x_k]$	Hernia Ratings, How Long Had Hernias, and BMI $[\partial E(p_{mi})/\partial x_k]$	Hernia Ratings, How Long, BMI, and Interaction Terms $[\partial E(p_{mi})/\partial x_k]$
	B. Controlling for skill intensity			
Intercept	-0.0950	-0.0879	-0.0914	-0.0745
Had hernias by 1900	0.0529			
Rated 0.1111–0.1667		0.2589**	0.2452**	0.2602**
Rated 0.2222		-0.0069	-0.0196	-0.0305
Rated 0.2500–0.5000				
Rated 0.5556–0.6250		-0.0180	-0.0442	-0.0288
Rated 0.6667–1.0000		-0.0477	-0.0637	-0.0628
Rating missing		-0.0046	-0.0354	-0.0663
Had hernias by 1910	-0.0461			
Rated 0.1111–0.1667		-0.3315	-0.3484*	-0.3196
Rated 0.2222		0.0926	0.0768	0.1446
Rated 0.2500–0.5000				
Rated 0.5550–0.6250		-0.0970	-0.1036	-0.0646
Rated 0.6667–1.0000		-0.0009	-0.0158	0.0243
Rating missing		0.0207	0.0107	0.0271
Years having contracted hernias by 1900			0.0027	0.0071
BMI at first exam	-0.0053	-0.0169	-0.0167	-0.0117
Square of BMI at first exam $\times 10^{-2}$	0.0344	0.0365	0.0273	-0.0265
Birth year				
1835–39	-0.0691*	-0.0700*	-0.0686*	-0.0621
1840–44	-0.1243***	-0.1250***	-0.1237***	-0.1193***
1845–51	-0.2379***	-0.2380***	-0.2368***	-0.2357***
Birth year missing	-0.1027	-0.0957	-0.0973	-0.0898

	(1)	(2)	(3)	(4)
1900 head of household	-0.0970*	-0.0934*	-0.0939*	-0.1003*
1900 number of residents in the household	-0.0131**	-0.0133**	-0.0133**	-0.0132**
1900 married	0.0258	0.0176	0.0176	0.0162
Native-born	0.0088	0.0107	0.0110	0.0098
Nativity missing	0.0300	0.0156	0.0175	0.0172
Able to read	0.0725	0.0795	0.0785	0.0739
1900 residence				
South region	-0.0320	-0.0281	-0.0283	-0.0105
West region	0.2512***	0.2566***	0.2576***	0.0302
Midwest region	0.1137***	0.1134***	0.1133***	-0.0083
Urban county	-0.0373	-0.0375	-0.0375	-0.1464**
Monthly pension award before and closest to 1910	0.0110***	0.0114***	0.0114***	0.0113***
1900 skilled occupation	-0.0103	-0.0035	-0.0047	-0.0958**
And residence West				0.2833*
And residence Midwest				0.1598***
And residence urban				0.1348*
And had hernias				-0.1836**
Interaction 1900 hernia and ruling amount $\times 10^{-2}$				0.0044

Notes: Sample III consists of men linked to surgeons' data who were in more manually demanding occupations in 1900.. In Classification I, farmers and farm managers are classified as more manually demanding occupations. The omitted hernias categories are 1900 hernia patients rated from 0.2500 to 0.5000, and 1910 hernia patients rated from 0.2500 to 0.5000. Other omitted categories are born between 1812 and 1834, and residence in the Northeast region in 1900, and 1900 unskilled occupation. We did not include the dummy variable indicating a zero hernia rating in 1900 and 1910. The number of observations in this category is so small that including this dummy variable in the regression would cause a convergence problem in the maximum likelihood estimation. The variables 1900 marital status missing, residential region unknown, household relationship missing, urban county unknown, and literacy unknown are perfectly correlated with the variable nativity missing, and thus are omitted from the regression.

***Significant at the 1 percent level.

**Significant at the 5 percent level.

*Significant at the 10 percent level.

Table 10.21   **Variable Means of 688 Recruits Who Were in Labor Force by 1900 (Sample III, Classification II)**

Variable	Mean (dummies in %)
1900 in labor force, 1910 retired	20.93
Had hernias by 1900	14.53
Rated 0.0000	0.29
Rated 0.1111–0.1667	1.16
Rated 0.2222	1.45
Rated 0.2500–0.5000	3.34
Rated 0.5556–0.6250	2.47
Rated 0.6667–1.0000	1.02
Rating missing	4.80
Had hernias by 1910	20.20
Rated 0.0000	0.00
Rated 0.1111–0.1667	0.73
Rated 0.2222	0.44
Rated 0.2500–0.5000	1.74
Rated 0.5550–0.6250	2.03
Rated 0.6667–1.0000	0.87
Rating missing	14.39
Years having contracted hernias by 1900	1.71
BMI at first exam	22.82
Square of BMI at first exam	527.85
Birth year	
1812–34	7.27
1835–39	18.60
1840–44	45.64
1845–51	21.37
Birth year missing	7.12
1900 head of household	89.10
1900 household relationship missing	2.91
1900 number of residents in the household	3.12
1900 married	86.34
Native-born	82.56
Nativity missing	3.05
Able to read	92.59
Literacy unknown	2.91
1900 residence	
Northeast region	51.45
South region	2.33
West region	3.63
Midwest region	39.68
Unknown	2.91
Urban country	33.14
County unknown	2.91
1900 occupation classification	
Not Much Physically Intensive	3.20
Somewhat Physically Intensive	13.95
Very Physically Intensive	82.85
Unskilled	43.60
Skilled	56.40
Monthly pension award before and closest to 1910	$14.57

Notes: Sample III consists of men linked to surgeons' data who were in more manually demanding occupations in 1900. In Classification II, farmers and farm managers are classified as less manually demanding occupations.

Table 10.22 Effect of Hernias on the Marginal Probability of Retirement (Sample III, Classification II)

	Hernia Yes/No and BMI $[\partial E(p_l)/\partial x_k]$	Hernia Ratings and BMI $[\partial E(p_{ml})/\partial x_k]$	Hernia Ratings, How Long Had Hernias, and BMI $[\partial E(p_{ml})/\partial x_k]$	Hernia Ratings, How Long, BMI, and Interaction Terms $[\partial E(p_{ml})/\partial x_k]$
	A. Controlling for physical intensity			
Intercept	0.0690	0.0710	0.0562	0.0200
Had hernias by 1900	0.0384			
Rated 0.1111–0.1667		0.2076*	0.1835	0.2665*
Rated 0.2222		0.0996	0.0811	0.1842
Rated 0.5556–0.6250		0.0180	-0.0091	0.0438
Rated 0.6667–1.0000		-0.2411	-0.2611	-0.1343
Rating missing		-0.0338	-0.0765	-0.0024
Had hernias by 1910	-0.0215			
Rated 0.2222		0.0608	0.0424	0.0234
Rated 0.5550–0.6250		-0.2221	-0.2327	-0.1463
Rated 0.6667–1.0000		0.0828	0.0566	0.1587
Rating missing		0.0693	0.0598	0.0926*
Years having contracted hernias by 1900			0.0034	0.0104*
BMI at first exam	-0.0197	-0.0224	-0.0216	-0.0196
Square of BMI at first exam $\times 10^{-2}$	0.0398	0.0453	0.0443	0.0424
Birth year				
1835–39	-0.1140**	-0.1136**	-0.1090**	-0.1136**
1840–44	-0.1258***	-0.1222***	-0.1205**	-0.1300**
1845–51	-0.2332***	-0.2333***	-0.2319***	-0.2487***
Birth year missing	-0.1019	-0.0958	-0.0976	-0.1017
1900 head of household	-0.1281**	-0.1287**	-0.1291**	-0.1362**
1900 number of residents in the household	-0.0137*	-0.0129	-0.0127	-0.0129
1900 married	0.0005	-0.0111	-0.0109	-0.0041
Native-born	0.0252	0.0391	0.0404	0.0394
Nativity missing	-0.1543	-0.1476	-0.1436	-0.1582
Able to read	0.0414	0.0466	0.0449	0.0429

(*continued*)

Table 10.22   (continued)

	Hernia Yes/No and BMI $[\partial E(p_i)/\partial x_k]$	Hernia Ratings and BMI $[\partial E(p_{ml})/\partial x_k]$	Hernia Ratings, How Long Had Hernias, and BMI $[\partial E(p_{ml})/\partial x_k]$	Hernia Ratings, How Long, BMI, and Interaction Terms $[\partial E(p_{ml})/\partial x_s]$
1900 residence				
South region	-0.0826	-0.0663	-0.0706	-0.0631
West region	0.0815	0.0936	0.0934	0.0768
Midwest region	-0.0030	-0.0016	-0.0020	-0.0022
Urban county	-0.0544	-0.0505	-0.0508	-0.0474
Monthly pension award before and closest to 1910	0.0131***	0.0139***	0.0139***	0.0146***
1900 occupation classification				
Somewhat Physically Intensive	0.0711	0.0826	0.0819	0.1050
Not Much Physically Intensive	0.0280	0.0343	0.0350	0.0365
Somewhat Physically Intensive and residence West				0.0455
Somewhat Physically Intensive and residence Midwest				0.0087
Somewhat Physically Intensive and residence urban				-0.0182
Somewhat Physically Intensive and had hernias				-0.1157
Interaction 1900 hernia and ruling amount $\times 10^{-2}$				-0.0123*
B. Controlling for skill intensity				
Intercept	0.2693	0.2968	0.2924	0.2213
Had hernias by 1900	0.0598			
Rated 0.1111–0.1667		0.2947*	0.2493*	0.2551
Rated 0.2222		0.1289	0.0903	0.1257
Rated 0.5556–0.6250		0.0418	-0.0245	0.0221
Rated 0.6667–1.0000		-0.1964	-0.2443	-0.1646
Rating missing		-0.0163	-0.1169	-0.1059
Had hernias by 1910	-0.0407			
Rated 0.2222		0.0024	-0.0516	0.0461
Rated 0.5550–0.6250		-0.2058	-0.2324	-0.1336
Rated 0.6667–1.0000		0.0689	0.0042	-0.0104
Rating missing		0.0363	0.0120	0.0410
Years having contracted hernias by 1900			0.0080*	0.0165***
BMI at first exam	-0.0347	-0.0365	-0.0366	-0.0277
Square of BMI at first exam $\times 10^{-2}$	0.0708	0.0729	0.0738	0.0566

Birth year				
1835–39	-0.1156**	-0.1109**	-0.1015**	-0.1045**
1840–44	-0.1283***	-0.1258***	-0.1243***	-0.1277***
1845–51	-0.2335***	-0.2219***	-0.2197***	-0.2336***
Birth year missing	-0.1165	-0.1055	-0.1129	-0.1256*
1900 head of household	-0.1195**	-0.1159**	-0.1169**	-0.1382**
1900 number of residents in the household	-0.0147*	-0.0140*	-0.0137*	-0.0142*
1900 married	0.0117	0.0002	0.0006	-0.0034
Native-born	0.0227	0.0330	0.0361	0.0358
Nativity missing	-0.0969	-0.1115	-0.1020	-0.1171
Able to read	0.0592	0.0579	0.0551	0.0524
1900 residence				
South region	-0.0819	-0.0662	-0.0766	-0.0499
West region	0.0923	0.0914	0.0902	0.0098
Midwest region	-0.0059	-0.0055	-0.0065	-0.0167
Urban county	-0.0421	-0.0422	-0.0434	-0.1010*
Monthly pension award before and closest to 1910	0.0130***	0.0127***	0.0128***	0.0127***
1900 skilled occupation	-0.0690**	-0.0505*	-0.0539*	-0.0645
And residence West				0.1246
And residence Midwest				0.0307
And residence urban				0.0908
And had hernias				-0.2245**
Interaction 1900 hernia and ruling amount $\times 10^{-2}$				-0.0044

Notes: Sample III consists of men linked to surgeons' data who were in more manually demanding occupations in 1900. In Classification II, farmers and farm managers are classified as less manually demanding occupations. The omitted hernias categories are 1900 hernia patients rated from 0.2500 to 0.5000, and 1910 hernia patients rated from 0.2500 to 0.5000. Other omitted categories are born between 1812 and 1834, and residence in the Northeast region in 1900, and 1900 occupation unskilled. We did not include the dummy variable indicating a zero hernia rating in 1900 and 1910, and hernias rated from 0.1111 to 0.1667 in 1910. The number of observations in these categories are so small that including these dummy variables in the regression would cause convergence problems in the maximum likelihood estimation. The variables 1900 marital status missing, residential region unknown, household relationship missing, urban county unknown, and literacy unknown are perfectly correlated with the variable nativity missing, and thus are omitted from the regression. For panel A, values of 1900 occupation Not Much Physically Intensive interacting with regional dummies, residence urban, and having hernias are so small that including those interaction terms in the regression would cause a convergence problem in the maximum likelihood estimation.

***Significant at the 1 percent level.

**Significant at the 5 percent level.

*Significant at the 10 percent level.

from chronic conditions." This difficulty applies to the mortality measure as well, because mortality can be viewed as the flip side of life expectancy. Calorie intake, height, and BMI are measures of past and current nutritional status and thus reflect demands made upon the body, including those of disease, labor, and even climate (Costa 1996). Yet those are indirect measures of disabilities, and they do not always have strong predictions on the prevalence of each condition. Zero-one disease indicators are interpreted as probabilities of contracting diseases. However, they do not contain information on the severity of each disease, and they do not reflect attitudinal bias that can affect pension compensation, as found in Blanck (2001).

This paper is a first step to construct a more sophisticated chronic disability index from comprehensive medical records and to use this index to forecast the labor supply of older men. We narrowed the scope of this first step by focusing on hernias, a chronic disability that could be extremely debilitating in its later development. We captured the severity of hernias by quantifying descriptions in all symptoms: subtype, location, size, and morbidity. Previous studies (Blanck 2001; Song 2000) show that hernia ratings matched hernia severity under each symptom. In particular, patients who had hernias of the more morbid kind received higher ratings and the ratings were consistent across time and states. One implication from those studies is that instead of using symptoms as health indicators in the retirement study, we could replace symptoms with hernia ratings. The ratings variable is a fraction with the denominator being the maximum scale assigned to the most severe hernias, and the numerator being the scale assigned to a particular hernia patient. Alternatively, we could directly incorporate all symptoms in the labor participation regressions. The inconvenience with this alternative is that the regressions become cumbersome. Each symptom enters the regressions via a set of categorical dummies. For example, there can be three categorical dummies representing hernia location: single hernia, double hernias, and location nonspecified or nonclassified. The number of right-hand-side variables can easily go up as we deal with multiple symptoms.

We find weak evidence of the influence of hernias on the labor force participation of the Civil War veterans, controlling for a general health measure (BMI) and demographic characteristics. Age was a highly significant factor in the labor force participation of older veterans. Consistent with the literature (e.g., Costa 1998; Kanjanapipatkul, ch. 9 in this volume), we find monthly pension award to be a significant predictor for retirement. Every one-dollar increase in the monthly pension raises the odds of retirement by almost 1 percent. The observed income effect applies to all recruits in our sample. We did not find an additional income effect on retirement among hernia patients. Everything else being constant, patients in more manually demanding occupations were equally likely to retire as patients in less manually demanding occupations, even though the latter had, on average, higher pay. There existed regional effects on retirement for veterans in the West and Midwest regions, relative to those residing in the Northeast region. Farmers and farm managers living in the West or the Midwest were more likely to retire, perhaps because of the lack of labor market alternatives. We obtain consistent results using a sample of men with hernias versus those without hernias but with other disabilities, a sample of men with hernias versus healthy men, and a subsample of men linked to surgeons' data in 1900 manually demanding occupations.

The Pension Bureau defined disability as the incapacity to perform manual labor. The interpretation of "manual labor" expanded from tasks that required "severe and continuous exertion" in 1862 to include "lighter kinds of labor which require education and skill" in 1872 (Glasson 1918, 131). Recruits in our 1900 and 1910 snapshots benefited from a liberal concept of disability, because both more and less manually demanding occupations fit the 1872 interpretation of manual labor. Despite the more favorable definition of disability over time in the pension system, we did not find that hernias influenced labor force decisions. There are two possible explanations for this result. First, what the pension surgeons (or even modern medical practice) believes to be debilitating, as in the case of hernias, may in fact be historically only discomforting. As a result, retirement was not much influenced by this condition. Second, older veterans in our sample endured hernias as long as the hernias did not pose a mortal threat. In this case, contracting hernias and the worsening of hernias would not cause a reduction in earnings from exiting the labor force—but they would induce a reduction in welfare from the disutility of coping with the pain and possibly from rising medical costs.

Appendix

Standardization of Diagnoses

Of the disease variables in the Surgeons' Certificates, hernia variables were among the most robust because the clinical diagnosis of hernias has not changed significantly since the nineteenth century. This allowed interpretation and standardization of the hernia findings without confounding issues, such as differences in medical knowledge and medical language. Among hernia variables, three were chosen for their clinical significance: the anatomic location of the hernia (h_knd); the characteristics of the hernia (h_cls); and the size of the hernia (h_siz).

After the initial transcription and classification of the free-form exam findings into disease variables, finer classification was performed using disease outlines. These outlines contained a multilevel system for classifying the many disease observations into a workable and clinically relevant number. At the base of the outline for each variable was the answer class (AC), which contained the major medical finding. Two supplemental categories added more detailed information to the AC. The middle modifier (MM) contained anatomic or descriptive information while the severity modifier (SM) contained severity information. Furthermore, the other variations in spelling, word orientation, and synonyms could be coded with a similar description. This compacted the free-form observations into a few clinically relevant and easily workable categories. Two special AC codes were created for ambiguous data. When the medical description by the Pension Bureau surgeons indicated the presence of an abnormal exam finding or disease, but the specific finding or disease was indeterminate, the observation would be coded as unspecified. When the observation was too vague for medical interpretation or significance, it was coded as unclassified. Table 10.2 demonstrates the standardization process with examples under each diagnostic dimension.

Disability Ratings

In estimating the overall degree of disability from having a hernia or hernias, two variables may be indicative. The first variable is a nominal dollar amount increasing with the severity of hernias. The second candidate is the ratio variable referred to as the hernia disability rating, where the denominator is the maximum severity of hernias and the numerator is the severity of hernias observed in a patient. The nominal pension amount is unattractive to use as a hernia disability index for four reasons: First, there is a large number of missing observations in this variable (out of 6,395 patient-exam pairs, only 1,311 are nonmissing). Second, the nominal amount depended on military rank. Third, the nominal amount depended on various versions of pension provisions. Fourth, the nominal amount attributed to hernias is highly correlated with the overall dollar amount of pension granted to a recruit. Since we use the overall monthly pension award as a proxy for income, including the dollar award corresponding to hernias as well would contaminate the income proxy. Because of those shortcomings, we used the ratio variable, our second candidate.[21]

The ratio variable is referred to as the disability rating. For example, hernia was considered a disability less than the third grade. Based on the 1873 Consolidation Act,[22] for a private, a single inguinal hernia of a minor protrusion translated to a disability rating of 6/18,[23] a double inguinal hernia of a minor protrusion translated to 10/18, and a single femoral hernia trans-

---

21. For examples of disability dollar compensations, see Sanders (2000).
22. For a detailed description of the history of pension laws, see Costa (1998, appendix A).
23. Examples are taken from the same sources given in note 5.

lated to 10/18. Within the same disability category, the rating unambiguously reflected a surgeon's belief about a patient's disability that is independent of military rank and pension-law updates.[24]

Reliability of Surgeons' Reports

There have been speculations that the examining surgeons appointed by the Pension Bureau to assess the degree of disability of pension claimants had been biased in their medical judgment. In particular, the surgeons were suspected of exaggerating the symptoms and granting higher disability ratings to veterans, therefore putting an additional strain on the already astronomical Civil War pension costs. Blanck (2001) studied the correlation between an individual symptom under a particular disability and the rating value.[25] He found that in general, there was a significant positive correlation between a "yes" answer to a particular symptom and the rating value, and there was a significant negative correlation between a "yes" answer to a particular symptom and the granting of a zero rating that corresponded to no pension. This result shows that there was a reasonable mapping from a symptom to a rating. However, this result does not prove that surgeons were unbiased in examinations, because they could have exaggerated the symptoms to justify asking for larger ratings. Song (2000) tested the claim that the examining surgeons intentionally skewed the disability severity measure of Civil War veterans. She found a close association between the surgeons' ratings and the pension applicants' symptoms in the case of hernias. Furthermore, she found that this association does not change over time and among states with different political party majority votes. This result indicates that surgeons who served for different pension boards and who served during different time periods followed the same examination rule and made consistent medical judgments. She concluded that the Pension Board had administered the UA pension program in a fair manner and that the examining surgeons had carried out their duties accurately.

The finding of a close association between the hernia disability ratings and the hernia symptoms is valuable for our study. Instead of sorting

24. Consider a private and a lieutenant, both of whom had hernia disability ratings equivalent to 0.5000. A lieutenant would receive a much higher dollar amount (say, $15 per month out of the $30 maximum total) while a private would receive only $4 per month out of the $8 maximum total. Regardless of a higher nominal pension received by the lieutenant, both men were judged by the surgeons to be equally disabled from hernias. New laws might increase dollar amounts of pensions for the same disability ratings, but in the case of hernia, they barely altered the ratings themselves. It is because of the unique meaning of the hernia rating variable that we deem it an appropriate index to measure the severity of this disability.

25. See Blanck (2001, appendix 2). He used disease screen variables for the correlation analysis. For example, under the cardiovascular screen, doctors were asked to give yes or no answers to the following symptoms: palpitations; murmurs; dilation, displacement, or enlargement; anasarca, dropsy, edema, or puffiness; cyanosis; dyspnoea; arteriosclerosis; or circulation impairment.

through numerous symptoms, we can rely on a single variable, the hernia disability ratings, to provide us with an unbiased measure of hernia severity.

References

Abramson, J., J. Gofin, C. Hopp, A. Makler, and L. Epstein. 1978. The epidemiology of inguinal hernia: A survey in western Jerusalem. *Journal of Epidemiology and Community Health* 32 (1): 59–67.
Bassini, E. 1889. *New operative method for the radical cure of inguinal hernias* (in Italian). *Atti del Congressa dell' Associazione Medica Italiana* 2:179–82.
Baxter, J. 1875. Introduction. In *Statistics, medical and anthropological: Provost Marshall General's Bureau, records of the examinations for military service in the armies of the United States during the late War of the Rebellion of over a million recruits, drafted men, substitutes, and enrolled men.* Washington, D.C.: GPO.
Blanck, P. D. 2001. Civil War pensions and disability. *Ohio State Law Journal* 62:109–249.
Blanck, P. D., and C. Song. 2001. "With malice toward none; with charity toward all": Civil War pensions for native and foreign-born Union Army veterans. *Journal of Transnational Law and Contemporary Problems* 11 (1): 1–76.
Blau, D., and D. Gilleskie. 2001. Retiree health insurance and the labor force behavior of older men in the 1990s. *Review of Economics and Statistics* 83 (1): 64–80.
Bound, J., M. Schoenbaum, T. Stinebrickner, and T. Waidmann. 1999. The dynamic effects of health on the labor force transitions of older workers. *Labour Economics* 6 (2): 179–202.
Bull, W. 1890. On the radical cure of hernia, with the results of one hundred and thirty-four operations. *Trans American Surgical Association* 8:99–117.
Center for Population Economics. 1998. *Public use tape on the aging of veterans of the Union Army.* Chicago: University of Chicago, Graduate School of Business, Center for Population Economics.
Chan, S., and A. Stevens. 2001. Job loss and employment patterns of older workers. *Journal of Labor Economics* 19 (2): 484–521.
Cheek, C. M., M. I. Williams, and J. R. Farndon. 1995. Trusses in the management of hernia today. *British Journal of Surgery* 82:1611–13.
Coile, C., and J. Gruber. 2000a. Social Security incentives for retirement. NBER Working Paper no. 7651. Cambridge, Mass.: National Bureau of Economic Research.
———. 2000b. Social Security and retirement. NBER Working Paper no. 7830. Cambridge, Mass.: National Bureau of Economic Research.
Coley, W., W. Keen, and J. DaCosta (eds.). 1910. *Surgery, its principles and practice.* Philadelphia: W. B. Saunders.
Cooper, A. 1804. *The anatomy and surgical treatment of inguinal and congenital hernia.* London: T. Cox.
———. 1807. *The anatomy and surgical treatment of crural and umbilical hernia.* Part II. London: Longman, Hurst, Rees, and E. Cox.
Costa, D. 1993. Height, weight, wartime stress, and older age mortality: Evidence from the Union Army records. *Explorations in Economics History* 30:424–49.

———. 1996. Health and labor force participation of older men, 1990–1991. *Journal of Economic History* 56 (1): 62–89.

———. 1998. *The evolution of retirement: An American economic history 1880–1990.* Chicago: University of Chicago Press.

———. 2002. Changing chronic disease rates and long-term declines in functional limitation among older men. *Demography* 39 (1): 119–37.

———. 2003. Understanding mid-life and older age mortality declines: Evidence from Union Army veterans. *Journal of Econometrics* 112 (1): 175–92.

Costa, D., and R. Steckel. 1997. Long-term trends in health, welfare, and economic growth in the United States. In *Health and welfare during industrialization,* eds. Richard H. Steckel and Roderick Floud. Chicago: University of Chicago Press.

Cutler, D., and B. Madrian. 1998. Labor market responses to rising health insurance costs: Evidence on hours worked. *RAND Journal of Economics* 29 (3): 509–30.

Dwyer, D., and O. Mitchell. 1999. Health problems as determinants of retirement: Are self-rated measures endogenous? *Journal of Health Economics* 18 (2): 173–93.

Fogel, R. 1993. New sources and new techniques for the study of secular trends in nutritional status, health, mortality, and the process of aging. *Historical Methods* 26 (1): 5–43.

———. 2000. *Public use tape on the aging of veterans of the Union Army: Military, pension, and medical records, 1860–1940.* Version M-5. Chicago: University of Chicago, Graduate School of Business, Center for Population Economics.

Glasson, W. H. 1918. *Federal military pensions in the United States.* New York: Oxford University Press.

Gustman, A., and T. Steinmeier. 2000. Retirement outcomes in the Health and Retirement Study. *Social Security Bulletin* 63 (4): 57–71.

Haines, M., L. Craig, and M. Weiss. 2000. Development, health, nutrition, and mortality: The case of the "antebellum puzzle" in the United States. NBER Working Paper no. H130. Cambridge, Mass.: National Bureau of Economic Research.

Halsted, W. 1889. The radical cure of hernia. *Johns Hopkins Bulletin* 1:12–13.

Hesselbach, F. 1806. *Anatomic-surgical treatise on the origin of inguinal ruptures* (in German). Wurzburg: Baumgartner.

———. 1814. *Latest anatomic-pathologic investigations concerning the origin and progress of inguinal and femoral ruptures* (in German). Wurzburg: Staheliano.

Iason, A. 1941. The incidence of hernia in man. In *Hernia,* 156–79. Philadelphia: Blakiston.

Kemp, T. R. 1990. Community and war: The Civil War experience of two New Hampshire towns. In *Toward a social history of the American Civil War,* ed. Maris A. Vinovskis. Cambridge: Cambridge University Press.

Law, N. W., and J. E. Trapnell. 1992. Does a truss benefit a patient with inguinal hernia? *British Medical Journal* 304:1092.

Lee, C. 1998. Long-term unemployment and retirement in early-twentieth-century America. *Journal of Economics History* 58 (3): 844–56.

Lichenstein, I. 1987. Herniorrhaphy: A personal experience with 6,321 cases. *American Journal of Surgery* 153 (6): 553–59.

Margo, R. A. 1993. The labor force participation of older Americans in 1900: Further results. *Explorations in Economic History* 30 (4): 409–23.

McVay, C. 1948. Inguinal and femoral hernioplasty: Anatomic repair. *Archives of Surgery* 57:524–30.

Mitchell, O., and J. Phillips. 2000. Retirement responses to early Social Security benefit reductions. NBER Working Paper no. 7963. Cambridge, Mass.: National Bureau of Economic Research.

Ponka, J. 1980. *Hernias of the abdominal wall.* Philadelphia: W. B. Saunders.

Ransom, R. L., and R. Sutch. 1986. The labor of older Americans: Retirement of men on and off the job, 1870–1930. *Journal of Economic History* 46:1–30.

Riley, J. C. 1991. Working health time: A comparison of preindustrial, industrial, and postindustrial experience in life and health. *Explorations in Economic History* 28:169–91.

Rubenstein, R., S. Beck, and K. Lohr. 1983. *Conceptualization and measurements of physiologic health for adults.* Santa Monica, Calif.: RAND.

Rutkow, I. 1998. A selective history of groin hernia surgery in the early-nineteenth-century." *Surgical Clinics of North America* 78 (6): 921–40.

Sanders, Matthew. 2000. History of the Civil War pension laws. Appendix 12 in *Public use tape on the aging of veterans in the Union Army: Military, pension, and medical records, 1860–1940. Data user's manual,* by R. W. Fogel. Chicago: University of Chicago, Graduate School of Business, Center for Population Economics.

Scarpa, A. 1809. *Hernia, anatomic-surgical notes* (in Italian). Milan, Italy: dalla Reale Stamperia.

———. 1821. *Perineal hernias* (in Italian). Pavia, Italy: Pietro Bizzoni.

Shearburn, E., and R. Myers. 1969. Shouldice repair for inguinal hernia. *Surgery* 66 (2): 450–59.

Song, C. 1999. Obtaining years of birth and cleaning exam ages in the Union Army Military and Surgeons' Certificates data sets. University of Chicago, Center for Population Economics. Unpublished manuscript.

———. 2000. Justice or politics: New evidence on surgeons' performance during the United States Civil War pension process. University of Chicago, Center for Population Economics. Unpublished manuscript.

Spraycar, Marjory (ed.). 1995. *Stedman's medical dictionary.* 26th ed. Baltimore, Md.: Williams and Wilkins.

U.S. Bureau of Census. 1989. *Historical statistics of the United States, colonial times to 1970.* Part 1. Washington, D.C.: GPO.

Waaler, H. T. 1984. Height, weight, and mortality: The Norwegian experience. *Acta Medica Scandinavica* 679 (Supplement): 1–56.

Welsh, D., and M. Alexander. 1993. The shouldice repair? *Surgical Clinics of North America* 73 (3): 451–69.

Conclusion

Dora L. Costa

Certain common themes recurred in the papers in this volume. These have been the relationship between socioeconomic factors and health; the relationship between infectious disease, environmental hazards, and migration and subsequent morbidity and mortality; and the roles of income, health, and social class in the retirement decision. The papers in this volume all brought new data to bear on these questions and shared a common methodological approach: Large data sets that cover the life histories of past populations who lived under very different institutions, disease environments, and technologies than populations today can help us understand long-run trends in health and in health differentials, the impact of disease on morbidity and mortality, and migration and retirement decisions.

In "The Rich and the Dead," Ferrie analyzed a new sample of 175,000 individuals to assess the effect of socioeconomic status on mortality in the nineteenth-century United States. Although the lower mortality of those higher in socioeconomic status has received a great deal of attention in the recent public health literature, few historical studies have documented such disparities in the period before 1960. The sample consisted of decedents from the mortality schedules and survivors from the population schedules of the 1850 and 1860 federal censuses. In 1850, for males aged twenty to forty-four in fifty rural counties, occupation was a poor predictor of all-cause mortality, although deaths from consumption (tuberculosis) were substantially more likely among craft and white-collar workers than among farmers and unskilled laborers. For males and females of

Dora L. Costa is associate professor of economics at the Massachusetts Institute of Technology and a research associate of the National Bureau of Economic Research.

nearly all ages in eleven rural counties in Alabama and Illinois in 1850 and 1860, there was no clear relationship between family real estate wealth and mortality. There was, however, a large and statistically significant negative relationship between family personal wealth and mortality in 1860. For example, among both infants and adults aged twenty to forty-four, those in families with no personal wealth were more than twice as likely to die in the year before the census as those in families with any personal wealth. Even when the United States was largely rural and agricultural, then, disparities in mortality by socioeconomic status of the sort observed in modern data were quite common. Although previous studies have characterized the nineteenth-century pattern of death as egalitarian, by disaggregating cause of death and by focusing on adult deaths in rural areas, Ferrie found inequality in death rates.

Chulhee Lee's "Prior Exposure to Disease, and Later Health and Mortality" used the Union Army data to examine the effects of socioeconomic factors and local disease environment on the morbidity and mortality of recruits while in the service. One of his findings was that greater household wealth reduced the chances of a recruit's contracting disease while in the service, although not his chances of dying, suggesting that in the past there were substantial morbidity disparities. The major result of Lee's paper was that prior exposure to an unfavorable epidemiological environment reduced the chances of contracting and dying from disease while in service. Farmers and rural residents, native recruits, and recruits from areas with high child mortality rates—all men who were on average healthier prior to enlistment—were more likely to contract disease while in the service than nonfarmers, urban dwellers, foreigners, and those from areas with low child mortality rates. Explanations included differences in immunity to such common army diseases as typhoid, knowledge of how to avoid contracting disease, and population selection caused by differential mortality (i.e., individuals who survived an unhealthy environment were on average more robust). This study provided a counterexample to "insult accumulation" models in which repeated stresses lead to higher morbidity and mortality. Instead, it implied that a prior insult leads to future disease resistance, especially when in a severe disease environment such as Civil War army camps. The findings suggested that changing human resistance to disease may explain in part the deterioration in health in the mid-nineteenth century during a time of increased geographical mobility, industrialization, and urbanization, and the subsequent turnaround in health in the late nineteenth century.

Daniel Scott Smith's "Seasoning, Disease Environment, and Conditions of Exposure" focused on the effect of both locales of enlistment and regions of service during the war on wartime mortality. Smith examined Union Army soldiers and units from New York State because he augmented the Union Army data set with a detailed tabulation of the outcomes of military service by New York regiments. He stressed the effect of the environment encountered during service, whereas Lee emphasized the prewar environment, interpreting the low incidence of disease among soldiers from cities as the legacy of having survived earlier exposure. Using the detailed, aggregate tabulations for New York, Smith showed that there was a positive relationship between the mortality of one company and that of all the others in the regiment. Among regiments, a similar relationship existed between the levels of disease mortality of officers and enlisted men, although officers died at much lower rates than enlistees. Regiments organized in counties characterized by lower mortality had higher disease death rates than regiments from higher-mortality environments such as cities. Units that were sent to the lower Mississippi Valley experienced particularly high disease death rates. Findings at the individual level, for New York soldiers in the Union Army data set, reinforced those evident at the aggregate level. Smith concurred with Lee that the lack of prior exposure to disease was the cause of the higher disease mortality of men who formerly were farmers. They were "seasoned," that is, they suffered higher mortality due to the novel and deadly disease environment of the army camps. After the first year of service, these background factors faded in importance in predicting death from disease. On the other hand, soldiering in the lower Mississippi Valley continued to be particularly deadly after the first year in the army as did the death rate of other men in the regiment. Thus, over time, the factors responsible for disease mortality shifted from attributes of men before they became soldiers to the environment they experienced during the war.

In "The Height of Union Army Recruits," Sven E. Wilson and Clayne L. Pope used the Union Army data to examine the effects of family and community on the height of recruits prior to their entering the army. (Recall that height is a measure of net nutritional status during the growing years.) They used the sample of recruits linked to the 1850 federal census schedules (which provide information on occupation, wealth, nativity, migration, school attendance, literacy, and family size) and matched the census records to county-level published data to obtain county-level economic and demographic data. They found that at the household level, the primary determinant of height was occupation, with farmers having a distinct advantage over nonfarmers. The migratory history of the recruit and his family also played an important role. Household wealth had only modest and statistically insignificant effects on height. This measure of health, in contrast to adult mortality (Ferrie's paper) and army camp morbidity (Lee's paper), showed an egalitarian pattern. The persistent positive effect of farming remained even after controlling for other household and county-level characteristics, including urbanization. Wilson and Pope concluded that farmers were better off, at least in part, because of better access to nutrition. However, it was among farmers that the effect of urbanization was strongest, implying that the farming advantage was a function of disease exposure as well as nutrient supply. Their conclusion was reinforced by the negative effect on height of the level of agricultural capital within the county (a potential indicator of trade and commerce) and of proximity to rail and waterways. Their findings suggest that changes in both nutrition and infectious disease, changes that arose from economic development and migration, can explain the significant decline in mean heights that began with the cohort born after 1830 and bottomed out with the cohorts born in the 1880s.

Sven E. Wilson's "The Prevalence of Chronic Respiratory Disease in the Industrial Era" examined how economic development in the decades following the Civil War affected the prevalence of chronic respiratory disease among older men using the sample of Union Army soldiers who survived to receive a pension. The paper developed a disease classification system that can be used to summarize the historical data from the medical examinations of Union Army veterans in a manner consistent with modern disease classifications. The analysis made divisions between upper and lower respiratory disease, with the latter broken down into asthma and chronic obstructive pulmonary disease. The paper found that among men aged fifty-five to seventy-four the prevalence of chronic respiratory disease was rising between 1895 and 1910 across all age groups. For instance, the prevalence of respiratory disease among sixty-five- to sixty-nine-year-olds in the most comprehensive category (those ever diagnosed with a chronic respiratory disease) rose from 25 to 46 percent. The rise in prevalence was fairly widespread across occupational groups and level of urbanization. Those in rural communities had the highest prevalence of respiratory disease, although whether this was due to the higher incidence of disease (perhaps because of farmers' exposure to organic particles) or to lower all-cause mortality in rural communities remains unclear.

Wilson's paper also found evidence of the negative effect of wartime exposure to infectious respiratory disease and of stunted growth, evidenced by shorter adult heights, on respiratory disease later in life. In contrast to the papers by Lee and Smith the findings therefore provide support for an insult accumulation model. Prior exposure may have enabled men to survive the harsh disease environment of the army camps, but prior exposure also left permanent scars.

Werner Troesken and Patricia E. Beeson's "The Significance of Lead Water Mains in American Cities" examined whether living in 1900 in a city that had lead water mains affected the health of Union Army veterans. Lead water mains were pervasive, and pollution at the source, corrosion of lead water mains, and corrosion of household plumbing (which was made of lead) led to high levels of exposure. Troesken and Beeson reported that in Massachusetts in 1900, all cities and towns in the state that were surveyed by the state health department had drinking water that contained lead levels several orders of magnitude greater than those set by the federal government today. Deaths from lead poisoning occurred in Lowell and in Milton. Troesken and Beeson found modest effects from the use of lead mains on the health of Union Army veterans. Veterans living in cities with lead mains in 1900 reported higher rates of dizziness and ear problems than veterans living in cities without lead, but they did not report higher levels of more serious lead-related ailments such as kidney failure. Given the relatively high levels of geographic mobility among Union Army veterans, their results are probably lower-bound estimates of the impact of lead water mains on health.

Mario A. Sánchez's "Internal Migration, Return Migration, and Mortality" used the rich residential information in the Union Army data to document the extent of internal migration, examine the characteristics of migrants across counties, and determine the effect of migration on health. He found that Union Army veterans were quite mobile, even at mature ages, and that many moved temporarily. The young, the single, and those with smaller families were less likely to move. The findings imply that workers were responsive to local economic shocks and therefore suggest that the degree of labor market integration in the United States during the late nineteenth century was fairly high. Migration, however, reduced workers' life expectancies. Life expectancies of migrants were significantly shorter than those of their counterparts who did not migrate because of migrants' higher probability of dying from infectious disease. Infectious diseases were particularly important in explaining the reduced life expectancies of migrants to urban counties. However, even migrants across rural areas suffered higher mortality rates relative to rural nonmovers. Migration was stressful in and of itself. Higher wages in cities relative to rural areas may therefore have compensated only for the increased risk of death faced by migrants.

The Union Army pension data are also a rich source of information on the retirement decision. Tayatat Kanjanapipatkul's "Pensions and Labor Force Participation of Civil War Veterans" examined the impact of Civil War pensions on the labor force participation, using a much larger data set than that which was available to previous researchers. In addition to using the Union Army data set, he also used the public use sample of the 1910 census to compare participation rates between Union and Confederate veterans, controlling for individual as well as regional characteristics. The results confirmed that the availability of pensions substantially reduced labor force participation rates among Union Army veterans. However, the results also showed that the magnitude of the effect varied with the measure of pension income and with occupation. Using lifetime income increased the estimated magnitude. Professionals and proprietors were more sensitive than blue-collar workers to pension income. Perhaps they were the only group with enough combined wealth to retire comfortably.

Chen Song and Louis L. Nguyen's "The Effect of Hernias on the Labor Force Participation of Union Army Veterans" examined the effect of health on the retirement decision by focusing on one specific health condition that can be extremely debilitating and that was uncurable—hernias. They used detailed health information from Union Army data to quantify the severity of recorded cases of hernias using such symptoms as size, subtype of hernia, and location. They found weak evidence of the influence of hernias on the labor force participation of Union Army veterans, controlling for general health and demographic characteristics, regardless of whether they compared men with hernias to those without hernias but with other disabilities or to those with no disabilities. They also found that even among men in more manually demanding occupations, hernias had relatively small effects on labor force participation rates. Why wasn't retirement influenced by hernias so severe that they were described as being the size of a large grapefruit or the size of a man's two fists? Song and Nguyen argue that there are two possibilities. One of these is that what the pension surgeons, or even physicians today, believed to be extremely debilitating may only have been discomforting and therefore did not influence the retirement decision. The second possibility is that in a society where incomes were low and medical care was of limited efficacy, older veterans simply worked with pain either because they could not afford to retire or because suffering from ill health was so common that men simply endured.

The papers in these volumes raised several issues for future research. One is the need to reexamine the role of social class, wealth, and occupation on morbidity and mortality in the past. In a world where death from infectious disease was common and where there were large mortality differentials by city size, geographic differences may have been more important than socioeconomic disparities, but, controlling for geography, substantial socioeconomic disparities may still have been there. Another important topic dealt with the effect of infectious disease on later outcomes. Did prior exposure provide protection against later disease or did it have a permanent scarring effect that raised future morbidity and mortality? The papers in this volume suggested that the answer to both questions was yes. Prior exposure could protect against extreme conditions but there was also a cost to prior exposure. As the disease environment changed over the twentieth century, the costs of prior exposure may have increasingly dominated the benefits. Further analyses of the interactions between individual life histories and the environment are needed. Because it is impossible to obtain a full medical history from birth until death, these life histories should also include the characteristics of past environments, both residential and workplace. Work is underway to augment the Union Army data set with data on city and county characteristics. Another issue raised by this volume is the need to adjust wage or income numbers to reflect the costs of morbidity and mortality. The mortality penalty paid by migrants suggests that during periods of high migration in the nineteenth century we may be overstating economic growth. Finally, this volume suggested that disability needs to be examined within a social context. In the past, men continued to work in pain with severe disabilities. Rising incomes allowed them to leave the labor force. Improvements in health did not lead them to remain in the labor force longer. As incomes continue to rise and as medical care becomes more efficacious, our notions of disability will continue to evolve.

Appendix A
Merged Mortality and Population Schedules from the U.S. Federal Censuses, 1850 and 1860

Joseph P. Ferrie

The data were constructed to take advantage of the information on decedents in the mortality schedules and on survivors in the population schedules. These schedules were filled out by census marshals as they went from household to household. After the information on the living family members was inserted into the population schedule, the household was to report information on any deaths that had occurred in the twelve months preceding the census for insertion into the mortality schedules. The population schedules record each individual's place of residence (state, county, township), name, age, sex, race, marital status, occupation, wealth (real estate in both 1850 and 1860; personal wealth as well in 1860), birthplace, literacy, school attendance, and disability. The mortality schedules record each individual's name, age, sex, race, marital status, occupation, cause of death, month of death, and number of days ill before death, as well as the location (state, county, township) of the family that reported the death. Two data sets were constructed by merging these sources.

Males Aged Twenty and Over in Fifty Rural Counties in 1850

Fifty counties were chosen for which computerized mortality and population schedules now exist.[1] Male decedents aged twenty and over from the mortality schedules were merged with male survivors aged twenty and over

Joseph P. Ferrie is associate professor of economics and faculty fellow at the Institute for Policy Research, both at Northwestern University, and a research associate of the National Bureau of Economic Research.

1. Alabama: Baldwin, Blount, Conecuh, Henry, Jackson, Jefferson, Lowndes, Madison, Marengo, Monroe, Shelby, Washington, and Wilcox; Illinois: Clark, Crawford, Gallatin, Grundy, Hamilton, McDonough, Perry, Saline, Sangamon, Schuyler, Scott, Stark, Washington, and Wayne; Indiana: Boone, Fayette, Kosciusko, and White; Iowa: Appanoose and Cedar; Kentucky: Simpson and Spencer; Michigan: Ionia and Lapeer; North Carolina:

from the population schedules for the same counties. This yielded a sample of 83,173 individuals (927 decedents and 82,246 survivors). For each individual, the sample contains

- Location (state and county);[2]
- Name;
- Age;
- Race;
- Marital status (single, married, widowed, divorced);
- Occupation;
- Birthplace;
- Whether the individual died in the twelve months preceding the 1850 census; and
- If the individual died, the month and cause of death.

All Family Members in Eleven Rural Alabama and Illinois Counties in 1850 and 1860

Eleven counties were chosen for which computerized transcriptions of the population schedules exist and for which transcriptions of the mortality schedules with families in the order they were visited by the census marshal have been published.[3] By arranging both the population and mortality schedules in the order they were originally written by the census marshals and setting the two lists side by side, it was possible to merge 85 percent of the decedents in the mortality schedules back to the families in the population schedules that reported their deaths. Decedents who could not be linked to surviving families were generally younger adults living away from their families, or the elderly. Families with more than $10,000 in real estate, or with fewer than two or more than nine members, were excluded. This yielded 39,300 individuals in 1850 (304 decedents and 38,996 survivors) and 52,779 individuals in 1860 (511 decedents and 52,268 survivors). For each individual, the sample contains

- Location (state, county, and township);
- Name;
- Age;
- Sex;
- Race;
- Marital status (single, married, widowed, divorced);

Northampton and Wake; Ohio: Henry, Pike, Sandusky, and Williams; Pennsylvania: Carbon, Sullivan, and Tioga; Texas: Galveston; Virginia: Charlotte, Fauquier, and Madison.

2. Although the computerized population schedules also report township, neither this variable nor "number of days ill" was included in the computerized mortality schedules. The manuscripts of these schedules will be examined to recover these variables.

3. For 1850, five counties in Illinois (Morgan, Jackson, Union, Saline, and Washington) and one in Alabama (Shelby) were used. For 1860, three counties in Illinois (Perry, Shelby, and Vermilion) and two in Alabama (St. Clair and Tuscaloosa) were used.

- Occupation;
- Individual and family wealth (real estate in 1850 and 1860; personal wealth as well in 1860);
- Birthplace;
- Whether the individual died in the twelve months preceding the 1850 census;
- If the individual died, the number of days ill and the month and cause of death; and
- If the individual survived, his or her level of literacy, school attendance, and any disabilities.

Appendix B
Properties and Availability of the Union Army Life-Cycle Sample

Peter Viechnicki

Sample Properties

The Life-Cycle Data on the Aging of the Veterans of the Union Army, cited by the authors in this volume, have been collected by the program project entitled "Early Indicators of Later Work Levels, Disease, and Death," funded by the National Institute on Aging (NIH P01 AG10120) and the National Science Foundation (NSF SBR 9114981). Generous support has also been provided by the National Bureau of Economic Research. The data were collected and coded by the Center for Population Economics (CPE) at the University of Chicago's Graduate School of Business, and by the Department of Economics at Brigham Young University, between 1991 and 2001. Further information on the development of the program project can be obtained from Larry T. Wimmer (author of ch. 1 in this volume), as well as from the CPE Web site: www.cpe.uchicago.edu/welcome/history.html. The data sets described below can be downloaded from the CPE's interactive data extraction system, located at http://www.cpe.uchicago.edu/data/data.html.

The Union Army Life-Cycle Sample consists of longitudinally linked observations for a sample of 39,616 white males mustered into the Union Army. A one-stage cluster sample, it consists of all enlisted men belonging to 331 randomly selected white infantry companies drawn from the 20,000-odd companies who fought for the Union in the Civil War (Dyer 1959). Due to budgetary considerations, data have not yet been collected on individuals belonging to 30 of the 331 companies in the original sample: 15 companies from Indiana and 15 from Wisconsin. The sample collected so far thus consists of 35,747 veterans from 303 Union Army companies. The remain-

Peter Viechnicki is managing director of research at the Center for Population Economics.

ing 30 companies' data will be collected and made available as described below. Since the demographic composition of the Union Army as a whole contained a disproportionate number of soldiers from Midwestern states relative to the general U.S. population (Smith 2000), this omission makes the database more geographically representative of the U.S. population.

A large fraction of the Northern military-age population served in the Union Army. Sixty-five to 98 percent of the cohorts born between 1838 and 1845 were examined for military service, and 48 to 81 percent of these cohorts served, the remainder being rejected for poor health. The men who served are representative of the Northern population of military age in terms of real estate and personal property wealth in 1860 (Fogel 1993).

Union Army veterans became eligible for pensions. This pension program was the most widespread form of assistance to the elderly prior to Social Security, covering 85 percent of all Union Army veterans by 1900 and 90 percent by 1910 (Costa 1998, 160). The program began in 1862 when Congress established the basic system of pension laws, known as the General Law pension system, to provide pensions to both regular and volunteer recruits who were severely disabled as a direct result of military service (see Costa, 197–212, for a history of the Union Army pension program). The Union Army pension program became a universal disability and old age pension program for veterans with the passage of the act of 27 June 1890, which specified that any disability entitled the veteran to a pension. Even though old age was not recognized by statute as sufficient cause to qualify for a pension until 1907, the Pension Bureau granted the minimum pension to those aged sixty-five or older unless they were "unusually vigorous." In 1912 the law changed yet again, granting larger pensions to veterans who had served for longer lengths of time and who met the age requirements. (For a review of changes in Civil War pension legislation, see Linares 2001).

The Pension Records contain complete medical examinations conducted by a board of three examining surgeons because those with severe chronic conditions were eligible for larger pensions, particularly if the disability could be traced to wartime experience. The surgeons rated the severity of specific conditions using detailed guidelines provided by the Pension Bureau. Several tests indicate that the population is representative of the general population circa 1900 in terms of mortality experience (Fogel 1993).

A variety of sources provide data on military, socioeconomic, and health characteristics for the men in the Life-Cycle Sample. Table B.1 lists the primary record types that served as sources for the linked Life-Cycle Sample. Linkage to the 1880 U.S. Census manuscript schedules is currently underway. No attempt was made to link veterans to the 1890 U.S. Census, since the majority of its schedules were destroyed by fire early in the twentieth century.

Not every individual in the Life-Cycle Sample could be linked to all record types. Successful linkage depended on a variety of factors, including

Table B.1   **Principle Data Sources for the Union Army Life-Cycle Sample**

Source	Abbreviation
Main sources	
Descriptive books of Union Army regiments	RR
Carded Medical Records, Union Army	CMR
Military Service Records, Union Army	MSR
Pension Records, Union Army	PEN
U.S. Census of 1850, manuscript schedules	C50
U.S. Census of 1860, manuscript schedules	C60
U.S. Census of 1870, manuscript schedules	C70
U.S. Census of 1880, manuscript schedules	C80
U.S. Census of 1900, manuscript schedules	C00
U.S. Census of 1910, manuscript schedules	C10
Regimental histories	RH
Supplemental sources	
Public health records	PHR
Muster-out rolls, Union Army	MO
Pension payout cards	PAY
Rejection records, Union Army	REJ
U.S. Census of Mortality, 1850, 1860, 1870, 1880	CMOR
Manual of American Water Works (Baker 1897)	WW
U.S. Army Morbidity and Mortality Reports, 1829–75	MM
State censuses, 1855, 1865, 1875	S55, S65, S75
General and Social Statistics of Cities, U.S. Census Bureau 1880, 1890, 1909, 1915–16	GSSC
Records of the Grand Army of the Republic	GAR

longevity, geographical location, and surname frequency. Linkage rates for the six primary record types are given in table B.2, which shows how linkage rates varied between the different record types. Because the 1850 and 1860 censuses lack adequate soundexes (phonetic indexes), linkages rates for these censuses are lower than they are for the 1900 and 1910 censuses. The linkage rate to the 1910 census is lower than that for 1900 because not all states in 1910 are soundexed.

Regression analysis of the probability of being linked to the seven record sources[1] revealed that most of the variance in the linkage rates was random noise. Characteristics that did predict linkage had a relatively small effect on the variance. In 1850 and 1860 farmers and farm laborers and the native-born were more likely to be linked because many of the foreign-born had not yet immigrated, and because it is easier to find men in rural than in urban areas. Being foreign-born decreased the probability of linkage by 0.26 in 1850 and by 0.14 in 1850. White-collar workers' probability of linkage to the 1860 census was smaller by 0.08 than that of farmers and farm laborers. The coefficients on other personal variables such as region of birth were

1. Full details of the regression analyses are available from Viechnicki (2002).

Table B.2   Linkage Rates for the Major Data Sources for the Life-Cycle Sample

Data Set	Number at Risk to be Linked	Number Linked	Percentage Linked
Military Service Records	35,571	34,775	98
Carded Medical Records	35,571	30,286	85
Pension Records	30,277[a]	24,185	79
U.S. Census of 1910	9,158[b]	6,376	70
U.S. Census of 1900	13,549[c]	11,049	82
U.S. Census of 1860	27,737[d]	11,278	41
U.S. Census of 1850	26,978[e]	9,794	36

[a] All recruits who survived the war were considered at risk for linkage to pension.
[b] In 1910, 9,158 veterans from the primary sample were alive.
[c] In 1900, 13,549 veterans from the primary sample were alive.
[d] Excludes veterans who were foreign-born and had not immigrated by 1860.
[e] Excludes veterans who were foreign-born and had not immigrated by 1850.

small. Among veterans at risk of being linked to the 1900 and 1910 censuses, a veteran was more likely to be linked if he lived in a rural area (defined as a county with no city of at least 25,000 residents), was retired, or lived in the North. Professionals were more likely to be linked, while laborers were less likely. Older veterans were also less likely to be linked.

Pension law determined the best predictors of linkage to the pension records. Deserters were ineligible, and until 1890 only a veteran with a war-related disability qualified for a pension. Veterans wounded in the war increased their probability of being linked to the pension records by 0.22 and deserters decreased their probability by 0.32. Substitutes and the foreign-born also had a lower probability of being linked to the pension records (about 0.14). Farmers were more likely to be linked to the pension records, but this increased their probability of linkage by only 0.11 relative to non-farmers. All other predictors had relatively little effect on linkage rates. Approximately 66 percent of all men with pension records have at least one examining surgeon's record. Linkage is much higher, though, if we exclude men who died during the war and have pension records only because their dependents filed for pension. After 1892, Surgeons' Certificates are available for roughly 83 percent of veterans who have pensions. Those without Surgeons' Certificates are men who were either so severely wounded or disabled during the war that they did not need to prove eligibility, or those who applied under the 1907 or 1912 laws on the basis of age and length of service.

In summary, regression analysis of linkage failures reveals that any selection bias issues raised by failure to link the Union Army recruits to the censuses, Pension Records, Surgeons' Certificates, or Military Service Records will have minimal impact; and what little bias may exist can easily be corrected by post-weighting where appropriate.

The records used to create the Union Army sample provide a wealth of information on soldiers' prewar characteristics, wartime experiences, and postwar health and socioeconomic status. In addition to these individual-level variables, ecological variables were also created to measure the severity of the disease environments in the localities in which the veterans lived at different points over the life course. The principal variables that have been collected for each veteran are listed in table B.3, together with their sources. As can be seen from panels A, B, and C of table B.3, the variables collected in the Union Army Life-Cycle Data set give an almost complete picture of the life history of each veteran, from the war until the veteran's death. For some veterans, prewar information is available as well.

Particular care has been focused on assessing the reliability of the medical information contained in the Pension Bureau's Surgeons' Certificates, which record physical examinations of the veterans in the sample. Analysis reveals that the examining surgeons' records provide reliable indicators of the health status of Union Army veterans. During an examination, a veteran would undergo several subexams, each of which targeted a specific organ or system. The number of subexams increased sharply after 1890, when the law waived the requirement that only war-related disabilities qualified for a pension, and declined after 1912, when many men sought increases in their pensions on the basis of age and length of service rather than changes in disability (cf. Linares 2001). Injury was the most common subexam until 1889. Between 1890 and 1903 the more common conditions examined were cardiovascular, rheumatism, respiratory, and gastrointestinal. From 1904 to 1914, genitourinary problems are added to the list of more common conditions. After 1914, eye problems become common, as would be expected in an aging population. Subexams served as regular check-ups and were not examined only when a recruit claimed to have a specific condition. The examining surgeons were particularly careful in screening for cardiovascular, gastrointestinal, respiratory, spleen, kidney, and liver problems. The same recruits were examined for the same basic problems across their life cycles. On average, 70 percent of subexams in an examination were the same types of subexams as in a previous examination, suggesting that the examining surgeons were consistent in their work. Consistency falls after 1914 as recruits develop more age-related problems, again suggesting that there are no systematic biases in the work of the examining surgeons.

The examining surgeons rated conditions in terms of how disabling each was, and these disability ratings appear to reflect accurately the severity of the related conditions. In a case study of the determinants of hernia ratings, Song (2000) finds that symptoms alone explained 44 percent of the variation in hernia ratings. The incremental ratings on each type of hernia are consistent with hernia severity. For example, relative to hernias in advanced stages of development that were more morbid, having a reducible hernia decreased the rating by 0.034 and having a hernia that could be held effectively

Table B.3   **Principle Variables in the Union Army Life-Cycle Sample**

Source		Variable
A. Preservice characteristics		
For individual and his family	C50, C60, RR, PEN	Year of birth
		Age at enlistment
		Height at enlistment
		Geographic origin (urban/rural, county/state/region)
		Place of birth and enlistment
		Date of enlistment (early/middle/late in war)
		Household wealth in 1850, 1860
		Ethnicity of parents
		Family size in 1850, 1860
		Birth order among surviving siblings
		Migration history of parental family
		Literacy of individual and family members
Ecological variables	C50, C60, S55, S65, PHR, CMOR, MM, WW	Causes of mortality and morbidity in nation as a whole
		Causes of morbidity and mortality in locality from early childhood to recruitment
		Nature of water supply and sewage system
Rejection data	REJ	Causes of rejection
		Relation of rejection to above
B. Wartime experiences		
Morbidity and mortality	RR, CMR, MSR, PEN	Illnesses and hospitalizations (cause, duration, treatment, outcome)
		Battle injuries
		Other accidents and trauma
Potential stress	RR, MSR, CMR, MO, PEN, RH	Rank
		Combat experience
		Casualties in company
		Wounded, fired-on, in-zone (number of battles for each)
		Severity of each battle
		Movements of company between battles
		Prisoner of war (when, where, duration, conditions)
		Tour of duty (duration, state of war, transfers)
		Service record (desertions or AWOL, citations for bravery, reprimands or punishments, promotions, demotions)
C. Postwar history		
Health of veteran	PEN, PAY	Testimonial history of health before pension application
		Complaints of veteran at each examination by Pension Bureau surgeons
		Height, weight, pulse, respiration, urinalysis at each exam by surgeons
		Conditions diagnosed at each examination
		Date of becoming bedridden

Table B.3   (continued)

	Source	Variable
		Dates of admission to veterans' hospitals or homes and the diagnoses on entry
		Date and cause of death
Occupations and work	PEN, C70, C80, C00, C10	Occupations at each pension examination and in 1870, 1880, 1900, 1910
		Surgeon's estimates at each examination of degree of impairment from manual labor for each condition
		Pension Bureau's estimate of overall impairment for manual labor
		Months worked in 1900 and 1910
Personal and family structure and characteristics	PEN, PAY, C70, C80, C00, C10, GAR	Marriages, divorces, deaths of spouses, with dates of each
		Births and deaths of children, with dates
		Residences at pension examinations, and when receiving payments from Pension Bureau
		Household structure in 1870, 1880, 1900, 1910
		Grand Army of the Republic membership
Environmental factors	PHR, GAR, WW, GSSC	Strength of GAR presence in locality
		Water supply and sewerage characteristics in town of residence
		Weekly infectious disease rates in town of residence
		Public spending on police, fire prevention, public health infrastructure, and recreation

Notes: C50, C60, C70, C80, C00, C10 = censuses of 1850, 1860, 1870, 1880, 1900, 1910; CMOR = Census of Mortality; CMR = Carded Medical Records; GAR = Records of Grand Army of the Republic; GSSC = General and Social Statistics of Cities; MM = Army Morbidity and Mortality Reports; MO = Muster-out Rolls; MSR = Military Service Records; PAY = Pension payout cards; PEN = Pension Records; PHR = Public Health Reports; REJ = Rejection Records Sample; RH = Regimental Histories; RR = Regimental Records; S55, S65 = State censuses of 1855 and 1865; WW = Water Works Data.

by a truss decreased the rating by 0.053. Larger hernias received higher ratings. Double hernias received higher ratings than single hernias. Controlling for nonmedical variables does not change the coefficient estimates on the medical variables, nor does it increase the explanatory power of the regression. Year of application, political party affiliation of the state, and whether the state was a swing state have no significant impact on hernia ratings. Filing with attorneys and filing under laws that were passed in later years decreased hernia ratings, because only those who were particularly healthy filed later and filed with an attorney. Hernia symptoms and ratings are also consistent across different groups of examining surgeons. Among hernia patients who had subsequent medical examinations in states or cities other than where they had their first examination, there is no evidence of regional discrepancies in hernia diagnoses and hernia ratings. The Pension

Bureau appears to have administered the Union Army pension program in a just manner and the examining surgeons appear to have carried out their duties accurately and fairly.

The examining surgeons' diagnoses and descriptions depended upon symptoms, signs, and conditions that did not require any diagnostic equipment. Cancer rates in the data are therefore underreported. Prevalence rates for other conditions such as hypertension are unknown because the examining surgeons had no way of diagnosing these. Considerable time has been devoted to understanding how to interpret many of the common conditions noted by the examining surgeons. Table B.4 compares some conditions in the Union Army Life-Cycle Sample among veterans aged sixty to seventy-four to men in the same age group in the 1988–94 National Health and Nutrition Examination Survey, and in the 1994 National Health Interview Survey, both based upon random samples of the noninstitutionalized population. Note the very high prevalence in the Union Army sample of heart murmurs, irregular pulse, and tachycardia. Some of this may reflect the more careful examinations of surgeons accustomed to direct observations as well as looser

Table B.4   Prevalence Rates of Chronic Conditions, Symptoms, and Signs, Men Aged 60 to 74

	UA, 1910	NHANES, 1988–94	NHIS, 1994
Decreased breath sounds	15.4	8.3	
Adventitious sounds	29.1	4.0	
Back problems	47.5	30.2	
Pain, tenderness, swelling in joints	54.1	35.2	
Heart murmur	38.7	3.8	1.7
Valvular heart disease (mitral or aortic origin murmurs)	27.4		
Congestive heart failure (edema, cyanosis, and dyspnea)	8.9	7.0	
Arteriosclerosis	9.2		4.7
Ever diagnosed stroke	0.6	5.2	
Irregular pulse	43.7	8.6	
Tachycardia	27.0		3.4
Varicose veins	10.1		3.4
Hemorrhoids	36.1		4.7
Poor circulation	4.1		1.4
Cataracts	6.6	16.1	
Blindness in at least one eye	4.9	3.1	
Deafness in at least one ear	4.5	2.7	
Paralysis	6.9	2.7	

Source: Costa (2000b).

Notes: UA = Union Army; NHANES = National Health and Nutrition Examination Survey; NHIS = National Health Interview Survey. Sample weights were used for NHANES and NHIS. With the exception of stroke, congestive heart failure, and cataracts, NHANES results are based upon physical exams. Stroke, congestive heart failure, and cataracts in NHANES are based upon a condition ever having been noted by a doctor. A condition is noted in NHIS if the person had the condition in the last twelve months. In UA a condition is noted if it was ever mentioned in an exam.

definitions. However, the high prevalence rates for irregular pulse, tachycardia, poor circulation, and varicose veins are consistent with the high prevalence rate of valvular heart disease. (The relationship between valvular heart disease and varicose veins or tachycardia is much looser than for irregular pulse or tachycardia.) The high prevalence of joint and back problems are consistent with analyses of skeletal remains from the American frontier, which report a high prevalence of degenerative joint disease (osteoarthritis), nonarthritic joint changes resulting from habitual postures, and fractures arising from traumas (e.g., Larsen et al. 1995). The increased specificity of diagnoses makes comparisons with modern data difficult for some conditions. The examining surgeons' use of hard arteries as a detection criterion for atherosclerosis provides evidence of peripheral arteriosclerosis, which may be evidence of either atherosclerosis (cholesterol and fatty plaques in the blood) or such other disease states as diabetes mellitus or systemic or local inflammation. Congestive heart failure could be defined either by using edema, cyanosis, and dyspnea as the diagnostic criteria or by using these criteria together with cardiomegaly and excluding respiratory conditions. For conditions such as cataracts or stroke, examining surgeons may have been more likely to note the final outcome (blindness or paralysis) rather than the cause. Nonetheless, even when prevalence rates cannot be compared with modern data, it is still possible to examine whether chronic conditions at older ages arose from infectious disease contracted while in the army, occupational stress, or such stresses as living in a large city at a young age.

Analysis of the antecedents of the chronic conditions, symptoms, and signs recorded by the examining surgeons provides further confirmation of the reliability of the diagnoses. Contracting acute respiratory infections while in the army increased the probability of chronic respiratory problems at older ages; measles, the probability of chronic respiratory problems and valvular heart disease; typhoid fever, of valvular heart disease and irregular pulse; tuberculosis, of chronic respiratory problems; rheumatic fever, of valvular heart disease, arrythmias, congestive heart failure, joint problems, and back problems; and malaria, of joint problems (Costa 2000b). These relationships were expected from a reading of the medical literature (although the links between malaria and joint problems are not well established and therefore represent new findings). The infections likely to exert the larger effect on chronic disease rates in fact did so: rheumatic fever on joint problems, and tuberculosis on respiratory difficulties.

Subsidiary Data Sets

The individual-level information in the Union Army Life-Cycle Sample can be supplemented with a variety of aggregate-level and ecological variables. These variables have been collected in a series of auxiliary data sets distributed by the Center for Population Economics (CPE). The data sets described below are all available via the CPE data extraction system, at http://www.cpe.uchicago.edu/data/data.html, under "Subsidiary Union Veterans Datasets."

The Regimental Histories Dataset focuses on the combat experiences of each Union Army company during the Civil War. It is drawn from Dyer's (1959) *Compendium of the War of the Rebellion.* This data set can be used to construct measures of wartime stress, military movement patterns, and regional disease environments for the veterans in the Union Army Life-Cycle Sample.

A number of subsidiary data sets record health conditions in different localities at different times. These can be linked to the Union Army Life-Cycle Sample to provide information on the disease environment in each veteran's region of residence over time. The earliest such data come from the United States Army's Morbidity and Mortality Reports for its military installations, which cover the period between 1829 and 1874. These reports provide quarterly case-rates and fatality rates for a series of infectious and chronic conditions for the regions of the country that contained military posts. The United States Census of Mortality from 1850, 1860, 1870, and 1880 can provide similar information on causes of death at the county level. Between 1899 and 1927, the American Public Health Association published case rates and fatality rates for infectious diseases in all U.S. cities possessed of more than 10,000 inhabitants. These three data sets thus provide measures of disease rates in various localities for most of the nineteenth century and the early twentieth century as well.

Several data sets describe the social and civic conditions of the towns and cities in which the veterans in the Union Army Life-Cycle Sample inhabited. The *Social and General Statistics of Cities,* published by the United States Census Bureau in 1880, 1890, 1909, and 1915–16, collects information on public infrastructure, expenditures, governance, and regulation for the period around the turn of the twentieth century. Baker's (1897) *Manual of American Water Works* is currently being computerized; by 2003, this data set will allow detailed information on water supply and sewerage to be accessed for every municipality in the United States that had a public water supply in 1897 (more than 4,000 such municipalities). Finally, the GAR Posts Dataset contains information about the number and location of Grand Army of the Republic posts for each U.S. county; it can be used to create measures of local influence for this most important Union Army veterans' organization.

Improvements and Extensions to the Life-Cycle Sample

Although the original data collection for the Union Army Life-Cycle Sample is essentially complete,[2] a series of improvements and extensions to

---

2. Linkage to the 1880 census, the last remaining record-type to be mined, was approximately 20 percent complete as of May 2002.

the sample are planned or underway. Chief among these improvements are the following steps. First, in order to allow comparisons of African American aging experiences to those of whites, a life-cycle sample of African American Union Army veterans is being collected from the National Archives. This sample will consist of longitudinally linked observations for a sample of 6,164 African American veterans, and will take the same form as the previous Union Army Life-Cycle Sample. Initial versions of the African American Sample will be available in the second half of 2003. Second, data from the thirty Union Army companies from the original Life-Cycle Sample that were not collected for budgetary reasons (discussed at the beginning of this appendix) will now be collected. The inclusion of these companies in the Union Army Life-Cycle Sample will make the resultant data into a random sample of Union Army infantry companies. Finally, in order to understand more clearly the relative health status of Union Army veterans as compared to the general population, a larger sample of rejection records from the Union Army service examination will be collected. Ten thousand rejection records will be collected and computerized from the National Archives. This sample will allow prevalence rates of various conditions to be estimated by recruitment district and year.

References

Baker, M. N. 1897. *The manual of American water works, 1897, compiled from special returns.* New York: Engineering News Publishing.

Costa, Dora. 1998. *The evolution of retirement: An American economic history.* Chicago: University of Chicago Press.

———. 2000a. Long-term declines in disability among older men: Medical care, public health, and occupational change. NBER Working Paper no. 7605. Cambridge, Mass.: National Bureau of Economic Research, March.

———. 2000b. Understanding the twentieth-century decline in chronic conditions among older men. *Demography* 37 (1): 53–72.

Dyer, Frederick. 1959. *A compendium of the War of the Rebellion.* 3 vols. New York: Thomas Yoseloff. Originally published in 1909.

Fogel, Robert. 1993. New sources and new techniques for the study of secular trends in nutritional status, health, mortality, and the process of aging. *Historical Methods* 26 (1): 5–43.

Larsen, C. S., J. Craig, L. E. Sering, M. J. Schoeninger, K. F. Russell, D. L. Hutchinson, and M. A. Williamson. 1995. Cross homestead: Life and death on the Midwestern frontier. In *Bodies of evidence: Reconstructing history through skeletal analysis,* ed. A. L. Grauer, 139–60. New York: Wiley.

Linares, Claudia. 2001. The Civil War Pension Law. In *Public use tape on the aging of veterans of the Union Army, Surgeon's Certificates 1862–1940.* Version S-1 Standardized, ed. Robert Fogel. Chicago: University of Chicago, Graduate School of Business, Center for Population Economics.

Smith, Daniel. 2000. Who fought for the North during the Civil War? The roles of nativity and region among white men. CPE Working Paper Series 2000. Available at [http://www.cpe.uchicago.edu/publication/publication.html].

Song, Chen. 2000. Justice or politics: New evidence on the surgeons' performance during the United States Civil War pension process. University of Chicago, Graduate School of Business, Center for Population Economics. Unpublished manuscript.

Viechnicki, Peter. 2002. Regression analysis of linkage biases in the Union Army Life-Cycle Datasets. CPE Working Paper Series 2002-2. Available at [http://www.cpe.uchicago.edu/publication/publication.html].

Contributors

Patricia E. Beeson
Department of Economics
4A30 Forbes Quad
University of Pittsburgh
Pittsburgh, PA 15260

Dora L. Costa
Department of Economics,
    E52-274C
Massachusetts Institute of
    Technology
50 Memorial Drive
Cambridge, MA 02142

Joseph P. Ferrie
Department of Economics
Northwestern University
Evanston, IL 60208-2600

Tayatat Kanjanapipatkul
Center for Population Economics
Graduate School of Business
The University of Chicago
1101 East 58th Street
Chicago, IL 60637

Chulhee Lee
School of Economics
Seoul National University
San 56-1, Sillim-dong, Kwanak-gu
Seoul, 151-742, Korea

Louis L. Nguyen
Department of Surgery
Barnes-Jewish Hospital
Washington University in St. Louis
1701 West Building
Barnes-Jewish Plaza
St. Louis, MO 63110

Clayne L. Pope
Department of Economics
990 SWKT; P.O. Box 25535
Brigham Young University
Provo, UT 84602-5535

Mario A. Sánchez
Inter-American Development Bank
1300 New York Avenue, NW
Washington, DC 20577

Daniel Scott Smith
Department of History
921 University Hall (M/C 198)
601 South Morgan Street
University of Illinois at Chicago
Chicago, IL 60607-7109

Chen Song
Resolution Economics, LLC
Suite 400
9250 Wilshire Boulevard
Beverly Hills, CA 90212

Werner Troesken
Department of History
3P30 Posvar Hall
University of Pittsburgh
Pittsburgh, PA 15260

Peter Viechnicki
Managing Director of Research
Center for Population Economics
1101 East 58th Street, Room 118
Chicago, IL 60637

Sven E. Wilson
Department of Political Science
732 SWKT
Brigham Young University
Provo, UT 84602

Larry T. Wimmer
Department of Economics
Brigham Young University
130 Faculty Office Building
Provo, UT 84602-2363

Author Index

Subject Index